Merger Control in Europe

This book addresses the phenomenon of mergers that may result in non-coordinated effects in oligopolistic markets. Such cases are sometimes referred to as "non-collusive oligopolies", or "gap cases" and there is a concern that they might not be covered by the substantive test that some member states of the EU use for merger assessment. Ioannis Kokkoris examines the argument that the EC Merger Regulation (Regulation 4064/89) did not capture gap cases and considers the extent to which the revised substantive test in Regulation 139/2004 deals with the problem of non-collusive oligopolies.

The author identifies actual examples of mergers that gave rise to a problem of non-coordinated effects in oligopolistic markets, both in the EU and in other jurisdictions, and analyses the way in which these cases were dealt with in practice. The book considers legal systems such as those in the United Kingdom, the United States, Australia, and New Zealand. The book investigates whether there is any difference in the assessment of non-collusive oligopolies between the various substantive tests that have been adopted for merger assessment in various jurisdictions. The book also looks at the various methodological tools available to assist competition authorities and the professional advisers of merging firms to identify whether a particular merger might give rise to anticompetitive effects and explores the type of market structure in which a merger is likely to lead to non-coordinated effects in oligopolistic markets.

Ioannis Kokkoris is a Reader at the University of Reading (UK). He is an international consultant on competition policy at the Organisation for Cooperation and Security in Europe (OSCE). He is also a Visiting Professor at Bocconi University (Italy), and City University (UK) and a Visiting Fellow at Durham University (UK).

Routledge Research in Competition Law

Available titles in this series include:

The Internationalisation of Competition Rules
Brendan J. Sweeney

Forthcoming titles in this series include:

Merger Control in Post-Communist Countries
EC Merger Regulation in Small Market Economies
Jurgita Malinauskaite

Merger Control in Europe

The Gap in the ECMR and National Merger Legislations

Ioannis Kokkoris

Routledge
Taylor & Francis Group
LONDON AND NEW YORK

First published 2011
by Routledge
2 Park Square, Milton Park, Abingdon, Oxon OX14 4RN

Simultaneously published in the USA and Canada
by Routledge
270 Madison Avenue, New York, NY 10016

Routledge is an imprint of the Taylor & Francis Group, an informa business

Typeset in Baskerville by
Wearset Ltd, Boldon, Tyne and Wear
Printed and bound in Great Britain by
CPI Antony Rowe, Chippenham, Wiltshire

British Library Cataloguing in Publication Data
A catalogue record for this book is available from the British Library

Library of Congress Cataloging in Publication Data
Kokkoris, Ioannis
Merger control in Europe: the gap in the ECMR and national merger legislations/Ioannis Kokkoris.
p. cm.
Includes bibliographical references.
1. Consolidation and merger of corporations–Law and legislation–European Union countries. I. Title.
KJE6467.K65 2010
346.24′06626–dc22 2010003792

ISBN13: 978-0-415-56513-4 (hbk)
ISBN13: 978-0-203-84672-8 (ebk)

Contents

List of tables

Table of cases

European Union

European Commission

General Court

Court of Justice

United Kingdom

Finland

Germany

United States

New Zealand

Table of statutory materials

European Union

Ireland

Germany

United States

New Zealand

Australia

Preface

This book aims to address the issue of mergers leading to non-coordinated effects in oligopolistic markets ("non-collusive oligopolies" or "gap" cases); to examine how the legal substantive test deals with non-collusive oligopolies; and to identify such cases in the current case law of the EC as well as of other jurisdictions. An improved understanding of mergers leading to non-coordinated effects in oligopolistic markets, as well as of the contributing factors, firmly rooted in economic theory is essential in three respects: reducing the number of transactions with adverse impact on competition, increasing the number of beneficial transactions, and reducing the uncertainty surrounding merger approval.

The Commission faced intense criticism following the *Airtours/First Choice* case, which appeared to illustrate the existence of the so-called "gap" in the application of the old EC Merger Regulation ("ECMR") and emphasized the need for an economically sound basis of merger assessment. The "gap" corresponds to the situation where the post-merger entity's market power would not amount to single firm or collective dominance but where the merger may nonetheless lead to non-coordinated effects in oligopolistic markets.

Even though the legal substantive test has been changed from the "dominance test" to the Substantial Impediment to Effective Competition ("SIEC") in the recast ECMR, and thus would appear to rectify the "gap" in the European Community merger regime, the occurrences of such "gap" cases may not cease under national laws that still adhere to the traditional dominance test. Such regimes are still likely to experience cases where they will be facing mergers which will have the features of a non-collusive oligopoly but will be unable to apply the current dominance test. They may thus resort to other methods of trying to deal with mergers having an adverse impact on competition.

Chapter 1 addresses how the "gap" resulted from the application of the dominance test as the legal substantive test in the assessment of mergers. Chapter 2 examines amendments in the ECMR designed to rectify the "gap". Chapter 3 presents important issues in the assessment of "gap" cases such as the quantitative methods used to accurately assess the adverse impact of a merger on competition. Chapter 4 identifies "gap" cases and demonstrates that the amendments in the ECMR were justifiable, and Chapter 5 presents economic evidence of the existence of such cases. Finally, criteria for the assessment of "gap" cases are presented.

Dr. Ioannis Kokkoris
London, 22 January 2010

Foreword

The debate that led to the 2004 adoption of the recast EU Merger Regulation was lively, stimulating and, at times, quite contentious. The original Merger Regulation of 1989 provided for the prohibition of a merger that "creates or strengthens a dominant position as a result of which effective competition would be significantly impeded". Over a period of time case-law of the Community Courts, most notably *Gencor* v *Commission* in the General Court (then the Court of First Instance) and *France* v *Commission* in the Court of Justice, established that a "dominant position" could include a "collective dominant position"; but it was not entirely clear what phenomena were included within the concept of collective dominance. There was a growing consensus that what we now call coordinated effects in oligopolistic markets were covered; but what was less clear was whether the enhanced ability of a non-dominant firm, following a merger, to exercise individual, as opposed to collective, market power, could be addressed. This phenomenon came to be known as "non-collusive oligopoly"; and its possible exclusion from the concept of collective dominance was commonly referred to as the "gap" in EU merger control.

If such a gap existed – and if it was sufficiently large that it needed to be filled – it seemed that a change in the legislation was required. The debacle of the *Airtours/First Choice* decision of the Commission added to the confusion in this area, since the General Court's annulment of the Commission's decision seemed to restrict the concept of collective dominance to "conventional" coordinated effects cases.

The appropriate standard of merger control was hotly debated throughout 2002 and 2003. A strong body of opinion believed that there was no need to change the dominance test at all; perhaps the gap did not exist; perhaps it could, even after *Airtours*, be covered by collective dominance; or perhaps it was so theoretical that it was simply not worth the disruption of legislative change that would undermine the decisional practice of the Commission and the jurisprudence of the Community Courts acquired over a period of more than a decade. However, an equally strong body of opinion pointed out that many jurisdictions, particularly in the "Anglo-Saxon" world, used the language of "substantial lessening of competition" for merger control, an expression that seemed both more intuitively natural for this purpose – will there be less competition in the market after the merger than before it? – and more "dynamic" than "static". As is well-known, the matter was finally resolved by the deceptively simple device of reversing the word order of the 1989 Regulation: henceforth a merger would be prohibited that would impede effective competition, "in particular" as a result of the creation or strengthening of a dominant position. Recital 25 of the 2004 Regulation explained that this reformulation should be interpreted as extending, beyond the concept of dominance, only to the anti-competitive effects of a merger resulting from the non-coordinated behaviour of undertakings which would not have a dominant position in the market concerned. In other words, the point was to fill the gap.

I vividly remember the debates on this subject, and the passions that were sometimes aroused. But I also recall a particular frustration: the dearth of "gap cases" in history to use as a basis for argument. That is not to say that there had never been gap cases; but rather that they had never been articulated as such. Mergers may have been prohibited (or modified) because of an anxiety about non-collusive oligopoly, but the competition authority may not have used that language in its decision. A finding that a merger would substantially lessen competition need not necessarily have identified non-collusive oligopoly as a theory of harm; and cases decided on the basis of creation or strengthening of dominance might, for example, have proceeded on the basis of a fairly suspect (unduly narrow) market definition. To quite a large extent, therefore, the debate took place at a somewhat theoretical level, unsupported by empirical evidence.

What was needed at that time was a book that covered precisely the ground explored in this one. Dr Kokkoris, after explaining the nature of the problem, proceeds to look at cases in various jurisdictions – the EU of course, but also the US, UK, New Zealand and Australia, for example – in which there have been cases that were, or probably were, gap cases. There is much research here that anyone interested in this subject will find invaluable. *Airtours* of course is discussed; but then several other important EU cases are also reviewed, including, for example, *Oracle/PeopleSoft*, *Sony/BMG*, *Johnson & Johnson/Guidant* and *T.Mobile/tele.ring*. *LloydsTSB/Abbey National* in the UK and *Heinz/Beech-Nut* in the US are discussed; and the interesting situation in Australia, which went from the "SLC" test to dominance and then back to SLC is also looked at: the author suggests that more research on the experience in Australia might be useful. The author's conclusion – with which I agree – is that there was indeed a gap in the dominance test, and that it needed to be filled.

Does this matter, now that the EU Regulation was been reformulated? The answer, surely, is yes, not least since there are many Member States of the EU that retain the dominance test: the author usefully summarizes the various tests in Europe in an Appendix to the book. This book usefully draws together the arguments for and against the gap and the need to fill it; reviews the relevant decisional practice; and discusses methodologies for identifying gap cases. Dr Kokkoris is to be congratulated on producing this extremely interesting and well-researched book which casts important light on an intriguing aspect of merger control.

Richard Whish
June 2010

Introduction

I Purpose of the book

This book aims to address the economic phenomenon of mergers that might result in non-coordinated effects in oligopolistic markets. Such cases are sometimes referred to as "non-collusive oligopolies",[1] and the fear that they might not be covered by the substantive test in the original EC Merger Regulation, Regulation 4064/89 ("ECMR"),[2] led to their sometimes being called "gap" cases. The book will examine the argument that the original regulation did not capture gap cases and will consider the extent to which the revised substantive test in Regulation 139/2004[3] deals with the problem of non-collusive oligopolies.

The book will also attempt to identify actual examples of mergers that gave rise to a problem of non-coordinated effects in oligopolistic markets, both in the EU and in other jurisdictions, and will analyse the way in which these cases were dealt with in practice. In some of these cases, there was no explicit articulation of the phenomenon of non-collusive oligopoly; however, at least in the EU, there are now a few examples of mergers where this problem has been specifically identified. The book will also consider various methodological tools available to assist competition authorities and the professional advisers of merging firms to identify whether a particular merger might give rise to anticompetitive effects (for example non-collusive oligopolies) and will also consider the type of market structure in which a merger is likely to lead to non-coordinated effects in oligopolistic markets.

The book will conclude that the dominance test was inadequate in capturing non-collusive oligopolies and that the reform of the substantive test was justified and necessary. Although the Council of Ministers, after the European Commission's ("Commission") proposal, adopted a new substantive test, which rectifies the gap in the applicability of the dominance test, many member states continue to use the dominance test and thus are likely to experience cases that will lead to anticompetitive effects but will not be caught due to the inapplicability of the dominance test to non-collusive oligopolies.

Improved understanding of mergers leading to non-coordinated effects in oligopolistic markets, including the contributing factors, firmly rooted in economic theory is essential in three respects: reducing the number of transactions with an adverse impact on competition, increasing the number of beneficial transactions, and reducing the uncertainty surrounding merger approval.

I.1 Non-coordinated effects in oligopolistic markets

The concept of non-collusive oligopoly was not explicitly addressed in the decisional practice of the European Commission or the community courts under Regulation 4064/89. Until the adoption of the recast ECMR in May 2004, there was no published decision under the original ECMR that unequivocally challenged the phenomenon of non-coordinated effects in oligopolistic markets.[4]

In the *Oracle/PeopleSoft* case,[5] one of the last decisions under the original ECMR, the Commission did not address the issue in its final decision whether the original ECMR applies to such mergers, although this had been a concern during the course of the administrative procedure.[6] The Commission initiated a Phase II examination of the proposed transaction but, on the basis of new evidence after the oral hearing, it concluded that the transaction did not, after all, raise any concerns.

However, although there were no explicit decisions dealing with non-collusive oligopoly, the Commission's decision in the *Airtours/First Choice*[7] case was controversial and ambiguous. It was not entirely clear what the Commission was arguing in this decision, but one possibility was that it was a so-called "gap" case: the Commission argued that the merger would lead to collective dominance, but, depending on how one interprets the decision, it was possible that it considered that the merger would lead to non-coordinated effects in an oligopolistic market.[8]

The Commission's argumentation was not clear on whether it was attempting to capture non-collusive oligopolies by expanding the notion of collective dominance or whether it misunderstood concerns related to non-collusive oligopolies with collective dominance. The decision was appealed to the General Court.[9] On appeal, the Commission's decision was annulled in its entirety. This was in large part because the General Court considered that the Commission had failed to establish the primary facts of the case and had been guilty of a manifest error of assessment in the inferences drawn from the facts. However, the General Court also laid down criteria for determining what is meant by the concept of collective dominance, and it seems clear that the phenomenon of non-collusive oligopoly would not be captured by the *Airtours* definition.

After the *Airtours/First Choice* merger, in 2001 the European Commission published a green paper analysing the proposed reforms to the European merger regime. Through this Green Paper,[10] the Commission tried to address the "gap". The comments on the green paper received by the Commission clearly indicated that the application of the original ECMR to mergers leading to non-coordinated effects in oligopolistic markets was unclear, both in the case law of the community courts[11] and in the practice of the Commission.[12]

In the draft *Horizontal Merger Guidelines*,[13] the Commission used the term "non-collusive oligopolies"[14] to describe mergers that can lead to post-merger firms adopting conduct having an adverse impact on competition in the post-merger market, without enjoying single-firm dominance and, at the same time, without tacitly colluding. This terminology created legal uncertainty as indicated by the comments received by the Commission during the consultation phase on the *Draft Commission Notice on the appraisal of horizontal mergers*".[15] Consequently, the term "non-collusive oligopolies" was not used in the final guidelines.[16]

The term "non-coordinated effects in oligopolistic markets" was introduced in Recital 25 of the ECMR.[17] The recast ECMR explicitly recognized the concept of non-collusive oligopolies (or "gap" cases) as a result of the prevailing perception that some mergers could lead to a harmful effect on competition that could not be addressed using the existing concepts of single-firm and/or collective dominance.[18]

The two terms "mergers leading to non-coordinated effects in oligopolistic markets" and "non-collusive oligopolies" refer to situations in which the remaining firms in the post-merger market have both the incentive and ability to adopt conduct inducing an adverse impact on competition, and thus profit from exerting their market power in the post-merger market, without being dependent on a coordinated response on the part of the other members of the oligopolistic market structure.[19] The adverse impact on competition is induced by the merger.

The most direct impact on competition will be the elimination of the competitive constraints that the merging firms exerted on each other prior to the merger. In addition, non-merging firms can also benefit from the reduction of competitive pressure that results from the merger since the merging firms' price increase or output reduction may induce the switching of some demand to the rival firms, which, in turn, may find it optimal to increase prices. This might happen in particular in differentiated product markets[20] where a merger can lead to incentives for conduct having an adverse impact on competition, without creating a single leading player, and without significantly increasing the feasibility of tacit collusion. The latter situation, which cannot be dealt either as single-firm dominance or as collective dominance, is known, as noted earlier, as the "gap" in the application of the dominance test.

I.2 Implications of the existence of non-collusive oligopolies for member states

Even though the legal substantive test has been changed from the "dominance test" to the "substantial lessening of competition ("SIEC") in the recast ECMR,[21] and thus would appear to rectify the "gap" in the European Community merger regime, the occurrences of such "gap" cases may not cease under national laws that still adhere to the traditional dominance test. Such regimes are still likely to experience cases where they will be facing mergers that will have the features of a non-collusive oligopoly but will be unable to apply the current dominance test. They may thus resort to other methods of trying to deal with mergers having an adverse impact on competition.[22]

I.3 Structure of the book

This book is structured as follows. The first chapter addresses the question of whether there was "gap" in the application of the dominance test of the original ECMR. After briefly introducing the original ECMR, the answer to this question will be provided by the analysis of the *Airtours*[23] case and, in particular, how that case illustrated the existence of a "gap" in the application of the dominance test. The historical origin of the term "dominance", along with the criteria that the General Court considered in *Airtours* as essential in the assessment of the likelihood of a merger leading to collective dominance, will be analysed. This part of the book will address the concept of collective dominance, as it is a necessary step in order to fully capture the issues addressed herein.

The second chapter will address the issue of whether the recast ECMR successfully captures gap cases: focus will be placed on the change of the legal substantive test from dominance to the SIEC test, as well as on the examination of whether the new test can be applied to "gap" cases.

The third chapter will address necessary steps in the assessment of mergers leading to non-coordinated effects in oligopolistic markets. Thus, this chapter will address the quantitative methods that can be used by the Commission in analysing the adverse impact of a merger on competition. In the early years of competition enforcement in the EU, market definition and structural analysis, that is to say analysis of competitive effects based on market shares, usually tended to dominate. Notably, however, the structural approach has tended to give way to a more economically sophisticated analysis of competitive effects. The analysis of merger simulation and critical loss analysis in this chapter will focus on the way that these methods have been applied under the Substantial Impediment to Effective Competition ("SLC") and dominance tests in the relevant jurisdictions, in an attempt to identify differences not only in the application of these methods under the two substantive tests but also in their efficiency, accuracy and predictability for the assessment of mergers leading to non-coordinated effects. Possible different application of these methods in merger cases, may have led to gap cases not being caught under the dominance test, not because of the gap in its application, but because of the different methods applied in the assessment of mergers.

The fourth chapter will consider the existence of evidence of "gap" cases in the current case law. The aim is to identify important merger cases that fell within the realm of non-collusive oligopolies. As mentioned already, until the adoption of the recast ECMR in May 2004, there was no published decision under the original ECMR that unequivocally challenged the phenomenon of non-coordinated effects in oligopolistic markets. In order to address the problem that there are few, if any, decisions adopted explicitly on the basis of non-collusive oligopoly theory, this book will include a comparative approach by examining mergers assessed under various different legal systems; these cases will include mergers that were prohibited as well as those that were allowed to proceed after the submission of undertakings by the parties.[24] Focus will be placed on mergers dealt with under the original ECMR. Some of these mergers were assumed to lead to collective dominance rather than non-coordinated effects in oligopolistic markets. When the decisions in these merger cases were taken, the concept of non-collusive oligopolies was not recognized in the original ECMR.[25] However, the market features that contribute to non-collusive oligopolies might have been in existence and prevalent in certain market structures. Hence, this book will provide evidence of non-collusive oligopolies.[26]

Other legal systems that will be included in the analysis are the United States, the United Kingdom, Finland, and New Zealand. Some of these jurisdictions have adopted the SLC test (for example the United Kingdom in the last 5 years);[27] for one, namely the USA, the SLC test has been used as the substantive legal criterion since the early 1900s.[28] Thus, it will be interesting to consider whether any difference in the assessment of non-collusive oligopolies can be detected between the two tests.

In order to evaluate the Commission's assessment of "gap" cases from a different viewpoint, the fifth chapter employs an event study in addressing the issue of whether the Commission's assessment of a "gap" case is supported by the stock market. A means of assessing the impact that mergers giving rise to non-coordinated effects in oligopolistic markets will have on competition is to evaluate the market perception of the competitive effects of such mergers. Event study methodology provides an ex ante evidentiary tool of merger assessment. Although it cannot solely determine the outcome of the merger, event studies can provide useful insights in the likely impact of the merger on competition. The analysis in this chapter will attempt to assess the stock market's perception of the non-collusive oligopolies identified in Chapter 4 and examine whether the Commission's decisions to prohibit or allow these mergers are reflected in the stock market's expectations. As mentioned earlier, since investors' perception is an indication of whether the merger is expected to have adverse effects on competition, it will illustrate whether the Commission's assessment was correct. Thus, it will provide a technical method of proof of the existence of gap cases, in addition to the theoretical support provided in Chapter 4.

The event study analysis will include:

- Cases that were examples of non-collusive oligopolies and that were not prohibited. If the share prices of the merging firms as well as of their rivals indicated a positive abnormal return[29] on the day of the merger announcement, shareholders expected these mergers to be profitable for the firms as well as for the other incumbents in the post-merger market. Firms increase profitability mainly by increasing prices (reducing output) in the market, thus inducing an adverse impact on competition.
- Cases that were examples of non-collusive oligopolies and which were prohibited. The intention is to evaluate whether prohibiting the merger was correct according to investors' perceptions. If investors believed that the merger would not be profitable for the merging firms and their competitors (that is to say they did not consider that the firms were likely to increase prices/reduce output, and thus were not likely to adopt conduct having an adverse impact on competition), the merging firms' as well as the competitors' share prices would be likely to have indicated a negative abnormal return on the day of announcement.

In order to evaluate the investors' perceptions and expectations, the abnormal return of the share prices of the merging firms and of their competitors on the announcement day will be calculated by deducting the share price of the both merging firms as well as of the competitors from an index of all market shares. Data on share prices will be taken from databases such as Datastream, Bloomberg, Factset as well as from public information data sources such as the *Financial Times*.

Our earlier analysis aims at assessing the stock market's perception of non-collusive oligopolies and examining whether the Commission's decisions to prohibit or allow such mergers are reflected in the expectation of the stock market. The conclusion will summarize the main findings, present some criteria for the assessment of mergers leading to non-coordinated effects in oligopolistic markets as they have been formulated through the case law, and suggest further areas of research for the future.

In the next chapter, the purpose and history of the ECMR is briefly outlined. The chapter also addresses the concept of dominance, on which the legal substantive test of the original ECMR, the dominance test, was both formulated and applied.

Notes

1 For the purposes of this book, the terms "mergers leading to non-coordinated effects in oligopolistic markets", "gap cases" and "non-collusive oligopolies" will be used interchangeably. The main focus of this book is non-coordinated in oligopolistic markets, rather than non-coordinated effects in general. As the following analysis will illustrate, the gap in the application of the dominance test relates to oligopolistic markets characterized, inter alia, by differentiated products as compared to oligopolistic structures with homogeneous products, which may give rise to collective dominance concerns.

2 Council Regulation (EEC) No. 4064/89 of 21 December 1989 on the control of concentrations between undertakings, OJ L395, 30.12.1989, pp. 1–12.

3 Council Regulation (EC) No. 139/2004 of 20 January 2004 on the control of concentrations between undertakings (the EC Merger Regulation), ("recast ECMR"), OJ L24, 29.01.2004, pp. 1–22.

4 Assonime, "*Comments on the Draft EC Commission Notice on the Appraisal of Horizontal Mergers*", http://europa.eu.int/comm/competition/mergers/review/contributions.html. Although there are cases that were arguably decided based on a rationale that resembles the one under the SIEC test. Such cases include Case M1672 *Volvo/Scania* [2001] OJ L143/74, Case M2817 *Barilla/BPL/Kamps* [2002] OJ C198/4, as well as Case M2861 *Siemens/Drägerwerk/JV* [2003] OJ L291/1 and Case M3083 *GE/Instrumentarium* [2004] OJ L109/1.

5 Case M3216 *Oracle/PeopleSoft* [2005] OJ L218/6.

6 See para 187 of *Oracle/PeopleSoft*: "In the statement of objections the Commission based its concerns in part on the finding that significant non-coordinated effects would arise from the transaction. In the reply to the statement of objections, Oracle contested the Commission's competence to assess such effects under the dominance test incorporated in Regulation (EEC) No. 4064/89. It is not necessary to address Oracle's submission on the lack of competence as, on the basis of the new evidence obtained after the Oral Hearing, it has been concluded that no such anticompetitive effects are likely to result from the merger."

7 Case M1524 *Airtours/First Choice* [2000] OJ L93/1 ("*Airtours/First Choice*"). The Commission faced criticism because it did not make an efficient use of evidence, for example, by not taking into consideration the conclusions of the UK Competition Commission in 1997 according to which the market was competitive with no significant barriers to entry. In addition, the Commission attempted to extend the law by applying the collective dominance concept in a merger between the second and third largest firms, in a market which did not exhibit the features that render it likely to be conducive to collective dominance. Furthermore, the merger would not lead to a situation of single firm dominance. See Chapters 2 and 4 of this book for further analysis. See also: UK Competition Commission, Cm 3813, *Foreign package holidays: A report on the supply in the UK of tour operators' services and travel agents' services in relation to foreign package holidays*, 19.12.97, www.competition-commission.org.uk.

8 See Chapters 2 and 4 for further analysis of the *Airtours/First Choice* merger. See also para 54 of the Commission's decision.

9 Case T-342/99 *Airtours v Commission* [2002] ECR II-2585. It can also be argued that the *Airtours* decision came at the right moment for the European Commission. The limitations of the dominance test and the benefits of adopting an SLC-type test were identified from the application of the SLC test in other jurisdictions, such as the United States. It can arguably be said that *Airtours* provided an "opportunity" to reform the substantive test.

10 *Green Paper on the Review of Council Regulation (EEC) No. 4064/89*, COM(2001) 745/6, 11.12.2001.

11 Court of Justice, General Court.
12 One of the major criticisms of the green paper was that the definition of "non-collusive oligopolies" was so wide that it could capture mergers in which the post-merger firm had considerable market power but was not dominant.
13 *Commission Notice on the appraisal of horizontal mergers under the Council Regulation on the control of concentration between undertakings*, COM/2002, 11.12.2002.
14 For the purposes of this book the terms "mergers leading to non-coordinated effects in oligopolistic markets", "gap cases" and "non-collusive oligopolies" will be used interchangeably.
15 See further: http://europa.eu.int/comm/competition/mergers/review/contributions.html.
16 *Guidelines on the assessment of horizontal mergers under the Council Regulation on the control of concentrations between undertakings* ("*Guidelines*"), OJ C31, 05.02.2004, 5–18.
17 Council Regulation (EC) No. 139/2004 of 20 January 2004 on the control of concentrations between undertakings (the EC Merger Regulation), ("recast ECMR"), OJ L24, 29.01.2004, 1–22.
18 The merged entity and one or more incumbents in the post merger market could hold a collectively dominant position.
19 See further: para 25, *Guidelines on the assessment of horizontal mergers under the Council Regulation on the control of concentrations between undertakings* ("*Guidelines*"), OJ C31, 05.02.2004, 5–18.
20 The significance of product differentiation may be diminished if it is possible for competitors to reposition their products to compete directly with the merging parties' products, (for example, by engaging in brand repositioning or introducing new brands).
21 *Guidelines on the assessment of horizontal mergers under the Council Regulation on the control of concentrations between undertakings* ("*Guidelines*"), OJ C31, 05.02.2004, 5–18.
22 See Appendix for the substantive tests in each EU member state.
23 Case T-342/99 *Airtours v Commission* [2002] ECR II-2585.
24 The request for submission of undertakings implies that the merger was found to be incompatible with the appropriate law and was cleared after the proposed remedies were considered sufficient to rectify the adverse impact on competition.
25 As the *Financial Times* mentioned in an article, the Commission may be constrained by current rules, which do not explicitly permit it to ban mergers that could give rise to "non-collusive oligopolies", such as the one Brussels suspects may arise between Oracle and SAP. See www.ft.com, article of 28 March 2004.
26 Such cases include: *Airtours/First Choice, Oracle/PeopleSoft,* Case M3333 *Sony/BMG* [2005] OJ L62/30 ("*Sony/BMG*").
27 The SLC was adopted with the Enterprise Act 2002. See further: www.oft.gov.uk.
28 See further: Clayton Antitrust Act 1914, 15 USC § 12–27, 29 USC § 52–53.
29 The abnormal return is computed as the difference between the return on the stock and the return on an appropriate index on the day of announcement. A normal rate of return for the stock would be the same return as the one for the index.

1 European Community Merger Regulation – Council Regulation (EC) No. 4064/89

This chapter addresses the question of whether there was a "gap" in the application of the dominance test of the original ECMR. After briefly analysing the purpose of the ECMR the answer to this question will be provided by the analysis of the *Airtours*[1] case and, in particular, how that case illustrated the existence of a "gap" in the application of the dominance test. The historical origin of the term "dominance", along with the criteria that the General Court considered in *Airtours* as essential in the assessment of the likelihood of a merger leading to collective dominance, will be analysed. This analysis will also address how the concept of dominance and collective dominance under the ECMR draws from the case law of Article 102 TFEU.[2] This part of the book will address the concept of collective dominance, as it is a necessary step in order to fully capture the issues addressed herein.

1.1 Purpose of the European Community Merger Regulation

The importance of this book is illustrated by the increased role of merger control. The purpose of merger laws is to capture mergers that may have adverse effects on competition. There are several reasons for firms to engage in mergers. A merger or an acquisition is a common method that firms choose in order to be profitable and sustain their viability and profitability through time. Mergers consolidate the ownership and control of business assets, including physical assets (for example, plant) and intangibles (for example, brand reputation). They can enhance corporate – and wider economic – performance by improving the efficiency with which business assets are used. Further reasons for firms to engage in mergers and acquisitions include efficiencies arising from the mergers,[3] and the tendency of some countries to endorse the concept of "national champions".[4] In addition, mergers provide the means to a firm to exit the industry while at the same time reap a monetary reward or compensation for the risks and the initial investments. Furthermore, mergers may also satisfy the ambitions of executives for more power and greater control.[5]

The purpose of the ECMR lies in sustaining an effective and well-functioning internal market by effectively ensuring that reorganizations in the market will not induce an adverse impact on competition.[6] Mergers may eliminate any competition that exists between the merging parties and may lead to a reduction in the number of firms competing in the market. Where this reduction has a substantial adverse effect on overall market competition, the market will be less oriented to consumer and efficiency goals, even in the absence of breaches of competition legislation.

In order to accomplish the target of sustaining the competitive structure of the post-merger market, a competition authority must apply a legal substantive test in order to determine the likelihood of an adverse impact of the merger on competition; it must also know what level and quality of evidence it needs in its assessment of whether the merger should be prohibited. The Recast ECMR applies the Substantial Impediment to Effective Competition ("SIEC") test[7] as the legal substantive test for the assessment of concentrations. The issue of evidence is a matter that has been determined by the General Court and the Court of Justice.

As has been discussed already, this chapter addresses the question of whether there was a "gap" in the application of the dominance test and how the *Airtours* case, in which the merger was prohibited on collective dominance grounds, illustrated the existence of a "gap" in the application of the dominance test. The Commission argued that the merger would lead to collective dominance, but, depending on how one interprets the decision, it was possible that it considered that the merger would lead to non-coordinated effects in an oligopolistic market. Thus, there was confusion in the Commission's interpretation of collective dominance. After presenting the General Court's interpretation of collective dominance, and illustrating the possibility of the existence of a gap in the dominance test, the next chapter will address the adoption of the new substantive test, which addressed the abovementioned gap. The following chapters will present extensive case law that indicates the gap in the application of the dominance test.

Before embarking on an analysis of the concept of non-collusive oligopolies, it is important to further define two concepts that are at the heart of the ECMR. These two concepts are non-coordinated effects (unilateral effects) and coordinated effects. A merger may either lead to the post-merger firm unilaterally engaging in conduct having an adverse impact on competition or may lead the remaining firms after the merger to collectively coordinate their behaviour.

Mergers can produce non-coordinated effects if the elimination of the competitive restraints that the merging firms exercised on each other increases the combined firm's market power. Non-coordinated (or unilateral) effects refer to the overall detrimental welfare effects resulting from changes or adjustments in prices and output made unilaterally by the post-merger firm. Such effects do not entail any coordination of decisions by the firms in the post-merger market. On the contrary, coordinated effects refer to the overall detrimental welfare effects of anti-competitive conduct as a result of a merger that renders collusion likely in the post-merger market.[8]

Furthermore, nonmerging firms in the same market can also benefit from the reduction of the competitive pressure resulting from the merger, since the merging firms' price increase may switch some demand to the rival firms, which, in turn, may find it profitable to increase their prices (non-collusive oligopoly scenario). Thus, even if rival firms pursue the same competitive strategies as they did prior to the merger, this can result in their increasing prices in the post-merger market. In such cases, the firms in the marketplace are not coordinating their competitive behaviour, but merely reacting to changes in each other's behaviour.

It has been argued that these non-coordinated (unilateral effects) and coordinated effects are mutually inconsistent[9] since non-coordinated effects arise when the merged group enjoys market power without depending for its success and profitability on coordinated interaction with other firms in the market, whereas coordinated effects depend on the successful coordinated interaction of the merged entity with the incumbents in the market. The creation of non-coordinated effects implies that the merged entity will be in a position to unilaterally adopt anticompetitive conduct. This is likely to be the case when it will have a market share which will be significantly higher than the second biggest firm in the market.[10] In contrast, the creation of coordinated effects requires the collectively dominant firms to have similar market share levels in order to face similar incentives as well as ability in sustaining a collectively dominant position.[11]

Although non-coordinated and coordinated effects are unlikely to occur simultaneously, it is possible that the merger may lead to non-coordinated and coordinated effects occurring sequentially. This can be the case in a merger between two firms, one of which is a maverick and/or the closest competitor of the other firm. The elimination of the maverick will enhance the likelihood of the firms in the post-merger market being collectively dominant. In addition, merging with a maverick and/or closest competitor enhances the firm's incentives for a unilateral price increase on products whose price was influenced by the maverick's pricing.[12] The non-coordinated effects would appear initially whereas coordinated behaviour would become rational for the remaining firms in the post-merger market.

The market structure in which mergers are likely to lead to non-coordinated effects in oligopolistic markets resembles the market structure in which mergers could lead to unilateral effects (or non-coordinated effects).[13] Non-coordinated effects in oligopolistic markets can arise in concentrated markets where firms compete with differentiated products and the products of the merging firms are particularly close substitutes. If firms producing close substitutes merge, the combined entity is more likely to increase price post-merger than if competitors that do not produce close substitutes merge. If the incumbents can alter their product line and become close substitutes to the merged entity, the induced non-coordinated effects will be mitigated.[14]

In contrast, coordinated effects arise in market structures that are prone to collusion. The General Court in *Airtours* articulated three criteria for coordination to be likely in the post-merger market. These criteria are transparency, retaliation mechanisms, and lack of countervailing reactions from consumers and competitors. The market structure that is prone to coordinated effects is characterized, inter alia, by product homogeneity,[15] low demand growth,[16] low price sensitivity of demand,[17] symmetric cost structures,[18] and multi-market contacts.[19]

In order to illustrate that these non-coordinated effects in oligopolistic markets and coordinated effects are mutually inconsistent, we should note that one of the elements conducive to a collusive equilibrium is the homogeneous nature of the products of the collectively dominant firms. Homogeneous products make comparison of prices easier leading consequently to improved detection of cheating and thus enhance the sustainability of collusive outcomes. The imbalance created by differentiated products reduces the incentives for collusion.[20]

One factor conducive to the creation of non-coordinated effects in oligopolistic markets is the differentiated nature of the products of the incumbents in the post-merger market. Under the assumption of one market, the products cannot be both differentiated and homogeneous. Thus, non-coordinated effects and coordinated effects cannot be simultaneously alleged in the same market.[21]

1.2 Origins of the notion of dominance

The EU has its origins in the common market established by the European Coal and Steel Treaty in 1952 ("ECSC").[22] The aim of the ECSC Treaty, as stated in Article 2, was to contribute, through the common market for coal and steel, to economic expansion, growth of employment, and a rising standard of living. In the light of the establishment of the common market, the ECSC Treaty introduced the free movement of products without customs duties or taxes. It prohibited discriminatory measures or practices, subsidies, aids granted by states or special charges imposed by states and restrictive practices. The Treaty dealt specifically with three elements that could distort competition: agreements,[23] concentrations, and the abuse of dominant positions.

Article 66 expressly dealt with merger control. Article 66(7) of the ECSC Treaty was based on dominance.[24] The origins of the notion of dominance can be traced back to German competition law. German competition law (*Gesetz gegen Wettbewerbsbeschränkungen* ("GWB"))[25] used the term "dominance" in Section 22(1); it was a concept already familiar due to the previous Abuse Regulation of 1923.[26] One reason for adopting the term dominance rather than the term monopolization, which is used in the Sherman Act,[27] is the influence that German competition law had on the drafter of the ECSC Treaty, Jean Monnet.

The notion of dominance has been addressed both in law and economics. In the realm of economics, dominance has been addressed by theories dealing with oligopolistic and monopolistic market structures. In the realm of law, the concept of dominance is found in two sets of legal provisions, namely Article 102 TFEU[28] and the ECMR.[29] The legal definition of dominance has been an issue of intense debate. The standard legal definition of dominance was laid down by the Court of Justice in *United Brands*. The Court of Justice stated that:

> The dominant position thus referred to (by Article [102 TFEU]) relates to a position of economic strength enjoyed by an undertaking which enables it to prevent effective competition being maintained on the relevant market by affording it the power to behave to an appreciable extent independently of its competitors, customers and ultimately of its consumers.[30]

In *Hoffmann-La Roche*,[31] the Court of Justice defined the notion of dominance as "a position of economic strength enjoyed by an undertaking, which enables it to behave to an appreciable extent independently of its competitors, its customers and ultimately of consumers".

The legal definition of dominance has been addressed by several cases brought before the Court of Justice. In *Continental Can*,[32] the Commission, in defining a "dominant position", focused on the ability of entities to behave independently in making decisions that affect the market as a whole. Regarding its definition in merger cases, the formulation of dominance in *United Brands* was echoed in the Court of Justice's *Kali und Salz* decision with respect to collective dominance.[33]

The legal definition of dominance as it has emerged through the case law still entails certain drawbacks. The essence of the Court of Justice's definition of dominance is the ability to act independently to an appreciable extent of competitors, customers, and consumers. It is this essence that entails problems. One of the criticisms of the definition of dominance is that firms cannot act to an appreciable extent independently of their consumers, due to the downward sloping demand curve, which implies that the higher the price of the product the lower the quantity demanded. This inverse relationship between price and quantity may not hold for products that are price inelastic, such as medicines, meaning that the increase in price may not affect the quantity demanded. This argument holds both for dominant and non-dominant firms, and as Azevedo and Walker (2002) argue, "trying to define dominance with respect to the ability of a firm to behave to an appreciable extent independently of its consumers will not distinguish adequately between dominant and non-dominant firms".[34]

A further criticism related to the difficulty in measuring the ability of firms to behave independently from competitors. Every firm that faces competitors (that is to say, all firms apart from monopolists) is constrained to some extent by the conduct of these competitors. The pricing policy of even a dominant firm is dependent on the pricing of its competitors. A dominant firm will raise prices above the competitive level to a point that will be determined by its demand curve, as well as by the constraints imposed on the firm by its competitors' strategy. So the dominant firm does not act independently of its competitors. This argument is also true in case the market is focused on other dimensions of competition such as quality and innovation.[35]

Azevedo and Walker (2002) argue that the definition of dominance as was outlined in *United Brands* could be made more economically coherent by replacing the "behave to an appreciable extent independently" with "restrained by the independent actions".[36] They also suggest an approach that mitigates the drawbacks related to the definition of dominance in *United Brands*. They argue that dominance can be defined as the ability to restrict output[37] substantially in the marketplace. Dominant firms have power over price and thus, by restricting output in the market, decrease consumer welfare. According to the authors, focusing on output restriction is consistent with most of the standard factors that are usually considered relevant in the appraisal of dominance.[38] In addition, in cases where the observation of price and costs cannot be easily achieved, concentrating on the ability to reduce quantity may provide an alternative means of assessing dominance. Thus, according to the authors, this definition would be consistent with current practice and would have a firm economic foundation.

However, focusing the definition of dominance on the restriction of output may be considered to be too narrow and possibly inadequate to incorporate conduct that has an adverse impact on competition entailing limited or no output restriction. Adverse effects on competition can be induced due to, among other things, lower quality. The criticisms already mentioned notwithstanding, for the purposes of this book dominance is defined according to Court of Justice's definition in *United Brands*.[39]

As stated earlier, in addition to Article 102 TFEU, the concept of dominance was used in the ECMR. As the Court of Justice confirmed in *Kali und Salz*,[40] there must be a causal link between the creation or the strengthening of dominance under the original ECMR and the adverse impact on effective competition. On the contrary, in the context of Article 102 TFEU, as the Court of Justice in *Continental Can* argued, "there is no need for a causal link to be established between the dominant position and the abuse. It is necessary only that the conduct strengthens the undertaking's dominant position and fetters competition on the market".[41] This distinction on the necessity of the "causal link" illustrates the different application of the dominance test under Article 102 TFEU and the ECMR.

Turning now to collective dominance, we can readily observe that it occurs in highly concentrated markets with a small number of players who recognize their interdependence and the futility of aggressive competitive behaviour. As a result, market structures are conducive to tacit coordination.[42] Collective dominance is dealt with by Article 102 TFEU as well as by the ECMR. As regards abuses of a collective dominant position, Article 102 TFEU applies to an abuse "by one or more undertakings of a dominant position within the Common Market or in a substantial part of it".[43]

As far as the application of Article 102 TFEU on dominance/collective dominance is concerned, dominance/collective dominance does not constitute infringements to Article 102 TFEU per se. An abuse of a dominant position is, however, a breach of Article 102 TFEU. The main types of abuse include: excessive pricing[44] (*United Brands*), predatory pricing[45] (*AKZO*),[46] discriminatory pricing[47] (*United Brands*), refusal to supply[48] (*Commercial Solvents*),[49] tying in[50] (*Hilti, Tetra Pak II*),[51,52] loyalty rebates (*Hoffman–La Roche*), abuse of intellectual property ("IP") rights (*Magill*),[53] and vexatious litigation (*Promedia*).[54] As the judgment in *Continental Can*[55] clarified, however, Article 102 TFEU did not set out an exhaustive enumeration of the types of abuse of a dominant position prohibited by the EC Treaty.[56]

At this point it would be useful to refer to cases of collective dominance dealt under Article 102 TFEU in order to have a concrete idea of the development of the concept of collective dominance.

In *Flat Glass*, the General Court condemned three firms for agreements and practices breaching Article 101 TFEU.[57] The Commission found three producers of flat glass as holding a collectively dominant position. The General Court for the first time applied the notion of collective dominance under Article 102 TFEU and considered that the definition of the term "undertaking" is the same under both Articles 101 TFEU and 102 TFEU. The General Court also considered the conceptual difference between infringements falling under Article 101 TFEU and 102 TFEU. Article 102 TFEU could apply to a situation where two or more independent undertakings being united by economic links, acted on the market as a single entity and not as individual entities (as would be required for application of Article 101 TFEU). However, the General Court left the term "economic links" undefined. Later cases such as *Almelo, CEWAL,*[58] *Irish Sugar*[59] (alleged breach of Article 102 TFEU), as well as cases such as *Nestlé,*[60] *France v Commission,*[61] and *Gencor*[62] (alleged breach of the ECMR), shed further light on the definition of the term "economic links".

In *Almelo,* the undertakings were found to be collectively dominant due to the adoption of the same conduct in the market (§1519–§1520). Collective dominance was also found in the *CEWAL* case, where, however, the Court of Justice emphasized the importance but at the same time the non-indispensability of economic links to a finding of collective dominance.

In the *Irish Sugar* case, the Commission found that the links between a distributor and a producer of sugar led to vertical collective dominance. However, the ability to adopt the same conduct in the market and not the issue of vertical or horizontal relationship is what was essential in the finding of collective dominance.

In contrast to Article 102 TFEU, the ECMR refers to the prospective assessment of collective dominance in seeking to determine the effects of a prospective merger. This fact reflects the different roles of Article 102 TFEU and of the EMCR and the different application of these two legal provisions in cases of collective dominance. Article 102 TFEU is designed to control market behaviour,[63] while the focus of the ECMR is on the future market structure rather than on the past development of competition. In addition, there have been relatively few findings of abuse, indicating the importance of the concept of collective dominance for mergers since it prevents collective dominance from arising in the post-merger market.[64] In general, the introduction of the concept of dominance pointed in the direction of the Court of Justice in Article 102 TFEU cases, even though jurisprudence focused on abusive commercial conduct by dominant firms rather than on the preservation of competitive market structures.[65]

As regards mergers that may lead to collective dominance the legal substantive test in the Recast ECMR states that "a concentration which would significantly impede effective competition, in the common market or in a substantial part of it, in particular as a result of the creation or strengthening of a dominant position, shall be declared incompatible with the common market".[66] Mergers leading, inter alia, to collective dominance are incompatible with the common market.[67]

In cases that formulated the concept of collective dominance, such as *Kali und Salz*, *Gencor* and *Airtours*,[68] the Community courts had considered collectively dominant firms in oligopolistic markets rather than firms adopting anti-competitive conduct individually in oligopolistic markets. Thus, there is no indication that the concept of mergers leading to non-coordinated in oligopolistic markets had been addressed.

In the following part of this chapter, we focus on the original ECMR and its development from its inception to its reform. Reform of the original ECMR came following the wide criticism received by the Commission in landmark cases such as *Airtours*, *Schneider*,[69] and *Tetra Laval*.[70]

Before embarking on an analysis of the so-called non-collusive oligopoly gap that *Airtours/First Choice*[71] appears to illustrate, this book briefly deals with the concept of collective dominance on which *Airtours/First Choice* was decided. As we shall see in the analysis herein, the features that exist in a market in which a merger can lead to non-coordinated effects in oligopolistic markets are similar to the features that render a market prone to collective dominance.

1.3 History of Council Regulation 4064/89 and its applicability on collective dominance

The original EC Treaty did not include any specific provision for the control of mergers. Articles 101 TFEU and 102 TFEU of the Treaty focus on controlling the behaviour of undertakings rather than dealing with mergers. The Commission sought to persuade the Council to enact a merger control provision, while at the same time attempted to apply Articles 101 TFEU and 102 TFEU to prevent conduct arising from some mergers that had an adverse impact on competition.

The application of Articles 101 TFEU and 102 TFEU on mergers entails certain drawbacks. This book will focus on the application of Articles 101 TFEU and 102 TFEU and their shortcomings when dealing with mergers in oligopolistic markets. Mergers permanently change the structure of the market. Undertakings in oligopolistic markets may realize their interdependence and behave "as if" they have colluded, hence producing an adverse impact on efficiency and consumer welfare. As they have not actually colluded or concerted, Article 101 TFEU(1) cannot apply: tacit coordination is not prohibited by the Article. Furthermore, Article 101 TFEU is not applicable to agreements whose purpose is the acquisition of total or partial ownership of an enterprise or the reorganization of the ownership of enterprises.

Controversy arose in situations where an undertaking acquired by agreement a minority shareholding in another undertaking without assuming legal or de facto control. Such a situation was encountered in *BAT*.[72] The Commission approved an agreement giving control of Rembrandt to Philip Morris. BAT and Reynolds brought an action before the Court of Justice on the basis of Article 230 EC to challenge the clearance decision of the Commission. The Court of Justice rejected the applicants' argument. The Court of Justice also held that agreements that lead to concentrations could be reviewed under Article 101 TFEU. The decision contributed to a substantial degree of uncertainty for mergers occurring within the Community. However, if an acquisition of shares leads to coordination of competitive behaviour of two undertakings, Article 101 TFEU(1) would still apply.[73] As Furse further argues, application of Article 101 TFEU(2) to a fully consummated merger could have disastrous and unpredictable consequences.[74]

In *Re Continental Can*,[75] the Commission found an abuse of Article 102 TFEU where a takeover bid was made by a dominant undertaking for a smaller competitor. The Commission argued that such an acquisition might constitute an abuse since it would adversely affect the structure of competition in a market where competition was weakened from the presence of the allegedly dominant undertaking. The Court of Justice annulled the Commission's decision on the basis that it did not identify the market accurately. However, the Court of Justice confirmed that

Article 102 TFEU could apply in a situation where a dominant undertaking was acquiring another undertaking.

As far as Article 102 TFEU is concerned, its shortcomings relate to the fact that it applies to concentrations already enjoying a dominant position. A transaction that creates a dominant position, as may be the case with a merger or acquisition, falls outside the ambit of Article 102 TFEU. In addition, Article 102 TFEU focuses on market behaviour,[76] while the focus of both the original and the Recast ECMR is on the future market structure rather than on the past development of competition in the market.

The shortcomings mentioned earlier were also indicated in Recital 7 of the Recast ECMR according to which:

> Articles 81 and 82 [102 TFEU], while applicable, according to the case law of the Court of Justice, to certain concentrations, are not sufficient to control all operations which may prove to be incompatible with the system of undistorted competition envisaged in the Treaty.

Motivated by such shortcomings the Council of Ministers, on 21 December 1989, adopted Council Regulation 4064/89[77] (original ECMR); this Regulation came into force on 21 September 1990. The Regulation is based both on Article 83, which provides for the making of Council Regulations to implement the provisions of Articles 101 TFEU and 102 TFEU, and on Article 232, which grants the Council the residual power to take appropriate measures where action proves necessary in order to attain one of the Commission's objectives and the Treaty of Rome has not provided the necessary powers.[78] The main aim of the original ECMR was to provide a means for the prevention of concentrations having an adverse impact on competition, as well as to provide a single framework within which such transactions can be assessed (the "one-stop shop" principle).[79]

As regards the applicability of the ECMR on collective dominance, the wording of the original ECMR lends no support for the view that it applies to concentrations leading to the creation or strengthening of a collective dominant position.[80] However, case law[81] has confirmed that both the original ECMR and the Recast ECMR[82] deal with the likelihood of creating or strengthening of a collective dominance in the post-merger market.

The Commission initially mentioned that the original ECMR operated to prevent the creation or strengthening of a collective dominant position in *Alcatel*.[83] The applicability of the original ECMR to the creation or strengthening of a dominant position enjoyed collectively by two or more firms was also confirmed in *Nestlé*[84] where, for the first time, the Commission accepted divestiture measures as a remedy in order to clear the merger. The acquisition of Perrier by Nestlé would lead to the two remaining big firms in the French market holding 75 per cent share of the market. High market shares, price parallelism, high entry barriers as well as market transparency rendered collective dominance likely in the post-merger market. The merger was approved after considerable divestiture measures were proposed by the parties.

In *Kali und Salz*,[85] the Court of Justice held that the ECMR did apply to situations of collective dominance. Kali und Salz proposed to conclude a joint venture with Treuhandanstalt. The Commission argued that the merger would lead to collective dominance. The Court of Justice annulled the Commission's decision, on the grounds that the Commission had failed to prove the likelihood of the creation or strengthening of a dominant position.

Although the original ECMR did not expressly refer to the concept of collective dominance, the Court of Justice considered that it should be interpreted widely with reference to its general purpose and structure in order to avoid distortions in the Common Market created by conduct having an adverse impact on competition. Hence, the creation or strengthening of a collective dominant position is incompatible with the original ECMR. The Court of Justice further stated that the ability of parties to adopt the same conduct in the market as well as the existence of "connecting factors" and other "economic links", which were left undefined, were essential in the sustainability of collective dominance.

In *Gencor*,[86] the notion of collective dominance was implicitly matched to the notion of tacit coordination by the General Court (at §§270–277). *Gencor/Lonrho*[87] was the first case in which the Commission prohibited a merger on the grounds that it created or strengthened a position of collective dominance and hence impeded effective competition. Gencor and Lonrho would jointly control platinum group metals in South Africa through a joint-owned entity, Implants Ltd. Hence, as the Commission argued, a dominant duopoly would be created with an adverse impact on effective competition within the Common Market. Gencor appealed, but the General Court upheld the Commission's decision. In its judgment, *Gencor*, the General Court clarified some ambiguous issues regarding collective dominance. The term "economic links", used in *Flat Glass*[88] in the ambit of Article 102 TFEU, was substituted for "structural links". In mentioning the *Flat Glass* case (at §273) the General Court did not distinguish between the way that cases of collective dominance would be dealt with under Article 102 TFEU and under the original ECMR. Furthermore, the General Court ruled that it was not necessary for the Commission to establish links between collectively dominant firms.[89]

After having briefly analysed the origin and case law related to collective dominance the book now intends to focus on the criteria that the Commission applies in its assessment of mergers that may contribute to collective dominance in the post-merger market. The significance and impact of the *Airtours*[90] case will be illustrated. This case contributed not only to improving the assessment criteria for collective dominance but also to illustrating the "gap" of the traditional dominance test and the need for the reform of the legal substantive test.

1.4 Appraisal criteria for assessing collective dominance

This part of the chapter will briefly address the assessment criteria for collective dominance that have been developed through the case law under the original ECMR. The characteristics of industries vary to the extent that collusion may be likely among four firms in one industry but not in another. Hence, evaluating the impact of a merger on competition and assessing the likelihood of collective dominance requires assessment of the characteristics of each industry separately. Article 2(1)[91] of the Recast ECMR sets out a list of "appraisal criteria" that should be taken into account in the assessment of concentrations. These criteria are essential in determining whether or not a concentration would significantly impede effective competition, in particular as a result of the creation or strengthening of a dominant position, in the common market or a substantial part of it, as these notions are incorporated in Article 2(3) of the Recast ECMR. This list of criteria is not exhaustive and their importance and relevance will depend on each case brought before the Commission, the General Court and Court of Justice.

In order for a collusive equilibrium to arise and be sustained, certain criteria need to be fulfilled including barriers to entry and exit,[92] a small number of firms, ability to coordinate towards equilibrium, ability to enforce compliance, as well as ability to monitor and deter any prospective maverick[93] firms. These criteria depend on features such as product homogeneity,[94] low demand growth, low price sensitivity of demand,[95] symmetric cost structures,[96] and multi-market contacts.[97] One of the possible classifications of these factors is a two-step procedure investigating the feasibility and likelihood of a significant impediment to effective competition resulting from the creation or strengthening of a dominant position. The first step comprises the identification of the post-merger market structure, while the second step establishes whether conduct inducing an adverse impact on competition is likely and whether there remains any competitive constraint on the post-merger firms. The development of a list of factors has been the result of vast case law precedence.[98]

The next part of this chapter turns to the analysis of *Airtours*, which, as mentioned, illustrated the "gap" in the traditional dominance test and the need for the reform of the legal substantive test.

1.5 The *Airtours* case

In the *Airtours* case,[99] the General Court[100] clarified the law in one of the most ambiguous areas of the original ECMR, that is, its application to mergers inducing non-coordinated effects in oligopolistic markets. As Cook and Kerse[101] (2000) argue, the decision represents the most significant development in EC merger control since the adoption of the Regulation itself. In *Airtours/First* Choice,[102] the Commission investigated a proposed hostile acquisition of Airtours by First Choice. The major tour operators were Thomson (30.7 per cent of the market), Airtours (19.4 per cent of the market), Thomas Cook (20.4 per cent of the market), and First Choice (15 per cent of the market).[103] Certain features of the market such as the high degree of price transparency and multi-market contacts among the major airlines may facilitate coordinated behaviour.[104] The market was already concentrated with four large firms having 80 per cent of the market and several smaller firms occupying the rest. The acquisition would allegedly lead to three firms holding a collective dominant position.[105] *Airtours/First Choice* was the second outright prohibition under the original ECMR on the basis of collective dominance. The Commission's decision was appealed to the General Court.[106]

The Commission appeared to take the view that the ability of firms to engage in tacit collusion is not essential. It is sufficient that the merger makes it rational for firms having adequate market power to act independently of competitors and customers.[107] The Commission diverged from its previous practice and extended the concept of collective dominance from duopoly to a merger reducing the number of post-merger firms to three.[108] The Commission's decision in *Airtours/First Choice*, as Briones and Padilla (2001) argue,[109] extended the boundaries of the situations under which the Commission may find firms to be in a collective dominant position, by focusing on a notion of rational incentives, and decreasing the importance of other factors[110] that had been taken prominently into account in previous decisions.

The *Airtours/First Choice* judgment of the General Court set a markedly higher evidentiary standard that may be applied in any case before the Commission. The Commission in its decision undermined the credibility of the concept of collective dominance and induced legal uncertainty by adopting an approach markedly different from its approach in previous cases. As Korah (2001) stated,[111] rather than clarifying the notion of collective dominance, the *Airtours/First Choice* Commission decision "muddied the water".

The General Court, in annulling the Commission's decision, argued that the Commission had not proved to the required legal standard that the merger would lead to a collective dominant position.[112] Specifically, the demand was volatile, capacity planning was complex with slow capacity changes, the market was not transparent in the capacity planning period, there was lack of barriers to entry, and consumers could easily switch to other types of foreign package holiday such as long-haul. We should add that the UK Competition Commission published a report[113] on foreign package holidays in the United Kingdom in 1997, one and a half years before the *Airtours/First Choice* merger notification, which concluded that the market was competitive with no significant barriers to entry.[114]

The General Court's decision outlined three necessary conditions for a position of collective dominance[115] to be reached and sustained, namely transparency, the existence of credible retaliatory mechanisms, and the countervailing impact of customers and competitors.

1.5.1 Transparency

The General Court argued that it is not sufficient for each member of the oligopoly to be aware that interdependent market conduct is profitable. There must be an adequate degree of transparency so that firms are able to monitor other firms' conducts and detect deviations.[116] The coordinated behaviour of firms may be disrupted by the presence of a maverick firm, which declines to follow the industry consensus and thereby constrains effective coordination. The presence of a maverick in connection with low barriers to entry has been considered by the Commission as decreasing the likelihood of a stable and sustainable collusive outcome.

High market transparency depends on the ability of firms to observe transaction prices and levels of sales of competitors as well as on the degree of concentration of the market, since in concentrated, highly transparent markets deviations from tacit agreements are easily identifiable. It is essential for the firm to be able to distinguish between deviations from the common policy and alterations in behaviour due to external factors such as demand volatility, supply shocks, and exchange rate variations.

The Commission emphasized the importance of market transparency in *Nestlé*[117] as well as in *Gencor/Lonrho*,[118] where it considered actions such as publication of price lists and production and sales statistics as enhancing market transparency.

In addition, the Commission has considered bidding mechanisms as decreasing market transparency and hence the likelihood of tacit collusion, since firms are not fully aware of their competitors' prices and output.[119] However, the reliance on bidding mechanisms as a means of keeping transparency low must be read in light of the fact that bids are often made for specific products so that low transparency is the outcome of both the mechanism and the difficulty in establishing a comparison between products. This was the case in *Valeo/ITT Industries*. Moreover, the Commission should be aware, as was the case in *ABB/Daimler-Benz*,[120] that firms might collude in the bidding process. In particular, they might coordinate so that they take turns in putting forward a tender.[121]

1.5.2 Retaliatory mechanisms

The second condition for sustainable collective dominance in the post-merger market is the existence of a retaliation mechanism as a means for deterring and punishing deviations. If all firms tacitly reach an understanding to compete less vigorously by charging higher prices, then any firm will be induced to increase its profits by charging a lower price and thus deviating from the common policy. In order for tacit coordination to be sustainable over time, as economic analysis also suggests, there must be a credible incentive not to depart from the common conduct in the market. However, the threat of punishment may not always be credible due to the high costs it entails for the firms implementing the punishment.[122]

The Commission, in *Airtours/First Choice*, denied the necessity of a retaliatory mechanism, despite the importance it placed on it in *Gencor/Lonrho*. The General Court argued that the Commission is not required to prove that a retaliation mechanism existed, rather that deterrents exist that provide incentives not to cheat.[123] This argument would appear to be contradictory particularly in light of the General Court's own approach to analysing the viability of the punishment mechanism outlined by the Commission in its decision. However, as Nikpay and Houwen (2003) argue, this vagueness may have been deliberate so the General Court would not tie the Commission's hands in the development of the doctrine of collective dominance.[124]

1.5.3 Competitors and customers

The General Court also pointed out that the Commission, in order to ascertain the sustainability of a common policy, should have established that current and potential competitors could not counterbalance a collective dominant position by increasing their capacity in response to a reduction in supply by the dominant merged entity. Existing or potential competitive constraints by third parties were an essential factor for the clearance of the merger in the *Kali und Salz*[125] case.

The presence of strong buyer power may have a positive impact on the sustainability of tacit collusion.[126] A concentrated buyer structure can be effective in countervailing seller power,[127] by offering to buy at a lower price than the tacitly collusive price and thus by providing incentives for deviations from the common policy. A significant factor influencing the power of buyers is the cost associated in switching suppliers. Low switching costs induce buyers to switch suppliers as a reaction to increased prices and hence undermine the market power of dominant firms. The countervailing power exercised by buyers, in switching to other competitors as a reaction to an increase in price by the dominant merged entity, is regularly considered by the Commission but has not been given great importance in the current case law.[128]

Countervailing buyer power may induce entry of new firms,[129] impede integration, and motivate deviation from the tacitly collusive outcome. The impact of countervailing buyer power may be mitigated, although where buyers are not the final users of the product and they pass on the increased costs to their own buyers, as was the case in *Gencor/Lonrho*, or where, as in *Nestlé*, there is brand loyalty in the market influencing buyers' choice.

1.5.4 Conclusion on Airtours

As Korah (2001) argued, the *Airtours/First Choice* assessment is a "forced fit" in terms of collective dominance, as the market conditions were not conducive to the creation of tacit coordination.[130] As Rodger and MacCulloch (2001) further argue, the Commission's decision in *Airtours/First Choice* indicated its willingness to utilize the collective dominance jurisprudence, and even to extend it somewhat further than the General Court.[131] The Commission's decision led to uncertainty and the outcome of the appeal to the General Court was eagerly awaited. The General Court annulled the Commission's decision to block the merger and laid down a stricter standard for establishing collective dominance. The Commission should not simply reflect the normal economic conditions of the markets but should convincingly indicate not only the adverse impact of commercial links on competition but the likelihood and sustainability of the common policy as well.

Motta (1999) argues, however, that blocking the merger was the correct decision, because the merger was related to unilateral effects, and was an attempt by the Commission to prohibit mergers that otherwise could not be blocked.[132] As Airtours submitted, the references to undertakings acting "individually" indicated that the scope of collective dominance was extended from coordinated effects to unilateral effects.[133] It has further been argued that the single dominance test requires such overwhelming market power by the dominant firm that many mergers that should be blocked on the basis of unilateral effects cannot be blocked, and thus have to be dealt with under collective dominance.[134] The General Court, however, by focusing on the likelihood of tacit coordination, accepted that the *Airtours* decision referred to collective dominance rather than unilateral effects.

Three reservations can be identified in the General Court's judgment. First, the General Court may have delved too far into the substantive merits of the Commission's assessment; second, the General Court may have drawn too close an analogy between tacit collusion and explicit agreements with adverse effects on competition; and, third, the General Court conflated separate aspects of the test for merger prohibition leaving the judgment less helpful as a source of guidance for future cases.[135] According to Nikpay and Houwen (2003), the General Court judgment does not represent a radical development of the law in relation to the doctrine of collective dominance.[136]

Regarding the assessment of collective dominance, the Commission has accepted and used the analytical framework applied by the General Court in *Airtours*.[137] Criteria such as number of firms, level of market concentration, market transparency, and symmetry of firms are given significant weight in the Commission's assessment. However, the decisive factor is the interaction of these criteria and their combined impact on the post-merger market. The Commission in its appraisal should not confuse the normal functioning of an oligopolistic market with oligopolistic dominance.

As Levy (2003) argues, in affirming the notion of collective dominance based on the likelihood of sustainable tacit collusion, the Commission has aligned its approach to that of the United States.[138] By specifying the assessment criteria for collective dominance, the Commission made the distinction between collective dominance and non-coordinated effects in oligopolistic markets more robust.

The *Airtours* judgment has failed to clarify explicitly two issues. These issues relate to the standard of proof that the Commission must meet and, second, whether the collective dominance doctrine can be applied to unilateral effects. Furthermore, the *Airtours* judgment appears to leave a gap in the coverage of the original ECMR, as Motta's (1999)[139] and Kühn's (2002)[140] arguments indicate, in that mergers which can have adverse effects on competition by leading to a position of neither single firm dominance nor collective dominance cannot be dealt with under the dominance test. As Europe Economics (2002) argued,[141] "this gap can only be filled by amending the ECMR, most obviously by adopting the substantial lessening of competition test (SLC)".

In recent years the Commission has been confronted with arguably problematic cases that neither satisfied the single dominance test (post-merger the merged entity does not have the largest market share) nor gave rise to obvious coordinated effects (the market structure was not conducive to tacit collusion and thus firms were unlikely to engage post-merger in tacit coordination). In such cases, the Commission sought either to stretch the concept of single firm dominance, as it did in the *Carrefour/Promodés*[142] decision (where the merged firm combined share was between 25 per cent and 30 per cent), or to blur the dividing line between unilateral and coordinated effects as it did in *Airtours/First Choice*. The first case indicates the inadequacy of the dominance test in dealing with the adverse effects of certain mergers on competition, while the latter illustrates the "gap" in the application of the dominance test as the legal substantive test for the assessment of concentrations.[143]

This chapter has addressed the question of whether there is a "gap" in the application of the dominance test. The *Airtours/First Choice*[144] case provided an example of where the Commission, under the impression that the merger would lead, inter alia, to non-coordinated effects in oligopolistic markets,[145] blocked the merger based on the allegation of creation or strengthening of collective dominance. This decision was appealed to the General Court, which annulled the decision and set out criteria that need to be satisfied before an allegation of collective dominance can be made by the Commission. The concept of collective dominance, based on which the *Airtours/First Choice* case was decided, refers only to coordinated effects and illustrates the inability of the original ECMR to apply to non-coordinated effects in oligopolistic markets.

After illustrating the possibility of the existence of a gap in the dominance test, the next chapter will analyse the Recast ECMR and evaluate how the Commission, after intense debate, changed the substantive test for assessing mergers, in an attempt to address and rectify the "gap" in the application of the dominance test. The chapter will also briefly address the procedural and jurisdictional reforms the Commission implemented in order to enhance legal certainty and efficiency in the assessment of concentrations. Finally, the chapter will present a brief account of the *Horizontal Merger Guidelines.*

Notes

1 Case T-342/99 *Airtours v Commission* [2002] ECR II-2585.
2 Pursuant to the Lisbon Treaty, Article 102 TFEU is now 102.
3 Including economies of scale and economies of scope. Economies of scale refer to the situation where long run average costs of production decrease as output rises. See further: Begg D., Fischer S. and Dornbusch R. (1997), *Economics,* 5th edn, McGraw-Hill, Maidenhead, 109. Economies of scope refer to the situation in which the joint output of a single firm is greater than the output that could be achieved by two different firms each producing a single product (with equivalent production inputs allocated between the two firms). See further: Pindyck, R. and Rubinfeld, D. (1998), *Microeconomics,* 4th edn, Prentice Hall International, Upper Saddle River, NJ, 227. Economies of scope are conceptually similar to economies of scale. Economies of scale apply to efficiencies associated with increasing or decreasing the scale of production and refer to changes in the output of a single product type. Economies of scope refer to efficiencies associated with increasing or decreasing the scope of marketing and distribution and refer to changes in the number of different types of products. In addition, economies of scale refer primarily to supply-side changes (such as level of production) whereas economies of scope refer to demand-side changes (such as marketing and distribution).
4 The concept of "national champion" refers to domestic firms that are able post-merger to successfully compete in international markets.
5 Managers may be interested in the size, growth or risk diversification of the company they run. Owners of firms may sometimes give managers incentives in their contracts to achieve some of these targets (that is to say increasing the firm's size in the marketplace). See further: Motta M. (2004), *Competition Policy-Theory and Practice,* Cambridge University Press, Cambridge, 243.
6 Recitals 2 and 3 of the preamble of the Recast ECMR, *Council Regulation (EC)* No. 139/2004 of 20 January 2004 on the control of concentrations between undertakings (the EC Merger Regulation), ("Recast ECMR"), OJ L24, 29.01.2004, 1–22.
7 Article 2(3), Council Regulation (EC) No. 139/2004 of 20 January 2004 on the control of concentrations between undertakings (the EC Merger Regulation), ("Recast ECMR"), OJ L24, 29.01.2004, 1–22.
8 For a definition of unilateral and coordinated effects see further: *Joint US Department of Justice and Federal Trade Commission Horizontal Merger Guidelines 1992,* www.ftc.gov/bc/docs/horizmer.htm, sections 2.1 and 2.2.
9 Europe Economics (2001), *Study on Assessment Criteria for Distinguishing between Competitive and Dominant Oligopolies in Merger Control,* http://europa.eu.int/comm/enterprise/library/lib-competition/libr-competition.html, vi, 62–3.

10 This paragraph does not refer to non-coordinated effects in oligopolistic markets. It only refers to unilateral effects. The possibility of non-coordinated effects in oligopolistic markets and coordinated effects occurring simultaneously will be addressed in the following paragraphs.

11 Kokkoris I. (2007b), "The Development of the Concept of Collective Dominance in the ECMR. From its Inception to its Current Status", *World Competition*, 30(3), 419–48.

12 Lindsay A. (2003), *The EC Merger Regulation: Substantive Issues*, Sweet & Maxwell, London, 151.

13 Non-coordinated effects in oligopolistic markets refer to a more specific type of competitive harm (specifically in oligopolistic markets, that is to say non-collusive oligopolies) induced from a merger compared to the more generic concept of non-coordinated effects (unilateral effects).

14 WilmerHale (2004), *Guide to EC Merger Regulation*, 4th edn, www.wilmehale.com, 51.

15 This factor was considered in cases such as: M619 *Gencor/Lonrho* [1997] OJ L11/30 (*Gencor/Lonrho*), Case M190 *Nestlé/Perrier* [1992] OJ L356/1 (*Nestlé*), M308 *Kali und Salz/MdK/Treuhand* [1998] OJ C275/3 (*Kali und Salz*).

16 This factor was considered in cases such as: *Gencor/Lonrho, Airtours/First Choice.*

17 This factor was considered in cases such as: *Gencor/Lonrho, Nestlé, Airtours/First Choice.*

18 This factor was considered in cases such as: *Gencor/Lonrho, Nestlé, Enso/Stora.*

19 This factor was considered in cases such as: *Gencor/Lonrho, Nestlé.*

20 See Kokkoris I. (2007b), "The Development of the Concept of Collective Dominance in the ECMR. From its Inception to its Current Status", *World Competition*, 30(3), 419–48.

21 The Commission in the Case M3916 *T-Mobile/Tele.ring*, 26 April 2006, alleged the creation of both non-coordinated effects and coordinated effects. However, the decision does not elaborate on the alleged coordinated effects.

22 The ECSC Treaty expired on 23 July 2002. Thus, the coal and steel sectors are now subject to Articles 101 TFEU and 102 TFEU, rather than Articles 65 and 66 ECSC. The consequences of this expiry are explained in the Commission's document *Communication from the Commission concerning certain aspects of the treatment of competition cases resulting from the expiry of the ECSC Treaty*, OJ [2002] C152/5, [2002] 5 CMLR 1036, Section 2: http://europa.eu.int/eur-lex/pri/en/oj/dat/2002/c_152/c_15220020626en 00050012.pdf.

23 Agreements or associations between undertakings could be cancelled by the High Authority if they directly or indirectly prevented, restricted, or distorted normal competition.

24 Article 66(7) was concerned with the concept of a dominant position: If the High Authority finds that public or private undertakings which, in law or in fact, hold or acquire in the market for one of the products within its jurisdiction a dominant position shielding them against effective competition in a substantial part of the common market are using that position for purposes contrary to the objectives of this Treaty, it shall make to them such recommendations as may be appropriate to prevent the position from being so used. If these recommendations are not implemented satisfactorily within a reasonable time, the High Authority shall, by decisions taken in consultation with the Government concerned, determine the prices and conditions of sale to be applied by the undertaking in question or draw up production or delivery programmes with which it must comply, subject to liability to the penalties provided for in Articles 58, 59 and 64.

25 Available from the Bundeskartellamt website www.bundeskartellamt.de/wDeutsch/index.shtml ?navid=27.

26 *Verordnung gegen Missbrauch Wirtschaftlicher Machtstellungen*, 1923, Reichsbesetzblatt, [R6B.1] I, 1067, 2 November 1923.

27 15 USC §2: monopolizing trade a felony; penalty: every person who shall monopolize, or attempt to monopolize, or combine or conspire with any other person or persons, to monopolize any part of the trade or commerce among the several States, or with foreign nations, shall be deemed guilty of a felony, and, on conviction thereof, shall be punished by fine not exceeding $10,000,000 if a corporation, or, if any other person, $350,000, or by imprisonment not exceeding three years, or by both said punishments, in the discretion of the court.

28 Articles 101 and 102 of the TFEU (ex 85 and 86 prior to the Treaty of Amsterdam which came into force on 1 May 1999. Article 12 of the Treaty of Amsterdam provided for the renumbering of the EC Treaty Articles). The EC Treaty was signed on 25 March 1957.

29 Article 102 TFEU deals with the abuse of an already existing dominant position (*ex post*), whereas the ECMR deals with the prospective assessment of dominance (*ex ante*).

30 Case 27/76 *United Brands Co. and United Brands Continental BV v Commission* [1978] ECR I-207, §65.

31 Case 85/76 *Hoffmann-La Roche & Co. AG v Commission* [1979] ECR I-461, at §38.

32 Case 6/72 *Europemballage Corp. and Continental Can Co. Inc. v Commission (Continental Can)* [1973] ECR I-215, §3.

33 See paragraph 221 of Cases C-68/94 and C-30/95 *France v Commission, Societé Commerciale des Potasses et de l'Azore (SCPA) v Commission* [1998] ECR I-1375. According to this paragraph: [I]n the case of an alleged collective dominant position, the Commission is therefore obliged to assess, using a prospective analysis of the reference market, whether the concentration which has been referred to it leads to a situation in which effective competition in the relevant market is significantly impeded by the undertakings involved in the concentration and one or more other undertakings which together, in particular because of correlative factors which exist between them, are able to adopt a common policy on the market and act to a considerable extent independently of their competitors, their customers, and also of consumers.

34 Azevedo, J. P. and Walker, M. (2002), "Dominance: Meaning and Measurement", *ECLR*, 23(7), 363–7. Additional work on the same definition on dominance includes: Dethmers, F. and Dodoo, N. (2006), "The Abuse of Hoffmann-La Roche: The Meaning of Dominance under EC Competition Law", *ECLR*, 27(10), 537–49, Jones, A. and Sufrin, B. (2004), *EC Competition Law*, 2nd edn, Oxford University Press, Oxford, 264, Church, J. and Ware, R. (2000), *Industrial Organization Strategic Approach*, McGraw-Hill, Singapore, 603, Cabral, L. (2000), *Introduction to Industrial Organization*, MIT Press, Cambridge, MA, 72–5, Dobbs, I. and Richards, P. (2005) "Output Restriction as a Measure of Market Power", *ECLR*, 26(10), 572–80.

35 As regards quality, firms might be lowering quality (and hence costs), but not price, up to the point at which further reductions in quality would not be profitable. As regards innovation firms might be slowing the pace of innovation (and hence R&D expenditures) as far as is consistent with maintaining long run profits. See further: Azevedo, J. P. and Walker, M. (2001), "Dominance: Meaning and Measurement", CRA Competition Policy Discussion Papers, 1–8, www.crai.co.uk, 4.

36 Azevedo, J. P. and Walker, M. (2002), "Dominance: Meaning and Measurement", *ECLR*, 23(7), 363–7.

37 The authors clarify that the definition refers to the restriction of total output in the market below its current level.

38 Factors such as market shares, barriers to entry, barriers to expansion, spare capacity, substitute products. Azevedo, J. P. and Walker, M. (2001), "Dominance: Meaning and Measurement", CRA Competition Policy Discussion Papers, 1–8, www.crai.co.uk, 6.

39 Case 27/76 *United Brands Co. and United Brands Continental BV v Commission* [1978] ECR I-207, §65. This book will adopt this definition as it is the one used by the Court of Justice in Article 102 TFEU and merger cases. Although, as it was illustrated, the definition entails drawbacks, this book will conform with the definition that the Court of Justice has given to the term.

40 Case M308 *Kali und Salz/MdK/Treuhand* [1998] OJ C275/3; on appeal Cases 68/94 and C-30/95 *France v Commission, Societé Commerciale des Potasses et de l'Azore (SCPA) v Commission* [1998] ECR I-1375.

41 Case 6/72 *Europemballage Corp. and Continental Can Co. Inc. v Commission (Continental Can)*, [1973] ECR I-215, at §§26–27.

42 Stiglitz, J. E. and Driffill, J. (2000), *Economics*, W.W. Norton & Company Ltd, London, 274.

43 Article 82 of the EC Treaty pursuant to 102 of the Lisbon Treaty.

44 On excessive pricing, see indicatively: Elliott, D. (2007), "What is an excessive price?", *Competition Law International*, 6(8), 13–15, Kon, S. and Turnbull, S. (2003), "Pricing and the Dominant Firm: Implications of the Competition Commission Appeal Tribunal's judgment in the Napp Case", *ECLR*, 24(2), 70–86, Glader, M. and Larsen, S. (2006), "Article 82: Excessive Pricing", *Competition Law International*, 5(7), 3–5, Geradin, D. and Rato, M. (2006), "Excessive Pricing: In Reply", *Competition Law International*, 5(10), 3–5, Oliver, P. (2006), "The Concept of 'Abuse' of a Dominant Position under Article 82 EC: Recent Developments in Relation to Pricing", *European CJ*, 1(2), 315–39.

45 On predatory pricing, see indicatively: Gal, M. (2007), "Below-cost Price Alignment: Meeting or Beating Competition? The France Telecom Case", *ECLR*, 28(6), 382–91, Gravengaard, M. (2006), "The Meeting Competition Defence Principle – A Defence for Price Discrimination and Predatory Pricing?", *ECLR*, 27(12), 658–77, Andrews, P. (1998), "Is Meeting Competition a Defence to Predatory Pricing? The Irish Sugar Decision Suggests a New Approach", *ECLR*, 49, Eilmansberger, T. (2005) "How to Distinguish Good From Bad Competition Under Article 82 EC: In Search of Clearer and More Coherent Standards for Anti-competitive Abuses", *CMLR* (PP), 129, OECD, "Competition Policy Roundtable on Predatory Foreclosure" (15 March 2005), pp. 1–279.

46 Case C-62/86 *AKZO Chemie BV v Commission* [1991] ECR I-3359.

47 On price discrimination/rebates see indicatively: OECD, "Competition Policy Roundtable on Loyalty and Fidelity Discounts and Rebates" (4 March 2003), pp. 1–239, Lang, J. T. (2005). "Fundamental Issues Concerning Abuse Under Article 82 EC", Regulatory Policy Institute 19, Lang, J. T. (2002) "Defining Legitimate Competition: How to Clarify Pricing Abuses Under Article 82", *FILJ*, 83, Lorenz, M., Lübbig, M. and Russel, A. (2005), "Price Discrimination: A Tender Story", *ECLR*, 355, Akman, P. (2007), "To Abuse, or not to Abuse: Discrimination between Consumers", *EL Rev.*, 32(4), 492–512, Gerard, D. (2005), "Price Discrimination under Article 82(c) EC: Clearing up the Ambiguities" in Global Competition Law Centre Research Papers on Article 82 EC 133, Lang, J. T. and O'Donoghue, R. (2002), "Defining Legitimate Competition: How to Clarify Pricing Abuses under Article 82 EC", *Fordham International Law Journal*, 26, 83, Armstrong, M. and Vickers, J. (1993), "Price Discrimination, Competition and Regulation", *Journal of Industrial Economics*, 41, 335,

Perrot, A. (2005), "Towards an Effects-based Approach of Price Discrimination" in *The Pros and Cons of Price Discrimination*, Swedish Competition Authority, Ridyard, D. (2002), "Exclusionary Pricing and Price Discrimination Abuses under Article 82 – An Economic Analysis", *ECLR*, 6, 286, Armstrong, M. (2005), "Recent Developments in the Economics of Price Discrimination", October 2005 Working Paper, http://129.3.20.41/eps/io/papers/0511/0511004.pdf, Schmalensee, R. (1981), "Output and Welfare Implications of Monopolistic Third-Degree Price Discrimination", *American Economic Review*, 71, 242, Varian, H. R. (1985), "Price Discrimination and Social Welfare", *American Economic Review*, 75, 870, Muysert, P. (2004) "Price Discrimination – An Unreliable Indicator of Market Power", *ECLR*, 6, 350.

48 On refusal to deal/essential facilities see indicatively: Nagy, C. (2007), "Refusal to Deal and the Doctrine of Essential Facilities in US and EC Competition Law: A Comparative Perspective and a Proposal for a Workable Analytical Framework", *EL Rev.*, 32(5), 664–85, Carlton, D. (2001), "A General Analysis of Exclusionary Conduct and Refusal to Deal – Why Aspen and Kodak Are Misguided", NBER Working Paper No. 8105, www.nber.org/papers/w8105, Chen, Z., Ross, T. and Stanbury, W. T. (1998) "Refusals to Deal and Aftermarkets", *Review of Industrial Organization*, 13, 131, Doherty, B. (2001), "Just what are Essential Facilities?", *CMLR*, 38, 397, Jones, A. (2006), "A Dominant Firm's Duty to Deal: EC and US Antitrust Law Compared", in Marsden, P. (ed.), *Handbook of Research in Transatlantic Antitrust*, Edward Elgar, Cheltenham, Lang, J. T. (1994), "Defining Legitimate Competition: Companies' Duties to Supply Competitors and Access to Essential Facilities", *Fordham International Law Journal*, 18, 437, Lao, M. (2005) "Aspen Skiing and Trinko: Antitrust Intent and Sacrifice", *Antitrust Law Journal*, 73, 171, OECD, "The Essential Facilities Concept", Background Note, OCDE/GD(96)113, Robinson G, (2002) "On Refusing to Deal with Rivals", *Cornell Law Review*, 87, 1177, Stratakis, A. (2006), "Comparative Analysis of the US and EU Approach and Enforcement of the Essential Facilities Doctrine", *ECLR*, 27, 434, Venit, J. (2005), "Article 82: The Last Frontier – Fighting Fire with Fire?", *Fordham International Law Journal*, 28, 1157.

49 Cases 6 and 7/73, *Instituto Chemioterapico Italiano SpA and Commercial Solvents Corp. v Commission (Commercial Solvents)* [1974] ECR 223.

50 On tying, see indicatively: Spector, D. (2006), "From Harm to Competitors to Harm to Competition: One More Effort, Please!", *Euro CJ*, 2(1) Supp. (Special issue), 145–62, Kühn, K-U., Stillman, R. and Caffarra, C. (2005), "Economic Theories of Bundling and their Policy Implications in Abuse Cases: An Assessment in Light of the Microsoft Case", *Euro CJ*, 1(1), 85–121, Ridyard, D. (2005), "Tying and bundling – cause for complaint?", *ECLR*, 26(6), 316–19, Furse, M. (2004), "Article 82, Microsoft and bundling, or 'The Half Monti'", *Comp. LJ*, 3(3), 169–178.

51 Case T-30/89 *Hilti v Commission* [1991] ECR II-1439, confirmed C-53/92P [1994] ECR I-666.

52 Case T-83/91 *Tetra Pak Rausing SA v Commission (Tetra Pak II)* [1994] ECR II-755.

53 *Magill TV Guide* [1989] OJ L78/43.

54 Case T-111/96 *ITT Promedia NV v Commission (Promedia)* [1998] ECR II-2937.

55 Case 72/71 *Re Continental Can Co. Inc.* [1972] OJ L7/25.

56 See further: Case 6/72 *Europemballage Corp. and Continental Can Co. Inc. v Commission (Continental Can)* [1973] ECR I-215, para. 26.

57 Pursuant to the Lisbon Treaty, Article 81 is now 101.

58 *CEWAL* [1993] OJ L34/20.

59 Case T-228/97 *Irish Sugar v Commission* [1999] ECR II-02969.

60 Case M190 *Nestlé/Perrier* [1992] OJ L356/1.

61 Cases 68/94 and C-30/95 *France v Commission, Societé Commercialed es Potasses et de l'Azore (SCPA) v Commission* [1998] ECR I-1375.
62 Case T-102/96 *Gencor Ltd v Commission* [1999], ECR II-753.
63 See further: Roth, P. (2001), *Bellamy and Child European Community Law of Competition*, 5th edn, Sweet & Maxwell, London, 405.
64 The ECMR also prevents collective dominance from being strengthened in the post-merger market.
65 See further: Cook, C. J. and Kerse, C. S. (2000), *E.C. Merger Control*, 3rd edn, Sweet & Maxwell, London, 131.
66 Article 2(3), Council Regulation (EC) No. 139/2004 of 20 January 2004 on the Control of Concentrations between Undertakings (the EC Merger Regulation), ("Recast ECMR"), OJ L24, 29.01.2004, 1–22.
67 As the following part of this chapter will illustrate, the applicability of the ECMR on collective dominance was confirmed through case law.
68 Council Regulation (EC) No. 139/2004 of 20 January 2004 on the Control of Concentrations between Undertakings (the EC Merger Regulation), ("Recast ECMR"), OJ L24, 29.01.2004, 1–22.
69 Case T-77/02 *Schneider Electric SA/Legrand v Commission* [2002] ECR II-4201, Case T-310/01 *Schneider Electric SA/Legrand v Commission* [2002] ECR II-4071.
70 Case T-80/02 *Tetra Laval v Commission* [2002] ECR II-4519, Case T-5/02 *Tetra Laval v Commission* [2002] ECR II-4381.
71 Case M1524 *Airtours/First Choice* [2000] OJ L93/1 ("*Airtours/First Choice*").
72 Cases 142 and 156/84 *BAT Ltd and RJ Reynolds Industries Inc. v Commission and Philip Morris* [1987] ECR I-4487.
73 Whish R. (2003), *Competition Law*, 5th edn, Butterworths, London, 794.
74 Furse M. (2004), *Competition Law of the UK & EC*, 4th edn, Oxford University Press, Oxford, 322.
75 Case 72/71 *Re Continental Can Co. Inc.* [1972] OJ L7/25.
76 See further: Roth, P. (2001), *Bellamy and Child European Community Law of Competition*, 5th edn, Sweet & Maxwell, London, 405.
77 Council Regulation (EEC) 4064/89 of 21 December 1989 on the Control of Concentrations between Undertakings, [1989] OJ L395/1, corrigendum [1990] OJ L257/14 ("original ECMR"). Council Regulation (EC) No. 1310/97 (OJ L180, 9.7.97) amended the original ECMR on the control of concentrations between undertakings, focusing mainly on issues such as multiple notifications, joint ventures, remedies and referrals to member states.
78 Articles 81, 82, 83 and 232 of the EC Treaty (ex 85, 86, 87 and 236 of the EC Treaty prior to the Treaty of Amsterdam which came into force on 1 May 1999. Article 12 of the Treaty of Amsterdam provided for the renumbering of the EC Treaty Articles). The EC Treaty was signed on 25 March 1957.
79 The Commission will consider whether the adverse effect of the transaction on effective competition is transitory or permanent and will only initiate an investigation in the latter case, as the approach in *Aerospatiale* indicated. See further: Case M53 *Aerospatiale-Alenia/de Havilland* [1991] OJ L334/42. This case was the first prohibition decision concerning single dominance. See further: Livingston, D. and Scott, J. (1995), *Competition Law and Practice*, FT Law & Tax, London, 768.
80 This is in contrast to Article 102 TFEU, which, according to each wording applies to an abuse by one or more undertakings.
81 Cases such as M308 *Kali und Salz/MdK/Treuhand* [1998] OJ C275/3, Cases 68/94 and C-30/95 *France v Commission, Societé Commerciale des Potasses et de l'Azore (SCPA) v Commission* [1998] ECR I-1375 as well as M619 *Gencor/Lonrho* [1997] OJ L11/30, T-102/96 *Gencor Ltd v Commission* [1999] ECR II-753.
82 Council Regulation (EC) No. 139/2004 of 20 January 2004 on the Control of

Concentrations between Undertakings (the EC Merger Regulation), ("Recast ECMR"), OJ L24, 29.01.2004, 1–22.

83 Case M165 *Alcatel/AEG Kabel* [1992] OJ C6/0. The Commission cleared the merger.

84 Case M190 *Nestlé/Perrier* [1992] OJ L356/1.

85 The first case in which the Court of Justice annulled a Commission decision under the original ECMR. Case M308 *Kali und Salz/MdK/Treuhand* [1998] OJ C275/3.

86 Case T-102/96 *Gencor Ltd. v Commission* [1999] ECR II-753.

87 Case M619 *Gencor/Lonrho* [1997] OJ L11/30.

88 Cases T-68, 77 and 78/89 *Societa Italiana Vetro SpA (SIV), Fabbrica Pisana and PPG Vernante Pennitalia v Commission* (*Flat Glass*) [1992] ECR II-1403.

89 Ibid., §273.

90 Case M1524 *Airtours/First Choice* [2000] OJ L93/1 ("*Airtours/First Choice*") and Case T-342/99 *Airtours v Commission* [2002] ECR II-2585.

91 In making this appraisal, the Commission shall take into account:

(a) the need to maintain and develop effective competition within the common market in view of, among other things, the structure of all the markets concerned and the actual or potential competition from undertakings located either within or outwith the Community;

(b) the market position of the undertakings concerned and their economic and financial power, the alternatives available to suppliers and users, their access to supplies or markets, any legal or other barriers to entry, supply and demand trends for the relevant goods and services, the interests of the intermediate and ultimate consumers, and the development of technical and economic progress provided that it is to consumers' advantage and does not form an obstacle to competition.

92 Forms of entry barriers include legal and administrative barriers (national regulations-*Hoffmann-La-Roche*), costs to customers of switching to a competitor (*Tetra Pak I,* Case T-51/89 *Tetra Pak Rausing SA v Commission* [1990] ECR II-309), IP rights (*Tetra Pak I*), sunk costs involved in entering the market (*United Brands*), vertical integration, efficient distribution and sale networks (*United Brands*), buying preferences (*Kali und Salz*), established brands (*Guinness/Grand Metropolitan,* Case M938 *Guinness/Grand Metropolitan* [1998] OJ L288/24) as well as superior technology of incumbent firms (*Michelin,* Case 322/81 *Michelin v Commission* [1983] ECR I-3461).

93 Kolasky, W. (2002), "Co-ordinated Effects in Merger Review: From Dead Frenchmen to Beautiful Minds and Mavericks", www.usdoj.gov/atr/public/speeches/11050.htm, 28. A firm is defined as maverick when it declines to follow the industry consensus and thereby undermines effective coordination.

94 *Gencor/Lonrho, Nestlé* as well as *Kali und Salz* involved homogeneous products.

95 The Commission took into account the price sensitivity of demand in several cases including *Gencor/Lonrho, Nestlé, Airtours/First Choice.*

96 A case that the Commission considered symmetric market conditions is: Case M1225 *Enso/Stora* [1999] OJ L254/9.

97 Multi market contacts were taken into consideration in: Case M222 *Mannesman/Hoesch* [1993] OJ L114/34.

98 For a detailed analysis of these factors see: Kokkoris, I. (2007b), "The Development of the Concept of Collective Dominance in the European Community Merger Regulation. From its Inception to its Current Status", *World Competition,* September.

99 Stroux, S. (2002), "Collective Dominance under the Merger Regulation: A Serious Evidentiary Reprimand for the Commission", *EL Rev,* 27(6), 736–46,

Nazerali, J. (2002), "A Merger of Minds or Split Opinion – Does the European Commission Address Current EU Merger Concerns?", *ICCLR*, 13(12), 480–84, Gordon, C. and Richardson, R. (2001) "Collective Dominance: The Third Way?", *ECLR*, 22(10), 416–23, Jephcott, M. and Withers, C. (2001) "Where to Go Now for EC Oligopoly Control?", *ECLR*, 22(8), 295–303, Rabassa, V. and Christensen, P. (2001), "The Airtours Decision: Is There a New Commission Approach to Collective Dominance?", *ECLR*, 22(6), 227–37, Niels, G. (2001), "Collective Dominance: More than Just Oligopolistic Interdependence", *ECLR*, 22(5), 168–72, Kloosterhuis, E. (2001), "Joint Dominance and the Interaction between Firms", *ECLR*, 22(3), 79–92, Black, O. (2003), "Collusion and Co-ordination in EC Merger Control", *ECLR*, 24(8), 408–11, Farrell, L. (2002), "*Airtours PLC v EC Commission*", *Comp. LJ*, 1(3), 207–15, Haupt, H. (2002), "Collective Dominance under Article 82 EC and EC Merger Control in the Light of the Airtours Judgment", *ECLR*, 23(9), 434–44, Parker, D. (2006), "A Screening Device for Tacit Collusion Concerns", *ECLR*, 27(8), 424–33.

100 Case T-342/99 *Airtours v Commission* [2002] ECR II-2585.

101 Cook, C. J. and Kerse, C. S. (2000), *E.C. Merger Control*, 3rd edn, Sweet & Maxwell, London, 173.

102 Case M1524 *Airtours/First Choice* [2000] OJ L93/1 ("*Airtours/First Choice*").

103 These figures refer to 1998. The next operator was Cosmos/Avro with 2.9 per cent of the market. In 1992 Thomson had 24 per cent, Airtours had 11 per cent, First Choice 6 per cent and Thomas Cook 4 per cent. See further: Motta, M. (2004), *Competition Policy-Theory and Practice*, Cambridge University Press, Cambridge, 272.

104 Biggar, D. (2000), "Airline Mergers and Alliances", *OECD Journal of Competition Law and Policy*, 2(2), 122–220.

105 A main feature of short-haul package holiday market is that the firms' activities are concerned with the capacity on the market. In the short-haul package holiday, market capacity is chosen by firms in the planning phase, 12–18 months prior to knowing demand, so profits are related to the levels of capacity that cannot change in the selling phase. Coordination can thus occur on capacity rather than on prices. *Airtours/First Choice* was not a typical collective dominance case in that the Commission was concerned with the likelihood of collective dominance in relation to capacity rather than prices.

106 The author of this book has written extensively about merger assessment and this part of the chapter incorporates some of his earlier work, including the following: Kokkoris, I. (2005d), "The Reform of the European Community Merger Regulation in the Aftermath of the Airtours Case. The Eagerly Expected Debate: SLC v Dominance test", *ECLR*, 26(1), 37–47.

107 The Commission did not allege that Airtours alone would have had a "dominant position" rather the Commission contended that the transaction would enable the three largest tour operators to engage in "collectively dominant" behaviour by reducing capacity and raising prices of short-haul package tours.

108 For the first time it prohibited a merger on the grounds of collective dominance where the merger reduced the number of firms from four to three.

109 Briones, J. and Padilla, A. J. (2001), "The Complex Landscape of Oligopolies under EU Competition Policy. Is Collective Dominance Ripe for Guidelines?", *World Competition*, 24(3), 307–18.

110 The factors that have been mentioned so far in this book.

111 Korah, V. (2001), *Cases and Materials on EC Competition Law*, 2nd edn, Hart Publishing, Portland, OR, 606.

112 Europe Economics (2002), "One's a Monopoly, Two's Collectively Dominant, Three's Alright?", www.europe-economics.com. The General Court in its judgment notes that the Commission's decision was vitiated by a series of

errors of assessment of the factors contributing to a collective dominant position. See further: Case T-342/99 *Airtours v Commission* [2002] ECR II-2585, §294.

113 UK Competition Commission, Cm 3813, "Foreign Package Holidays: A Report on the Supply in the UK of Tour Operators' Services and Travel Agents' Services in Relation to Foreign Package Holidays", 19.12.97, www.competition-commission.org.uk.

114 As Chapter 4 of this book will illustrate, according to the perception of the stock market, the *Airtours/First Choice* merger would not have induced adverse effects on competition in the post-merger market.

115 The main feature of oligopoly is the existence of a sustainable mechanism of coordination of behaviour that may lead to parallelism of prices and capacity. In an oligopolistic market, there are a small number of operators who are able to behave in a parallel manner and derive benefits from their collective market power, without necessarily entering into an agreement or concerted practice. This phenomenon is called *tacit collusion*. The General Court in *Gencor* implicitly equated the notion of collective dominance with the notion of tacit collusion, broadening thus the reach of the ECMR.

116 Stroux, S. (2002), "Collective Dominance under the Merger Regulation: A Serious Evidentiary Reprimand for the Commission", *European Law Review*, 27(6), 736–46.

117 This factor was considered in cases such as: M619 *Gencor/Lonrho* [1997] OJ L11/30 (*Gencor/Lonrho*), Case M190 *Nestlé/Perrier* [1992] OJ L356/1 (*Nestlé*), M308 *Kali und Salz/MdK/Treuhand* [1998] OJ C275/3 (*Kali und Salz*), at §84.

118 This factor was considered in cases such as: M619 *Gencor/Lonrho* [1997] OJ L11/30 (*Gencor/Lonrho*), Case M190 *Nestlé/Perrier* [1992] OJ L356/1 (*Nestlé*), M308 *Kali und Salz/MdK/Treuhand* [1998] OJ C275/3 (*Kali und Salz*), at §150.

119 See cases: Case M1245 *Valeo/ITT Industries* [1998] OJ C288/5, Case M1597 *Castrol/Carless/JV* [2000] OJ C16/5, Case M1432 *Agfa-Gevaert/Sterling* [1999] OJ C228/11.

120 Case M580 *ABB/Daimler Benz* [1997] OJ L11/1.

121 See further: Europe Economics (2001), "Study on Assessment Criteria for Distinguishing between Competitive and Dominant Oligopolies in Merger Control", http://europa.eu.int/comm/enterprise/library/lib-competition/libr-competition.html, vi, 62, 63, 83.

122 As Bishop and Walker (2002) argue, coordination on a long-term variable, such as the introduction of new capacity or new investment, is less likely to be adopted and sustained since the retaliation mechanism is not as effective and credible as in the case where coordination is on a short-term variable such as price or output. See further: Bishop, S. and Walker, M. (2002), "The Economics of EC Competition Law: Concepts, Application and Measurement", Sweet & Maxwell, London, 286.

123 Case T-342/99 *Airtours v Commission* [2002] ECR II-2585, §§194–195. The General Court dismissed all the deterrents adduced by the Commission in its decision, due to practical difficulties such as insufficient reaction time for the deterrents to be punitive, volatility of demand as well as economic losses suffered by the perpetrators themselves. See: Field Fisher Waterhouse (2002), "Collective Dominance: The Airtours Appeal", www.ffwlaw.com/download/Docs1944387_1.PDF.

124 Nikpay, A. and Houwen, F. (2003), "Tour de Force or a Little Local Turbulence? A Heretical View on the Airtours Judgment", *ECLR*, 24(5), 193–202.

125 Case M308 *Kali und Salz/MdK/Treuhand* [1998] OJ C275/3.

126 In the *Coca-Cola/Carlsberg* case (Case M833 *Coca-Cola/Carlsberg* [1998] OJ L145/41), the Commission argued that the question in assessing dominance is whether there is significant countervailing buyer power to neutralize the market power of the parties involved.

127 Europe Economics (2001), "Study on Assessment Criteria for Distinguishing between Competitive and Dominant Oligopolies in Merger Control", http://europa.eu.int/comm/enterprise/library/lib-competition/libr-competition.html, 84.
128 See, for example, Case M337 *Knorr-Bremse/Allied Signal* [1993] OJ C298/0. See further: Kokkoris, I. (2006a), "Buyer Power Assessment in Competition Law", *World Competition*, 29(1), 139–64.
129 Barriers to entry are essential in determining the level of *de novo* entry of potential competitors in the market, which entry must occur in a reasonable timescale.
130 See further: Korah, V. (2001), *Cases and Materials on EC Competition Law*, 2nd edn, Hart Publishing, Portland, OR, 609.
131 Rodger, B. and MacCulloch, A. (2001), *Competition Law and Policy in the EC and UK*, 2nd edn, Cavendish Publishing, London, 218.
132 Motta, M. (1999), "Economic Analysis and EC Merger Policy", European University Institute, www.iue.it/Personal/Motta?ECMergR.pdf, 27.
133 See §54 of *Airtours/First Choice*: "[I]t is sufficient that the merger makes it rational for oligopolists to act individually in ways which will substantially reduce competition between them."
134 Provided the criteria for the sustainability of collective dominance are satisfied. Cases where these criteria are not satisfied are an illustration of the abovementioned "gap" of the dominance test. See further: Kühn, K. U. (2002), "Closing Pandora's Box? Joint Dominance after the Airtours Judgment", in *The Pros and Cons of Merger Control*, Swedish Competition Authority, www.kkv.se/epdf/skrift_proscons.pdf, 48.
135 Scott, A. (2002), "An Immovable Feast? Tacit Collusion and Collective Dominance in Merger Control after Airtours", www.ccr.uea.ac.uk/workingpapers/ccr02–6.pdf, 12.
136 The authors argued that, in relation to the doctrine of collective dominance, the judgment is no more than a distillation and summation of the status of the law as established in *Gencor*. They add that it leaves a number of issues unanswered and provides the Commission with sufficient freedom to develop its interpretation of the scope of application of the doctrine of collective dominance. See further: Nikpay, A. and Houwen, F. (2003), "Tour de Force or a Little Local Turbulence? A Heretical View on the Airtours Judgment", *ECLR*, 24(5), 193–202.
137 See, for example, the *Sony/BMG* case.
138 Levy, N. (2003), "EU Merger Control: From Birth to Adolescence", *World Competition*, 26(2), 195–218.
139 Motta, M. (1999), "Economic Analysis and EC Merger Policy", European University Institute, www.iue.it/Personal/Motta?ECMergR.pdf, 27.
140 Kühn, K.U. (2002), "Closing Pandora's Box? Joint Dominance after the Airtours Judgment", in *The Pros and Cons of Merger Control*, Swedish Competition Authority, www.kkv.se/epdf/skrift_proscons.pdf.
141 Europe Economics (2002), "One's a Monopoly, Two's Collectively Dominant, Three's Alright?", www.europe-economics.com, 4.
142 Case M1684 *Carrefour/Promodés* [2000] OJ C164/5. The Commission cleared the merger subject to conditions and obligations by the parties.
143 Recent merger cases that the Commission cleared, although initially it alleged that the merger may lead to collective dominance, include Case M3099 *Areva/Urenco/ETC JV* (4064) [2006] OJ L61/11, Case M3333 *Sony/BMG* [2005] OJ L62/30 and Case M3216 *Oracle/PeopleSoft* [2005] OJ L218/6.
144 Case M1524 *Airtours/First Choice* [2000] OJ L93/1 ("*Airtours/First Choice*").
145 As illustrated in para. 54 of *Airtours/First Choice*.

2 The new European Community Merger Regulation – Council Regulation (EC) No. 139/2004

As already mentioned, the *Airtours/First Choice* decision illustrated a "gap" in the application of the dominance test. In that case, the Commission, assuming that the merger would lead to adverse effects on competition,[1] prohibited the merger based on the concept of collective dominance, since the post-merger market structure would not sustain an allegation of single firm dominance. The Commission argued that the merger could lead to oligopolists adopting unilateral conduct, resulting in an adverse impact on competition.[2] The General Court annulled the prohibition of the merger. Had the merger been assessed under the SIEC test, the General Court would have taken into account the fact that the merger could lead to non-coordinated effects in oligopolistic markets.

Mario Monti[3] claimed that the Commission's decisions, overturned on appeal by the General Court in the cases of *Airtours*,[4] *Schneider*[5] and *Tetra Laval*,[6] as well as the resultant and unprecedented criticism faced by the Commission, provided an opportunity for an even deeper reform in the way the Commission assessed concentrations than was originally envisaged.

Article 1(4) of the original ECMR required the Commission to report to the Council before 1 July 2000 on the operation of the thresholds and on the criteria for determining whether a concentration has a community dimension. The Commission submitted a report that considered several jurisdictional, procedural and substantive issues that needed to be addressed. The Commission published these issues in a Green Paper[7] in December 2001. In December 2002 the European Commission published its proposals for reform of the original ECMR[8] together with a draft notice on the appraisal of horizontal mergers, as well as draft "Best Practices on the Conduct of EC Merger Control Proceedings".[9] The draft notice was the response of the Commission to a widespread demand for enhanced legal certainty surrounding the Commission's assessment of mergers. The reforms aimed at clarifying the criteria applied by the Commission in the appraisal of concentrations.[10]

"Council Regulation (EC) No. 139/2004 of 20 January 2004 on the Control of Concentrations between Undertakings (the EC Merger Regulation)"[11] entered into force in May 2004 and coincided with the expansion of the EU from 15 to 25 member states. The reform aimed at improving both the parties' rights of defence and the Commission's decision-making process,[12] both of which are essential for the application of the Recast ECMR, especially in an enlarged EU of 27 member states. The ECMR reform further aimed at minimizng transaction costs for firms through the "one-stop-shop"[13] principle and at augmenting the transparency and the speediness of the procedural assessment of concentrations, leading thus to enhanced legal certainty.

In a nutshell, the adopted reforms concerned procedural, jurisdictional and substantive issues. The Green Paper clearly reflected the Commission's belief that the merger assessment process should offer a high degree of efficiency and transparency.[14] In an attempt to enhance legal certainty and predictability related to the assessment of mergers,[15] the Commission proposed a clarification of the law and the introduction of checks and balances in its merger assessment procedure.

The most important difference between the Recast ECMR and the original ECMR is the change of the substantive legal test from the traditional dominance test to the SIEC test. As mentioned earlier, this change came as a result of widespread criticism of cases that illustrated the "gap" in the application of the dominance test. The Recast ECMR aims at filling the gap so that the problem of non-collusive oligopolies can be addressed in merger investigations.

Apart from substantive reforms, procedural and jurisdictional reforms were also adopted in the Recast ECMR. An extensive account of these reforms is outside the scope of this book. Procedural changes included enhanced flexibility for companies in deciding when to file merger notifications, allowing firms to better organize their transactions without being obliged to fit their planning around unnecessary regulatory rigidities, and changes in the deadlines for Commission decisions. In addition, amendments to the time schedule provide more time to the Commission to consider remedies proposed by firms. In combination with the Regulation[16] for the enforcement of Articles 101 and 102 TFEU adopted on 26 November 2002, the procedural and jurisdictional reforms to the ECMR strengthen the Commission's enforcement powers.

Regarding jurisdictional issues, a pre-notification process that determines the allocation of jurisdiction between the Commission and national competition authorities ("NCAs"), tackles the phenomenon of intra-EU multi-jurisdictional filings, while at the same time enhances the effectiveness of the "one-stop-shop" principle according to which parties may request the Commission to take jurisdiction in cases where the turnover thresholds are not met but the merger needs to be notified in at least three member states. The "one-stop-shop" principle[17] is essential for the efficient application of the Recast ECMR, especially in the enlarged EU.

As mentioned earlier, the substantive proposed reforms concerned the change from the dominance test to the SLC test. After an extensive debate the Commission finally adopted the SIEC test, a hybrid of the dominance and SLC tests. The new legal substantive test is regarded as a compromise between the two tests. The following part of this chapter addresses in detail the arguments submitted to the Commission in favour and against both the dominance and the SLC tests. It also presents the Commission's choice of the substantive test for merger assessment and gives a brief account of the new *Horizontal Merger Guidelines* ("*Guidelines*").

2.1 Arguments for and against SLC test and dominance test

2.1.1 Dominance test

The dominance test is mentioned in Article 2(3) of the original ECMR. According to this article: "[A] concentration which creates or strengthens a dominant position as a result of which effective competition would be significantly impeded in the common market or in a substantial part of it shall be declared incompatible with the common market."[18]

The Green Paper[19] launched a debate on the dominance test used under the original ECMR comparing it to the SLC test used in other jurisdictions such as those in the United States,[20] the United Kingdom,[21] Australia,[22] New Zealand,[23] and Ireland.[24]

During that debate, apart from Europe Economics (2002),[25] John Vickers[26] (2002) also argued that the General Court judgment in *Airtours* has left a considerable gap in policy.[27] In addition, he doubted that it is possible for merger policy to have all three: the dominance wording of the original ECMR, the effect of catching non-collusive oligopolies, as well as rigorous case analysis.

Most EU member states adhere to the dominance test. Hence, it was argued that it would have been unreasonable for the Commission to switch to the SLC test, since such a move would inhibit the harmonization of national competition laws and would enhance legal uncertainty.[28]

Another argument against the change of the dominance test was that the two tests, while differently worded, pursue the same objective of preventing an adverse impact on competition. In addition, both tests had similar interpretations in the EU and the United States and had produced broadly convergent outcomes.[29]

However, there were cases where the two tests may deliver different results. One example of divergent outcomes of the two tests was a case brought before the Commerce Commission of New Zealand. In the *Progressive Enterprises Limited*[30] case, the proposed transaction concerned the acquisition of Woolworths (New Zealand) Limited ("Woolworths") by Progressive Enterprises Limited ("Progressive"), the country's third and second largest supermarket chains respectively. New Zealand's competition regulator, the Commerce Commission, assessed this acquisition under the dominance test, subsequently (as explained later), it assessed it a second time, but this time under the SLC test. There were three major competitors in the supermarket industry, Foodstuffs had 58 per cent market share, Progressive had 24 per cent and Woolworths 18 per cent. Under the dominance test, the Commerce Commission cleared the proposed acquisition since the merged entity would be effectively constrained by Foodstuffs from unilaterally exercising market power in markets where Foodstuffs had a significant presence.[31]

When the clearance of the proposed acquisition was resubmitted to the Commerce Commission to be assessed under the new SLC test,[32] the Commerce Commission concluded that the merger would not lead to a substantive lessening of competition on the basis of unilateral effects, thus coinciding with its decision under the dominance test. However, on the issue of coordinated conduct, the Commission viewed barriers to *de novo* entry of new supermarket chains as a significant factor and thus concluded that the merger would lead to a substantial lessening of competition due to the enhanced coordination in the supermarket industry that would result from the merger. In the analysis of the case under the two tests, market definition remained the same and unilateral effects, although tested under a new lower threshold, did not give rise to different conclusions. However, although the analysis of entry barriers was similar, the impact of entry barriers was different under the SLC test and led to enhanced likelihood for coordinated behaviour in the post-merger market.[33]

Turning to the arguments in favour of changing the dominance test, as Philip Lowe (2002) had argued,[34] before a change in the dominance test was decided a cost-benefit analysis of the change must be carried out. The issue that must be assessed under both the dominance and the SLC tests is whether substantial competition exists between the companies operating in the post-merger market. The threshold of market power triggering the Commission's intervention in mergers ought to be lower than that triggering liability for breach of the competition law provisions (Articles 101 and 102).[35] The dominance test follows a structural approach that places excessive emphasis on market definition and market shares and gives greater weight to competitor concerns.[36]

The most robust argument against the dominance test was that it may fail to forbid mergers between non-dominant firms having an adverse impact on competition.[37] The "gap" corresponds to the situation where the post-merger entity's market share falls below the level required for dominance but the merger may, however, lead to non-coordinated effects. Non-coordinated effects may arise in a concentrated market with differentiated products where, because of the small number of firms, the incumbents are able to adopt conduct having an adverse impact on competition, without the need to coordinate their behaviour and thus without adopting collectively dominant conduct. Attempting to capture non-collusive oligopolies by applying the single firm dominance concept is inadequate since it omits the incumbents' responses to the actions of the merged entity. In addition, collective dominance may not be applicable due to the fact that in the post-merger market the incumbents do not act in a collusive manner, but individually adopt conduct having an adverse impact on competition.

The *Heinz*[38] case presented an example of this alleged "gap".[39] This merger was assessed by the Federal Trade Commission ("FTC"), which applied the SLC test.[40]

Heinz was a worldwide producer and distributor of a wide variety of food products. Worldwide, Heinz was the largest seller of prepared baby foods, with over $1 billion in sales. Beech-Nut was a subsidiary of Milnot, a food product company. Beech-Nut had over $100 million in sales in prepared baby food sales. The direct competition between Heinz and Beech-Nut for shelf space at the wholesale level was intense, forcing these companies to compete aggressively, leading to better prices for consumers as well as to innovation, and forcing Gerber to compete on price and innovation.

Heinz and Beech-Nut also competed at the retail level through advertising, couponing, loyalty card discounts, product quality, innovations, shelf positioning, and product variety.[41] The head-to-head competition for supermarket accounts resulted in very substantial price concessions to retailers and promotional programs directed to consumers ("slotting fees" and "pay-to-stay arrangements").

The merger, between the second and third largest companies in the market, would eliminate competition at both wholesale and retail levels. This merger to duopoly raised very serious concerns that consumers would be harmed as a result of higher prices, less innovation, and less consumer choice.

The FTC assembled evidence that the proposed merger would, in fact, substantially reduce competition in the prepared baby food market in two ways. First, the proposed merger would eliminate substantial head-to-head competition between Beech-Nut and Heinz, thus enabling the merged firm to increase its prices unilaterally. Second, by reducing the number of competitors in the prepared baby food market from three to two, the proposed merger would significantly increase the likelihood that the merged firm and Gerber would engage in coordinated behaviour.[42]

The FTC further identified the likelihood of tacit collusion as a consequence of the merger. There would be significantly less incentive for the merged entity and Gerber to engage in head-to-head competition to displace each other, since there would be space on the shelves for both firms' products.[43]

The FTC decided to seek a court order enjoining the merger as it substantially impaired competition. This case would not be covered by the dominance test of the original ECMR since it involved the second and third largest producers, and the post-merger entity was not the biggest in the market, it would not lead to individual dominant position. Similar concern is raised in cases where firms will be in a position to exercise market power by raising prices, although without engaging in coordination and without holding the largest market share.

Thus, the dominance test was said to include "blind spots", as certain types of merger, having an adverse impact on competition, could not be classified as creating or strengthening either a position of single firm dominance or of collective dominance.[44] The dominance test as applied by the Commission might have failed to capture mergers between firms producing differentiated products that gave rise to unilateral effects unless markets are narrowly defined.

Such an approach was taken in the *Office Depot*[45] case, dealt with under the SLC test in the United States.[46] The FTC assessed the impact of the proposed acquisition by Staples of Office Depot by focusing on the impact that Office Depot's presence had on Staples' pricing. The FTC found that retail prices were higher in towns where there was only one office superstore than in towns where there were two or more local competitors.[47] The FTC argued that an SLC would occur in locations where the merger brought together the only office superstores under common ownership.

As has been illustrated, merger assessment under the two tests can result in different outcomes although the economic rationale underpinning merger control by enforcement authorities and courts in the jurisdictions implementing the two tests is very similar.[48] Thus, any discrepancy in the outcomes of the two tests will not be the result of different analysis or different assessment factors but will depend on the diverse implications that these factors may have under each substantive test. Lowe (2002) argued that the debate on the substantive test should focus on the economic targets that merger legislation should achieve, including restrictions of competition by firms which are not dominant.[49]

2.1.2 SLC test

The main thrust of arguments in favour of the change to the SLC test[50] concerned the suitability of the test as an economics-based tool used to assess the competitive effect of mergers, since it allows emphasis to be placed on inter-firm competitive dynamics, on empirical evidence, and on economic analysis, and permits greater identification of the competition problems and associated remedies, especially in cases dealing with collective dominance, where as aforementioned, there are "gaps" in the scope of the dominance test.[51] In addition, the SLC test would bring the ECMR in line with other international competition regimes, making international cooperation in competition issues more likely to be achieved.[52]

In its response to the Green Paper, the United Kingdom mentioned that the SLC test, especially in oligopolistic markets, is fundamentally better adapted to merger control, primarily because it is directly grounded on economic analysis and on the impact of the merger on competition in a way that the concept of dominance is not.[53] The SLC test may be assumed to deal more effectively with cases where one cannot state that there is a risk of concerted practices but concentration enables the company to act to the detriment of consumers.[54] Thus, the alleged "gap" that has been mentioned already in the context of the criticisms that the Commission received after the *Airtours/First Choice* case, was one of the main shortcomings of the dominance test. The United Kingdom further argued that the benefits from the change to the SLC test outweigh the relatively small risks of change.

In addition, the use of the SLC test detaches the substantive test for mergers from the control of abusive behaviour under Article 102 TFEU.[55] Article 82 is applied *ex post*, and thus the focus is on the past conduct of the undertaking and on the operation of the market during that period. The Recast ECMR is applied *ex ante*, and thus the focus is on the changes in the structure of the market that come as a consequence of the merger. The purpose of the merger control is not to prevent future abuses of a dominant position, but to ensure that the post-merger market structure will not be less competitive.

Volcker[56] (2004) argued that the Commission may already have applied an SLC type analysis in certain cases (equivalent to the unilateral effects analysis as it has been laid out in the *Guidelines*).[57] The Commission had in the past claimed that dominance will be created or strengthened where the predicted market shares were below 40 per cent.[58] The *Guidelines* state that it matters more whether the merged entity's products are "closest substitutes" for a substantial group of customers than whether it has the highest combined share in the relevant market.

Volcker (2004) cites many cases where the Commission had taken into account the "closeness" of the merging parties' products or the elimination of "rivalry between them" as an aggravating factor in the analysis of whether the proposed transaction would lead to the creation or strengthening of a dominant position. Such cases include *Volvo/Scania*,[59] *Barilla/BPL/Kamps*,[60] as well as *Siemens/Drägerwerk/JV*[61] and *GE/Instrumentarium*,[62] where the Commission analysed bidding markets.[63]

By way of contrast, the Commission had accepted the fact that the parties did not offer close substitutes as a defence in prima facie[64] cases of dominance. Cases include *Philips/Agilent Health Care Solutions*,[65] *Philips/Marconi Medical Systems*,[66] and *Pfizer/Pharmacia*.[67] In general, the Commission had relied on unilateral effects analysis to substantiate a dominance argument only in cases in which market shares were at a level that would strongly indicate single dominance in any event.

Arguments against the adoption of the SLC test included the unpredictability and legal uncertainty that might arise due to the enhanced discretion that the Commission would acquire by implementing the SLC test in adopting an interventionist approach to mergers. Moreover, since a considerable body of precedent had been founded on the dominance test, unpredictability would arise regarding the interpretation of the new standards of the SLC test, a test without established EU case law precedence. It can though be argued that the SLC test has an established legal precedence in other jurisdictions such as the United States and Canada. In addition, the notion of dominance is also inherently unclear and the key jurisprudence as regards, notably, collective dominance, is relatively recent since the *Gencor/Lonrho*[68] decision where the Commission, in 1999, outlined market characteristics that contribute to collective dominance.

An additional drawback in adopting the SLC test concerned the harmonization of merger laws. The legal substantive test of a significant number of member states is based on the notion of dominance.[69] The convergence of substantive standards will be beneficial for firms engaging in substantial cross border transactions, since it will reduce the uncertainty that is caused by dealing with jurisdictions that apply different legal standards for the same transaction. However, the facts of the merger case may be evaluated differently by various competition agencies even if a uniform test (either SLC or dominance test) is applied as the substantive prohibition criterion. The change from the dominance test to the SLC test made no fundamental difference in the analysis that needs to be conducted and the requirements that need to be fulfilled.

2.2 SLC test v dominance test

As was illustrated earlier, several arguments have been voiced regarding the advantages and disadvantages of each substantive test. This section will attempt to ascertain under what circumstances the two tests may lead to the same conclusions as regards the assessment of a merger.

The main difference between the SLC and the dominance test appears to be the structural and formalistic approach according to which the dominance test is applied. The SLC test is concerned with the changes in the market that the merger induces, rather than merely with the post-merger market conditions. The emphasis that each test places on market definition differs as well. Under the dominance test, market definition plays a crucial role in a prima facie indication of adverse effects on competition,[70] while the SLC test focuses on the impact of the merger on existing competitive constraints.

In a narrowly defined market, focusing entirely on market shares would render the merger likely to create or strengthen a dominant position. If limited weight is placed on market shares as an indication of dominance, the outcome of both tests could converge and the outcome of merger assessment could be similar under both tests. Less emphasis on market shares implies that dominant firms will not be only the biggest firms in a market. Firms with significant market power may also be deemed dominant irrespective of having the highest market share in the market. Mario Monti (2002) had argued[71] that the case for and against the switch to the SLC test appears to be a finely balanced one.[72]

Regarding the assessment of mergers leading to non-coordinated effects in oligopolistic markets (the alleged "gap" cases), Voigt and Schmidt (2004) argue that the two tests may not lead to different conclusions.[73] The relevance of unilateral effects is determined by the degree of homogeneity in the relevant market. In homogenous product markets, unilateral effects are identical to single firm dominance. The post-merger firm will be able to increase the price by reducing its output. However, if the remaining competitors are able to compensate the reduction in output, the increase in price is only sustainable if the post-merger firm is in a dominant position. A non-dominant firm will not find it profitable to increase prices due to the switching of demand to other incumbents. The compensation in output and the switching of demand as a result of the merger will depend on capacity constraints as well as on the diversion ratio between the incumbents.[74]

The negative effects of the merger only materialize if a dominant position is created by the proposed merger and thus the merger would be blocked both under the SLC/SIEC and dominance tests. Thus, for mergers involving homogeneous products, the SLC/SIEC and the dominance tests can achieve the same outcome as regards the assessment of mergers.

In markets characterized by homogeneous products and capacity constraints faced by the incumbents, mergers may lead to a similar adverse impact on competition as non-collusive oligopolies. When the merger takes place in such a market it is possible that the merged entity as well as its rivals may raise prices and that no firm will be able to increase capacity in order to absorb the switching of demand attributed to that price increase. In the post-merger market, all firms may increase prices due to the capacity constraints. However, the merger induces neither such constraints nor the price increase and, thus, such price increase is likely to happen in the absence of the merger as well. In addition, as Willig (2002) argues, this post-merger effect is unilateral, in the sense that the action that creates harm for consumers in the post-merger market, and is induced by the merger, is the likely price increase by the merged entity, rather than the likely responses of the incumbents.[75] Thus, it cannot be argued that non-collusive oligopolies can arise in markets where firms produce homogeneous products and face capacity constraints. Any anticompetitive effects in the post-merger market will be due to the unilateral actions of the merged entity, rather than due to non-coordinated reaction of the firms in the post-merger oligopolistic market which may lead to harmful effects on competition.

In the case of heterogeneous product markets the lessening of competition does not depend primarily on market shares but on the degree of competition before the merger. The closer substitutes the merging firms' products were before the merger, the higher unilateral price effects will be after the merger. If the definition of the relevant market under the dominance test is sufficiently narrow then the two tests may again lead to the same substantive assessment and outcome.[76]

However, such narrow market definition may not always be accurate and may lead to complications as regards the creation of precedent for future merger, as well as Article 102 TFEU, cases. The market definition in a merger case should be done objectively, without being influenced by the impact of the merger on competition. Only after the market has been defined can there be an accurate assessment of the impact of the merger on competition.

Thus, although for mergers involving homogeneous products, the SLC/SIEC and the dominance tests can achieve the same outcome in the merger assessment, the application of the dominance test is inadequate in capturing the adverse effects on competition of some mergers involving heterogeneous products.[77]

2.3 The Commission's choice

The importance of the substantive test in the assessment of mergers is immense. The criteria that the test must satisfy include a focus on the dynamic change in competition rather than on the static pre- and post-merger levels of competition. Moreover, the substantive test should take into account the rivals' reaction to the merged entity's conduct, have consumer welfare as its objective,[78] and avoid any link with Articles 81 and/or 82, as well as avoiding legal uncertainty.[79]

The Commission decided to retain an altered version of the dominance test. The Commission considered that the aim of improving legal certainty and enhancing transparency regarding the scope of the dominance test is best served by clarifying the Recast ECMR itself. The new test (SIEC test) is outlined in Article 2(3) of the Recast ECMR, which states that "a concentration which would significantly impede effective competition, in the common market or in a substantial part of it, in particular as a result of the creation or strengthening of a dominant position, shall be declared incompatible with the common market".[80] Thus, the creation or strengthening of a dominant position is only one example, albeit the principal example, of a significant impediment to effective competition.

There was considerable debate in the Council,[81] with Germany, Italy and the Netherlands being in favour of the current dominance test[82] whereas the United Kingdom, Ireland and Sweden preferred a move to the SLC.[83] Denmark and Portugal supported the Commission's proposal, while France and Spain suggested a compromise wording based on their own domestic tests. Finally, the Franco-Spanish compromise prevailed, supplemented by a last-minute German addition to a recital[84] which provided that the new substantive test will serve to efficiently assess non-collusive oligopolies.

Factors that will be taken into account in the appraisal of concentrations include[85] the market position of the undertakings concerned and their economic and financial power, the alternatives available to suppliers and users, their access to supplies or markets, any legal or other barriers to entry, supply and demand trends for the relevant goods and services, the interests of the intermediate and ultimate consumers, and the development of technical and economic progress provided that it is to consumers' advantage and does not form an obstacle to competition.

The legal substantive test in the Recast ECMR, the SIEC test, is intended to fill the perceived gap in the application of the dominance test, which was illustrated by cases such as *Airtours/First Choice*[86] and *Heinz*.[87] As has already been mentioned in this book, the "gap" corresponds to the situation where the post-merger entity's market share falls below the level required for dominance and where the merger may nonetheless still lead to unilateral effects.

According to Recital 25 of the Recast ECMR:[88]

> In view of the consequences that concentrations in oligopolistic market structures may have, it is all the more necessary to maintain effective competition in such markets. Many oligopolistic markets exhibit a healthy degree of competition. However, under certain circumstances, concentrations involving the elimination of important competitive constraints that the merging parties had exerted upon each other, as well as a reduction of competitive pressure on the remaining competitors, may, even in the absence of a likelihood of coordination between the members of the oligopoly, result in a significant impediment to effective competition. The Community courts have, however, not to date expressly interpreted Regulation (EEC) No. 4064/89 as requiring concentrations giving rise to such non-coordinated effects to be declared incompatible with the common market.
>
> Therefore, in the interests of legal certainty, it should be made clear that this Regulation permits effective control of all such concentrations by providing that any concentration which would significantly impede effective competition, in the common market or in a substantial part of it, should be declared incompatible with the common market. The notion of 'significant impediment to effective competition' in Article 2(2) and (3) should be interpreted as extending, beyond the concept of dominance, only to the anticompetitive effects of a concentration resulting from the non-coordinated behaviour of undertakings which would not have a dominant position on the market concerned.

According to this Recital, the SIEC extends, in a disciplined way, beyond dominance, and makes clear that the new test covers non-coordinated effects, thus rectifying the problem of the gap in the application of the dominance test. In the formulation of Recital 25, the Commission has attempted to enhance legal certainty by creating the impression that the interpretation of the SIEC test is compatible with former court judgments.[89]

Even though the new wording of the legal substantive test rectifies the "gap", the application of the SIEC test may be quite wide and allow increased scrutiny of transactions between smaller firms in concentrated markets, where the reduction in the number of players may lead to a possible reduction in competition due to the loss of competitive constraints in the post-merger market. Although the wording used in the new provision[90] could be read as extending the reach of the ECMR further than the SLC test could have, Voigt and Schmidt (2004) argue that the SIEC in rectifying the "gap" does not make the European merger policy more restrictive, but, gives the Commission more discretion in its assessment of concentrations. According to the authors, the enhancement of the restrictiveness of the European merger policy due to the introduction of the new substantive test is mitigated and balanced by the explicit introduction of the efficiency defence.[91] However, both the new test and the efficiency defence increase the Commission's discretion and, hence, may make merger policy less predictable.

In addition, Recital 32 of the Recast ECMR states that:

> Concentrations which, by reason of the limited market share of the undertakings concerned, are not liable to impede effective competition may be presumed to be compatible with the common market. Without prejudice to Articles 81 and 82 of the Treaty, an indication to this effect exists, in particular, where the market share of the undertakings concerned does not exceed 25 per cent either in the common market or in a substantial part of it.

This Recital seems to counterbalance the alleged enhanced ability of the Commission for intervention derived from the SIEC test, since it implies that concentrations leading to market shares below 25 per cent are not likely to induce any significant impediment to effective competition. However, legal uncertainty remains on two issues. The first relates to the discretion of the Commission due to the adoption of the SIEC, factoring in all the factors that enhance or mitigate such discretion. The second issue regards the possibility that a merger may lead to a post-merger market structure where the post merged entity and/or a small number of incumbents will each have less than 25 per cent, and the remaining market share belonging to a multitude of firms, none of which will be an effective competitor to this small number of incumbents.

In that case, if Recital 32 is read without any emphasis placed on *indication* and without noting Recital 25 according to which: "The notion of 'significant impediment to effective competition' in Article 2(2) and (3) should be interpreted as extending, beyond the concept of dominance, only to the anticompetitive effects of a concentration resulting from the non-coordinated behaviour of undertakings which would not have a dominant position on the market concerned", this merger, although it may lead to an adverse impact on competition, will not be blocked by the SIEC test.

Thus, in treating the threshold of 25 per cent, as stated in Recital 32, as not binding and as constituting a mere indication of a market share which is not liable to impede effective competition, the Commission has the discretion of capturing mergers in which the post merger entity will have less than 25 per cent and the merger will be likely to induce anticompetitive effects.[92]

It would be counterintuitive to argue that Recital 32 prohibits the Commission from alleging that a merger must be prohibited because it will lead to a post-merger market where one of the incumbents will hold less than 25 per cent (for example 24 per cent). The SIEC test was introduced to rectify the gap (that is to say mergers leading to non-coordinated effects in oligopolistic markets). Such mergers are likely to involve firms with less than 25 per cent market share in highly differentiated markets. Thus, the Commission is unlikely to have adopted a new substantive test to deal with mergers leading to non-coordinated effects in oligopolistic markets, but be prevented from doing so, by constraining itself due to a strict reading of Recital 32, in isolation of the wording of the substantive test, as well as of Recital 25.

Except from "closing the gap" in the application of the dominance test, an additional benefit (and one of the aims) of the SIEC test is to introduce a separation between the concept of dominance for the purposes of Article 102 TFEU and those of the Recast ECMR, as well as to include mergers having non-coordinated effects in oligopolistic markets,[93] and take into account unilateral effects in such markets.[94] Furthermore, the new substantive test, apart from addressing the "gap" in the application of the dominance test, facilitates consideration of merger-specific efficiencies, and, by encompassing dominance, it preserves existing precedents.[95]

Furthermore, the new substantive test aims at clarifying the notion of collective dominance as well. As Mario Monti has argued,[96] the advantage of such a definition of collective dominance under the Recast ECMR will have the advantage of not linking it with any interpretations of dominance given by the Court of Justice in cases falling within the ambit of Article 102 TFEU. In addition, the proposed substantive legal test not only aims at "closing the gap" of the traditional dominance test but also seeks to maintain the established case law and practice.[97]

As the Regulatory Policy Institute (2001)[98] notes, some of the issues underpinning competition are, and will remain, controversial after the adoption of the Recast ECMR. The relative importance of competition versus what it delivers as well as the combination of the necessary degree of discretion with a proper regard for legal certainty in the competition regime remain some of the highly controversial issues.

2.4 The horizontal merger guidelines

The *Guidelines*[99] describe both the theoretical basis and the analytical methodology for evaluating the potential for adverse effects on competition resulting from a horizontal merger. More importantly, in line with the desire to improve its economic reasoning, the *Guidelines* focus on the nature of the analysis needed in order to identify the competitive constraints that each of the merging parties currently poses on the other. The aim is to provide greater predictability with a view to increasing legal certainty for all parties concerned.

The *Guidelines* present the Commission's method of assessment of non-coordinated or unilateral effects, coordinated effects as well as non-coordinated effects in oligopolistic markets. The criteria for assessing each of these theories of harm are different.[100]

Unilateral effects typically arise where the combined entity has an appreciably larger market share than the next competitor in the post-merger market.[101] A significant impediment to effective competition can also result from a reduction in the competitive constraints that the merging parties previously exerted on each other, which could include a situation in which the combined entity does not have the largest market share in the relevant market.[102]

The Commission will also examine whether a proposed merger in a concentrated market will increase the likelihood that companies will coordinate their behaviour with a resulting increase in prices (coordinated effects).

The *Guidelines* outline a non-exhaustive list of factors, which taken separately are not necessarily decisive, but may influence the assessment of non-coordinated effects that may result from a merger. These factors are:[103]

- large market shares held by the merging firms (an analysis of market share thresholds appears in paragraphs 17–21 of the *Guidelines*)
- the merging firms are close competitors
- customers have limited possibilities of switching between suppliers
- competitors are unlikely to increase supply if prices increase
- the merged entity is able to hinder expansion by competitors
- the merger eliminates an important competitive force.[104]

The *Guidelines* also explain that in differentiated products markets mergers between firms producing non-close substitute products are unlikely to restrict competition. The primary concern should be whether the merging parties' products are close substitutes, and whether the loss of competition between the merging parties will enable the merged entity, as well as rival firms, to raise prices. In addition, the competitor's ability to raise prices will depend on the substitutability of their products with the ones of the merged entity and on the barriers to expansion that they may face. The greatest impact that the new substantive test will have in the assessment of mergers is that it allows the degree of closeness of substitution of the firms' products, as well as the degree of rivalry between firms, to be taken into account. The *Guidelines* add some additional references to the Commission's existing practice regarding the ECMR's substantive test and provide a clear legal basis and framework for non-coordinated effects (unilateral effects) analysis.

As regards coordinated effects, decisive factors that the Commission will take into account in its assessment include the easiness of reaching a common perception as to the terms of coordination, the monitoring of deviations and available/possible deterrent mechanisms, and the reactions of outsiders (customers and competitors).[105,106] Coordination will also depend on several elements of the market structure including barriers to entry[107] and exit, the existence of a small number of firms, the ability to coordinate towards equilibrium, the ability to enforce compliance, as well as ability to monitor and deter any prospective maverick firms. These factors depend on features such as product homogeneity, low demand growth, low price sensitivity of demand, symmetric cost structures, and multi-market contacts (see Table 2.1).[108] It is noteworthy that the factors mentioned above are quite similar to the ones that the Commission took into account in assessing collective dominance in cases under the original ECMR.[109]

Regarding the Commission's analysis of coordinated effects in the *Guidelines*, Ridyard (2004) argues that the Commission has missed out on a chance to clarify that its focus lies on the changes that the transaction induces on the market. Thus, there is a danger that the Commission will blur the distinction between the state of pre-merger competition in an industry and the assessment of how the merger affects that competition. Such an outcome could significantly prejudice analytical clarity and predictability.[110]

Mergers involving a potential competitor may also generate horizontal adverse effects on competition, either coordinated or non-coordinated, if the potential competitor significantly constrains the behaviour of firms active in the market.[111] Two basic conditions must be fulfilled for a merger with a potential competitor to have an adverse impact on competition. First, the potential competitor must already exert a significant constraining influence or there must be a significant likelihood that it would grow into an effective competitive force. Second, there must not be a sufficient number of other potential competitors which could maintain sufficient competitive pressure after the merger.

Table 2.1 Conditions for coordinated conduct in oligopolistic markets

Necessary criteria	*Factors that contribute to the necessary criteria*
Very few firms	
Repeated interaction	No large and lumpy orders
Barriers to entry	
Capacity to reach a mutually acceptable equilibrium	Homogeneous products Market transparency Symmetry Stable market conditions Low buyer power
Ease of detection of cheating	Homogeneous products Market transparency Symmetry Stable market conditions Low buyer power
Enforceability of compliance	Symmetry Stable demand conditions No/short detection lags Multimarket contacts Excess capacity

The *Guidelines* also briefly deal with adverse effects on competition arising from horizontal mergers that give rise to buyer power.[112] Such effects include foreclosure of rivals in the downstream market and a decrease in the level of the merged firm's output in the final product market due to a reduction in its purchase of inputs in an attempt to obtain lower prices in the upstream market.

The *Guidelines* also examine situations whereby efficiencies may counteract the proposed transaction's adverse effects on competition. In most competition enforcement regimes, it is recognized that a merger that may have significant adverse effects on competition should nevertheless be permitted if it would also result in improvements in efficiency that outweigh the adverse effects of the transaction.[113] The key criterion outlined in the *Guidelines* in examining efficiency claims is that consumers should not be worse off as a result of the proposed merger. In order for any efficiency claim to counteract the adverse effects on competition, certain criteria must be satisfied. The alleged efficiency claim must benefit consumers in the relevant market and it must be a direct consequence of the merger. In addition, efficiencies must be likely to materialize and must be verifiable as well as substantial enough to outweigh any adverse effects of the proposed transaction on competition.[114]

The Commission will also, in line with case law of the Court of Justice,[115] consider the "failing firm defence". In vigorously competitive markets, mergers involving failing firms may often enhance general welfare either through increasing the efficiency of existing capacity, redeploying that capacity to socially more valued uses, or preserving jobs and having other socially beneficial advantages.[116] The burden of proof of such welfare benefits lies with the party that claims the defence. If one of the companies involved in the merger is a "failing firm" and would exit the market in the absence of the merger, then the merger may be deemed not to significantly impede effective competition. The basic requirement is that the deterioration of the competitive structure that follows the merger cannot be said to be caused by the merger.[117]

The Commission considers the following three criteria[118] as relevant for the application of a "failing firm defence". First, the allegedly failing firm would in the near future be forced out of the market because of financial difficulties if not taken over by another undertaking. Second, there is no alternative transaction inducing less damage to competition than the notified merger. Third, in the absence of a merger, the assets of the failing firm would inevitably exit the market.

As already illustrated, the *Guidelines* widen the potential scope of the Recast ECMR below the traditional threshold associated with findings of single firm dominance. By removing the safe harbour previously implicit in the definition of single firm dominance, the new substantive test and the *Guidelines* that accompany it imply that the Commission will intervene in a significantly large number of transactions.

This chapter has addressed the advantages and disadvantages of the SLC and the dominance tests. It has also presented the Commission's choice of substantive test and briefly analysed the new *Guidelines*. The change in the test aimed, at enhancing the applicability of the ECMR on mergers leading to non-coordinated effects in oligopolistic markets.

The third chapter addresses the quantitative methods that can be employed in the assessment of mergers leading to non-coordinated effects in oligopolistic markets, in an attempt to assess whether the application of these methods in merger assessment depends on the substantive test used and whether the alleged inability of the Commission to capture gap mergers under the dominance test is not due to the gap in the application of the dominance test but due to a different application of merger assessment methods.

Notes

1 The UK Competition Commission had conducted an analysis of the market two years before the notification of the *Airtours/First Choice* merger and concluded that the market was competitive. See further: UK Competition Commission, Cm 3813, "Foreign Package Holidays: A Report on the Supply in the UK of Tour Operators' Services and Travel Agents' Services in Relation to Foreign Package Holidays", 19.12.97, www.competition-commission.org.uk. Some parts of this chapter have been published in Kokkoris, I. (2005d), "The

Reform of the European Community Merger Regulation in the Aftermath of the Airtours Case. The Eagerly Expected Debate: SLC v Dominance Test", *ECLR*, 26(1), 37–47.

2 See §54 of *Airtours/First Choice*: "[I]t is sufficient that the merger makes it rational for oligopolists to act individually in ways which will substantially reduce competition between them."

3 Monti, M. (2002), "Merger Control in the European Union: A Radical Reform", European Commission/IBA Conference on EU Merger Control, 7 November, Brussels, http://europa.eu.int/rapid/start/cgi/guesten.ksh?p_action.gettxt=gt&doc+SPEECH/02/545|0|RAPID&lg=EN&display+.

4 Case T-342/99 *Airtours v Commission* [2002] ECR II-2585.

5 Case T-77/02 *Schneider Electric SA/Legrand v Commission* [2002] ECR II-4201, Case T-310/01 *Schneider Electric SA/Legrand v Commission* [2002] ECR II-4071.

6 Case T-80/02 *Tetra Laval v Commission* [2002] ECR II-4519, Case T-5/02 *Tetra Laval v Commission* [2002] ECR II-4381.

7 See further: *Green Paper on the Review of Council Regulation (EEC) No. 4064/89*, COM(2001) 745/6, 11.12.2001. Green Papers are typically issued at an early stage in the legislative process, setting out the various options for change under discussion and establishing the overall framework of debate. See further: Clifford Chance (2002), "Green Paper on the Merger Regulation. A Summary of the Main Issues", www.cliffordchance.co.uk/uk/pdf/ECMR_Summary_of_Main_issues.pdf, 2.

8 *Proposal for a Council Regulation on the Control of Concentrations between Undertakings*, COM/2002/0711 final – CNS 2002/0296, OJ C020, 28.01.2003, 0004–0057.

9 See: *DG Competition Best Practices on the Conduct of EC Merger Control Proceedings*, http://europa.eu.int/comm/competition/index_en.html.

10 For further details on the history of the debate concerning the change of the legal substantive test, see: Fountoukakos, K. and Ryan, S. (2005), "A New Substantive Test for EU Merger Control", *ECLR*, 26(5), 277–96.

11 OJ L24, 29.01.2004, 1–22.

12 William, Cutler and Pickering (2002), "The European Commission Adopts Merger Control Reform Package", www.wilmer.com/docs/frameset.cfm?SECTION=practice&P.=index, 1.

13 According to the "one-stop shop" principle, a single authority, this being the Commission, assesses mergers having a Community dimension within a strict and short timetable and has exclusive Community-wide competence.

14 Freshfields Bruckhaus Deringer (2001), "EC Merger Regulation Green Paper: The Best of all Possible Worlds?", www.freshfields.com/practice/corporate/publications/pdfs/2322.pdf.

15 After the *Airtours/First Choice* decision, there was the implication that the Commission could rely on collective dominance to prohibit any merger in an oligopolistic industry. See further: Nicholson, M. and Cardell, S. (2002), "Airtours v Commission: Collective Dominance Contained", IBA EC Merger Control Conference, www.ibanet.org.

16 Council Regulation (EC) No. 1/2003 of 16 December 2002 on the implementation of the rules on competition laid down in Articles 81 and 82 of the Treaty, OJ L1, 04.01.2003, 1–25.

17 See further: William, Cutler and Pickering (2002), "The European Commission Adopts Merger Control Reform Package", www.wilmer.com/docs/frameset.cfm?SECTION=practice&P.=index, 2.

18 The author of this book has written extensively about merger assessment and this part of the chapter incorporates some of his earlier work, including the following: Kokkoris, I. (2005d), "The Reform of the European Community

Merger Regulation in the Aftermath of the Airtours Case. The Eagerly Expected Debate: SLC v Dominance Test", *ECLR*, 26(1), 37–47.

19 *Green Paper on the Review of Council Regulation (EEC) No. 4064/89*, COM(2001) 745/6, 11.12.2001.

20 Section 7 of the Clayton Act. See further: "Clayton Act, 15 U.S.C. §§12–27, 29 U.S.C. §§52–53", www.usdoj.gov/atr/foia/divisionmanual/ch2.htm.

21 Implemented by the Enterprise Act 2002, www.legislation.hmso.gov.uk/acts/acts2002/20020040.htm.

22 The SLC was adopted with the Trade Practices Act 1974.

23 Implemented by the Commerce Act 1986.

24 Implemented by the Competition Act 2002.

25 Europe Economics (2002), "One's a Monopoly, Two's Collectively Dominant, Three's Alright?", www.europe-economics.com.

26 Ex-director General of Fair Trading, UK Office of Fair Trading ("OFT").

27 Vickers J. (2002), "How to Reform the EC Merger Test? A Speech at the EC/IBA Merger Control Conference", Brussels, 2. See further: www.oft.gov.uk.

28 See further: International Chamber of Commerce (2002), "Comments on the EC Green paper on the Review of Merger Regulation 4064/89", www.iccwbo.org/home/statements_rules/statements/2002/review_of_merger regulation.asp.

29 There are notable exceptions where EU and the United States diverged in the outcome of their assessment. Cases include the *GE/Honeywell* merger, which was cleared in the United States and blocked in the EU (Case M2220 *General Electric/Honeywell* [2004] OJ L48/1). However, this case does not constitute a "gap" case and was treated differently because of the different impact of the merger in the two markets. The General Court upheld the Commission's decision as far as the horizontal effects arising from the merger were concerned (T-210/01 *General Electric v Commission*, Judgment of 14 December 2005).

30 Commerce Commission, *Progressive Enterprises Limited and Woolworths (New Zealand) Limited*, Decision No. 438 (13 July 2001). This case is analysed in Chapter 4.

31 Under the dominance test, the Commerce Commission concluded that *de novo* entry could not be relied on to constrain the merged entity (Progressive and Woolworths). For a detailed analysis of the case see: Goddard, G. and Curry, E. (2003), "New Zealand's New Mergers Test: A Comparison of Dominance and Substantially Lessening of Competition in the Supermarket Industry", *ECLR*, 24(7), 300–11.

32 New Zealand adopted the SLC test in May 2001.

33 Goddard, G. and Curry, E. (2003), "New Zealand's New Mergers Test: A Comparison of Dominance and Substantially Lessening of Competition in the Supermarket Industry", *ECLR*, 24(7), 300–11.

34 Lowe, P. (2002), "Review of the EC Merger Regulation – Forging a Way Ahead", European Merger Control Conference, Conrad Hotel, 8 November, Brussels, http://europa.eu.int/comm/competition/speeches/text/ sp2002_035_en.pdf, 9.

35 See further: Vickers, J. (2002), "How to Reform the EC Merger Test? A Speech at the EC/IBA Merger Control Conference", Brussels, 2. See further: www.oft.gov.uk, 3.

36 McDavid, J. (2002), "Proposed Reform of the EU Merger Regulation: A U.S. Perspective", *Antitrust*, 7, 52–5.

37 EEA Standing Committee of the EFTA States (2002), "EEA EFTA Comments on the Commission's Green Paper on the Review of Council Regulation

(EEC) No. 4064/89 (COM(2001) 745/6 Final)", secretariat.efta.int/Web?EuropeanEconomicArea/OngoingWork/100w149.doc, 7.

38 *FTC v H.J. Heinz, Co.*, 116 F.Supp. 2d 190 (D.D.C. 2000), appeal pending, No. 00–5362 (D.C. Cir.).

39 Boge, U. and Muller, E. (2002), "From the Market Dominance test to the SLC Test: Are There Any Reasons for a Change?", *ECLR*, 23(10), 495–8, 496.

40 For a detailed analysis of this case, see Chapter 4.

41 *FTC v H.J. Heinz Company, et al.*, Brief for Plaintiff-Appellant Federal Trade Commission. No. 00–5362, 8.

42 *FTC v H.J. Heinz Company, et al.*, Civ. No. 1:00CV01688 JR, Memorandum in Support of Plaintiff's Motion for Preliminary Injunction, www.ftc.gov/os/2000/07/heinzmemo.htm.

43 *FTC v H.J. Heinz Company, et al.*, Civ. No. 1:00CV01688 JR, Memorandum in Support of Plaintiff's Motion for Preliminary Injunction, www.ftc.gov/os/2000/07/heinzmemo.htm.

44 See further: Bishop, S. and Walker, M. (2002), *The Economics of EC Competition Law: Concepts, Application and Measurement*, Sweet & Maxwell, London, 310.

45 *Federal Trade Commission v Staples Inc.*, No. 97–701, 1997, US Dist.

46 Although the dominance test may include "blind spots", it has also been argued that the dominance test can be applied and adapted to a wide variety of situations where market power exists. See further: *Proposal for a Council Regulation on the control of Concentrations between Undertakings*, COM/2002/0711 final – CNS 2002/0296, OJ C020, 28.01.2003, 0004–0057.

47 Baker, S. (2002), "Unilateral Effects in Retail Chain Mergers: An Application to Supermarkets", *ECLR*, 23(4), 180–92.

48 Lowe, P. (2002), "Competition Policy in the European Union", speech at the American Antitrust Institute, Washington, DC, 1 July, www.eurunion.org/news/speeches/2002/020701 phillowe.htm.

49 Lowe, P. et al. (2002), "Substantive Standards for Mergers and the Role of Efficiencies", in Hawk, B, *International Antitrust Law and Policy*, Fordham University Law School, Corporate Law Institute.

50 The same arguments can be made for the SIEC test as well, since both SIEC and SLC have similar wording and will reach broadly the same outcome following the of a merger.

51 Snelders, R. and Dolmans, M. (2002), "Cross-Border Mergers in Company Law and Competition Law: Removing the Final Barriers", at the XX Congress of the Fédération Internationale pour le Droit Européen (FIDE), London 30 October–2 November, www.fide2002.org/pdfs/cbmnetherlands.pdf, 8.

52 As McDavid (2002) argues, the Green Paper provided an important opportunity to improve merger regulation in the EU and to take a significant step toward multilateral convergence. See further: McDavid, J. (2002), "Proposed Reform of the EU Merger Regulation: A U.S. Perspective", *Antitrust*, 17, 52–5.

53 "UK Response to the Commission Green Paper on the Review of Council Regulation (EEC) NO 4064/89", www.dti.gov.uk/ccp/topics2/pdf2/ukresponsetoecmegersgp.pdf, 9.

54 The so-called "unilateral effects". See further: Ministry of Industry, Employment and Communications (2002), "Statement of opinion on Green Paper COM(2001) 745 final on the Review of Council Regulation (EEC) No. 4064/89 (the so-called Merger Regulation)", Sweden, www.industry.ministry.se/pdf/ eun2002_ 880_nl.pdf, 6.

55 See further: Whish, R. (2002), "Substantive Analysis under the EC Merger Regulation: Should the Dominance Test be replaced by Substantial Lessening of Competition"?, in "EU Competition Law and Policy, Developments and Priorities", Hellenic Competition Commission, 19 April, Athens, 19.

56 Volcker, S. (2004) "Mind the Gap: Unilateral Effects Analysis arrives at the Merger Control", *ECLR*, 25(7), 395–409.
57 "*Guidelines on the Assessment of Horizontal Mergers under the Council Regulation on the Control of Concentrations between Undertakings*" ("*Guidelines*"), OJ C31, 05.02.2004, 5–18.
58 The Commission has argued that market shares as low as 36 per cent in *Hutchinson/ECT/RMPM* (Case M1412 *Hutchinson/RMPM/ECT* [2002] OJ C113/7), less than 30 per cent in *Carrefour/Promodes* (Case M1684 *Carrefour/Promodés* [2000] OJ C164/5), rendered undertakings dominant. Volcker, S. (2004), "Mind the Gap: Unilateral Effects Analysis Arrives at the Merger Control", *ECLR*, 25(7), 395–409.
59 Case M1672 *Volvo/Scania* [2001] OJ L143/74.
60 Case M2817 *Barilla/BPL/Kamps* [2002] OJ C198/4.
61 Case M2861 *Siemens/Drägerwerk/JV* [2003] OJ L291/1.
62 Case M3083 *GE/Instrumentarium* [2004] OJ L109/1.
63 For a brief analysis of such markets, see Chapter 1.
64 Due to high combined market shares.
65 Case M2256 *Philips/Agilent Health Care Solutions* [2001] OJ C292/10.
66 Case M2537 *Philips/Marconi Medical Systems* [2001] OJ C321/12.
67 Case M2922 *Pfizer/Pharmacia* [2003] OJ C110/24.
68 M619 *Gencor/Lonrho* [1997] OJ L11/30 (*Gencor/Lonrho*), Case M190 *Nestlé/Perrier* [1992] OJ L356/1 (*Nestlé*), M308 *Kali und Salz/MdK/Treuhand* [1998] OJ C275/3 (*Kali und Salz*).
69 See Appendix for a detailed analysis of all the substantive tests in the 27 member states.
70 See further: EEA Standing Committee of the EFTA States (2002), "EEA EFTA Comments on the Commission's Green Paper on the Review of Council Regulation (EEC) No. 4064/89 (COM(2001) 745/6 Final)", secretariat.efta.int/Web?EuropeanEconomicArea/OngoingWork/100w149.doc, 30 July 2003, 6.
71 See further: Monti, M. (2002), "Review of the EC Merger Regulation – Roadmap for the Reform Project", Conference on Reform of European Merger Control, British Chamber of Commerce, 4 June, Brussels, http://europa.eu.int/rapid/start/cgi/guesten.ksh?paction.gettxt=gt&doc= SPEECH/02/252|0|RAPID &lg=EN& display=, 6.
72 The Hungarian Office of Economic Competition has argued that the dominance test could be used in cases concerning the creation of a dominant position, while the SLC test can be applied, in an economically more flexible manner, to cases leading to the strengthening of existing dominance positions. See further: Hungarian Office of Economic Competition (2002), "Comments of the Hungarian Office of Economic Competition to some Issues by the Green Paper of the Commission on the Review of Council Regulation No. 4064.89", http://europa.eu.int/comm/competition/mergers/review/comments/ref029hungarianoffice.pdf, 4.
73 Voigt, S. and Schmidt, A. (2004), "Switching to Substantial Impediments to Competition (SIC) can have Substantial Costs", *ECLR*, 25(9), 584–90.
74 Diversion ratio is the percentage of the total sales lost by a product when its price increases that is captured by all the other products in the candidate market.
75 Willig, R. et al (2002), "Substantive Standards for Mergers and the Role of Efficiencies", in Hawk, B., *International Antitrust Law and Policy*, Fordham University Law School, Corporate Law Institute.
76 Voigt, S. and Schmidt, A. (2004), "Switching to Substantial Impediments to Competition (SIC) can have Substantial Costs", *ECLR*, 25(9), 584–90.
77 Further details on the criteria that gap mergers must meet are provided in the last chapter.

78 Competition law has a consumer welfare objective. In para. 25, Case 6/72 *Europemballage Corp. and Continental Can Co. Inc. v Commission (Continental Can)* [1973] ECR I-215 and para. 118 of T-168/01 *GlaxoSmithKline Services/Commission*, decision of 27 September 2006, the Court of Justice and General Court respectively clarify that the objective of competition law is consumer welfare. Although *Continental Can* is prior to the 4064/89 Regulation, *Glaxo* is after the original ECMR.

79 Fingleton, J. (2002), "Does Collective Dominance Provide Suitable Housing for All Anti-competitive Oligopolistic Mergers", in Hawk, B., *International Antitrust Law and Policy*, Fordham University Law School, Corporate Law Institute, 196.

80 Article 2(3), Council Regulation (EC) No. 139/2004 of 20 January 2004 on the control of concentrations between undertakings (the EC Merger Regulation), ("Recast ECMR"), OJ L24, 29.01.2004, 1–22.

81 See www.internationallawoffice.com/ld.cfm?Newsletters__Ref=7850#substantive, for the stance that these member states adopted.

82 We may assume that Germany may have been one of these countries, since Germany has the dominance test as its substantive test. Ulf Boge, head of the German Federal Cartel Office, was in favour of the dominance test. See further: Boge, U. and Muller, E. (2002), "From the Market Dominance test to the SLC Test: Are There Any Reasons for a Change?", *ECLR*, 23(10), 495–8.

83 We may assume that the United Kingdom and Ireland may also have been included in this list of countries, since both have the SLC test as their substantive test. The Directors General of the UK OFT and the Irish Competition Authority were in favour of the SLC test. See further: Vickers, J. (2002), "How to Reform the EC Merger Test? A Speech at the EC/IBA Merger Control Conference", Brussels. See further: www.oft.gov.uk, and Fingleton, J. (2003), "Competition for the Merger Test Market", presentation to the CRA Conference on Economics and Merger Policy for the 21st Century, 4 June, www.crai.com/.%5CAgenda%5General Courtngletonpr.pdf.

84 When interpreting provisions of regulations and directives, the European courts look at the aim of the provision and frequently examine recitals to elicit that aim. It is therefore likely that the German amendment will have the effect of narrowing the plain meaning of the SIEC test. See further: www.internationallawoffice.com/ld.cfm?Newsletters__Ref=7850#substantive.

85 Article 2(1)b of the Recast ECMR.

86 Case M1524 *Airtours/First Choice* [2000] OJ L93/1 ("*Airtours/First Choice*").

87 US District Court, Columbia, *FTC v HF Heinz Company et al.*, 00–5362a, 2000.

88 Recital 25 of the Recast ECMR, see: Council Regulation (EC) No. 139/2004 of 20 January 2004 on the Control of Concentrations between Undertakings (the EC Merger Regulation), ("Recast ECMR"), OJ L24, 29.01.2004, 1–22.

89 Voigt, S. and Schmidt, A. (2004), "Switching to Substantial Impediments to Competition (SIC) can have Substantial Costs", *ECLR*, 25(9), 584–90.

90 Wording such as "appreciable" rather than "substantial" as well as the reference to foreclosure of competitors. See further: William, Cutler and Pickering (2002), "The European Commission Adopts Merger Control Reform Package", www.wilmer.com/docs/frameset.cfm?SECTION=practice&P.=index, 2.

91 See further: Voigt, S. and Schmidt, A. (2004), "Switching to Substantial Impediments to Competition (SIC) can have Substantial Costs", *ECLR*, 25(9), 584–90.

92 For example, in markets with highly differentiated products, and a few significant firms where the post-merger entity and/or a small number of incumbents will each have less than 25 per cent market share.

93 As is the case in a merger between the second and third largest producers in

highly concentrated market encountered in the *Heinz* case. US District Court, Columbia, *FTC v HF Heinz Company et al.*, 00–5362a, 2000.

94 Sweet & Maxwell (2003), "*In Competition*", February, www.smlawpub.co.uk/online/newslet/incm/.

95 Padilla, J. (2004), "The Economics of Merger Control. An Overview of Quantitative Methods for the Assessment of Competitive Effects", a presentation to the UK Competition Commission, www.lecg.com.

96 See further: European Commissioner for Competition Policy, Monti, M. (2002), "Merger Control in the European Union: A Radical Reform", European Commission/IBA Conference on EU Merger Control, 7 November, Brussels, http://europa.eu.int/rapid/start/cgi/guesten.ksh?p_ action.gettxt=gt&doc=SPEECH/02/545|0|RAPID&lg=EN&display=, 5.

97 Fingleton, J. (2003), "Competition for the Merger Test Market", presentation to the CRA Conference on Economics and Merger Policy for the 21st Century, 4 June, www.crai.com/percent5CAgenda percent5C Fingletonpr.pdf.

98 Regulatory Policy Institute (2001), "Developments in Competition Policy: Mergers and Oligopolies", International Competition Policy Conference, 26 June, http://216.239.37.104/search?q=cache:u8EUV_ TO3TYJ:www.competition-commission.org.uk/inquiries/rpiconf.pdf+developments+in+ competition +policy:+ Mergers+and+Oligopolies&hl=el&ie=UTF-8, 14.

99 "*Guidelines on the Assessment of Horizontal Mergers under the Council Regulation on the Control of Concentrations between Undertakings*" ("*Guidelines*"), OJ C31, 05.02.2004, 5–18. Commission's notices and guidelines are not legally binding. However, they strongly indicate the Commission's position on a variety of important issues.

100 The Commission does not analyse specific criteria for assessing non-coordinated effects in oligopolistic markets. This book will analyse these criteria at a later stage. An analysis of the criteria for assessing unilateral or coordinated effects is essential for understanding the following parts of this book.

101 Firm with a paramount market position as was termed in the draft notice.

102 §25 of the *Guidelines*. Non-collusive oligopolies as was termed in the draft notice.

103 *Guidelines* at §§26–38. The discussion of factors (ii) and (iv) is of greatest interest for the discussion of unilateral effects.

104 The *Guidelines* refer to two cases where the market shares do not clearly indicate the non-coordinated effects that the merger may have. Such cases are the elimination of an entrant who was expected to exert significant competitive pressure or the elimination of important innovators with products in the pipeline. See further §§37–38 of the *Guidelines*.

105 In order for buyers to exert significant influence on the merged entity, they must be able to, inter alia, switch to other suppliers with no significant time delays or without incurring costs, sponsor expansion by competitors, credibly threaten to integrate vertically, as well as cease or delay purchases from the merged firm. See further §§64–67 of the *Guidelines*.

106 These three criteria are analysed in the assessment of the *Airtours/First Choice* merger case.

107 For entry to be considered a sufficient competitive constraint on the merging parties, it must be shown to be likely, timely and sufficient to deter or defeat any potential adverse effects on competition of the merger. See further: *Guidelines*, §68.

108 See further: Kokkoris, I. (2005d), "The Reform of the European Community Merger Regulation in the Aftermath of the Airtours case. The Eagerly Expected Debate: SLC v Dominance test", *ECLR*, 26(1), 37–47, Kokkoris, I. (2007b), "The Development of the concept of Collective Dominance in the

European Community Merger Regulation. From its Inception to its Current Status", *World Competition*, September.

109 See for example: Case M2256 *Philips/Agilent Health Care Solutions* [2001] OJ C292/10, Case M2537 *Philips/Marconi Medical Systems* [2001] OJ C321/12, and Case M2922 *Pfizer/Pharmacia* [2003] OJ C110/24.

110 Ridyard, D. (2004), "The Commission's New Horizontal Merger Guidelines – An Economic Commentary", http://gclc.coleurop.be/documents/DR %20GCLC %20paper%20March%2004.pdf.

111 Guidelines, §59.

112 See further: *Guidelines*, §§61–63.

113 Clark, J. (1999), "Efficiency Claims in Horizontal Mergers", *OECD Journal of Competition Policy*, 1(3), 245–62. Motta (2000) argued that the Commission in the *Airtours/First Choice* should consider efficiency gains from the prospective merger. See further: Motta, M. (2000), "EC Merger Policy and the Airtours Case", *ECLR*, 21(4), 206–207.

114 Case M4000 *Inco/Falconbridge*, 20 January 2006.

115 Applied in Case M308 *Kali und Salz/MdK/Treuhand* [1998] OJ C275/3. In addition, the defence has been successfully invoked in Case M2314 *BASF/Pantochem/Eurodial* [2002] L132/45. Additional cases where the failing firm defence has been invoked include: Case M53 *Aerospatiale-Alenia/de Havilland* [1991] OJ L334/42, Case M774 *Saint-Gobain/Wacker-Chemie/NOM* [1997] OJ L247/1, Case M993 *Bertelsmann/Kirch/Premiere* [1999] OJ L53/1, Case M1221 *Rewe/Meinl* [1999] OJ L274/1, Case M2876 *Newscorp/Telepiù* [2004] OJ L110/73. See further: Kokkoris, I. (2006c), "Failing Firm Defence in the European Union. A Panacea for Mergers?", *ECLR*, 27(9), 494–509.

116 Hewitt, G. (1999), "The Failing Firm Defence", *OECD Journal of Competition Law and Policy*, 1(2), 113–33.

117 *Guidelines*, §89. The prerequisite of causality was argued by the Commission in: Case M308 *Kali und Salz/MdK/Treuhand* [1998] OJ C275/3.

118 *Guidelines*, §90. The criteria have been developed through case law. See further: Kokkoris, I. (2006c), "Failing Firm Defence in the European Union. A Panacea for Mergers?", *ECLR*, 27(9), 494–509.

3 Merger assessment and the legal substantive test: quantitative methods in merger analysis

3.1 Quantitative methods in merger assessment

One of the most important trends in merger control in recent years has been a movement towards the use of empirical economic methods to assess the likely adverse effects of mergers on competition. This advanced sophistication of merger analysis is due to several factors including the enhanced quantity and quality of data available as well as the increased focus on the possibility of competitive harm arising from "unilateral" market conduct.[1] The lack of advanced quantitative methods in the past was due to insufficient data or to the different focus of merger analysis. As the complexity of merger cases increased, so did the need for supplementing qualitative evidence with quantitative evidence, the combination of which could provide a more accurate assessment of the effects of the merger in the relevant market.

Economic analysis regarding the non-coordinated effects in the post-merger market as well as the accurate definition of the market is amenable to quantification. Such types of economic analysis include merger simulation,[2] critical loss analysis,[3] price correlation analysis (*BP/E.ON (Aral)*[4] and *Nestlé/Perrier*),[5] price elasticity analysis (*Guinness/GrandMet*),[6] stationarity analysis (*Nutreco Holding NV/Hydro Seafood GSP*),[7] price concentration analysis (*Federal Trade Commission v Staples Inc.*,[8] *Nordic Capital/Mölnlycke/Kolmi*,[9] *Reed Elsevier Plc and Harcourt General, Inc*),[10] natural experiments (*Kimberly Clark/Scott*)[11] and bidding studies (*Oracle/PeopleSoft*,[12] *GE/Instrumentarium*,[13] *CHC Helicopter Corporation and Helicopter Services Group ASA*,[14] *Price Waterhouse/Coopers & Lybrand*).[15]

While quantitative analysis is essential in the assessment of mergers, qualitative evidence and analysis verifies and completes the results derived from quantitative analysis. Qualitative evidence, including company documents, market surveys and marketing studies, provides quite important insights and adds significant value and accuracy to quantitative evidence. Thus, the two types of analysis should be jointly used for an accurate and coherent assessment of a merger.

The chapter will address two methods of empirical analysis that relate to two essential stages in the assessment of a merger.[16] One such type of empirical analysis is used for the assessment of the non-coordinated effects of a merger; the other is used both in the definition of the relevant market and in the assessment of the non-coordinated effects of a merger. These two methods are merger simulation and critical loss analysis respectively. Specifically, merger simulation can predict price increases or decreases for a merger involving firms in the same market, depending on efficiencies and changes in market structure including repositioning and divestitures. Critical loss analysis can be used to accurately define the market, using the "Small but Significant Non-transitory Increase in Price" ("SSNIP") test, by estimating the percentage of customers that would need to switch in the presence of a 5 to 10 per cent price increase in order to make this price increase unprofitable for the hypothetical monopolist.

Merger analysis is an *ex ante* analysis. Although perhaps complicated, it is also very important to be able to predict the post-merger competitive conditions in the market, as they are determined by the post-merger features of the market such as prices, quantities and innovation. The accurate measurement of the competitive effects of mergers is essential for competition authorities and practitioners alike in their assessment of mergers. In recent years there have been significant developments in the use of empirical economic methods, including merger simulation models, to study the likely competitive effects of mergers. These developments have been shaped by the increased use of unilateral/non-coordinated effects analysis. Both the SIEC and SLC tests focus on post-merger price increases, a fact that makes them more accurate for merger assessment than the dominance test.[17]

In assessing a merger under the two substantive tests, the competition authorities must be able to accurately predict the post-merger competitive situation. As Werden, Froeb and Scheffman (2004) state: "[W]ith suitable models indicating what actions market participants take under particular circumstances, it is straightforward to predict the likely outcome, or 'equilibrium,' of their interaction, and it is similarly straightforward to compute the likely effects of a merger on the equilibrium, provided that the same, well-specified model of competitor interaction applies before and after the merger."[18] The value of this statement, as well as of merger simulation models, may be mitigated if the application of merger simulation differs according to the substantive test that is used for the assessment of the merger.

If the outcome of the merger simulation model changes depending on whether the dominance test or the SLC test is used for assessing the merger, a particular merger case that may not fall within the ambit of the dominance test, but would fall within the ambit of the SLC, may not, in reality, be a "gap" case. This underestimates the scope of application of the dominance test. In this case, the inability of the dominance test to apply to mergers leading to non-coordinated effects in oligopolistic markets, compared to the SIEC test, will not be due to the inherent limitation in the scope of the application of the dominance test but due to the different applications, under the dominance test and the SIEC test, of the method used to assess the competitive effects of the merger.

Merger simulation evaluates the ability of the post-transaction firm to raise the prices of some or all of its products through unilateral decisions and without resorting to overtly collusive activities. Merger simulation models provide a mechanism for explicitly trading off a reduction in the degree of competition against cost reductions from merger synergies. Firms may present such cost reductions as efficiencies arising from the merger. Thus, merger simulation can prove useful in assessing the non-coordinated effects arising from a merger.

Turning to critical loss analysis, this is one of the most advanced and widely used empirical methods in the definition of the relevant market. It has also application in the assessment of competitive effects of a merger. Its use by competition authorities as well as its acceptance by the courts as an accurate and representative tool indicates the importance it has for the assessment of competition cases. Critical loss analysis is important both in the assessment of a merger but also for the analysis of effects of agreements, concerted practices[19] and conducts that constitute abuses of dominant position.

The accuracy and outcome of the market definition process can substantially alter the assessment of the Commission of a particular merger since the degree of competition in a market crucially depends on how the boundaries of the market in product and geographical terms determine the presence and extent of competitive constraints.

Although there are a number of methods to define a market including price correlation studies, price concentration studies, stationarity analysis these methods entail drawbacks relevant to data availability and accuracy that mitigate their accuracy and value for market definition purposes.[20] When reliable data on consumer-switching behaviour is available the market definition analysis will be more accurate and will avoid errors due to preconceived notions of substitutability. Critical loss analysis can exploit such econometric evidence and may assist in analysing the impact of the marginal consumers' choices on the profitability of a price increase. Thus, critical loss analysis enhances the value of the SSNIP test which is used by lawyers, economists and competition practitioners in dealing with cases raising competition concerns. The SSNIP test is a constructed hypothetical test and critical loss analysis puts practical value to it by ensuring that the results of the SSNIP test will be accurate and will be interpreted in a way representative of the facts of the assessed merger.

The concept of critical loss analysis is essential in addressing the issue of mergers leading to non-coordinated effects in oligopolistic markets and in examining how the legal substantive test deals with non-collusive oligopolies, as well as in attempting to identify such cases in the current case law. Under the dominance test, market definition plays a crucial role as a prima facie indication of adverse effects on competition,[21] while the focus of the SLC/SIEC test lies on the impact of the merger on existing competitive constraints.

The aim is to evaluate whether the application of critical loss analysis in mergers under the two substantive tests might have led to a different assessment of the relevant market, and thus to a different assessment of the adverse effects of a merger on competition. In such a case, the inability of the dominance test to capture non-collusive oligopolies compared to the SLC/SIEC may be due to the different results of the assessment tools rather than due to a gap in the application of the dominance test.

Taking into account the importance of market definition for cases assessed under the dominance test, it might have been the case that the application of critical loss analysis on a particular merger case indicated a different market than the one that would be identified under the SLC/SIEC test, and thus the different assessment of the merger under the two substantive tests would not be the result of any alleged "gap" in the application of the dominance test but due to the different outcome of the critical loss analysis. If that is the case, then there may have been cases where the inability of the dominance test to apply to mergers leading to non-coordinated effects in oligopolistic markets would not have been due to the limited scope of the dominance test but due to an inaccurate definition of the market based on an inaccurate application of critical loss analysis. If the analysis herein shows that the application of the critical loss analysis is the same under the two substantive tests, then any limitation in the application of the dominance test, compared to the SLC/SIEC test, is likely to be due to a "gap" in the scope of the dominance test, rather than due to a different application of the quantitative method used in the process of market definition.

This chapter will investigate the theoretical background of these two quantitative methods in order to evaluate how these two methods are applied in practice in cases brought before courts in jurisdictions applying the dominance test and the SLC/SIEC test. The jurisdictions of focus for the purpose of this chapter are the United States and the EU.[22] The aim of this chapter is to evaluate whether the application of these two methods in these jurisdictions was different due to the application of a different legal substantive test and whether the choice of substantive test affected these methods' effectiveness in assessing mergers in general, but more specifically in assessing mergers leading to non-coordinated effects. In order to achieve this aim, reference will be made not only to cases decided in the courts of these jurisdictions but also to the theoretical background of these methods and evaluation will be undertaken as to whether the different legal substantive test led to different applications of the economic analysis or to different assessments of mergers leading to non-coordinated effects by courts, based on the same economic analysis.

A clear and concise idea of what merger simulation and critical loss analysis entail both in theory and as they have been applied in cases is necessary in order to assess whether the choice of the legal substantive test has any implications for the methodology and results of these two quantitative methods. The aim is to look into merger simulation and critical loss analysis in more detail and assess the impact of the legal substantive test on their implementation and their efficiency in assessing mergers leading to non-coordinated effects in oligopolistic markets.

Before embarking on actual evidence of gap cases,[23] we should clarify whether the existence of gap cases is due to the inability of the dominance test to capture such mergers, or due to some erroneous application of the assessment methods (for example merger simulation, critical loss analysis). If the latter is the case, then there was no need to adopt a new substantive test. What would have been adequate would be to amend these assessment techniques. Thus, an analysis of merger simulation and critical loss analysis will illustrate whether the gap cases are due to the inadequacy of the dominance test (and thus the substantive reforms of the ECMR were necessary) or due to erroneous application of these methods.

This chapter will thus examine whether the choice of the substantive test for the assessment of the merger can affect the application and the outcome of merger simulation models in estimating the competitive effects of mergers leading to non-coordinated effects in oligopolistic markets.

3.1.1 Merger simulation

Merger simulation models have been extensively used by parties and antitrust authorities in the United States, and they have started to be used in Europe with cases such as *Volvo/Scania*[24] and *Lagardere/Natexis/VUP*.[25] The new legal substantive test in the ECMR,[26] the SIEC, which resembles the equivalent substantive test used in the United States, the SLC, focuses on consumer harm. Both these tests focus on post-merger price increases, a fact that makes merger simulation more relevant to merger assessment than in the past. Unilateral effects simulation can predict price increases or decreases for a merger involving firms in the same market, depending on efficiencies and changes in market structure including repositioning and divestitures. Employing a combination of game-theoretic and econometric methods, there is the capability to estimate consumer demand using industry data and, based on these demand estimates, to derive specific predictions regarding post-merger prices.[27]

As mentioned earlier, merger simulation makes quantitative predictions for the likely post-merger firm's unilateral conduct that may have an adverse impact on competition. Unilateral or non-coordinated effects arise when the merged group enjoys market power[28] without depending for its success and profitability on coordinated interaction with the other firms in the market. Merger simulation analysis evaluates the ability of the post-transaction firm to raise the prices of some or all of its products through unilateral decisions and without resorting to overtly collusive activities.[29]

Thus, accurate merger simulation can provide competition authorities with an indication of the competitive effects of the merger and identify whether the merger would lead to unilateral effects and more specifically to non-coordinated effects in oligopolistic markets. Such econometric methods can prove invaluable to lawyers, economists, and competition practitioners alike in their assessment of such merger cases.

Merger simulation facilitates the assessment of the differing implications of alternative assumptions and can be very useful in identifying the factors that determine the impact of a transaction in the post-merger market. Models generally are abstract descriptions of real-world situations that assist in determining the consequences of a given set of hypothetical actions or the implications of a certain set of facts. Merger simulation models increase the focus and accuracy of the analysis of a differentiated products merger by providing a mechanism for explicitly trading off a reduction in the degree of competition against cost reductions from merger synergies. In addition, it provides a mechanism for evaluating possible remedies particularly in cases where brands are not all equally good substitutes for each other, or if there are synergies from the combination of some of the merging firms' brands. As Werden and Froeb (2004) argue, merger simulation models contribute to predicting the net short-term effects of a merger and thus to assessing the net effect of a merger on standard measures of economic welfare.[30]

Merger simulation models may also be used in assessing efficiencies and possible remedies that may not be measurable by other quantification methods. Specific efficiencies may be adequately significant to offset predicted price increases. In addition, merger simulation can contribute to the evaluation of the adequacy of proposed divestitures.[31]

Merger simulation practice has indicated the complexity in the variety of competitive processes resulting in different outcomes of the merger simulation depending on the modelling assumptions. The predictions of the merger are at best reasonable but rough estimates of the likely effects of mergers. Although merger simulation models can predict the short-term impact of the merger on output and prices, issues relating to the longer term evolution of the market such as entry and product repositioning must be separately considered since they are not included in the merger simulation model.[32] Merger simulation models may complement a fact-based analysis of the market but they can never be a *substitute* for such an analysis.

The following part of this chapter will analyse merger simulation models and their effectiveness in assessing the impact of mergers. A non-technical analysis of merger simulation will be provided in order to assess the practical issues that confront competition authorities and practitioners in the assessment of a merger. The following section will briefly describe the merger simulation process. The next section will deal with the effectiveness of merger simulation models in the various models of competition that may characterize a market. Then this chapter will briefly describe in more detail the economic models that can be utilized as the basis for a simulation analysis. Subsequently, evidence of the application of merger simulation models in the assessment of merger cases will be provided. Finally, some of the limitations of merger simulation models that have been indicated by the use of such models by antitrust authorities will be addressed.

3.1.1.1 Merger simulation process

This section will address the procedure that can be used to apply a merger simulation model; this will be achieved by looking at the stages of the merger simulation process itself. Merger simulation uses economic models founded on the theory of industrial organization to predict the effects of the merger on post-merger prices in the market; it is based on information about a set of pre-merger market conditions and certain assumptions about the behaviour of the firms in the relevant market. Such models attempt to estimate the effect that a merger will have on market prices by combining estimates of elasticities of demand as well as other variables such as data on price and quantity, with an economic model of how firms interact (that is to say, with a model reflecting the nature of competition). With merger simulation models, it is straightforward to compute the likely impact of the transaction on post-merger prices and quantities if the same model of competitor interaction (that is to say, the nature of competition) before and after the merger is applied.

Simulation models are essential in predicting the increase in the price of the products of the merging firms if these products are substitutes, since any substitution between the two firms' products will merely redistribute revenues between the two partners of the merged firm after the merger. Prior to the merger such substitution between the merging firms' products would translate into a loss in the revenues of the firm that increased its price. Simulation models may also contribute to predicting the impact of the merger on the prices charged by rival suppliers in certain market structures. An increase in the price by the post-merger firm will enhance the demand for competing firms' products, which may encourage them to increase their prices as consumers will be substituting towards their products.[33]

The computational approach of merger simulation involves two distinct steps: estimating a structural demand model; and computing or "simulating" the post-merger equilibrium to predict post-merger prices and quantities, which can be used to calculate measures of economic welfare.[34] With the first stage, assumptions are made for the value of the market shares as well as of the own-price and cross-price elasticity for each product in the market prior to the merger. With the second stage, an assumption is made about the nature of the competition in the market in order to assess the impact of the change in the merged firm's prices compared to the prices charged by the two firms prior to their merger.[35]

With the first stage of merger simulation, estimates of the own-price and cross-price elasticity for each product in the market prior to the merger can be obtained in two ways. They can be econometrically estimated, which relates to issues on price elasticity analysis. Alternatively, strong assumptions can be made about the structure of consumer demand, and then elasticities for all the products can be calculated using data on the prices and outputs of the main products and estimates of the own-price and cross-price elasticity for just one product.[36]

Merger simulation requires a functional form of demand that specifies the relationship between prices charged and quantities sold in the relevant market. An efficient merger simulation model must satisfy certain demand and supply conditions.[37] Regarding demand conditions the own-price elasticity[38] of each product should be negative since increases in a product's own price should reduce the quantity demanded of that product. In addition, cross-price elasticities would normally be expected to be positive, since a price increase for one product normally leads to an increase in the quantity demanded of the remaining products in the market, provided that the products are substitutes. Implementation of the model requires particular values for the own- and cross-price elasticities. These elasticities are used to estimate what prices and outputs would be if one supplier controlled the brands of a rival supplier.[39]

The supply conditions that the merger simulation model must meet relate to the cost function and the relationship determining the nature of competition in the market. The cost function is the economic description of the technology that firms face in an industry.[40] Knowledge of the cost function allows one to measure economies of scale and scope[41] as well as to evaluate cost complementarities, which would be useful in the perspective of assessing efficiency gains from mergers.[42]

With the second stage, after taking into account the estimated demand elasticities and the assumption about the nature of competition, post-merger prices and outputs are obtained by calculating the prices that the merging parties would set to maximize the merged firm's profits. This process involves taking into account two factors. First, the merged firm takes into account that, in setting its prices following the merger, any substitution between the two firms' products prior to the merger will merely redistribute revenues between the two partners of the merged firm after the merger; a merger mainly internalizes the competition between formerly separately owned firms.

Second, as already mentioned, an increase in price by the post-merger firm will enhance demand for competing firms' products as consumers switch their demand towards these alternatives, and will, therefore, encourage rival firms to raise their prices. This turns the "unilateral" effect into what can be called a "non-coordinated" effect or a "multilateral" effect of price increases. The evaluation of the latter type of effect is essential in the assessment of mergers leading to non-coordinated effects in oligopolistic markets. The post-merger equilibrium is reached when no firm in the market has an incentive unilaterally to change its prices.

The model depicting the nature of competition and its underlying demand and supply implications is essential in the outcome of the merger simulation model. Merger simulation uses economic models based on the theory of industrial organization to predict the effects of the merger on prices in the relevant markets. The following part of this chapter will address the outcome of merger simulation in markets with Cournot and Bertrand models of competition as well as in markets that are characterized by auctions.

3.1.1.2 Merger simulation: from theory . . .

Before analysing the exact methodology behind merger simulations, it would be useful briefly to analyse the theory behind the effects in the market of a merger between firms producing either homogeneous or differentiated products. After establishing what in theory is likely to be the result of the merger, the focus will turn to the merger simulation model and to evaluating the extent to which the theoretical predictions for the aftermath of a merger are observed in practice and to what extent the choice of the substantive test of the assessment of the merger affects these predictions. It would be useful to start by analysing some of the types of market structure in which merger simulation models can apply and by observing the effects of a merger in these markets.[43]

In the theory of industrial organization, two models that describe the nature of competition in a market are the Cournot and the Bertrand models.[44] A distinction can be made between markets in which firms compete primarily in output/capacity and markets in which firms compete primarily in prices. The first type of market structure resembles Cournot oligopoly; the second Bertrand oligopoly. The Cournot model of oligopoly assumes that firms produce homogeneous products and compete by setting output to maximize profits and takes the output of other firms as fixed, while that of Bertrand assumes that firms set price in order to maximize profits and takes as given the prices of other firms in the market.

As in the Cournot model of competition, firms compete by setting quantities, firms' quantities are substitutes. A reduction in the output of the merged firm producing homogeneous products typically leads competing firms to expand their own output, although not to the extent of fully compensating the initial output reduction.[45] Thus, because of the substitutability of the quantities, the direct impact of the merger on the market. Hence, such mergers may not necessarily lead to a reduction in output or increase in prices of the post-merger market, since the decrease in the output by the merged firm will be compensated by the increase from the incumbent firms in the market.[46]

In the Bertrand model of competition, firms will converge on the equilibrium price and quantity whether products are perfectly homogeneous (to the price that would prevail in a perfectly competitive market) or horizontally differentiated[47] (to prices above to the price that would prevail in a perfectly competitive market). With product differentiation, firms are able to adjust prices without losing the entire market. In such cases, prices do not rapidly collapse to marginal cost (as would be the case under perfect competition) and hence mergers are profitable for all the firms in the market. The adverse impact of the merger on competition in the market may be substantial, even if the differentiated products of the merging firms are not close substitutes.

When firms compete in prices, these prices are often complements. This implies that an increase in the price of one good will typically lead competing firms to increase their own prices, although probably to a lesser extent. An increase in the merging firms' prices triggers a positive response from the other firms, thereby further encouraging the merging firms to raise their own prices. Because of the complementarity of the prices, the direct impact of the merger on the market is exacerbated by the rival firms' adaptation to the new market structure.[48]

After this brief theoretical evaluation of the effects of a merger in these markets, this chapter continues with the mechanics of merger simulation. Merger simulation models in Cournot industries entail a process that includes the specification of the functional forms for demand; the calibration of parameters of these functions (for example, own price as well as cross-price elasticities) to make them correspond to the pre-merger prices and market shares in the market prior to the merger; and the estimation of the post-merger prices and market shares in the relevant market.[49]

Merger investigations gather information about average prices, aggregate annual output, and market shares. Although this information will vary over time, in merger simulations the market share and prices that are used for the equilibrium prior to the merger are generally estimates that are averaged over a recent time period. If the data are characterized by volatility, averaging over a long-term period will account for this volatility. Contrariwise, if the data exhibit trends, short-term averages may mitigate the fact that the data may not be consistent over time.

For a merger in the Cournot model of competition, with competitors distinguished by their costs and production capacities, the merger simulation model must reflect the cost and capacity conditions that the firms face. If the pre-merger capacities are the Cournot outputs, it follows that nonmerging firms are capacity constrained immediately following a merger. Until capacities are adjusted to the new equilibrium levels after the merger, the merged firm may find that a substantial price increase maximizes its short run profits, since the rival firms will not be able to react by increasing their production to the merged firm's price increase. Thus, the Cournot model is of major interest to the assessment of adverse effects of a merger on competition only if there are capacity constraints. If there are no capacity constraints, the incumbent firms will react to the reduction in the quantity by the merged firm by increasing their production, mitigating thus the adverse impact on quantity in the post-merger market.

In the case of a market with differentiated products, however, capacity constraints are not so important, as in markets with homogeneous products, since the output of the nonmerging firms is unlikely to change much after the merger, in contrast to the case of the Cournot type of competition, where, since the products are homogeneous, inability of the rival firms to increase their capacity may lead the merged firm to increase its price.

Turning to the Bertrand model of competition in the market, merger simulation models entail the same stages as in Cournot models, that is to say, specification of the functional forms for demand, calibration of parameters of these functions and estimation of the post-merger prices and market shares in the relevant market. The difficulty of calibrating the parameters of demand functions in a differentiated products environment is higher than in the case of homogeneous products, a fact that complicates the use of merger simulation models in Bertrand-type markets.[50]

Defining the relevant market for a merger simulation model in a Bertrand type of competition may undermine a challenge to a merger. Unilateral effects merger simulation does not require that a relevant antitrust product market be defined. Instead, the merger simulation procedure may be viewed as a way to model price effects for any given set of firms and brands, regardless of whether they constitute a formal relevant market.[51] With highly differentiated consumer products, the relevant market delineated by the hypothetical monopolist paradigm may be as narrow as the two merging products (if they are next best substitutes), yet such narrow markets are not alleged before the US courts because of a well-founded belief that judges would reject them out of hand.[52]

Since a merger in a market with a Bertrand type of competition will increase all firms' post-merger prices any exclusion of substitute products from merger simulation models biases downward the price-increasing effects of the merger. Excluding substitute products merely narrows the list of products for which prices may increase after the merger, and because the prices of excluded products generally would not be substantially affected by a merger, excluding them induces a downward bias to the price increase predictions. Products whose prices are excluded from a merger simulation model are assumed to be unaffected by the merger.

Before proceeding to analyse some economic models of demand specification that can be used in merger simulation models, the efficiency of simulation models in markets involving auctions should be addressed. Merger simulation with an auction model is much like that in a Cournot or Bertrand market, but instead of specifying functional forms for demand and cost, valuation or cost distributions for competing bidders are specified.

Auction models vary depending on the detailed specifications of the bidding process. Bidders in private values auctions are distinguished by the valuations they place on the item auctioned.[53] In a private values English auction,[54] each bidder bids up to his valuation of the item. The merger of two bidders in such a market (by forming a coalition that eliminates competition between them) would affect the auctions, in which the merging firms have the first and second highest valuations.[55] The average effect of the merger is determined by the frequency with which the merging bidders have the two highest valuations and by the difference between the second and third highest valuations when they do.

There is much in common between the effects of mergers in industries characterized by the private values English auction model and their effects in industries characterized by the Bertrand model, but there are also significant differences. All customers face the same prices in a Bertrand model, but each faces its own set of prices in an auction model. Consequently, the unilateral exercise of market power following a merger in a private values English auction market does not affect the identity of the winner bidder in any auction. In contrast, the unilateral exercise of market power following a merger in a market characterized by Bertrand type of competition causes some customers to switch their purchases. Hence, there may be a reduction in consumer welfare from a merger in a Bertrand market but not in a market in which English auctions are used.[56]

3.1.1.3 Demand estimation and merger simulation

Merger analysis requires models that can be estimated, have a unique equilibrium, and can capture loss of competition. In order for merger simulation models to have such characteristics they must satisfy certain requirements. Such models must be able to capture the likely loss of competition, must be able to be estimated or calibrated to parameters that will be used as inputs to the models, and be tractable enough so that post-merger equilibria regarding prices and quantities can be easily estimated.

As mentioned earlier, an efficient merger simulation model must satisfy certain demand conditions. Thus, a functional form of demand that will satisfy these conditions needs to be used. Since estimation of elasticities is essential for the outcome of the merger simulation model and thus the calculation of post-merger prices, it is important to use a demand model that will not predetermine the values of the elasticities and will allow the data to determine the elasticities and thus the degree of substitutability or complementarity between the two merging firms' brands.

Crooke, Froeb, Tschantz and Werden (1997) compared the results of a merger simulation model under the logit, the linear, the "Almost Ideal Demand System" (AIDS) and the constant elasticity functional forms of demand. The model using the logit and linear functional forms resulted in very low post-merger prices, while under the AIDS and constant elasticity functional forms the merger simulation model resulted in post-merger prices that are much higher. For small mergers, however, a merger simulation model using the AIDS functional form can result in lower price and quantity reductions for the merging firms' products. Thus, the functional form of demand substantially determines the magnitude of price increases from a merger: linear and logit demand yield the smallest price increases; the constant elasticity and AIDS demand models yield price increases that are substantially higher than those resulting from using linear or logit functional forms of demand.

The main obstacles that merger simulation models must overcome are the large number of demand parameters that need to be estimated as well as data limitations regarding the merging firms and their competitors. Rubinfeld, Roy and Epstein (2001) proposed a simulation model that overcomes these obstacles by requiring the estimation of a limited number of parameters and the use of limited data. The "Proportionality-Calibrated AIDS" (PCAIDS) model can estimate the AIDS functional form of demand in case of limited data availability.[57] PCAIDS provides analytical flexibility while retaining many of the desirable properties of the AIDS model.[58]

The PCAIDS model offers a simplified version of AIDS that requires only market shares, an estimate of the market's demand elasticity, and an estimate of the price elasticity of demand for a single brand in the market in order to generate a prediction of the effect of a horizontal merger in the prices and quantities in the post-merger market. The limited requirement of the PCAIDS model in relation to data, which makes it quite employable in merger simulation models, implies that the unilateral effect of a merger on the merging firms' prices is constrained to be directly related to the market share of the merging firms. Thus, its ability to explain the conditions present in an industry that is characterized by significant differentiation is severely mitigated.

More efficient merger simulation models would require a larger quantity of data, and thus may derive more realistic results based on the actual interaction between brands. Such improved models should also allow the analysis to be less constrained by specific market definitions, since the degree of substitutability between brands can be evaluated through the estimation process. In order for the model to capture the dynamics of a market and accurately predict the impact of the merger in the post-merger market it will require the necessary quality and quantity of data to assess the reactions of consumers, buyer power, likely efficiencies, as well as supply-side reactions.

A theoretical background on the mechanics of merger simulation models has now been detailed; the following section assesses how merger simulation models have been used by antitrust authorities in transactions brought before them and the limitations such models have illustrated.

3.1.1.4 Merger simulation: . . . to practice

This section will deal with the practical application of merger simulation models in mergers that were brought before antitrust authorities.[59] The merger simulation models[60] in the cases *Centrica/Dynegy*,[61] *Oracle/PeopleSoft*,[62] *Volvo/Scania*,[63] and *GE/Instrumentarium*[64] will be assessed.

In *Centrica/Dynegy*, Centrica acquired Rough, Dynegy's largest gas storage facility in the United Kingdom.[65] Centrica was formed by the 1997 demerger of British Gas Plc into two parts, Centrica and BG Plc. Dynegy, a US energy company, acquired Rough from BG Group in 2001. Centrica was involved in retail gas supply but it also owned the large Morecambe Bay gas fields. It had also diversified, by entering the UK electricity industry.

The UK Competition Commission defined markets for the wholesale supply of gas and the retail supply of gas. It concluded that supply to domestic gas and electricity customers was converging towards a single market.

As a result of the *Centrica/Dynegy* merger, Centrica would be likely to withhold sources of flexible gas in order to force up wholesale gas prices. The transaction would give Centrica not only the incentive to raise the wholesale price of gas in winter, which determines Rough prices, and thus to increase the price of storage "units"' in Rough, but also the ability to raise these wholesale prices by restricting capacity of its flexible gas.

As mentioned earlier, to conduct a merger simulation model, a reliable estimate of the elasticity of demand for the merging parties' products is necessary in order to assess the impact of a price increase on the quantity demanded of the product. In addition, the firm's cost function needs to be estimated, in order to evaluate the impact of restricting capacity on costs and therefore profits.

Lexecon[66] conducted a merger simulation model to assess the impact of the transaction in the price of storage "units" in Rough in the post-merger market.[67] The first step in the simulation analysis was to estimate Centrica's residual demand for gas in order to assess the quantity of winter gas Centrica would have to reduce in order to raise the wholesale price of gas in winter and thus to increase the price of storage "units" in Rough by a penny per storage unit. Initially the residual supply curve[68] for wholesale gas was estimated and this estimate was used to derive Centrica's residual demand curve.[69] The likely costs and benefits of restricting capacity were quantified using the estimate of Centrica's residual demand curve, along with estimates of various other factors, such as Centrica's ability to pass on increased gas costs to final customers in the downstream gas market.[70]

The outcome of the merger simulation model was that Centrica's direct benefit from an increase in winter prices would have been an increase in the value of Rough storage in the order of £10 million per annum. The assessment of the net effect rested on three key empirical questions that determined the cost to Centrica of making this happen: the elasticity of Centrica's demand for gas, the opportunity cost of holding back sufficient winter gas to generate the price increase, and the ability to pass on higher procurement costs to customers. The results of the analysis showed that the cost to Centrica of withholding gas would exceed the benefit it would receive from higher Rough prices. Therefore, Centrica would have no incentive to withhold gas in the wholesale market following the merger. The UK Competition Commission accepted the conclusions of the merger simulation model and recommended that the transaction should be cleared subject to negotiation of undertakings to address other concerns.[71]

As with the *Centrica/Dynegy* merger, a merger simulation model was also used in the *Oracle/PeopleSoft* case.[72] Oracle was a publicly listed company that was active in the design, development, manufacture, and distribution of enterprise application software, database, and application server software and related services. PeopleSoft was a publicly listed company that was active in the design, development, manufacture, and distribution of enterprise application software and related services. Oracle Corporation would acquire sole control of the undertaking PeopleSoft Inc.

The Commission found that the relevant product markets for the assessment of the present transaction were the markets for high function financial management systems ("FMS") and human resources ("HR") software applications. As FMS and HR applications were not substitutable for buyers, the Commission considered these as two distinct markets. In addition, the market investigation showed that characteristics of high-function HR and FMS software were different from those of mid-market products. The underlying architecture of high-function solutions was fundamentally different from the one of mid-market products. The Commission concluded that the market for software applications for mid-size enterprises formed a separate market from the markets for high-function FMS and HR solutions. The Commission also concluded that the geographic scope of these markets might not be wider than European Economic Area ("EEA") wide. However, the exact delimitation was left open.

As regards the market for high-function FMS and HR solutions or software, based on a definition of the market that, after the merger, would consist solely of Oracle and SAP, the Commission had raised concerns in its Statement of Objections that there would be a significant group of customers for whom there would essentially be only one supplier left after the transaction. However, in light of conclusions after the oral hearing regarding the existence of additional firms in the market, the Commission could not uphold its preliminary conclusion that customers would be confronted with a de facto absence of choice after the merger.

The Commission could not conclude that the merger would lead to a collective dominant position of a combined Oracle/PeopleSoft and SAP. The other vendors, Lawson, Intentia, IFS, QAD, and Microsoft, appeared to be suitable alternatives as the Commission's data and the dataset submitted by Oracle after the oral hearing showed that those vendors had won bids for software in the relevant markets. In addition, the highly differentiated nature of the FMS and HR high-function software,[73] the lack of structural links, the asymmetric market shares, the large number of incumbents, the limited transparency, and inadequate retaliatory mechanisms made the achievement of a tacitly collusive outcome very unlikely.

The merger simulation model was based on estimated market shares and predicted that a reduction from three to two bidders would not harm customers since prices were not likely to increase and the product variety was not likely to decrease. The scope of the econometric analysis in this case, and the weight given by the Commission to its conclusions, indicated the importance that the European Commission places on such quantitative methods of analysing the effects of mergers.

In addition, merger simulation was employed in the assessment of the merger of Volvo and Scania which was prohibited by the European Commission. For the European authority, the combined market shares held by Volvo and Scania would be sufficiently high to raise concerns that the proposed acquisition could create a dominant position. Volvo and Scania are Swedish companies whose principal businesses include the manufacturing and sale of trucks, buses, and marine and industrial engines. The market investigation conducted by the Commission confirmed that Volvo and Scania had been each other's closest competitors and had competed strongly. In addition, the barriers to entry or expansion in the relevant markets were high since any competitor who wanted to challenge the merged entity would have to make large investments over a significant period of time.

The Commission was concerned that Volvo and Scania could be one another's closest competitors in that both seemed to pursue similar market strategies. In its decision it indicated that it had commissioned an econometric study designed "to measure *directly* what the effects of the merger could be on the prices charged by heavy truck producers in the various national markets" (emphasis added).[74]

The quantitative analysis of the likely unilateral effects of the merger included an econometric study for the estimation of demand elasticities for the main heavy truck brands in each EU country. The results of the econometric analysis were used as inputs in a merger simulation model that was developed to quantify the price effects of the proposed transaction. The study was based on a panel dataset of 16 countries in the EEA over two years (1997 and 1998) for each of the seven major truck manufacturers. The market shares for each truck model were estimated as a function of price, horsepower, and other factors that may affect demand (for example, factors that are unique to each country and firm).[75]

The results of the merger simulation suggested that the merger would have substantial unilateral effects, with the prices of both Volvo and Scania trucks increasing by about 5 per cent in many EU countries and by more than 10 per cent in the Scandinavian countries. The prices of rival suppliers' heavy trucks were largely unaffected by the merger. The Commission's merger simulation analysis was strongly contested by the parties on the ground that the data had serious limitations.[76] The authors of the Commission's merger simulation analysis argued that: "[T]he model involves assumptions about cost conditions, demand conditions and market equilibrium. All together they produce a model that is parsimonious in the number of parameters to be estimated. This approach is necessary given European merger investigations provide rather limited time to collect data and perform a quantitative analysis. However, we believe that the model still provides a good approximation of the working of the heavy truck market."[77]

They added that several of the assumptions used in the model can be debatable, but they attempted to ensure that the assumptions would lead to no clear bias, or would lead to conservative estimates of the price effects. They concluded by noting that it is because of a quantified model that one is able to assess the effects of the assumptions.

The *GE/Instrumentarium* decision approved the acquisition by General Electric Medical Systems (GE) of Instrumentarium, a leading hospital equipment manufacturer. In its assessment of the effect of the merger the Commission analysed market share data, as well as qualitative information regarding the nature of the process by which hospitals purchase patient monitors. To obtain an estimate of the likely price effect of the proposed transaction at the EEA level the Commission analysed bidding situations involving a third-party manufacturer of patient monitors (Philips).

Based on an econometric analysis the Commission found that the elimination of GE or Instrumentarium as an independent competitor was likely to lead to higher prices by a third-party supplier of patient monitors. Alongside a high market share the merged entity would have the ability to appreciably increase prices for a significant proportion of its customers without being challenged by its competitors. In such a situation, the takeover of the closest rival would lead to a considerable loss of competition since, in any new bidding round, the merged entity would have the ability to increase its price in the knowledge that the dissatisfied customer would tend to buy its alternative product line. The analysis of the submissions made by customers and competitors and the econometric studies conducted by the Commission on the basis of bidding data also revealed that the transaction would remove a particularly close competitor from the market, therefore significantly increasing GE/Instrumentarium's market power in perioperative patient monitors vis-à-vis its customers, that is to say the hospitals.

The Commission also concluded that the rivalry between GE and Instrumentarium was a source of competitive pressure for other manufacturers.

Thus, the merger was likely to lead to higher prices for other manufacturers as well. In its final decision, the Commission cleared the acquisition subject to commitments intended to preserve competition in the market.[78]

This type of econometric analysis does not in itself provide an estimate of the likely impact of the merger on price. Such estimates can be obtained only at the price of imposing extreme assumptions as to the nature of competition between firms in the relevant market as well as by taking into account the possibility of either demand- or supply-side responses as a result of the merged entity's attempt to increase prices in the post-merger market.[79]

Most merger simulation models are a proxy for the actual situation in a market and thus would have to be supplemented with critical analysis and judgment in order to accurately predict the effects of a transaction in the post-merger market. Calibrated economic models provide concrete, quantitative analysis of market delineation and the competitive effects of mergers. Econometrics-based merger simulation substantially increases the accuracy and persuasiveness of merger analysis by basing price-increase predictions directly on the underlying data from which the relevant demand elasticities are estimated. This analysis is firmly rooted in the facts of the case and based on the nature of competition in the market. The choice between the SLC and the dominance test does not affect either the method or the results of merger simulation.[80] However, it should always be kept in mind that, since price increase predictions always are subject to modelling error, the predictions of merger simulation are at best reasonable, albeit rough, estimates of the likely effects of mergers.

In order to be able to rely on merger simulation models for accurate predictions of the impact of the transaction in the post-merger market, they must reflect critical features of the nature of competition in the market, such as whether the product is homogeneous or highly differentiated. The ability of a merger simulation model to explain the impact of mergers in the past in an industry may indicate its ability accurately to predict the impact of mergers in the future. The use of accurate merger simulation models significantly enhances the focus, accuracy, and persuasiveness of merger analysis. Such models constitute a very useful tool in estimating the effects of a merger and may be of great value in identifying the competitive effects of mergers leading to non-coordinated effects in oligopolistic markets.

After having analysed the theoretical and practical issues behind merger simulation models, this chapter now turns to addressing critical loss analysis.

3.1.2 Critical loss

Critical loss analysis and interpretation of quantitative evidence is essential in predicting and quantifying the magnitude of competitive harm that firms' conduct may induce in a market. In addition, such evidence significantly enhances the focus, accuracy and persuasiveness of the assessment analysis. The importance of empirical evidence may be given different weight by different decision makers. Thus, quantitative evidence can be regarded as complementary to qualitative evidence and the two methods are used jointly to assess the adverse effects of mergers on competition.

A type of empirical analysis used in the definition of the relevant market as well as in the assessment of the adverse effects of a merger on competition is critical loss analysis ("CLA"). Since the early 1980s there has been a considerable amount of research into developing economic approaches that are appropriate to competition analysis. Economists started to focus on devising new methods for defining markets.

As Stigler (1982) argued: "[E]xcept for a casual flirtation with cross-elasticities of demand and supply, the determination of markets has remained an undeveloped area of economic research at either the theoretical or empirical level."[81] Coate (1992) referring to market definition argues: "[T]he Courts have struggled with the issue for years while economists with rare uniformity have suggested that the analysis be based either directly or indirectly on the demand and supply elasticities."[82] Critical loss analysis may assist in identifying the correct boundaries of the market and accurately assessing the competitive effects of a merger and thus in indicating whether the dominance test does have a "gap" in its application to mergers leading to non-coordinated effects in oligopolistic markets.

Critical loss analysis was introduced by Harris and Simons (1989), who define the critical loss "for any given price increase as the percentage loss in sales necessary to make the specified price increase unprofitable".[83] It has gained increasing importance in competition law since market definition plays a crucial role in assessing practices of firms having an adverse impact on competition. The accuracy and outcome of the market definition process can substantially alter the assessment by the competition authorities of competitive harm since the evaluation of the degree of competition in a market crucially depends on how the boundaries of the market in product and geographical terms are defined.

The next section of this chapter deals with the mechanics of critical loss analysis, presenting an explanation on how critical loss can be implemented for the definition of the market as well as for the assessment of competitive effects. This chapter continues with an assessment of how critical loss analysis can be applied in practice; this assessment looks at some cases in which critical loss analysis was used by the parties.

3.1.2.1 Critical loss analysis: mechanics

CRITICAL LOSS ANALYSIS AND MARKET DEFINITION

Critical loss analysis makes the SSNIP test (Small but Significant Non-transitory Increase in Price, also known as the hypothetical monopolist test) operational. According to the SSNIP test, if a small (in the range of 5 to 10 per cent) permanent increase in the price of a good ("starting price") leads to such an increase in purchases of another good that the price increase would be unprofitable, then the two goods belong to the same market.[84] The test seeks to establish the smallest product group as well as the geographic area such that the hypothetical monopolist controlling that product group in that area would be able to profitably sustain prices that are higher than the competitive level of prices even by a small amount.[85] The equivalent analysis is applicable in cases concerning the concentration of buying power, where the starting point would be the supplier, and the price test would identify the alternative distribution channels or outlets for the supplier's products.[86]

Critical loss analysis involves three stages: estimation of the hypothetical monopolist's profit margin per unit before the increase in prices; determination of the percentage of customers that the hypothetical monopolist would lose before the price increase becomes unprofitable; and whether the hypothetical monopolist would lose this percentage of customers if he increased prices. Thus, critical loss analysis can be used to accurately define the market, using the SSNIP test, by estimating the percentage of customers that would need to switch in the presence of a 5 to 10 per cent price increase in order to make this price increase unprofitable for the hypothetical monopolist. For example, 90 per cent of the customers may switch to another product and the price increase may still be profitable.

Critical loss analysis estimates how much the hypothetical monopolist's sales would have to fall in order to make the hypothetical price increase unprofitable. The price increase contemplated in the SSNIP test has two opposing effects on the hypothetical monopolist's profits. It has a negative effect on profits because sales will fall as some consumers substitute to rival products in response to the increase in price. However, there is an offsetting positive effect on profits as the hypothetical monopolist now earns higher margins on all of its remaining sales. If the negative effect on profits is greater than the positive effect, the price increase will be unprofitable for the hypothetical monopolist, and the relevant market will be wider.[87] The critical loss is the percentage reduction in quantity such that these two effects just balance. If the reduction in unit sales is greater than the critical loss, the price increase will reduce profits. If the reduction in unit sales is less than the critical loss, the price increase will increase profits.

As already mentioned, critical loss analysis estimates the percentage price increase of a product for the percentage loss in unit sales that is required to make the price increase unprofitable. The argument is that the larger the profit margins, the greater the reduction in profits from sales lost after a price increase. It takes a smaller critical loss to make a given price increase by a hypothetical monopolist unprofitable. For any given price increase, the critical loss is smaller the higher the gross profit margin. This is so because when the gross margin is higher there is a larger negative effect on profits arising from the fall in sales (caused by the increase in price). Thus, profit margins determine the amount of substitution needed to expand a provisional relevant market definition. It should be noted that large margins can be observed as a result of conduct having an adverse impact on competition as well as in industries with differentiated products in which the products of different firms are not close substitutes.

The argument that the larger the profit margins the greater the reduction in profits from sales lost after a price increase is contested by Katz and Shapiro (2003); they believe that the argument is incomplete as high margins also tend to imply that the actual loss is small, and thus a price increase might be profitable even when the critical loss is small.[88] They suggest an alternative approach based on the aggregate diversion ratio, the percentage of the total sales lost by a product when its price increases that is captured by all the other products in the candidate market. They argue that an aggregate diversion ratio greater than the critical loss creates a presumption that the candidate product market is, in fact, a relevant antitrust market.

Although critical loss estimates the percentage loss in unit sales to make the price increase unprofitable, it does not clarify whether the reduction will actually occur. Thus, the second stage in critical loss analysis is to calculate the actual loss in sales due to the price increase. This estimation requires analysis of the reaction of consumers (demand side of the market) as well as of producers (supply side of the market).

The price effects of a merger depend crucially on the magnitude of the lost sales that would be diverted to competitors as the result of a price increase, and the allocation of that diversion among the competing firms. If the evidence on the likely loss of sales associated with a price rise (which can be compiled using a range of techniques, including demand estimation, shock analysis, and switching surveys) suggests that the actual loss would be greater than the critical loss, then the products in question do not form a relevant market (the price increase would not be profitable). If the actual loss is greater than critical loss, then the price increase is not profitable and the market must be expanded. Depending on the context, an actual loss greater than critical loss implies that a unilateral or coordinated price effect equal to the given price increase is not of concern, or that the goods involved do not form a separate antitrust market.[89]

In other words, critical loss analysis involves estimating the maximum amount (in percentage terms) by which sales of the products in question can fall following the hypothesized price increase and yet still ensure that the hypothetical monopolist's profits do not decline. Thus, critical loss analysis estimates the point at which the two opposing effects of a 5 to 10 per cent price increase on the hypothetical monopolist's profits cancel each other out.

The computational method used to calculate the critical loss is simple and requires the initial price and average variable cost to allow the calculation of a proxy for the price cost margin. The formula[90] is the ratio of the hypothesized percentage price increase over the sum of the hypothesized percentage price increase and the price-cost margin (that is to say, percentage incremental profit margin, which is equal to initial price minus the average cost) and this outcome divided by the initial price.

Sheffman and Simons (2003), however, argue that firms seldom set price to equate marginal revenue[91] and marginal cost.[92] They claim that irregularities (kinks) in the industry demand curve or in marginal costs make this assumption unrealistic. They conclude that the actual loss for the hypothetical monopolist will be lower than for an individual competitor, whereas actual loss may be substantially greater than critical loss.[93]

As a quantity response to a price increase, critical loss analysis can be restated in terms of elasticities[94] under the assumption that firms maximize profits by equalizing marginal cost with marginal revenue. The industry elasticity facing the hypothetical monopolist should be smaller in magnitude than the price elasticity of each firm because the industry as a whole would face less competition than each firm individually. Critical elasticity analysis greatly enhances the accuracy of econometrics-based market definition by providing a specific value with which to compare the estimated elasticity for a candidate market.[95]

As just mentioned, apart from market definition, critical loss analysis plays an important role in assessing competitive effects. Critical loss analysis may assist in assessing the likelihood of coordinated behaviour in raising prices when not all members of a group of competitors adopt the same conduct. Furthermore, if different competitors have substantially different costs and/or face substantially different actual losses arising from a coordinated price increase, critical loss analysis might demonstrate that some competitors would not find it in their interest to participate in a coordinated price increase.[96]

The preceding section of this chapter examined the importance of critical loss analysis for the definition of the relevant market; the following section assesses the application of critical loss analysis in the assessment of the competitive effects of a merger.

CRITICAL LOSS ANALYSIS AND COMPETITIVE EFFECTS OF THE MERGER

As explained earlier in this chapter, critical loss analysis plays a crucial role in the definition of the relevant market. It also plays an important role in assessing the competitive effects of a merger. It can provide insights to the degree of closeness of the merging parties' products, as well as to the elimination of rivalry between the products as an indication of unilateral effects of the merger. It can also be used in order to assess the likelihood of sustaining a tacitly collusive outcome, by examining, inter alia, the incentives of firms to divert from the collusive outcome.

In assessing the competitive effects of a merger critical loss analysis entails the same steps as in the case of market definition:

- estimation of the hypothetical monopolist's profit margin per unit before the increase in prices
- determination of the percentage of customers that the hypothetical monopolist would lose before the price increase becomes unprofitable
- whether the hypothetical monopolist would lose this percentage of customers if he increased prices.

In differentiated products markets, however, the diversion from the products of the merging firms must be taken into account since it influences the amount of sales lost that would make the price increase unprofitable. In addition, the reactions of the incumbent firms must also be taken into account, since their pricing decisions will influence again the amount of sales lost that would make the price increase unprofitable.

The aim in using critical loss analysis for the assessment of the unilateral effects of a merger is to evaluate whether the post-merger firm will be able to price unilaterally after the merger. What should be taken into account in differentiated product markets where firms produce substitute products is the diversion ratio, which will indicate the diversion of sales from the products of one of the merging firm, in case of a price increase by that firm, to the other's before the merger. After the merger this diversion is internalized since the two merging firms before the merger constitute one entity post-merger, a point which will be further analysed later.

In addition to the issue of substitutability between the merging firms' products, the unilateral reactions of other firms must also be taken into account.[97] The other incumbents in the market may increase prices to the same levels as the merged firm, may increase prices to a lower level than the merged firm, or may not increase prices at all. Where the firms are differentiated: in the second case, they may increase sales depending on their price relative to the merged entity's, while in the last case, they may gain a higher marker share due to the diversion of sales from the merged entity to them. In setting its prices *after* the merger, the merged firm takes into account the price reaction of the incumbents in the market and since the prices of these incumbents may also increase, the relative increase of the merged firm's prices is lower than the actual.

Thus, due to the price reaction of the nonmerging firms and the impact on the quantities demanded for their products as well as the merged firm's products, the actual loss of the sales of the merged firm due to an increase in its price will be smaller than it would be absent the price reaction of the nonmerging firms. Ignoring this price reaction would not only affect the market definition since it would lead to an underestimation of the profitability of the 5 to 10 per cent price increase but also to an incorrect assessment of the competitive effects of the merger since the impact on the profitability of the merged firm will be underestimated.

O'Brien and Wickelgren (2003) argue that critical loss analysis fails to recognize that a firm's margin provides information about the magnitude of the sales that it is likely to lose from a price increase and ignores the importance of the degree of substitutability[98] among the products of the firm implementing the price increase. If margins are high, so that the diverted sales are highly profitable, the merged firm will have a relatively higher incentive to raise price absent offsetting entry, product repositioning, or efficiency gains.[99] The authors' most important result is that higher margins typically make it more likely that a price increase by merging firms will be profitable.

However, this argument is contentious since large margins can be observed not only as a result of conducts having an adverse impact on competition but also in industries with differentiated products in which the products of different firms are not close substitutes. The degree of profitability of a price increase will depend on the elasticity of the product involved. If the product is highly elastic, then any price increase will divert sales to substitute products and therefore significantly affect profits. Such a result will, of course, depend on the extent to which substitute products exist and can be offered to consumers. If the firms producing substitute products face capacity constraints such as significant costs or time constraints or where entry in to the market of new players with substitute products is difficult then the price increase by the incumbent firm is likely to be very profitable.

O'Brien and Wickelgren (2003) also argue that the closer substitutes there are for a firm's product, the lower the firm's margin must be, and thus the lower the required price,[100] to prevent customers from switching to those products.[101] However, as our preceding analysis mentioned indicates, the closeness of substitution between products depends not only on the degree of differentiation of these products, but also on factors such as capacity constraints and barriers to entry and expansion.

An important assumption that O'Brien and Wickelgren (2003) make is that the merger enhances the degree of coordination between the merging firms' products.[102] The authors also argue that when two or more substitutes come under common ownership, the degree to which competition is reduced is greater when margins are high than when margins are low.[103] Enhanced coordination is vital if these products are substitutes, since any substitution between the two firms' products, due to the relative increase of one of the product's price, will merely redistribute revenues between the two partners of the merged firm in the post-merger market. As mentioned earlier in this chapter, prior to the merger such substitution between the merging firms' products would translate in to a loss in the revenues of the firm that increased its price. After the merger, this loss in revenues will be mitigated by the increase in revenues due to consumers switching to the substitute product that post-merger belongs to the merged firm.

Thus, if the merging firms' products can be significantly coordinated, the merged firm, in increasing its prices, takes into account that in setting its prices following the merger any substitution prior to the merger between the two merging firms' products due to the increase of one of the product's price will merely redistribute revenues between the two partners of the merged firm in the post-merger market.[104]

The statement that the merger enhances the degree of coordination between the merging firms' products is quite restrictive since in order for the degree of coordination between the merging firms' products to be enhanced these products must not be highly differentiated. The higher the degree of differentiation between the two products the less likely it is that their coordination will be successful. In addition, if the merging firms' products are complementary,[105] the increase in the price of one of the merging firms' products will lead to the reduction in the quantity of both goods. Thus, there will be no redistribution of the revenues, generated by the relative increase of one of the merged firm's products, between the two partners of the merged firm after the merger.

O'Brien and Wickelgren (2003) also argue that large margins imply that actual loss is low,[106] which will affect not only the definition of the market but also the profitability of any price increase by the post-merger firms and thus one of the criteria indicating the competitive effects of the merger. As Katz and Shapiro (2003) claim, if a firm makes more money per unit sold (that is to say, it has large margins), then it will take fewer new sales to offset the profitability losses associated with a given price decrease. High margins indicate the supplier perceives demand for its product to be relatively insensitive to its own price reductions.[107] As they further argue, a high margin indicates that the product faces inelastic demand, a typical reason being that the product is differentiated from other products in the market. When products are differentiated, those customers who like a particular brand's attributes are likely to continue to purchase that brand even after its price increases by a small amount.

However, inelastic demand for the product may not be the only or the most important factor of high margins. Factors such as economies of scale and scope as well as other efficiencies in production may also explain the high margins without giving any information regarding the price sensitivity of the firm's product. In addition, the extent of low elasticity of the product (inelastic demand) will crucially depend on the degree of differentiation of the products. Furthermore, the degree to which buyers will remain loyal to a product due to its characteristics even after an increase in the price of the product depends not only on the particular features of the product but on the magnitude of the price increase as well. Thus, no accurate conclusions can be drawn regarding the relationship and the link between high margins and low elasticity, as well as between high margins and low actual loss.

Critical loss analysis may also be used in the assessment of the likelihood of a merger to lead to collective dominance.[108] A type of market structure in which price elasticity is low but margins are not necessarily high is a post-merger market that is prone to collective dominance. The substantive test that is applied to assess the likelihood of collective dominance is irrelevant to the actual results of the critical loss analysis, as this will later illustrate. In order for a collusive equilibrium to arise and be maintained, certain criteria need to be fulfilled including transparency, barriers to entry and exit, a small number of firms, ability to coordinate towards equilibrium, ability to enforce compliance as well as ability to monitor and deter any prospective maverick firms. In addition, consumers and competitors must be unable to counterbalance the collective dominant position by switching demand or by increasing their capacity in response to a reduction in supply by the post-merger dominant firm respectively. These criteria depend on features such as product homogeneity, low demand growth, low price sensitivity of demand, symmetric cost structures, and multi-market contacts.[109]

Thus, a collectively dominant market may exhibit low price elasticity but firms therein may not necessarily benefit from high margins due to all the factors mentioned above that make the sustainability of high margins quite difficult. As an example, there may be collectively dominant firms in a market with stagnant demand facing significant costs. These are just two of the many factors that may decrease the margins of firms and their ability to set higher prices. In addition, some firms may have higher costs than others although the market as a whole may exhibit low price elasticity. Such differences in costs induce some firms to lose more sales than their critical loss even though the group could collectively raise its profits, thus affecting the likelihood of firms adopting a common conduct and consequently affecting the sustainability of a likely tacitly collusive equilibrium.

In *Nestlé*,[110] the Commission argued[111] that although in a price-inelastic market the likelihood of collusion in prices is significant, the asymmetries in cost structure would inhibit parallel behaviour. Thus, in collectively dominant markets the extent of high margins may differ among firms in a low elasticity market due to, inter alia, differences in costs.[112]

A firm's incentive to cheat is significantly influenced by the contribution margin and thus the level of its individual critical loss. The extent of this incentive is measured by the level of sales an individual firm can afford to lose before the price increase becomes unprofitable. If a firm expects that cheating will increase sales by more than its critical loss, it will cheat on the price agreement.[113] The incentive of the firm to cheat makes the tacitly collusive equilibrium unlikely to be sustained and thus the merger is unlikely to lead to collective dominance.[114]

The Commission has discussed the incentive to collude based on critical loss considerations in a number of cases including *VNU/WPP/JV*,[115] *Alcoa/British Aluminium*[116] and *Pirelli/BICC*.[117]

Although O'Brien and Wickelgren (2003) argue that large margins indicate a low actual loss, a determining factor of the importance of low actual loss in the presence of high margins is the post-merger structure of the market. Irrespective of whether the actual loss will be low or high its importance for the firms will depend on the market share of the firms. In assessing the degree of dominance of the firms, the choice of substantive test is relevant. However, in estimating the market shares and the impact of high or low market shares on the profitability of a price increase as well as on the actual loss the substantive test is irrelevant. As was the case with merger simulation, the choice between the SLC and the dominance test affects neither the method nor the results of critical loss analysis, regarding not only the definition of the relevant market but also the competitive effects of mergers and in particular of mergers leading to non-coordinated effects in oligopolistic markets.

It should be emphasized that, in the case where the post-merger market is one with no substantially dominant firm, the importance of a decrease in the quantity demanded as a result of a price increase is likely to be higher than in the case of a dominant firm that has a significant share in the market. In the former case, each firm will have lower incentives to increase prices even in the presence of high margins because the actual loss may have substantial implications for the firm's profits. In the latter case, a single firm being the dominant player in the market will control a higher share of the market and will thus have an enhanced ability to increase prices, and to reduce the demanded quantity for its product, without significant implications for its total profits and viability.

In addition, in market structures characterized by decreased competition, the "cellophane fallacy" may mitigate the efficiency and accuracy of critical loss analysis. The large margins may be a result of the fact that the firm already has market power; consequently, no accurate conclusions can be drawn for the magnitude of the actual loss of the price increase.

Thus, the adverse implications of actual loss will be less severe for a dominant firm compared to the implications of actual loss for a non-dominant firm. So firms will not base their decision to increase prices strictly on whether the critical loss is greater or smaller than actual loss, but rather will take a decision based on the implications of the actual loss for the firms' profitability and viability.

As the analysis in this chapter has indicated, critical loss analysis is commonly used not only in delineating markets but also in assessing the adverse effects of mergers on competition. It provides a simple technique which can add more rigour to the assessment of market definition and market power. The methodology for critical loss analysis needs to make more complete use of pre-merger market facts and focus attention on demand-side issues such as substitutability, degree of differentiation of products and, in effect, the extent to which the products in the candidate relevant market compete directly with each other rather than with products outside the candidate market.

Critical loss analysis based on demand or cost assumptions at variance with actual market conditions should not be considered accurate either for the purpose of defining the market or for assessing mergers. This type of analysis remains an appropriate technique for these purposes, provided that the actual loss associated with hypothesized exercises of market power is accurately estimated. Critical loss analysis remedies a number of deficiencies in the current approach to market definition, which focuses excessively on product characteristics and absolute price differences, and ignores the profitability of hypothetical price increases.

The use of empirical methods is an indication of the great weight that is given to analyses that can quantify the likely price effects of a proposed transaction. However, it is unlikely that such analysis will replace the qualitative analysis of a thorough review of the documents and other evidence that shed light on important issues regarding the assessment of the merger, such as, inter alia, the nature of competition in the marketplace, the conditions for entry and expansion, and countervailing buyer power.

This chapter continues with an evaluation of how critical loss analysis has been applied in cases brought before the competition authorities and the courts.

3.1.2.2 Critical loss analysis: practical application

Before addressing the more complicated theoretical underpinnings of critical loss analysis, one should indicate how critical loss analysis has been applied in cases. The cases that will be briefly analysed include *Federal Trade Commission v Occidental Petroleum Corp.*,[118] *Federal Trade Commission, et al. v Tenet Healthcare Corporation, et al.*,[119] *Federal Trade Commission v Swedish Match North America Inc., et al.*,[120] *US v SunGard and Comdisco*,[121] *California v Sutter Health System*,[122] and *Royal Caribbean Cruises, Ltd/P&O Princess Cruises Plc* and *Carnival Corporation/P&O Princess Cruises Plc.*[123]

FEDERAL TRADE COMMISSION v OCCIDENTAL PETROLEUM CORP.

The concept of critical loss first appeared in the United States in *FTC v Occidental Petroleum Corp.*, a 1986 merger trial in which the FTC sought to block a merger between producers of polyvinylchloride resin (PVC) and alleged that the geographic market was confined to North American producers. The FTC failed to obtain a preliminary injunction.

Occidental was based in Los Angeles, California, and acquired Tenneco through its subsidiary, Occidental Chemical Corporation. Tenneco was based in Houston, Texas. The FTC decided that Occidental's acquisition of Tenneco would substantially lessen competition in the US market for mass and suspension PVC homopolymer, suspension PVC copolymer, and dispersion PVC. The FTC required Occidental to divest the Tenneco polyvinyl chloride (PVC) plant in Pasadena, California, and the suspension PVC and dispersion PVC plant in New Jersey.[124]

The analysis focused on the definition of the relevant geographic markets. According to the FTC, the geographic market was confined to North American producers while the parties claimed it was much wider and should include foreign producers as well. Critical loss analysis indicated that a sufficient number would purchase foreign-produced PVC resins if domestic-produced resin's price increased by 5 per cent and foreign producers had excess capacity and could supply the US market. The district court concluded that geographic market for both types of PVC resin was wider than the United States.

FEDERAL TRADE COMMISSION, ET AL. v TENET HEALTHCARE CORPORATION, ET AL.

In *FTC v Tenet Healthcare Corp.*, the FTC attempted to block a hospital merger of the only two hospitals in Poplar Bluff, a small Missouri city, on the ground that the geographic market was limited to Poplar Bluff, suggesting that the merger would have removed the main competitive constraints that the two hospitals faced. The hospitals in the market were differentiated by location and level of service.

The parties submitted a critical loss analysis to support their argument that the market was wider than Poplar Bluff. The critical loss analysis included estimation of the contribution margin for the merging hospitals. Defendants argued that because the merging hospitals had very large margins, the percentage of patients they would have to lose to other hospitals to make a price increase unprofitable was not very large. The contribution margin was estimated by directly considering the costs that would be saved by the hospital in the event of a decrease in quantity of 10 to 15 percent for a one-year period. The parties argued that a 5 per cent price increase would have been unprofitable if more than 7 per cent of the merged hospital's patients switched in response to the price increase; thus, the critical loss was 7 per cent. Given that about 55 per cent of the merged hospital's patients would have come from areas where a significant proportion of patients already used hospitals outside Poplar Bluff, the defendants argued that the merged hospital would have lost more than 7 per cent of their patients if they increased prices, and so the market was wider than Poplar Bluff.[125]

The Court of Appeals, based on critical loss analysis, overturned the district court and found for the defendants. It noted that: "[A] critical loss analysis would identify the threshold number of patients who, by seeking care at other hospitals, could defeat a price increase by making it unprofitable. The purchasing behaviour of these patients or 'marginal customers' would discipline or constrain any potential price increase by a merged entity."[126]

In reaching its decision, the court found important the "significance of the consumers who live outside Poplar Bluff, particularly those patients within the FTC's proposed geographic market who actually live or work closer to a hospital outside that geographic market than to either of the Poplar Bluff hospitals".[127]

The Circuit Court did not take into account either the diversion between the products of the two merging firms or the fact that other hospitals could have increased their price in response to an increase in the price by the merged hospital affecting thus the profitability of this price increase. O'Brien and Wickelgren (2003) have argued that, as is often the case in standard critical loss analysis, the large margins asserted by the defendants' expert were not consistent with testimony about the willingness of customers to switch. In this case, a telephone survey presented by the experts purported to show that many patients would switch to other hospitals if faced with a 5 percent price increase.[128]

FEDERAL TRADE COMMISSION v SWEDISH MATCH NORTH AMERICA INC., ET AL.

In this case, the FTC relied on critical loss analysis to stop a proposed acquisition by Swedish Match of the loose-leaf chewing tobacco business of National Tobacco Company.

Swedish Match and National Tobacco were the first and third largest sellers of loose-leaf chewing tobacco in the United States. The companies contested the FTC's claim that loose-leaf chewing tobacco and moist snuff constituted separate antitrust markets. The defendants' expert report argued that because margins were high, a significant price increase by a hypothetical monopolist or by the merging firms after the merger was very unlikely. The report did not consider the fact that the high margins it found indicated that the amount of sales lost from a given price increase is likely to be quite small. The critical loss for a 5 per cent price increase was compared to the actual loss implied by the estimate of the market elasticity of demand for loose-leaf chewing tobacco. The estimated actual loss exceeded the critical loss, and thus a 5 percent price increase by a hypothetical monopolist of loose-leaf chewing tobacco would be unprofitable. Thus, the relevant product market should be wider and include moist snuff in addition to loose-leaf chewing tobacco.

The FTC prevailed because it was able to establish that consumers would not substitute in sufficient numbers between loose-leaf chewing tobacco and moist snuff. The court agreed with the FTC that, although the products were functionally interchangeable, they did not constrain each other's prices and concluded that two firms would control approximately 90 per cent of the loose-leaf chewing tobacco market.[129] The court argued that the acquisition may substantially lessen competition by increasing the level of concentration in the relevant market, leading to increases in price for the relevant product, increasing barriers to entry and allowing Swedish Match unilaterally to exercise market power, through its control of the combined Swedish Match and National Tobacco portfolio of brands. The court granted the FTC's motion for a preliminary injunction against the merger.

The *Swedish Match* court explicitly addressed the possibility of using econometric analysis to estimate directly the elasticity of demand rather than inferring it from the observed gross margins.[130] Although the calculations of the margin in the critical loss analysis are correct, the estimated market elasticity is inconsistent with such high margins. Thus, econometric estimates of demand elasticities must be consistent with other evidence about substitution, such as that implied by margins.

US v SUNGARD AND COMDISCO

In 2001, in *US v SunGard and Comdisco*, a case concerning a market with pervasive price discrimination, the court concluded that SunGard's acquisition of the computer disaster recovery assets of Comdisco was not likely to harm competition. The central issue in the case was whether alternatives, especially internally provided hotsites, a particular type of recovery service, potentially providing even more rapid recovery, were in the relevant market.

The US Department of Justice ("DOJ") alleged a market consisting of shared "hotsite" recovery services. The defendants presented the court with a critical loss analysis purporting to show that the critical loss was only 5 per cent because margins were extremely high. That analysis indicated that very little substitution was enough to defeat a price increase, and it was impossible for the DOJ to show that even such little substitution would not occur.[131] Consequently, all customers could credibly threaten to use these alternative services, which, in turn, meant that the appropriate antitrust market to evaluate the SunGard/Comdisco transaction needed to include the full range of alternatives already being used.

The Court relied on critical loss analysis against the DOJ in concluding that SunGard's acquisition of the computer disaster recovery assets of Comdisco was not likely to harm competition.

CALIFORNIA v SUTTER HEALTH SYSTEM

Sutter Health is one of the largest healthcare systems in California. Its affiliate, Alta Bates Medical Center, is a large, tertiary care hospital in Berkeley, California. In 1998, Sutter Health would merge with Summit Medical Center, a large independent tertiary care hospital in Oakland, California, located a few miles from Alta Bates. The plaintiff produced, inter alia, a critical loss analysis to define the geographic boundaries of the market. The critical loss analysis calculated the number and percentage of patients that would need to divert from the hospitals within the boundaries of the proposed market definition in order to make the 5 to 10 per cent increase unprofitable. Given the profit margins identified by Sutter Health the hospitals would have to lose 15.5 per cent to 19.4 per cent of their patients before a 10 per cent price increase would be unprofitable.[132] However, such a decrease in the number of patients was unlikely to occur with a 10 per cent price increase.

The District Court ruled in favour of the defendants and rejected the critical loss analysis based on the fact that a 5 per cent increase should have been used and that under this price increase there would be enough patients to switch and thus make the price increase unprofitable. The Court did not take into account either the price reaction of firms within close range of the merging hospitals or the diversion of patients between the two merging hospitals in using critical loss analysis to assess the competitive effects of the merger.[133] As discussed already, an evaluation of the diversion ratios between the merging parties as well as of the reaction of the nonmerging undertakings in the post-merger market are useful in assessing the anticompetitive effects of a merger.

ROYAL CARIBBEAN CRUISES, LTD/P&O PRINCESS CRUISES PLC AND *CARNIVAL CORPORATION/P&O PRINCESS CRUISES PLC*

This case[134] concerned the proposed friendly creation of a "dual-listed company" combining Royal Caribbean Cruises, Ltd ("RCCL") and P&O Princess Cruises Plc ("Princess"), and the competing hostile tender offer by Carnival Corporation ("Carnival") for Princess. The main issue was whether the relevant product market included oceanic cruises, or was limited to oceanic cruises only, or included segments of oceanic cruises. The case was assessed by the FTC, the UK Competition Commission[135] and the European Commission. The FTC used critical loss analysis for the assessment of any anticompetitive effects arising from the merger, while the UK Competition Commission for the definition of the market.[136] The European Commission did not use critical loss analysis at all.[137]

In an attempt to assess the unilateral effects of the merger, the FTC conducted, inter alia, a critical loss analysis and concluded that the critical loss in terms of sales was lower for the merged entity than for the industry.[138] The FTC concluded that substantial increases in capacity reduced average fares, and implied that demand elasticities are large relative to standard critical loss measures. In view of a high elasticity of demand in the cruise industry relative to the critical loss, an *across-the-board* price increase would be unprofitable and unlikely under current market conditions. A hypothetical monopolist, however, could likely use yield management systems[139] to mitigate this effect and thus could likely increase *average* prices profitably.

Because most costs of cruising are fixed and a passenger generates incremental margins from onboard expenditures, standard critical loss estimates were small. Consistent with the low critical loss, the cruise lines made considerable efforts to maintain high "load factors".

In addition, the econometric analysis that was conducted for this merger included the consideration whether "list" or "early" prices could be used as a coordination device where no systematic relationship between "list" and "early" prices was found. There was substantial variability in the pricing movements across competitors, which was driven by the capacity of the ship that was booked rather than by changes in the competitors' prices. Finally, there appeared to be no evidence of capacity coordination.[140]

Carnival's takeover bid against P&O Princess was also assessed by the European Commission and the UK Competition Commission. The European Commission cleared the merger due to the high recent and projected growth rate in cruise markets that would constitute a significant competitive constraint on the incumbent cruise operators as high growth rates would provide an incentive for new operators to enter the market. In addition, it cleared the dual-listed company[141] combining the cruise activities of Carnival and P&O Princess since there had been no significant changes in the cruise markets in Europe after the clearance of the takeover bid from Carnival for P&O Princess.[142] The UK Competition Commission used critical loss analysis for the definition of the relevant market and assessed the effect of an anticipated price increase on the profits of the two parties.[143] It cleared the merger by concluding that the market for UK cruise customers was characterized by growth, variety and new entry, and that this could be expected to continue.

As this analysis of the case law has illustrated, critical loss analysis plays a crucial role in market definition and in the assessment of the mergers having an adverse impact on competition. In most of the cases we examined, it has been used as a tool for market definition. It can also provide insights to the degree of closeness of the merging parties' products, as well as to the elimination of rivalry between the products as an indication of unilateral effects of the merger. It can also be used in order to assess the likelihood of sustaining a tacitly collusive outcome, by examining, inter alia, the incentives of firms to divert from the collusive outcome. The application of critical loss analysis in market definition is more straightforward than its application in the assessment of the anticompetitive effects of a merger. In addition, critical loss analysis is, in my opinion, one of the most tractable methods when used for market definition, being simple to calculate and without any extensive data requirements. Finally, for the assessment of the effects of mergers, there are other methods that can be used which will provide more accurate results (for example, merger simulation).

However, it entails drawbacks that mitigate the efficiency and accuracy of its application. Some of these criticisms concern the percentage change in the base price.[144] The formulas for critical loss analysis indicate their dependence on the significance threshold for price increases and the price-cost margin[145] for the market. While a 5 per cent price increase would not be profitable for a hypothetical monopolist, a slightly larger price increase would be. This can occur if some existing consumers are more responsive to price changes than others. Whether a 5 per cent relative price increase is profitable will depend on whether the loss of sales resulting from the price increase can be offset by the increase in profits. As the analysis herein has indicated, it is not essential that all customers switch products as a result of the relative price increase, rather that an adequate number of customers do switch so as to make this price increase unprofitable.

In spite of these drawbacks, critical loss analysis can prove invaluable not only in the process of market definition but also in assessing the competitive effects of mergers leading to non-coordinated effects in oligopolistic markets.[146]

Merger simulation and critical loss analysis have now been analysed. The following section evaluates the effect of the SLC and the dominance tests on the applicability, efficiency, and results of these two methods in assessing mergers leading to non-coordinated effects in oligopolistic markets.

3.1.3 Merger simulation and critical loss analysis under the SLC and dominance test

Chapter 3 has thus far analysed the mechanics of the methodology of merger simulation and critical loss analysis as well as the theoretical background of these two methods of empirical analysis and has reviewed some of the cases in which these methods have been used. The aim of the chapter is not only to evaluate whether the legal substantive test has any implications for the methodology used to conduct merger simulation and critical loss analysis, but also to assess whether these two methods' efficiency in providing important input for the assessment of mergers in general, but more specifically for mergers leading to non-coordinated effects in oligopolistic markets, varies depending on the substantive test applied. If the outcomes of these quantitative methods vary depending on the legal substantive test, then the fact that a merger may not be captured by the dominance test is not due to the "gap" in the dominance test's applicability but is due to the different evaluation of the merger resulting from the outcome of merger simulation and critical loss analysis in the cases analysed in this chapter. The SLC test was applied in seven[147] of these cases and the dominance test in three.[148]

The difference in the assessment of a merger that arises from the application of the two substantive tests induces a different outcome regarding the evaluation of the adverse effects of a merger on competition. In case of a merger between two firms producing differentiated products, a price increase may be rational for the merged entity regardless of the reactions of the other firms in the market.[149] Even if rival firms do not increase their pre-merger prices in the post-merger market, the merging firms will still have the incentive to increase their prices since any substitution between the two merging firms' products that would occur prior to the merger will be captured by the merged firm after the merger. As mentioned earlier, a merger mainly internalizes the competition between formerly separately owned firms. Any substitution between the two firms' products prior to the merger will merely redistribute revenues between the two partners of the merged firm after the merger.

If the SLC/SIEC test is applied to assess a merger leading to non-coordinated effects, the prediction of a post-merger price increase may not necessarily depend on the combined entity being the largest player in the market, as would be required if the dominance test were applied. Thus, the closeness of substitution between the merging firms' products is more important than whether the merged firm has the highest market share. Merger simulation models are essential in predicting the post-merger price increase of the products of the merging firms if these products are substitutes, since any substitution between the two firms' products will merely redistribute revenues between the two partners of the merged firm after the merger.

Market definition is given different importance under the two tests. As already mentioned, under the dominance test, market definition plays a crucial role as a prima facie indication of adverse effects on competition,[150] while the focus of the SLC/SIEC test lies on the impact of the merger on existing competitive constraints.[151] When reliable data on consumer-switching behaviour are available, the market definition analysis will be more accurate and will avoid errors due to preconceived notions of substitutability. Critical loss analysis can exploit such econometric evidence and may assist in analysing the impact of the marginal consumers' choices on the profitability of a price increase.[152]

Even though the Commission had been applying a different legal substantive test than the SLC/SIEC test, its assessment of mergers has sometimes taken into account the closeness of the merging firms' products or the elimination of the rivalry between the merging firms' products, factors that are taken into account when the merger is assessed under the SLC/SIEC test. Thus, the Commission has taken these as factors indicating that a transaction may lead to the creation or strengthening of a dominant position. In addition, the Commission has accepted the fact that the merging parties do not offer close substitutes as a defence in prima facie cases of dominance.[153] As was mentioned in Chapter 2, the Commission has relied on unilateral effects analysis to substantiate a dominance argument only in cases in which market shares were at a level that would strongly indicate single dominance in any event.

As the preceding analysis indicates, some of the most important issues in the assessment of mergers are whether prices will increase post-merger and how the market should be defined. Merger simulation models and critical loss analysis play an essential role in dealing with these two issues. The emphasis that will be put on the outcomes of merger simulation and of critical loss analysis may vary depending on whether the legal substantive test that will be applied for the assessment of the transaction is the traditional dominance test or the SLC/SIEC test. The methodology and application of these two empirical methods, however, will not vary depending on the legal substantive test. The methodology and implementation of these two techniques for the assessment of a merger leading to non-coordinated effects in oligopolistic markets will be the same under both substantive tests.

3.1.3.1 Merger simulation under the SLC and dominance test

As the analysis of merger simulation models has illustrated, the merger simulation methodology is the same irrespective of the type of competition that characterizes the market. In the Cournot type of competition, in the absence of capacity constraints, a reduction in the output of the merged firm producing homogeneous products typically leads competing firms to expand their own output. In such industries, merger simulation models entail several stages, including the specification of the functional forms for demand and the calibration of parameters of these functions. In industries that are characterized by the Bertrand type of competition, merger simulation models entail the same stages as in Cournot models. Finally, as regards markets in which auctions represent the main vehicle of transactions, merger simulation models are similar to the ones used in a Cournot or Bertrand market. In auction markets, instead of specifying functional forms for demand and cost, valuation or cost distributions for competing bidders are specified.

The choice of the demand model is crucial in the accuracy of the results of the merger simulation model. The determinant of the demand model that is used in order to quantify the impact of the merger on prices in the post-merger market depends on the availability and accuracy of data. The choice of the demand model is irrelevant for the actual substantive test used to evaluate the implications of the merger simulation model's results for the effects of the merger in the post-merger market.

Although merger simulation allows the analysis of the competition effects of the transaction to be carried out without the requirement of market definition, merger simulation models omit non-price issues such as barriers to entry and expansion, buyer power and the potential for post-merger coordination. In addition, in the absence of counterbalancing efficiencies, merger simulation is likely to show a price increase and thus such models increase the likelihood of intervention below the level of single firm dominance.[154] Hence, a competitive effects analysis still needs to be carried out. If the results of a merger simulation are consistent with the rest of the analysis, then this provides support for the accuracy of the competitive effects analysis.

The choice of the legal substantive test does not affect either the stages of the merger simulation process or the choice of the demand model. In all the three types of market analysed herein, the stages of the merger simulation models are the same or exhibit minor variations. The demand specification depends on external factors such as the availability and accuracy of data. In effect, what merger simulation models do is calculate the effect on the price in the post-merger market. They do not have any individual impact on the price. These models constitute the means to quantify the impact of certain transactions on prices and to assess the competitive effects of a merger.

In addition, the choice of legal substantive test does not affect the stages of the merger simulation process. The choice of the substantive test plays a role after the last stage of the merger simulation process and does not affect the application and mechanics of the simulation process. Although, the merger simulation model's outcome is influenced by the theoretical input of the model, the evaluation of this outcome by the two substantive tests is irrelevant to the actual merger simulation process. This evaluation and the implications it may have for the legitimacy of the transaction depends on the choice of the substantive test. Thus, the methodology and application of merger simulation analysis are irrelevant to the choice of the substantive test employed for the assessment of mergers leading to non-coordinated effects.

As regards the transactions analysed in this chapter in which merger simulation models were used, *Centrica/Dynegy*,[155] was assessed by applying the SLC test whereas *Oracle/PeopleSoft*, *Volvo/Scania* and *GE/Instrumentarium* were assessed by applying the dominance test. In most of these cases, the quantitative analysis of the likely unilateral effects of the merger included an econometric study for the estimation of demand elasticities. This type of econometric analysis does not in itself provide an estimate of the likely impact of the merger on price. Such estimates can only be obtained by imposing assumptions regarding the nature of competition between firms in the relevant market as well as by taking into account likely responses of competitors and consumers as a result of the merged entity's attempt to increase prices in the post-merger market.[156] Thus, the analysis of these cases indicates that the implementation of merger simulation models did not depend on the legal substantive test but on issues such as demand elasticity and the nature of competition.

Irrespective of whether the SLC or the dominance test is applied in assessing a merger in general but more specifically to assess a merger leading to non-coordinated effects in oligopolistic markets, the way the actual merger simulation process is conducted and the outcome of the merger simulation remain the same. The use of the substantive test and the importance of the choice between SLC/SIEC and dominance tests is indicated when the competition authorities have to evaluate the results of the merger simulation model in order to assess whether the transaction will lead to a substantial lessening of competition, or to the creation or strengthening of a dominant position. The legal substantive test is the spectrum through which the quantified impact of the transaction is assessed.

Thus, the gap of the dominance test to capture mergers leading to non-coordinated effects in oligopolistic markets is not due to an alleged different outcome of merger simulation depending on the legal substantive test but due to the limits in the applicability of the dominance test.

3.1.3.2 Critical loss analysis under the SLC and dominance test

Turning to the critical loss analysis: this type of analysis constitutes an important empirical method that enhances the accuracy of market definition. Critical loss focuses not only on product characteristics and absolute price differences, but on the profitability of hypothetical price increases as well. As this chapter has illustrated, critical loss analysis identifies for any given price increase the quantity in sales that can be lost before the price increase becomes unprofitable. If the actual loss is less than the critical loss, the price increase would be profitable. If the actual loss is greater than the critical loss, the firm would not find it profitable to increase its product's price.

In evaluating the impact of the choice of the substantive test on the application of critical loss analysis on market definition, it should be noted that the variables that are included in the formula that calculates critical loss that is to say the hypothesized percentage price increase and the price-cost margin are unaffected by the choice of the legal substantive test. They depend on quantities that correspond to the pre-merger condition of the market and are unaffected by the substantive criterion according to which the merger will be assessed.

As mentioned earlier in this chapter, in conducting critical loss analysis the existence of a dominant firm (or a firm with significant market power) must be taken into account in order to reach representative and accurate results. Critical loss analysis takes into consideration the existence of such a firm in the pre-merger market rather than in the post-merger market since its existence in the pre-merger market will affect the assessment of the result of critical loss analysis. The results of critical loss analysis must be given the relative weight taking into consideration that the same numerical critical and actual loss may have different implications for a firm depending on the degree of market power it has as regards the desirability and viability of an increase in the price of the product.

In order to evaluate the impact of the choice of the substantive test on the application of critical loss analysis on the assessment of the effects of a merger, let us use the example of the application of critical loss analysis in assessing the sustainability of collective dominance. The incentive of firms to collectively raise prices will be affected by the level of sales an individual firm can afford to lose before the price increase becomes unprofitable. Critical loss analysis will indicate when there are discrepancies in the willingness of all members of a group of competitors to adopt the same conduct in the market and thus when cheating from the common target is likely to occur. Critical loss analysis may provide information regarding the factors that contribute to the sustainability of collective dominance in the market. Although such an analysis will give an assessment of some of the factors that contribute to collective dominance, the way competition authorities will use this assessment will depend on the substantive test used to assess the particular transaction. The likelihood, for example, that firms may renege on their common target will be the same irrespective of the substantive test. The implications of this factor and the extent to which this factor will affect the assessment of the transaction will, in turn, depend on the particular substantive test used by the competition authorities.

As our analysis illustrated, the application of critical loss analysis is irrelevant to the substantive test of merger assessment. Critical loss analysis is conducted taking the pre-merger market structure as the benchmark. The substantive test does not assess the degree of market power/dominance of the firm prior to the merger. The substantive test assesses the impact on competition in the post-merger market. Thus, the choice between the SLC/SIEC and the dominance test will not affect either the methodology/mechanics behind critical loss analysis or its efficiency in providing important input for the assessment of non-collusive oligopolies. The critical loss analysis is conducted in the same way irrespective of the substantive test, and the latter serves for the assessment of the impact of competition in the post-merger market taking the outcome of critical loss analysis into account.

Thus, the methodology and application of critical loss analysis remains unaffected by the choice of substantive test used to assess mergers. The inability of the dominance test to apply to mergers leading to non-coordinated effects in oligopolistic markets is not due to a different outcome of the critical loss analysis regarding the definition of the market or the competitive effects of the merger, but due to the limited scope in the application of the dominance test.

3.2 Conclusion

The cases briefly analysed in this chapter lead to the same conclusion regarding the impact of the choice of the substantive test as the analysis of the theory of critical loss analysis. In the cases referred to herein, the calculations of the margin in the critical loss analysis aimed at estimating the market elasticity. The courts have accepted critical loss analysis as an indication of the boundaries of the market in both product and geographical terms. The choice of the substantive test has no impact on the results of the critical loss analysis, an argument that is also reinforced by the case precedence. The courts have not emphasized the importance of the substantive test in their application of critical loss analysis. The results of the analysis for the effects of a merger leading to non-coordinated effects may be evaluated according to the substantive test, while the actual methodology and conduct of the analysis are independent of the choice of the test.

There are doubts, however, as to whether the use of econometric evidence before the Commission will reach the level of sophistication seen in US cases. The reasons that Volcker (2004) mentions for this lack in the impetus of sophistication in empirical analyses before the Commission include: the statutory deadlines governing the EU merger review, the Commission's lack of resources as well as its reliance on complainants, usually competitors.[157] The courts, in dealing with cases that involve econometric analyses, are in most cases reluctant to address the debate between the parties' economic experts, as the *Tetra Laval*[158] case indicated.[159]

As this chapter has suggested, choice of the substantive test is irrelevant to the methodology and application of both merger simulation and of critical loss analysis. This may be the case for other types of quantitative technique referred to in this chapter. All these techniques mainly focus and use quantitative data based on the pre-merger and post-merger situation of the market. The choice of the substantive test does not have any impact on the actual method and execution of these analyses for the assessment of mergers in general and more specifically of mergers leading to non-coordinated effects. The alleged inability of the dominance test to capture mergers leading to non-coordinated effects is irrelevant to the methodology and application of merger simulation models and critical loss analysis. The issue of whether a merger creates or strengthens a dominant position or leads to a substantial lessening of competition is important in the evaluation of the results of these methods; however, it does not affect the actual application of these types of analysis.

Any inability of the dominance test to capture mergers leading to non-coordinated effects in oligopolistic markets will be due to its limited scope of application, rather than to the quantitative method that lawyers, economists and competition practitioners will employ to assess the effects of such mergers.[160] The cases presented in the next chapter will illustrate the gap in the application of the dominance test.

This book has thus far addressed reforms in the legislation that aimed at rectifying the gap in the application of the dominance test. Subsequently, it examined whether this gap was due to the different application of quantitative method used in merger assessment. After illustrating that the alleged gap in the application of dominance is due to its applicability this book turns now to evidence of gap cases in the current case law. The next chapter will illustrate examples of this inability of the dominance test to capture non-collusive oligopolies.

Notes

1 Including non-coordinated effects in oligopolistic markets.
2 Cases where merger simulation has been used will be analysed in detail in this chapter.
3 Cases where critical loss analysis has been used will be analysed in detail in this chapter.
4 Case B8 – 130/01 *BP/E.ON (Aral)* Bundeskartellamt.
5 Case M190 *Nestlé/Perrier* [1992] OJ L356/1 (*Nestlé*).
6 Case M938 *Guinness/GrandMet* [1998] OJ L288/24.
7 Cm 5005, *Nutreco Holding NV and Hydro Seafood GSP Ltd*, 2000.
8 *Federal Trade Commission v Staples Inc.*, No. 97–701, 1997, US Dist.
9 Case M1075 *Nordic Capital/Mölnlycke/Kolmi* [1998] OJ C39/19.
10 Cm 5186, *Reed Elsevier Plc and Harcourt General, Inc.*, 2001.
11 Case M623 *Kimberly Clark/Scott* [1996] OJ L183/1.
12 Case M3216 *Oracle/PeopleSoft* [2005] OJ L218/6.
13 Case M3083 *GE/Instrumentarium* [2004] OJ L109/1.
14 Cm 4556, *CHC Helicopter Corporation and Helicopter Services Group ASA*, 2000.
15 Case M1016 *Price Waterhouse/Coopers & Lybrand* [1999] OJ L50/27.
16 Some parts of this chapter have been published in: Kokkoris, I. (2005c), "Merger Simulation: A Crystal Ball for Assessing Mergers", *World Competition*, 28(3), 327–48, Kokkoris, I. (2005b), "Critical Loss Analysis: Critically Ill?" *ECLR*, 26(9), 518–25.
17 Walker, M. (2004), "The Use of Empirical Analysis in Antitrust: Lessons from Merger Simulation Models", Network of Industrial Economists Meeting, 14 December 2004, Nottingham University Business School.
18 Werden, G., Froeb, L. and Scheffman, D. (2004), "A Daubert Discipline for Merger Simulation", www.ftc.gov/be/daubertdiscipline.pdf, 2.
19 However, it can be argued that the issue of market definition in cases involving cartels is not an issue of major importance and is only necessary to indicate that trade between member states has been affected. See further: para. 230, Case T-62/98 *Volkswagen AG v Commission* [2000] ECR II-2707.
20 For a detailed analysis of these methods as well as the drawbacks they entail, see: Lexecon, "Quantitative Techniques in Competition Analysis", www.lexecon.co.uk/assets/quantitative_techniques.pdf, 01/11/2003.
21 See further: EEA Standing Committee of the EFTA States (2002), "EEA EFTA Comments on the Commission's Green Paper on the review of Council Regulation (EEC) No. 4064/89 (COM(2001) 745/6 Final)", secretariat.efta.int/Web?EuropeanEconomicArea/OngoingWork/100w149.doc, 6.
22 The analysis of these cases will be limited to the application and outcomes of merger simulation and critical loss analysis. A detailed analysis of these cases is beyond the scope of this chapter.
23 See Chapter 4.
24 Case M1672 *Volvo/Scania* [2001] OJ L143/74.
25 Case M2978 *Lagardère/Natexis/VUP* [2004] OJ L125/54.
26 Council Regulation (EC) No. 139/2004 of 20 January 2004 on the control of concentrations between undertakings (the EC Merger Regulation), ("Recast ECMR"), OJ L24, 29.01.2004, 1–22. The SIEC is outlined in Article 2(3) of the ECMR which states that "a concentration which would significantly impede effective competition, in the common market or in a substantial part of it, in

particular as a result of the creation or strengthening of a dominant position, shall be declared incompatible with the common market".

27 Shapiro, C. (1995), "Mergers with Differentiated Products", before the American Bar Association International Bar Association "The Merger Review Process in the U.S. and Abroad", Willard Inter-Continental Hotel Washington, DC, 9 November, www.usdoj.gov/atr/public/speeches/shapiro.spc, 4.

28 DG Competition's Article 82 Discussion Paper defines market power as the power "to influence market prices, output, innovation, the variety or quality of goods and services, or other parameters of competition on the market for a significant period of time", DG Competition discussion paper on the application of Article 82 of the Treaty to exclusionary abuses, December 2005, http://ec.europa.eu/comm/competition/antitrust/art82/discpaper2005.pdf.

29 Merger simulation analysis is most efficiently applied in consumer products, since in order to determine demand parameters for large simulation models, econometric estimation using supermarket scanner data is proved to be the most reliable and accurate.

30 Werden, G. and Froeb, L. (2006) "Unilateral Competitive Effects of Horizontal Mergers", in Buccirossi, P. (ed.), *Handbook of Antitrust Economics*, MIT Press, Cambridge, MA, 34.

31 Jayaratne and Shapiro (2000) provide a straightforward way of predicting the net effect of a merger as well as of a curative divestiture. Jayaratne, J. and Shapiro, C. (2000), "Simulating Partial Asset Divestitures to Fix Mergers", *International Journal of the Economics of Business*, 7, 179–200.

32 Merger simulation analysis is most efficiently applied in consumer products, since in order to determine demand parameters for large simulation models, econometric estimation using supermarket scanner data is proved to be the most reliable and accurate.

33 Such an impact is likely to arise from a merger leading to non-coordinated effects in oligopolistic markets.

34 Crooke, P., Froeb, L., Tschantz, S. and Werden, G. (1997), "Draft: Comments Solicited, Properties of Computed Post-merger Equilibria", http://www2.owen.vanderbilt.edu/fmrc/pdf/wp9712.pdf, 2.

35 Detailed economic/econometric analysis of each stage of the merger simulation is beyond the scope of this chapter.

36 Lexecon, "Quantitative Techniques in Competition Analysis", www.lexecon.co.uk/assets/quantitative_ techniques.pdf, 01/11/2003, 25.

37 Rubinfeld, D., Roy, J. and Epstein, R. (2001), "Merger Simulation: A Simplified Approach with New Applications", Paper CPC01–026, Institute of Business and Economic Research, Competition Policy Center, University of California, Berkeley, http://repositories.cdlib.org/cgi/viewcontent.cgi?article=1000&context=iber/cpc, 5.

38 The term "own-price elasticity" refers to the percentage change in the quantity for a given percentage change in its own price. "Cross-price elasticity" refers to the percentage change in the quantity of a product for a given percentage change in another product's price.

39 Coscelli, A. and Van Reenen, J. (2004), "Empirical Analysis of Unilateral Effects in Merger Control", Presentation to the IBC Conference on "The Use of Economics in Competition Law", 11 March.

40 Most simulation analyses assume that incremental costs do not vary with output.

41 Economies of scale refer to the situation where long-run average costs of production decrease as output rises. See further: Begg, D., Fischer, S. and Dornbusch, R. (1997), *Economics*, 5th edn, McGraw-Hill, Maidenhead, 109. Economies of scope refer to the situation where the joint output of a single

firm is greater than the output that could be achieved by two different firms each producing a single product (with equivalent production inputs allocated between the two firms). See further: Pindyck, R. and Rubinfeld, D. (1998), *Microeconomics*, 4th edn, Prentice Hall International, Upper Saddle River, NJ, 227. Economies of scope are conceptually similar to economies of scale. Economies of scale apply to efficiencies associated with increasing or decreasing the scale of production and refer to changes in the output of a single product type. Economies of scope refer to efficiencies associated with increasing or decreasing the scope of marketing and distribution and refer to changes in the number of different types of product. In addition, economies of scale refer primarily to supply-side changes (such as level of production) whereas economies of scope refer to demand-side changes (such as marketing and distribution).

42 Ivaldi, M., Jullien, B., Rey, P., Seabright, P. and Tirole J. (2003), "The Economics of Unilateral Effects", IDEI, Toulouse, Interim Report for DG Competition, European Commission, http://europa.eu.int/comm/competition/mergers/review/the_economics_of_unilateral_effects_en.pdf#search="Economics%20of%20Unilateral%20Effects", 83.

43 This chapter will focus on price as the only aspect of competition taken into account in merger simulations models. There is limited academic literature on the accuracy of merger simulation models when price is not the only aspect of competition. Gandhi, Froeb, Tschantz and Werden (2004) analysed mergers in both their price and location aspects. They argue that all competitors raise price following a merger, but competitors also change locations, which, in turn, affects pricing. The merging firms move away from each other, to avoid interfering in each others' sales. The nonmerging firms change their locations in response, opting for the space the merging firms vacate. This repositioning increases variety in a way that benefits consumers and thereby offsets the loss in consumer welfare arising from price increases. Limitations in the Gandhi *et al.* approach include the assumption of costless change in the location of the firms as well as the issues of timeliness and costs entailed in altering product characteristics. Froeb, Tenn and Tschantz (2004) analyze mergers with competition in both price and "advertising". They show that erroneously modelling competition as being just in price can yield misleading predictions of a merger's price effects, depending on how optimal advertising expenditures vary with price. See further: Gandhi, A., Froeb, L., Tschantz, S. and Werden, G. (2004), "Post-Merger Product Repositioning", University of Chicago Working Paper, Froeb, L., Tenn, S. and Tschantz, S. (2004), "Mergers When Firms Compete by Choosing both Price and Promotion", FTC Working Paper.

44 In 1838 Antoine Augustin Cournot published the first systematic analysis of oligopoly, arguing that firms compete by setting quantities. In 1883 Joseph Louis Francois Bertrand, in reviewing Cournot's book, argued that competitors compete by setting their prices.

45 Provided there are no capacity constraints.

46 However, some mergers in markets characterized by the Cournot model of competition will lead to a reduction in quantities and an increase in prices. If the products of the merged entity and of the other incumbents in the market are complements, a reduction in the output of the merged firm will lead to a reduction in the rival firms' output and a consequent increase in all prices. In addition, if the rival firms are unable or unwilling to expand output sufficiently to offset the output reduction from the merging parties, prices of all the products will increase. Output expansion is unlikely where competitors

face binding capacity constraints, or where existing excess capacity is significantly more costly to operate than capacity currently in use as well as where there is limited spare capacity in the presence of barriers to expansion.

47 This will be the case unless the merger leads to a reduction in the marginal costs of the merging firms (for example, due to likely efficiencies) translating into lower prices, or unless the merger induces *de novo* entry or product repositioning affecting the preferences of consumers. See further: Werden, G. and Froeb, L. (2006), "Unilateral Competitive Effects of Horizontal Mergers", in Buccirossi, P. (ed.), *Handbook of Antitrust Economics*, MIT Press, Cambridge, MA, 13.

48 This impact resembles the non-coordinated or multilateral effects of a merger analysed earlier.

49 The Cournot model appears not to have been used in any court for the purpose of simulating a merger, but two courts in nonmerger antitrust cases have evaluated the fit of Cournot models employed in analogous tasks. The leading example is *Concord Boat* (*Concord Boat v Brunswick Corp.* (2000), 207 F.3d 1039 (8th Cir.)) and *Heary Bros* (*Heary Bros. Lightning Protection Co., Inc. v Lightning Protection Institute* (2003), 287 F. Supp. 2d 1038 (D. Ariz.)). See further: Werden, G. and Froeb, L. (2006), "Unilateral Competitive Effects of Horizontal Mergers", in Buccirossi, P. (ed.), *Handbook of Antitrust Economics*, MIT Press, Cambridge, MA, 44. It should be noted at this point that, the testimony of the liability expert was excluded because it ignored relevant data and issues. Not all relevant circumstances were incorporated into the expert's method of analysis related to antitrust liability. Dr Hall's opinion that Brunswick's discount programs imposed a tax on boat builders who chose to purchase engines from other manufacturers is not supported by the evidence that some boat builders chose to purchase 100 per cent of their engines from Brunswick when they only needed to purchase 80 per cent to qualify for the maximum discount. If Brunswick's market share had enabled it to charge supracompetitive high prices for its engines, presumably none of the boat builders would have chosen to purchase more than the minimum percentage required to receive the discount. See further: www.ca8.uscourts.gov/opndir/00/03/983732P. pdf, 26. In *Daubert v Merrell Dow Pharmaceuticals, Inc.*, 509 US 579, 592–93, 595 (1993), the Supreme Court required trial judges to make a "preliminary assessment" of whether expert testimony is "scientifically valid," focusing "solely on principles and methodology". The Court also held that expert testimony is admissible only if it is "sufficiently tied to the facts of the case that it will aid the jury in resolving a factual dispute," that is to say, only if there is a good "fit" between the testimony and the pertinent inquiry. As described in *Daubert*, in considering an expert's testimony, judges must ensure that the testimony is based on a scientifically valid methodology and that the analysis is properly applied to the facts of the case.

50 Calibration of the parameters needed in a merger simulation in a market characterized by Bertrand type of competition does not require widespread estimation of the values of these parameters. An alternative for the value of short-run marginal costs is the value of variable costs. Variable costs in turn can be estimated by accounting data. The outcome of the simulation model, the predicted price effects of the merger, is the difference between the simulated post-merger prices and market shares, and the prices and market shares in the market prior to the merger.

51 Epstein, R. and Rubinfeld, D. (2004), "Technical Report Effects of Mergers Involving Differentiated Products", COMP/B1/2003/07, http://europa.eu.int/comm/competition/mergers/others/effects_mergers_involving_differentiated_products.pdf, 19.

52 And when a broad relevant market is alleged, some judges take this to be a concession that all products in the market are very close substitutes for each other. Werden, G. and Froeb, L. (2002), "Calibrated Economic Models Add Focus, Accuracy, and Persuasiveness to Merger Analysis", www2.owen.vanderbilt.edu/luke.froeb/ papers/sca10.pdf, 13.

53 Procurement auctions also can be modelled as competitions among differentiated products. Buyers with heterogeneous tastes or needs perceive the products of competing bidders to differ in important respects.

54 Although there are many auction models, the English auction model is, in my opinion, the one most frequently encountered in merger cases under the ECMR as well as the most tractable.

55 Werden, G. and Froeb, L. (2006), "Unilateral Competitive Effects of Horizontal Mergers", in Buccirossi, P. (ed.), *Handbook of Antitrust Economics*, MIT Press, Cambridge, MA, 23. According to the authors, the effect of synergies also differs. In a Bertrand market, reduced marginal costs for the merging products are passed through to some extent in the form of lower prices of these products. In an auction model, a marginal cost reduction has no effect on prices when the merged firm wins the auction, but rather affects price when the merged firm has the second highest valuation and loses the auction, since the expected revenue from the auction is the second highest bid.

56 As mentioned in this section, in a private values English auction, each bidder bids up to his valuation of the item. The merger of two bidders in such a market would affect the auctions, in which the merging firms have the first and second highest valuations. If they do not have the first and second highest, then the winner of the bid does not change (it will be an undertaking other than two merging bidders). Since each bidder faces its own set of prices in an auction model, the merged entity's bid will be the maximum that he is willing to bid and will not "switch" and refrain from bidding (although he may bid at a lower price). In a Bertrand market, since some consumers switch in the post-merger market there is some loss in consumer welfare.

57 Knowledge of the own-price elasticity of any one product and the overall market price elasticity is sufficient to obtain estimates of all relevant demand parameters of the PCAIDS model from the market share data.

58 Epstein, R. and Rubinfeld, D. (2004), "Technical Report Effects of Mergers Involving Differentiated Products", COMP/B1/2003/07, http://europa.eu.int/comm/competition/mergers/others/effects_mergers_ involving_differentiated_products.pdf, 11.

59 Constance K. Robinson analyses some recent mergers in the USA and how quantitative methods have been used in those cases. She analyses the *Bread* (*United States v Interstate Bakeries Corp. and Continental Baking Co.*, N.D. Ill., filed July 20, 1995, 60 Fed. Reg. 40, 195, 7 August 1995). For a brief description of these merger cases see further: Robinson, C. K. (1996), "Quantifying Unilateral Effects in Investigations and Cases", US DOJ Before the George Mason Law Review Symposium Antitrust in the Information Revolution: New Economic Approaches for Analyzing Antitrust Issues, George Mason University School of Law, Arlington, Virginia, 11 October. We should note that the cases analysed herein do not necessarily relate to non-coordinated effects in oligopolistic markets. As analysed in the previous sections of this chapter, the application of merger simulation and critical loss analysis does not depend on the type of anticompetitive effects that the merger induces. Thus, we can use a merger case inducing unilateral effects, in order to evaluate how these two quantitative methods were applied, and extrapolate conclusions that will apply to the analysis of mergers inducing coordinated effects or non-coordinated effects in oligopolistic markets.

60 Without access to the confidential documents of the parties and/or DG Competition it is impossible to present the mechanics of merger simulation in these cases. The aim of this section is not to show the actual technical application but to make an assessment of the methodology and implications of the application of merger simulation.
61 Cm 5885, *Centrica Plc/Dynegy Storage Ltd and Dynegy Onshore Processing*, August 2003.
62 Case M3216 *Oracle/PeopleSoft* [2005] OJ L218/6.
63 Case M1672 *Volvo/Scania* [2001] OJ L143/74.
64 Case M3083 *GE/Instrumentarium* [2004] OJ L109/1.
65 A major issue for the inquiry was whether, as a result of the merger, Centrica would be likely to withhold sources of flexible gas in order to force up wholesale gas prices.
66 Commissioned by Centrica. See further: para. 5.71 of the CC report.
67 The UK Competition Commission conducted its own projection of the profitability to Centrica of withholding gas supply and outlined the differences between its projection and that done by Lexecon. See further: para. 5.75 of the CC Report. The UK Competition Commission's assessment of Lexecon's analysis is included in para. 5.71–5.81, and the Lexecon report itself is reproduced in Appendix 5.5 of the CC Report.
68 The residual supply curve indicates the market supply that is not met by consumers in other sectors at any given wage.
69 The residual demand curve shows how much demand is "left over" for the incumbent in the post-merger market.
70 For a detailed analysis of these methods as well as the drawbacks they entail, see: Lexecon, "Quantitative Techniques in Competition Analysis", www.lexecon.co.uk/assets/quantitative_techniques.pdf, 01/11/2003, 26.
71 For a detailed analysis of these methods as well as the drawbacks they entail, see: Lexecon, "Quantitative Techniques in Competition Analysis", www.lexecon.co.uk/assets/quantitative_techniques.pdf, 01/11/2003, 26.
72 For a detailed analysis of the *Oracle/PeopleSoft* case, see Chapter 4.
73 The products were very heterogeneous to the extent that they differed between products sold between the same vendor to different customers.
74 Case M1672 *Volvo/Scania* [2001] OJ L143/74, at para. 72.
75 Wu, L., Williams, M. and Hofer, P. (2004), "The Increasing Use of Empirical Methods in European Merger Enforcement: Lessons from the Past and a Look Ahead", www.nera.com, 10. For details regarding the methodology and conclusions of the econometric study, see: Ivaldi, M. and Verboven, F. (2001), "Quantifying the Effects from Horizontal Mergers in European Competition Policy", www.cepr.org/pubs/dps/DP2697. asp. The demand side of the model is based on the multinomial nested logit model, which generates the following substitution pattern. When the price of one product increases by 1 per cent, it increases the demand for the other products within the same segment by an equal percentage, whereas it increases the demand for products in a different segment by a lower percentage.
76 For a detailed analysis of these methods as well as the drawbacks they entail, see: Lexecon, "Quantitative Techniques in Competition Analysis", www.lexecon.co.uk/assets/quantitative_techniques.pdf, 01/11/2003, 27. The Commission argued that: "[U]sing this type of study is a relatively new development in European merger control. Furthermore, in its Reply Volvo contested the validity of the study, claiming that the analysis was seriously flawed and that the results cannot be relied on. Although Professors Ivaldi and Verboven have provided answers to these criticisms, Volvo still contests some of the fundamental elements of the study. Given the novelty of the approach and the

level of disagreement, the Commission will not base its assessment on the results of the study." See further: para. 75 of the Commission's decision.

77 Ivaldi, M. and Verboven, F. (2002), "Quantifying the Effects from Horizontal Mergers in European Competition Policy", September, www.idei.fr/doc/by/ivaldi/iv_merger_v04.pdf, 19.

78 Wu, L., Williams, M. and Hofer, P. (2004), "The Increasing Use of Empirical Methods in European Merger Enforcement: Lessons from the Past and a Look Ahead", www.nera.com, 10, 16. As regards the market for perioperative monitors, a package of remedies was submitted, "based on the divestiture of Spacelabs (a division of Instrumentarium) in conjunction with a series of OEM supply agreements (Instrumentarium anaesthesia machines, Instrumentarium/Datex-Ohmeda perioperative monitor Cardiocap5 and Instrumentarium latest gas module model) aiming at making the divested business more appealing to potential purchasers and a more effective competitive force" (para. 322 of the Commission's decision). In order to remove the Commission's serious doubts relating to the vertical issues and concerning the interoperability between anaesthesia machines, patient monitors and CIS, the Interface Commitment was submitted. According to the Commission, this commitment "removes foreclosure-related serious doubts by ensuring that it will continue to be possible in the future to connect the patient monitors, anaesthesia machines and CIS of third-party manufacturers to the merged entity's devices and CIS. The merged entity would be under an obligation to provide safe, seamless and effective interface options, to provide interface information on a non-discriminatory basis and to co-operate with third parties where certification of a configuration is necessary" (para. 356 of the Commission's decision).

79 RBB Economics, "Assessing Unilateral Effects in Practice: Lessons from GE/Instrumentarium", RBB Brief 14, www.rbbeconomics.com/publications/downloads/rbb_brief14.pdf, May 2004, 4.

80 As abovementioned, the assumptions used for the application of merger simulation, are irrelevant to the actual substantive test for the assessment of the merger.

81 Stigler, G. (1982), "The Economists and the Problem of Monopoly", *American Economic Review*, 72, 9.

82 Coate, M. B. (1992), "Economics, the Guidelines and the Evaluation of Merger Policy", *Antitrust Bulletin*, 37(4), 997–1024, 1003.

83 Harris, B. and Simons, J. (1989), "Focusing Market Definition: How Much Substitution is Necessary?", *Research in Law and Economics*, 12, 207–26.

84 See further: *US Department of Justice and Federal Trade Commission Horizontal Merger Guidelines 1992*, www.usdoj.gov/atr/public/guidelines/horiz_book/5.html, 19 March 2003.

85 Kokkoris, I. (2005a), "The Concept of Market Definition and the SSNIP test in the Merger Appraisal", *ECLR*, 26(4), 209–214.

86 *Commission Notice on the Definition of the Relevant Market for the Purposes of Community Competition Law* [1997] OJ C372/5. For cases concerning the assessment of a merger between companies enjoying buyer power the equivalent SSDIP (Small but Significant Non-transitory Decrease in Price) test can be used. See further: Kokkoris, I. (2006a) "Buyer Power Assessment in Competition Law", *World Competition*, 29(1), 139–64.

87 Wu, L., Williams, M. and Hofer, P. (2004), "The Increasing Use of Empirical Methods in European Merger Enforcement: Lessons from the Past and a Look Ahead", www.nera.com, 10, 18.

88 Katz, M. and Shapiro, C. (2003), "Critical Loss: Let's Tell the Whole Story", *Antitrust*, Spring, 50.

89 Epstein, R. and Rubinfeld, D. (2004), "Technical Report Effects of Mergers Involving Differentiated Products", COMP/B1/2003/07, http://europa.eu.int/comm/competition/mergers/others/effects_mergers_involving_differentiated_products.pdf, 28.
90 Critical Loss: [Y/(Y+PCM)]*100.
91 The revenue associated with one additional unit of production.
92 The marginal cost of an additional unit of output is the cost of the additional inputs needed to produce that output. The argument that firms maximize profits by setting marginal cost equal to marginal revenue is valid in a perfectly competitive market. The concept of a perfectly competitive market is a theoretical benchmark used in economics and does not resemble actual market conditions.
93 Sheffman, D. and Simons, J. (2003), "The State of Critical Loss Analysis: Let's Make Sure We Understand the Whole Story", www.antitrustsource.com, 5.
94 The economic concept of price elasticity of demand refers to the degree that the demand for a product changes as a result of a change in its price. If the market demand is inelastic/elastic, each individual firm's demand is also likely to be inelastic/elastic respectively. For a detailed definition of price elasticity, see further: Mas-Colell, A., Whinston, M and Green, J. (1995), *Microeconomic Theory*, Oxford University Press, New York, 27.
95 Werden, G. and Froeb, L. (2002), "Calibrated Economic Models Add Focus, Accuracy, and Persuasiveness to Merger Analysis", www2.owen.vanderbilt.edu/luke.froeb/papers/sca10.pdf, 6.
96 Werden, G. and Froeb, L. (2002), "Calibrated Economic Models Add Focus, Accuracy, and Persuasiveness to Merger Analysis", www2.owen.vanderbilt.edu/luke.froeb/papers/sca10.pdf, 2.
97 Such reactions constitute the impact of non-collusive oligopolies in the post-merger market.
98 The degree of substitutability between two products is indicated by the cross-price elasticity. The concept of cross-price elasticity of demand refers to the responsiveness of the quantity demanded of one good to changes in the price of another good. See further: Bannock, G., Baxter, R. E. and Rees, R. (1985), *The Penguin Dictionary of Economics*, 3rd edn, Penguin Books, Basingstoke, 106.
99 O'Brien, D. and Wickelgren, A. (2003), "A Critical Analysis of Critical Loss Analysis", www.ftc.gov/be/workpapers/wp254.pdf, 3.
100 As mentioned earlier in this chapter, the percentage incremental profit margin is equal to initial price minus the average cost and this outcome divided by the initial price. Thus, assuming costs remain the same, for the firm's margin to be lower the price must also be lower.
101 O'Brien, D. and Wickelgren, A. (2003), "A Critical Analysis of Critical Loss Analysis", www.ftc.gov/be/workpapers/wp254.pdf, 30.
102 The authors make additional assumptions most of which are addressed by Sheffman and Simons: Sheffman, D. and Simons, J. (2003), "The State of Critical Loss Analysis: Let's Make Sure We Understand the Whole Story", www.antitrustsource.com.
103 O'Brien, D. and Wickelgren, A. (2003), "A Critical Analysis of Critical Loss Analysis", www.ftc.gov/be/workpapers/wp254.pdf, 31.
104 A merger will mainly internalize the competition between formerly separately owned firms.
105 Two goods are complements if their cross-price elasticity is negative. If the price of one good increases, then the quantity demanded of this good as well as of its complement good decreases.
106 As outlined in O'Brien, D. and Wickelgren, A. (2003), "A Critical Analysis of Critical Loss Analysis", www.ftc.gov/be/workpapers/wp254.pdf, 4.

107 Katz, M. and Shapiro, C. (2003), "Critical Loss: Let's Tell the Whole Story", *Antitrust*, Spring, 51.
108 For completeness, as regards the uses of critical loss analysis, this chapter will also briefly address the use of critical loss analysis on cases involving collective dominance.
109 Kokkoris, I. (2005d), "The Reform of the European Community Merger Regulation in the Aftermath of the Airtours Case. The Eagerly Expected Debate: SLC v Dominance test", *ECLR*, 26(1), 37–47.
110 M190 *Nestlé/Perrier* [1992] OJ L356/1.
111 *Nestlé/Perrier*, §124.
112 Although there may be asymmetries in costs, these asymmetries may not be adequate to change the collectively dominant nature of the market.
113 Harris, B. and Veljanovski, C. (2003), "Critical Loss Analysis: Its Growing Use in Competition Law", *ECLR*, 24(5), 213–18.
114 Additional factors that determine the existence of a tacitly collusive equilibrium include the existence of transparency and retaliation mechanisms in the market, as was outlined by the General Court in the *Airtours* decision. See: Case T-342/99 *Airtours v Commission* [2002] ECR II-2585.
115 Case M3512 *VNU/WPP/JV*, 15 September 2004.
116 Case M2111 *Alcoa/British Aluminium* [2000] OJ C348/14.
117 Case M1882 *Pirelli/BICC* [2003] OJ L70/35, 19 July 2000. See further: Baxter, S. and Dethmers, F. (2006), "Collective Dominance Under EC Merger Control-After Airtours and the Introduction of Unilateral Effects is There Still a Future for Collective Dominance", *ECLR*, 27(3), 148–60.
118 *Federal Trade Commission v Occidental Petroleum Corp.*, 1996–I Trade vs. (CCH) 67,071 (DDC 1986).
119 *Federal Trade Commission, et al. v Tenet Healthcare Corporation*, 186 F. 3d 1045 (Eight Circuit 1999).
120 *Federal Trade Commission v Swedish Match North America Inc., et al.*, 131 F. Supp. 2d 151, 160–62 (DDC 2000).
121 *US v SunGard and Comdisco*, 172 F. Supp. 2d 172, 182,186–92 and n.21 (DDC 2001).
122 *California v Sutter Health System*, 130 F. Supp. 2d 1109 (CD Cal. 2001).
123 *Royal Caribbean Cruises, Ltd/P&O Princess Cruises Plc and Carnival Corporation/ P&O Princess Cruises Plc*, FTC File No. 021 0041, 2002.
124 www.ftc.gov/opa/1995/11/ocal.shtm.
125 Lexecon, "Quantitative Techniques in Competition Analysis", www.lexecon.co.uk/assets/quantitative_ techniques.pdf, 01/11/2003, 20.
126 Harris, B. (2004), "Recent Observations about Critical Loss Analysis", www.ftc.gov/bc/mergerenforce/presentations/040217harris.pdf, 4.
127 Harris, B. (2004), "Recent Observations about Critical Loss Analysis", www.ftc.gov/bc/mergerenforce/presentations/040217harris.pdf, 4.
128 The authors also present five possibilities that can explain this outcome. O'Brien, D. and Wickelgren, A. (2003), "A Critical Analysis of Critical Loss Analysis", www.ftc.gov/be/workpapers/wp254.pdf, 27.
129 www.ftc.gov/opa/2000/12/swedish2.shtm.
130 Harris, B. (2004), "Recent Observations about Critical Loss Analysis", www.ftc.gov/bc/mergerenforce/ presentations/040217harris.pdf, 52.
131 Wu, L., Williams, M. and Hofer, P. (2004), "The Increasing Use of Empirical Methods in European Merger Enforcement: Lessons from the Past and a Look Ahead", www.nera.com, 10. For details regarding the methodology and conclusions of the econometric study, see: Ivaldi, M. and Verboven, F. (2001), "Quantifying the Effects from Horizontal Mergers in European Competition Policy", www.cepr.org/pubs/dps/ DP2697.asp, 7.

132 Langenfeld, J. and Li, W. (2004), "Critical Loss Analysis in Evaluating Mergers", in Evans, D. and Padilla, J. (eds), *Global Competition Policy, Economic Issues and Impacts*, LECG, Emeryville, CA, 7.
133 Langenfeld, J. and Li, W. (2004), "Critical Loss Analysis in Evaluating Mergers", in Evans, D. and Padilla, J. (eds), *Global Competition Policy, Economic Issues and Impacts*, LECG, Emeryville, CA, 59.
134 www.ftc.gov/os/2002/10/cruisestatement.htm#N_9_.
135 Cm 5536, *P&O Cruises and Royal Caribbean Cruises Ltd*, 19/6/2002, www.competition-commission.org.uk/rep_pub/reports/2002/468po.htm#full.
136 As it has been and will be further elaborated in the implications of this case law analysis (at a later stage of this section), critical loss analysis can be used both for market definition and for the assessment of the anticompetitive effects of a merger.
137 Case M2706 *Carnival Corporation/P&O Princess* [2003] OJ L248/1. Judging from the decision of the European Commission, critical loss analysis was not used. The Commission stated that no data was collected that would allow any quantitative tests related to market definition to be conducted. See footnote 10 of the Commission's decision.
138 See further: www.ftc.gov/be/hilites/ftcbeababrownbag.pdf.
139 Yield management uses estimates of predicted load factors relative to actual load factors as one indicator of whether prices should be changed.
140 See further: Coleman, M. and Sheffman, D. (2004), "Quantitative Analysis of Potential Competitive Effects from a Merger", in Evans, D. and Padilla, J. (eds), *Global Competition Policy, Economic Issues and Impacts*, LECG, Emeryville, CA, 102.
141 Case M3071 *Carnival Corporation/P&O Princess (II)* [2003] OJ C42/7.
142 The Commission argued that from a competition point of view, the dual listing was not materially different from the previous Carnival bid for P&O Princess, which the Commission had cleared.
143 It recognized that there was a wide range of uncertainty that depended on the fraction of sales and administrative costs.
144 Tom (2004) analyses instances when the SSNIP test should depart from the 5 per cent rate of increase. Suppose a situation in which a price increase of 5 per cent would lead to the loss of *x* units of sales. Suppose that the profit on those *x* units is greater than the increased profits on the sales that the seller would continue to make. Therefore, a 5 per cent price increase would not be profitable. If the next tranche of customers is highly price inelastic, an increase in the price will not divert many customers into other substitutes of the firm's product. Thus, with a price increase of 10 per cent, the seller still loses no more than *x* units of sales. But this time, with a 10 per cent instead of a 5 per cent price increase, the increased margin on the sales that are kept is great enough to outweigh the lost profits from the sales that are lost, which means that the price increase is profitable. Similar reasoning applies to price increases smaller than 5 per cent. A price increase of 1 per cent might cause a small enough loss of unit sales to be profitable, whereas a 5 per cent price increase would not.

According to Tom (2004), since it is not likely to accurately know what would happen if the merger did not occur, there needs to be some reasonable benchmarks, not only for legal certainty and for providing legal advice, but also to avoid unnecessary interference in pro-competitive mergers; the 5 per cent to 10 per cent benchmark is the most reasonable benchmark to date. See further: Tom, W. (2004), "Market Definition under the Merger Guidelines: Some Modest Proposals", comments submitted to the FTC/DOJ Merger Enforcement Workshop, Washington, DC, 17 February.

145 Price minus marginal cost, all divided by price. The marginal cost of an additional unit of output is the cost of the additional inputs needed to produce that output.
146 As has been mentioned, the Commission has discussed the incentive to collude based on critical loss considerations in a number of cases including *VNU/WPP/JV*, *Alcoa/British Aluminium* and *Pirelli/BICC*.
147 Six were in the United States and one in the United Kingdom.
148 All three were dealt by the European Commission.
149 This may also apply to homogeneous products if firms have high market shares and capacity is not unlimited.
150 See further: EEA Standing Committee of the EFTA States (2002), "EEA EFTA Comments on the Commission's Green Paper on the review of Council Regulation (EEC) No. 4064/89 (COM(2001) 745/6 Final)", secretariat.efta.int/Web?EuropeanEconomicArea/OngoingWork/100w149.doc, 30 July 2003, 6.
151 In merger cases brought before the European Commission and assessed based on the SIEC test market definition may still play a significant role due to the existence of legal precedents.
152 A 5 to 10 per cent increase as stipulated by the SSNIP test. As already mentioned in this book, the SSNIP test assists in the definition of the market.
153 Due to high combined market shares. Cases include: Case M2256 *Philips/Agilent Health Care Solutions* [2001] OJ C292/10, Case M2537 *Philips/Marconi Medical Systems* [2001] OJ C321/12, and Case M2922 *Pfizer/Pharmacia* [2003] OJ C110/24.
154 Baxter, S. and Dethmers, F. (2005), "Unilateral Effects Under the European Merger Regulation: How Big is the Gap?", *ECLR*, 26(7), 380–89.
155 Cm 5885, *Centrica Plc/Dynegy Storage Ltd and Dynegy Onshore Processing*, August 2003.
156 RBB Economics, "Assessing Unilateral Effects in Practice: Lessons from GE/Instrumentarium", RBB Brief 14, www.rbbeconomics.com/publications/downloads/rbb_brief14.pdf, May 2004, 4.
157 Volcker, S. (2004), "Mind the Gap: Unilateral Effects Analysis arrives at the Merger Control", *ECLR*, 25(7), 395–409.
158 Case T-5/02 *Tetra Laval v Commission* [2002] ECR II-4381, Case T-80/02 *Tetra Laval v Commission*, [2002] ECR II-4519.
159 Volcker, S. (2004), "Mind the Gap: Unilateral Effects Analysis arrives at the Merger Control", *ECLR*, 25(7), 395–409.
160 See further: Kokkoris, I. (2006b), "Do Merger Simulation and Critical Loss Analysis Differ Under the SLC and Dominance Test?" *ECLR*, 27(5), 248–59.

4 Mergers leading to non-coordinated effects in oligopolistic markets

4.1 Introduction

In this chapter,[1] an attempt will be made to provide evidence of mergers leading to non-coordinated effects in oligopolistic markets.[2] It will be interesting to assess whether any difference in treatment can be detected as to how non-collusive oligopolies have been analysed under the dominance and SLC tests.[3] This chapter will consider the existence of "gap" cases in the current case law. The aim is to identify important merger cases that fell into the realm of non-collusive oligopolies.

These cases were chosen after research that was conducted in the jurisdictions analysed herein. The initial sample of cases included cases that had features similar to the ones of collective dominance but were characterized by differentiated products. The cases herein are put in chronological order so as to illustrate the development of the case law related to non-coordinated effects in oligopolistic markets. The list of cases does not purport to be exhaustive, however, it clearly indicates the existence of a gap in the application of the dominance test. The number of cases not only of the European Commission but also of the national competition authorities that apply the dominance test is likely to be significant. The conclusion of this chapter will present the implications of the gap in the application of the dominance test for some of the new member states.

This chapter includes a comparative approach of examining mergers where the outcome of the assessment could be different under the dominance test and the SLC/SIEC test in various legal systems. The focus of the chapter will be mergers dealt under the original ECMR. When the decisions on these merger cases were taken, the concept of non-collusive oligopolies was not recognized in the ECMR.[4] Other legal systems that will be included in the analysis are the United Kingdom,[5] Finland, New Zealand,[6] the United States,[7] and Australia.[8] Some of these jurisdictions have adopted the SLC test (for example, the United Kingdom, New Zealand, Australia) while in others the SLC test has been used as the substantive legal criterion since the early 1900s (for example, the United States).[9]

4.2 The European Union

The cases that will be analysed in this part of the chapter include *Airtours/First Choice*,[10] *Oracle/PeopleSoft*,[11] *Sony/BMG*,[12] *Syngenta CP/Advanta*,[13] *Johnson & Johnson/ Guidant*,[14] and *T-Mobile Austria/Tele.ring*.[15]

4.2.1 Airtours/First Choice

4.2.1.1 Analysis of the case

In *Airtours/First Choice* the Commission investigated a proposed hostile acquisition of Airtours by First Choice. On 29 April 1999 Airtours Plc, a UK company whose main activity was as a tour operator and supplier of package holidays, announced its intention to acquire all the shares in the UK tour operator, First Choice Plc, one of its competitors. The major tour operators were Thomson (30.7 per cent of the market), Airtours (19.4 per cent of the market), Thomas Cook (20.4 per cent of the market) and First Choice (15 per cent of the market).[16] The relevant product market adopted as regards airline services was that for the supply to tour operators of seats on charter flights to short-haul destinations. The relevant geographic markets for each of the relevant product markets were, respectively, the United Kingdom and Ireland.

Certain features of the market such as the high degree of price transparency and multi-market contacts among the major airlines may facilitate coordinated behaviour. The market was already concentrated with four large firms having 80 per cent of the market and several smaller firms occupying the rest. The acquisition would allegedly lead to three firms holding a collective dominant position. The Commission concluded that the proposed operation would create a dominant position in the market for short-haul foreign package holidays in the United Kingdom, as a result of which competition would be significantly impeded. The Commission's decision was appealed to the General Court.

The *Airtours/First Choice* was the second outright prohibition under the ECMR on the basis of collective dominance. The Commission appeared to take the view that the ability of firms to engage in tacit collusion is not essential. It is sufficient that the merger makes it rational for firms having adequate market power to act independently of competitors and customers.[17] The Commission diverged from its previous practice and extended the concept of collective dominance from duopoly to a merger reducing the number of post-merger firms to three.

The General Court,[18] in annulling the Commission's decision, argued that the Commission had not proved to the required legal standard that the merger would lead to a collective dominant position. Specifically, the demand was volatile, capacity planning was complex with slow capacity changes, the market was not transparent in the capacity planning period, there was lack of barriers to entry, and consumers could easily switch to other types of foreign package holiday such as long-haul.

The General Court laid down a stricter standard for establishing collective dominance. The Commission should not simply reflect the normal economic conditions of the markets but should convincingly indicate not only the adverse impact of commercial links on competition but the likelihood and sustainability of the common policy as well. The General Court's decision outlined three necessary conditions for a position of collective dominance or tacit collusion to be reached and sustained, namely transparency, the existence of credible retaliatory mechanisms, and the countervailing impact of customers and competitors.

4.2.1.2 A gap case?

The Commission did not allege single firm dominance and did not sufficiently prove the likelihood of collective dominance arising from the merger. In the market definition, the Commission did not question either the fact that long-haul foreign package holidays are becoming increasingly attractive to consumers or address the market studies cited by the applicant in its reply to the Statement of Objections. Thus, the market might have been defined too narrowly with an ensuing overestimation of the parties' market shares.

Even in this likely narrowly defined market, the combined market share was 34.4 per cent below the 50 per cent threshold that has been identified in the case law (for example, *AKZO*).[19,20] Thus, the low market shares of the parties post-merger could not substantiate an argument of single firm dominance. The Commission considered whether the merger would lead to collective dominance. According to the case law, in order for a collusive equilibrium to arise and be sustained, certain criteria need to be fulfilled including barriers to entry and exit, a small number of firms, ability to coordinate towards equilibrium, ability to enforce compliance, as well as ability to monitor and deter any prospective maverick[21] firms. These criteria depend on features such as product homogeneity, low demand growth, low price sensitivity of demand, symmetric cost structures, and multi-market contacts. The Commission provided an extensive analysis of the reasons that would make the post-merger market prone to collective dominance in the aftermath of the merger of Airtours and First Choice.

However, these arguments were not persuasive, resulting in a successful appeal from Airtours against the Commission's decision. The General Court in its judgment noted that the Commission's decision was vitiated by a series of errors of assessment of the factors contributing to a collectively dominant position.[22]

In *Airtours*,[23] the General Court argued that the Commission was not entitled to treat the cautious capacity planning characteristic of the market as evidence substantiating its proposition that there was already a tendency to collective dominance in the industry. The Commission made errors of assessment in its analysis of the competition conditions (related to capacity setting) in the pre-merger market as regards the tendency in the industry towards collective dominance. In addition, the Commission did not consider that the main tour operators' market shares had been volatile in the past and that such volatility is evidence that the market was competitive.

Furthermore, the General Court stated that the Commission's interpretation of the data available to it concerning growth of demand was inaccurate in its disregard for the fact that the market had been marked by a clear tendency towards considerable growth over the last decade in general, despite the volatile nature of demand from one year to another, and that the pace of demand growth had increased during recent years.[24] In addition, the Commission failed to establish that volatility of demand was conducive to the creation of a dominant oligopoly by the three remaining major tour operators.[25] The Commission thus wrongly concluded that there was low growth, a factor conducive to the creation of a collective dominant position by the three remaining large tour operators.

The General Court also added that the Commission wrongly formed the view that market transparency was high for the four major integrated operators during the planning period and that the degree of market transparency was a characteristic that made the market conducive to collective dominance. The General Court emphasized that the crucial capacity decisions for the following season were taken during the planning period and thereafter the scope for increasing capacity was very limited. The Commission erred in concluding that if the transaction were to proceed the three major tour operators remaining after the merger would have an incentive to cease competing with one another.

The General Court further argued that the Commission underestimated the likely reaction of smaller tour operators, as well as potential competitors and consumers, as a counterbalancing force capable of destabilizing the collective dominant position. The Commission underestimated the ability of the small operators to increase capacity in order to take advantage of opportunities afforded by a situation of general undersupply brought about by the large tour operators and thus to counteract the creation of a collective dominant position following the concentration. In addition, it underestimated the ability of potential competitors to enter the market and, therefore, to take fast and effective action in the event of the large tour operators aligning their capacity strategies in order to induce a situation of undersupply. Finally, consumer demand might partly switch to other types of holiday if there were sufficient price convergence, since consumer tastes were evolving in favour of long-haul foreign package holidays.

The General Court concluded that the Commission had failed to prove that the result of the transaction would be to alter the structure of the relevant market in such a way that the leading operators would no longer act as they had in the past and that a collective dominant position would be created.

As this analysis indicates, the merger between Airtours and First Choice raised neither single firm dominance nor collective dominance concerns. Whish (2002) mentions *Airtours/First Choice* as one of the cases in which mergers were investigated and were not struck down under a dominance test but which might have been or were under the SLC test.[26]

In *Airtours/First Choice*, the Commission argued that the merger would lead to the creation of a collective dominant market position in short-haul package holidays in the United Kingdom. It added that active collusive conduct of any kind is not a prerequisite for collective dominance to occur. It is sufficient that adaptation to market conditions causes an anti-competitive market outcome.

The Commission made an attempt to widen the notion of collective dominance by applying it to a merger that it thought, was leading to non-coordinated effects in an oligopolistic market. As the Commission states in paragraph 54:

> It is sufficient that the merger makes it rational for the oligopolists, in adapting themselves to market conditions, to act, individually, in ways which will substantially reduce competition between them, and as a result of which they may act, to an appreciable extent, independently of competitors, customers and consumers.

The decision refers to oligopolists acting individually in substantially reducing competition. The concept of oligopolists acting individually in harming competition is equivalent to unilateral effects in an oligopolistic market rather than to collective dominance. The General Court defined collective dominance as the adoption of a common policy on the market. In paragraph 62, the General Court stated:

> A collective dominant position significantly impeding effective competition in the common market or a substantial part of it may thus arise as the result of a concentration where, in view of the actual characteristics of the relevant market and of the alteration in its structure that the transaction would entail, the latter would make each member of the dominant oligopoly, as it becomes aware of common interests, consider it possible, economically rational, and hence preferable, to adopt on a lasting basis a common policy on the market with the aim of selling at above competitive prices, without having to enter into an agreement or resort to a concerted practice within the meaning of Article 81 EC (see, to that effect, Gencor v Commission, paragraph 277) and without any actual or potential competitors, let alone customers or consumers, being able to react effectively.

As the General Court emphasized, each member of the dominant oligopoly will adopt a common policy. This contradicts the Commission's view as outlined in paragraph 54, where it stated that the oligopolists should be acting individually.

Market shares and the structure of the market may provide an indication of whether the merger would be likely to lead to non-coordinated effects. As the Commission states in its Guidelines, market shares and concentration levels provide useful first indications of the market structure and of the competitive importance of both the merging parties and their competitors.[27] In general, under the SIEC test it can be argued that even at a low market share of 34.4 per cent the Commission can argue that competition is significantly impeded if barriers to entry and expansion are high as well as in the presence of capacity constraints.

Although the market shares are low, the relative market shares draw a different picture. The relative market shares may be an initial rough indication of the competitive constraints that each firm is imposing on the other incumbents.[28] The importance of the market share as an indication of collective dominance depends on the level relative to that of the nearest competitor as well as on factors tending to entrench the leading position of the firm.[29]

In the pre-merger market Thomson had 30.7 per cent, Thomas Cook 20.4 per cent, Airtours 19.4 per cent and First Choice 15 per cent. In the post-merger market the merged entity would have 34.4 per cent, Thomson would have 30.7 per cent and Thomas Cook 20.4 per cent. The elimination of First Choice led to increased concentration in the market. The CR3[30] ratio in the pre-merger market was 70.4 per cent, which increased to 85.5 per cent in the post-merger market. The CR4 ratio was 85.5 per cent prior to the merger – 88.6 per cent after the merger. Such increased concentration in a market can lead to firms individually adopting conduct having an adverse impact on competition by increasing prices if the competitive constraints that exist between two firms diminish after the merger.

One stage in the assessment of a merger is the calculation of the HHI ratios. The HHI is calculated by summing the squares of the individual market shares of all the participants (see www.ftc.gov/bc/docs/horizmer.htm-N_17_#N_17_). Unlike the four-firm concentration ratio, the HHI reflects both the distribution of the market shares of the top four firms and the composition of the market outside of the top four firms. However, it gives proportionately greater weight to the market shares of the larger firms, in accordance with their relative importance in competitive interactions. Markets can be broadly characterized as unconcentrated (HHI below 1000), moderately concentrated (HHI between 1000 and 1800), and highly concentrated (HHI above 1800).[31] However, a DOJ/FTC study on HHIs in merger challenges between 1999 and 2003 shows, from nearly 1300 mergers challenged by US agencies over these five years, no merger with post-merger HHI below 1400, and change in the HHI of approximately 85 was challenged.[32]

While the absolute level of the HHI can give an initial indication of the competitive pressure in the market post-merger, the change in the HHI (known as the "delta" or "dHHI") is a useful proxy for the change in concentration directly brought about by the merger. The Commission is unlikely to identify horizontal competition concerns in a market with a post-merger HHI below 1000. The Commission is also unlikely to identify horizontal competition concerns in a merger with a post-merger HHI between 1000 and 2000 and a delta below 250, or a merger with a post-merger HHI above 2000 and a delta below 150, except where special circumstances such as where: a merger involves a potential entrant or a recent entrant with a small market share; one or more merging parties are important innovators in ways not reflected in market shares; there are significant cross-shareholdings among the market participants; one of the merging firms is a maverick firm with a high likelihood of disrupting coordinated conduct; indications of past or ongoing coordination, or facilitating practices, are present; and where one of the merging parties has a pre-merger market share of 50 per cent of more.[33]

In *Airtours/First Choice*, the pre-merger HHI was 2170.[34] The post-merger HHI was 2752. The dHHI was 582. From the HHI ratios as well as the concentration ratios it is clear that the market would be concentrated post merger. According to the Commission, in the post-merger market with three major competitors, high concentration and a highly polarized market structure, the merged entity as well as the other incumbents were likely to increase their prices in the aftermath of the merger. This analysis indicates that in the *Airtours* case due to, mainly, the low market shares, the merger would not lead to single firm dominance and the market structure in the aftermath of the merger was not prone to collective dominance.[35]

The UK Competition Commission had published a report on foreign package holidays in the United Kingdom in 1997, one and a half years before the *Airtours* merger notification, which concluded that the market was competitive with no significant barriers to entry.[36] In contrast, according to Motta (1999), the merger would lead to unilateral effects, and with increased concentration and unlikely entry, only efficiency gains would counteract the adverse impact of the merger. However, as the author mentions, it is unlikely that efficiency gains would occur from the merger.[37] The merger would decrease economic efficiency. He further mentions that the Commission might have been trying to extend the concept of collective dominance to cope with a distortion of the original ECMR, which did not prohibit welfare decreasing mergers unless they create or reinforce dominance. In addition, Nicholson and Cardell (2002) argue that the General Court ruled out the assessment of multilateral effects (or non-collusive oligopolies) under the original ECMR.[38] The General Court had the chance by elaborating on the Commission's thinking (for example paragraph 54 of the Commission's decision) to sustain the application of the dominance test to non-collusive oligopolies but rather it decided to argue that the merger would create collective dominance. It has also been mentioned that one aspect of the *Airtours/First Choice* regarded multilateral effects.[39]

Thus, the Commission might have been trying to use collective dominance to capture unilateral effects of mergers that do not lead to single firm dominance. In addition, as Ehlermann, Völcker and Gutermuth (2005) mention,[40] in this case the Commission appears to have viewed non-coordinated effects as a category of collective dominance. This is also illustrated from paragraph 54 of the Commission's decision which, as mentioned earlier, refers to oligopolists acting individually in substantially reducing competition. The concept of oligopolists acting individually in harming competition is equivalent to unilateral effects in an oligopolistic market rather than to collective dominance. Fingleton (2002) argues that the *Airtours/First Choice* was incorrectly characterized as a tacit collusion case instead of a multilateral effects case.[41]

The *Airtours/First Choice* merger should not have been blocked as leading to collective dominance. As the previous analysis has indicated, this merger satisfied the criteria neither for collective nor for single firm dominance. However, this case presented an example of how the Commission was trying to amend the gap in the application of the dominance test, since it considered that the merger would allow the incumbents in the post-merger market to act, individually, in ways which will substantially reduce competition between them.[42]

The results arising from the event study[43] indicated that the Commission's decision contradicts the investors' perception on the day of the initial significant dissemination of information. The market did not expect the *Airtours/First Choice* to have an adverse impact on competition.

In my opinion, the Commission wrongly considered that the merger would lead to adverse effects on competition. However, in an attempt to block it, it tried to expand the notion of collective dominance to cover non-coordinated effects in oligopolistic markets. The Commission recognized a gap in the application of the dominance test (even though the merger might not have led to adverse effects on competition) and mistakenly tried to amend it. The fact that the Commission erred in its assessment of the factual framework of the case does not mean that it also erred in its belief that there is a gap in the application of the dominance test. It is my belief that under the Commission's wrong assessment of the facts, the Commission realized that it would be difficult to block the merger under single firm dominance, and thus tried to expand the notion of collective dominance in order to block the merger and prevent the assumed post-merger adverse impact on competition.[44]

4.2.2 Oracle/PeopleSoft[45]

4.2.2.1 Analysis of the case

Oracle was a publicly listed company that was active in the design, development, manufacture and distribution of enterprise application software, database and application server software and related services. PeopleSoft was a publicly listed company active in the design, development, manufacture and distribution of enterprise application software and related services. In July 2003 PeopleSoft acquired control of JD Edwards, a US company also active in the application software business.

On 14 October 2003 the Commission received notification of a proposed concentration by which the undertaking Oracle Corporation would acquire sole control of the undertaking PeopleSoft Inc. by way of a public bid, within the meaning of Article 3(1)(b) of the original ECMR. On 7 April 2004, following the oral hearing, the Commission issued a request for information under Article 11 of the ECMR inviting Oracle to submit further information in order to enable the Commission to take a decision on a "broader factual basis". In the absence of a reply from Oracle, the Commission adopted a decision under Article 11(5) of the ECMR on 14 April 2004 suspending as of that date the periods laid down in Articles 10(1) and 10(3) of the original ECMR. Following Oracle's submission in response to the Commission's request for information, the timetable resumed again on 7 October 2004.

The operation was reviewed by the US authorities in parallel with the Commission. In the United States, a trial was held in front of the US District Court for the Northern District of California in San Francisco. The District Court of Northern California, by its judgment of 9 September 2004, refused to grant an injunction regarding the transaction. In the course of the trial, numerous documents concerning the transaction became public and were (partly) put on the website of the DOJ. Also transcripts of the statements made by around 30 witnesses in the trial became public. The Commission took into consideration parts of the evidence from the US trial.

Oracle and PeopleSoft were vendors of enterprise application software ("EAS"). EAS supported major business functions needed to manage a business effectively at a corporate or branch level, such as managing corporate finances, automating sales, and marketing functions of a company, or managing the resources involved in corporate projects. The industry generally grouped EAS into categories having functionality with broadly similar purposes. The relevant categories identified were financial management systems ("FMS") and human resources ("HR"), together often called enterprise resource planning ("ERP"). The FMS suite typically included software for accounting (accounts receivable, accounts payable, general ledger), planning and budgeting, reporting, time and expense management, and the financial supply chain. The HR suite combined software for personnel data, payroll management and benefits. Other EAS pillars were customer relationship management ("CRM") and supply chain management ("SCM").

The Commission found that the relevant product markets for the assessment of the present transaction were the markets for high-function FMS and HR software applications. As FMS and HR applications were not substitutable for buyers, the Commission considered these as two distinct markets. In addition, the market investigation showed that characteristics of high-function FMS and HR software were different from those of mid-market products. The underlying architecture of high-function solutions was fundamentally different from the one of mid-market products.

The high-function FMS and HR software applications were intended to serve the needs of large and complex enterprises ("LCEs"), which required software and accompanying services with a particularly high standard in terms of, inter alia, scalability, configurability, sophistication, pricing, reliability and quality of the software, and brand recognition of the vendor. High-function FMS and HR software had to offer compliance with the legal requirements and accounting rules of the main economic zones and legal jurisdictions (for example US-GAAP) and other national systems. Mid-market solutions typically had been optimized for use in a specific economic region, and as a result typically provided far less language and geographic support options.

High-function FMS and HR solutions were software that was typically purchased by complex organizations/companies which had a very high level of functional needs, expected high standards in product performance, and required short time and continuous availability of accompanying services. The Commission therefore came to the conclusion that there were distinct product markets for FMS and HR high-function solutions for large and complex enterprises.

The Commission further established who the vendors of FMS and HR high-function software were by looking at the bids made by suppliers for such customers, that is to say, for large and complex enterprises needing complex functionality in the field of FMS and HR applications.[46] The Commission concluded that Oracle, PeopleSoft and SAP were the main players in the markets for high-function FMS and HR for large and complex enterprises. The Commission's data and the submissions by Oracle showed that occasionally other players won bids for high-function FMS and HR software to serve the needs of large and complex enterprises including Lawson, Intentia, IFS, QAD, and Microsoft. The Commission further concluded that no significant distinction could be identified between the behaviour of Oracle when competing against SAP and PeopleSoft compared to the behaviour against other bidders even when attention was placed on large deals.

The market investigation clearly indicated that the geographic scope of the markets for high-function HR and FMS solutions for large and complex enterprises was worldwide.

The Commission concluded that the market for software applications for mid-size enterprises formed a separate market from the markets for high-function FMS and HR solutions, and possibly also from the markets for applications for small enterprises (that is to say, those with revenues below €30 million). Furthermore, the Commission found indications that applications software for small businesses only covered the basic needs of an enterprise with a uniform organizational structure. However, the Commission left the exact delineation of the product markets for mid-market FMS and HR solutions and the small business software open as the transaction did not lead to competition concerns on the basis of any of these possible market definitions. The Commission also concluded that the geographic scope of these markets might not be wider than EEA wide. However, the exact delimitation was left open.

The Commission's investigation as well as evidence stemming from the US trial in front of the District Court of Northern California demonstrated that FMS and HR high-function software was not interchangeable with simpler software (mid-market), or with best-of-breed or outsourcing options. Neither would a possible substantial non-transitory increase in price of this high-function software make mid-market FMS and HR applications, outsourcing, best-of-breed solutions, or software in-house development a suitable alternative, rendering the price increase unprofitable. Thus, best-of-breed and outsourcing were not part of the markets for high-function FMS and HR solutions.[47]

Turning to the assessment of the merger, calculation of market shares proved to be particularly difficult for the relevant markets, as neither publicly available industry studies nor the parties had provided a segmentation of vendors revenues according to the segmentation of the market (high-function market and mid-market) and vendors did not normally classify their customers according to their volume of revenue or their number of employees. Therefore, the Commission sought to establish the strength of the vendors on the basis of their total revenues as reported in industry reports, independently of whether these are achieved in the high-function market or the mid-market. Given their limited meaning for the markets at stake due to the inaccuracy of the data and the high degree of heterogeneity of the products, the Commission used the shares only as an indication of the relative strength of the different vendors in the markets.

According to the Gartner report,[48] the combined share of total licences revenues in 2002 was 46 per cent for Oracle/PeopleSoft/JD Edwards in the HR market and 28 per cent in the FMS market with SAP having 40 per cent and 51 per cent respectively, Microsoft MBS 2.5 per cent and 14 per cent respectively and Lawson 9 per cent and 4 per cent respectively. These revenues corresponded to the total revenues of the parties irrespective of whether they were achieved in the high-function market or in the mid-market. As mentioned earlier, these shares did not necessarily reflect the respective market shares of the vendors in the markets for high-function FMS and HR applications. These data showed that Oracle, PeopleSoft (including JD Edwards) and SAP were the main players in both the FMS and the HR market and that the share of other players might be estimated at between 10 and 15 per cent. SAP would still lead the market over a combined Oracle/PeopleSoft in FMS whereas a combined Oracle/PeopleSoft would take the lead in HR.[49]

Although the market shares play only a minor indicative role in this case, the Commission would have difficulty in arguing single firm dominance with such close relative market shares of SAP and Oracle/PeopleSoft in a bidding market characterized by a high degree of differentiation as well as innovation.

As regards the market for high-function HR and FMS solutions or software, in its Statement of Objections, the Commission, based on a definition of the market which after the merger would consist of only Oracle and SAP, had raised concerns that there would be a significant group of customers for whom there would essentially be only one supplier left after the transaction. However, in light of conclusions after the oral hearing regarding the existence of additional firms in the market, the Commission could not uphold its preliminary conclusion that customers would be confronted with a de facto absence of choice after the merger.

As regards FMS and HR mid-market software markets, significantly more players were active than in the markets for high-function FMS and HR solutions. No specific market shares for the mid-market applications were available, however. Nevertheless, the overall revenues achieved for 2002 (on the basis of analyst reports) showed that, on a worldwide basis, SAP would remain the strongest player in the FMS market, followed by a combined Oracle/PeopleSoft. Other significant players included Sage, Microsoft MBS, Hyperion, Systems Union, and Lawson. For HR mid-market solutions, the combined Oracle and PeopleSoft would become the strongest player, closely followed by SAP. Other significant players would include Kronos, Lawson, Sage, and Microsoft MBS.

In order to assess whether or not the notified concentration would lead to non-coordinated effects, the Commission investigated to what extent the competitive situation of a particular bid (measured by the number of final round bidders) had an impact on the discounting offered by the seller in question (that is to say PeopleSoft in PeopleSoft's dataset and Oracle in Oracle's datasets). The Commission found that there was a very strong relationship between the size of the deal and the discount offered. However, once the size of the deal was taken into account in the analysis the number of final bidders no longer provided any additional explanatory element over the discount offered and no general pattern emerged regarding the presence of a particular competitor prompting high discounts.[50]

A finding, as in this case, that the number and identity of competitors in a given bid appeared not to have an effect on a firm's behaviour did not, in itself, prove the lack of harmful effects of the merger on customers. There might have been a variety of reasons why such an effect was absent from the bidding data. One reason for the absence of any effects in the data could be that the quality of the data might have been low or that it might have been characterized from a bias in selection. Another could be that Oracle (and its competitors), when deciding what to bid, did not consider the information about actual competitors sufficiently reliable to want to base its behaviour on it. A third reason could be that the identity of bidders in the final round was an incomplete picture of the actual competitive process.[51] The absence of an appreciable effect of competition on Oracle's behaviour made the bidding data unsuitable to rely on as determinative proof of an adverse effect of the merger on competition.

The Commission argued that buyers were very sophisticated when acquiring software, and could structure the competitive bidding process as they preferred in order to exert competitive pressure on the bidders. In addition, they were in control of the flow of information to the bidders about who else was bidding. The market after the merger would still contain a significantly large number of bidders usually invited to the final round, and SAP remained a very strong competitor. Based on these findings, the Commission could not conclude that Oracle was likely to be in a position to profitably increase prices after the merger.[52]

In the Statement of Objections, the Commission had also based its concerns on the finding that, in addition to the non-coordinated effects, the two remaining players would be in a position to further soften competition by coordinating their competitive behaviour. The theory of coordination was based on a definition of the market which after the merger would consist of only Oracle and SAP and relied in particular on the symmetrical market shares of a combined Oracle/PeopleSoft and SAP and an alignment of incentives between them due to the fact that SAP was by far the largest reseller of Oracle databases. As parameters for adopting a common policy, the Commission identified the allocation of customers in a duopoly, a reduction in price competition and a common understanding to slow down the addition of further functionalities and the improvement of products.

However, based on the amended market definition (after documents of the US proceedings became available to the Commission), the Commission could not conclude that the merger would lead to a collective dominant position of a combined Oracle/PeopleSoft and SAP. The other vendors, Lawson, Intentia, IFS, QAD, and Microsoft, appeared to be suitable alternatives as the Commission's data and the dataset submitted by Oracle after the oral hearing showed that those vendors had won bids for software in the relevant markets. In addition, the highly differentiated nature of the FMS and HR high-function software,[53] the lack of structural links, the asymmetric market shares, the large number of incumbents, the limited transparency, and inadequate retaliatory mechanisms made the achievement of a tacitly collusive outcome very unlikely.

On a European level, given the limited strength of a combined Oracle/PeopleSoft in the mid-markets for FMS and HR applications and the numerous other players also active in these markets, the transaction would not lead to competition concerns, irrespective of the exact delineation of these markets.

The Commission declared the concentration compatible with the Common Market.

4.2.2.2 A gap case?

In paragraph 187, the Commission clearly stated that the initial concerns it had concerned the likely non-coordinated effects arising from the merger:

> In the Statement of Objections the Commission based its concerns in part on the finding that significant non-coordinated effects would arise from the transaction. In the reply to the statement of objections, Oracle contested the Commission's competence to assess such effects under the dominance test incorporated in Regulation (EEC) No. 4064/89. It is not necessary to address Oracle's submission on the lack of competence as, on the basis of the new evidence obtained after the Oral Hearing, it has been concluded that no such anticompetitive effects are likely to result from the merger.

The new evidence that the Commission refers to in the later part of this paragraph refers to the amended market definition, which included a larger number of vendors (albeit smaller than the three major suppliers SAP, Oracle, and PeopleSoft). As the remaining part of the analysis of this case will illustrate, the larger number of firms was not adequate, in itself, to counteract the adverse effects of this merger on competition. This merger, in my opinion, would lead to non-coordinated effects in the oligopolistic market for high-function FMS and HR software.

As Baxter and Dethmers (2005)[54] argue, the Commission relied on unilateral effects and the analysis was devoid of any single dominance considerations. The DOJ reviewed this transaction under a unilateral effects standard and dismissed coordinated effects. In addition, as Ehlermann, Völcker and Gutermuth (2005) mention,[55] in this case, the Commission appears to have viewed non-coordinated effects as a category of collective dominance. The Commission actually tried to close the enforcement gap in the application of the dominance test in this case, by stretching the concept of collective dominance. The market structure, as mentioned already, was not conducive to collective dominance and the fact that SAP and Oracle/PeopleSoft had similar market shares in an innovative market with differentiated products would render a credible allegation of single firm dominance difficult.

However, the merger would reduce the choices of customers as regards procuring products from major suppliers, without the remaining incumbents (smaller firms such as Lawson, Microsoft, etc.) being able to fully and effectively counteract this loss in choice with a selection of equal in quality and effectiveness products. The limited competitive constraint that smaller firms posed is also indicated, as will be shown, by the limited number of bids they won.

The concentration would result in the disappearance of PeopleSoft as an independent competitor, and would reduce the number of major firms that compete in the market for high-function FMS and HR software from three to two. This would decrease the intensity of competition in the market, leading to significant adverse effects on customers in terms of price, product variety, product quality, and innovation. Even under a wide definition of the market, when the market exhibits some degree of differentiation and it is difficult for undertakings to offer slightly different products from the ones they currently offer, the undertakings may devise strategies to apply localized price increases, leading thus to an adverse impact on competition in the market.

Competition in the market for high-function FMS and HR was characterized by vendors' attempts to offer a software solution that best met the specific demands of specific large customers, while, at the same time, decreased the total cost of ownership.[56] The products of software vendors exhibited a degree of product differentiation, characterized by a high degree of innovation. In addition, customers of high-function FMS and HR solutions often had specific needs requiring customization of the basic product offerings. In this respect, in order to be able to make a bid that best met the customer's requirements, competitors submitting a bid usually aimed to obtain as much knowledge as possible about customer needs.[57] The market investigation revealed that price was not necessarily the most important factor in the choice of a customer; a more important role was played by the breadth and depth of the functionality offerings, the proven track record of the supplier, the capability to offer EAS solutions to complex organizations and the scalability of those solutions.[58] Thus, the ability of alterative vendors to offer equal in quality and effectiveness products was essential in order to counteract the reduction in choices to customers induced by the merger.

These three factors (product differentiation, the ability to provide customization, and superior knowledge of the customer) might have provided each EAS vendor with a certain margin in its price setting vis-à-vis the other players which did not have the same product offering available, did not have the same capability to customize their product to the needs of the customer involved or did not have the same degree of insight into the needs of that customer.[59] Similarly, it provided for a certain margin in the extent to which each EAS vendor wanted to optimize the product it offered to a specific customer.

Each of the major vendors, SAP, PeopleSoft, and Oracle, was constrained to a significant degree by the existence of the other major market participants. As the merger removed an important independent player from the market, the combination of Oracle and PeopleSoft was likely to enhance the ability of the remaining firms in the post-merger market to adopt conducts harmful for competition by altering their pricing and product offerings.

The post-merger market structure was thus likely to lead to significant adverse effects in terms of price and product offerings for consumers. The group with particularly limited choice after the merger consisted, inter alia, of those customers who did not find one of the two products (of Oracle and PeopleSoft) suitable for their needs; those who preferred to run their software on a non-Oracle database;[60] those who, in order to avoid being dependent on one supplier, might prefer to purchase their FMS and HR software from two different suppliers; and those customers who might prefer not to have software and database provided by the same supplier.[61] Thus, as a result of the merger most customers could be faced with the prospect of significantly reduced competition between the two major remaining vendors.

For some customers, the extent of product differentiation, the ability to customize on the part of the vendor, and the required degree of company knowledge might have been such that Oracle and PeopleSoft could be characterized as the only two viable alternatives. Thus, the effects of the merger would be particularly acute for those customers that after the merger could be faced with essentially only the merged entity, and for whom SAP might be a distant second choice.

Those customers that had no technical or strategic restrictions on which of the major suppliers to choose, could face a significant reduction in their choices as well. They might effectively see the number of potential major suppliers being reduced from three to two. Prior to the merger such customers could organize a bidding contest where the three major EAS providers each proposed a package to the customer that differed in terms of scope, quality and price to provide the best "fit". After the merger, even if the two members of the duopoly were to continue to compete for a given contract, the reduction in potential providers in itself was likely, on average, to reduce the quality of the "fit" between the customer's preferred solution and its needs. In addition, the incentive for SAP and Oracle to offer extra non-standard functionalities might be diminished. For Oracle the absence of an offer from PeopleSoft might reduce the probability that the customer's preferred alternative would provide a very good "fit".

Customers who after the merger had preferences not to enter into a contract with Oracle might be left with SAP as the only major supplier able to provide a product of similar quality to the one of Oracle. In part, this might again have been due to the extent of product differentiation as well as to the ability of the supplier to customize the product.

Furthermore, it should be noted that, in such an innovative market, barriers to entry might have been high, and the likelihood of new entry low. The development of a product that would adequately compete might not have been likely to occur within a reasonable timeframe. In addition, the importance of software to a firm, and the risks associated with installing new systems (downtime, interoperability problems, or complete failure), might also have led to a degree of customer inertia.

As this analysis indicates, the Commission based its concerns in the Statement of Objections partly on the finding that there might be a significant group of customers for whom there could essentially be only one supplier left after the transaction. This concern was based on a definition of the market which, after the merger, would consist of only Oracle/PeopleSoft and SAP. In light of the conclusions regarding the market definition, the Commission did not uphold its preliminary conclusion that this group of customers would be confronted with a de facto absence of choice after the merger, since vendors such as Microsoft, Lawson, Intentia, IFS, QAD would also provide, according to the Commission, alternative options for customers.

The Commission mentioned that in the markets for high-function FMS and HR for large enterprises with complex functional needs, Oracle, PeopleSoft and SAP were the main players. Oracle, PeopleSoft and SAP were identified by 90 per cent or more of the respondents as possible suppliers of FMS or HR high-function solutions. Other players also occasionally won bids for high-function FMS and HR software to serve the needs of large enterprises with complex functional needs. Such other vendors of FMS and/or HR high-function software were Lawson, Intentia, IFS, QAD, and Microsoft. Those vendors won in only a limited number of bids, they qualified as runners-up in a larger number of bids for high-function FMS and HR software, and participated in bids with a licence value exceeding €1 million. Although, the Commission concluded that Lawson, Intentia, IFS, QAD, and Microsoft were vendors in the market for high-function FMS and HR software beside Oracle, PeopleSoft, and SAP,[62] the fact that these smaller firms had won a limited number of bids indicates the limited competitive constraints they would pose on the two remaining firms in the post-merger market.[63]

In addition, the extent to which Microsoft would provide such credible alternatives for customers in the high-function FMS and HR markets should be further doubted since, in its own publicly available information, Microsoft has mentioned that it will become even more important in the small and medium sized business market (which is the larger portion) through the supply of basic application functions.[64] In addition, in the Commission press release,[65] Microsoft is mentioned as a mid-market player that managed occasionally to win bids in the enterprise space. These comments do not confirm the Commission's argument that Microsoft would pose a significant competitive constraint on the two major firms in the post-merger market, so as to counteract the loss in the choices of consumers in the post-merger market.

As the DOJ argued, Oracle's proposed acquisition of PeopleSoft would substantially increase the already high concentration among vendors that sell high-function FMS and HRM software purchased by organizations. More specifically, the proposed transaction would eliminate aggressive head-to-head competition between Oracle and PeopleSoft and might result in higher prices, less innovation, and decreased support for these high-function integrated software applications.[66] The DOJ further stated that in the absence of continued competition from PeopleSoft, Oracle's incentives to continue to innovate and upgrade its products in order to win additional customers, and to maintain its current customers, would be substantially reduced.[67]

Finally, the DOJ suggested that the merger would lead to actual and potential competition between Oracle and PeopleSoft, and between these companies and others, in the development, provision, sale, and support of high-function HRM software, and that competition in the market for high-function FMS software would be eliminated or substantially lessened. Thus, the merger would lead to non-coordinated effects in oligopolistic markets since the competition between the merging parties as well as between these companies and other incumbents would be reduced.

As Werden (2005)[68] mentions in relation to this merger in the United States, significant unilateral effects can occur despite the presence of several rivals even if the merging products are not particularly close substitutes. Thus, the existence of a number of firms in the post-merger market (Microsoft, Lawson, etc.) offering products in the high-function FMS and HR markets, which arguably are not as efficient as the three majors' ones, does not preclude the existence of unilateral adverse effects on competition from the merger in the form of non-coordinated effects in the post-merger oligopolistic market.

As mentioned earlier, the Commission initially based its concerns on the finding of non-coordinated effects in the post-merger oligopolistic market. However, the Commission consequently focused and justified the lack of harm on competition on the existence of smaller players in the markets for high-function FMS and HR for large enterprises. Although, initially it claimed that the merger would lead to adverse effects on competition due to the limited choice available to customers, it subsequently argued that the existence of smaller players would provide credible and efficient alternatives to customers. However, as our analysis indicated, these remaining smaller players were not in a position to pose a significant competitive constraint on the merged entity as well as on SAP in the post-merger market and thus would not offer a credible alternative to SAP and

Oracle/PeopleSoft so as to prevent the last two firms from adopting conduct having an adverse impact on competition.

Thus, the Commission's analysis does not, in my opinion, clearly prove that the merger would not lead to any adverse effects on competition. Based on its analysis of the market structure post-merger, the nature of competition in this market, characterized by product differentiation, customization, knowledge of the customer, as well as innovation, the merger was likely to allow the two remaining suppliers Oracle and SAP to increase prices and reduce product offerings substantially, thereby acting independently of their competitors and customers and impeding effective competition. Although this effect would be particularly acute for the customers that after the merger would be faced with essentially only one potential supplier, the remaining competition between Oracle/PeopleSoft and SAP might have been insufficient to shield customers from significant harm.

The results arising from the event study[69] indicated that the Commission's decision contradicts the investors' perception on the day of the initial significant dissemination of information. The market expected *Oracle/PeopleSoft* to induce adverse effects on competition in the post-merger market.

Thus, *Oracle/PeopleSoft*, which was indeed consummated, could lead to non-coordinated effects in oligopolistic markets which the Commission, as is clearly mentioned in paragraph 187 of the decision, was not able to prevent due to the gap in the application of the dominance test on mergers leading to non-coordinated effects in oligopolistic markets.

4.2.3 Sony/BMG[70]

4.2.3.1 Analysis of the case

On 9 January 2004 the Commission received notification of a proposed concentration by which the undertakings Bertelsmann AG and Sony Corporation of America (the "parties") belonging to the Sony group would merge their global recorded music businesses. Bertelsmann was an international media company; its worldwide activities included music recording and publishing, television, radio, book publishing, magazines and newspapers, print and media services, and book and music clubs. Bertelsmann was active in recorded music through its wholly owned subsidiary, Bertelsmann Music Group ("BMG"). Sony was globally active in music recording and publishing, industrial and consumer electronics, and entertainment. In recorded music, it acted through Sony Music Entertainment.

The joint venture companies, which would be operated under the name SonyBMG, would be active in the discovery and the development of artists ("A&R") and the subsequent marketing and sale of recorded music. SonyBMG would not engage in related activities such as music publishing, manufacturing, and distribution.

The Commission defined a national market for recorded music which the parties considered as including A&R, and the promotion, sales and marketing of recorded music. However, it did not conclude whether the various genres constituted separate markets. In addition, the Commission defined a market for online music markets and distinguished the emerging wholesale market for licences for online music and the emerging retail market for distribution of online music, both of which were considered to be national in scope.

Finally, the Commission defined a market for music publishing which consisted of the acquisition by publishers of rights to musical works and their subsequent exploitation on remuneration, mostly in the form of a commission charged by the publisher to the author on the revenues generated by the commercial exploitation of musical works. The Commission left open further subdivision of this market but mentioned that there are some indications for the existence of separate product markets for music publishing according to the exploitation of the different categories of rights, namely mechanical, performance, synchronization, and printing. Regarding the geographic scope of the market for mechanical and performance rights, several elements pointed in the direction of national markets, in particular the fact that they were generally administered and collected by the national collecting societies on behalf of the publishers and/or authors/composers. The exact scope of the geographic market was, however, left open.

In assessing whether there was an existing collective dominant position in the markets for recorded music, the Commission analysed whether in the last three to four years prior to the merger a coordinated price policy of the majors[71] could be identified. In order to assess whether the majors' wholesale prices had been coordinated, the Commission first analysed the majors' pricing behaviour on the basis of their average wholesale net prices.[72] The Commission further examined whether any price coordination, on the basis of parallelism in average prices, could have been reached in using list prices (PPDs) as focal points. Finally, the Commission analysed whether the different majors' discounts were aligned and sufficiently transparent in order to allow efficient monitoring of any price coordination on the level of net prices.

On the basis of net average real prices, the Commission found some parallelism and a relatively similar price development of the majors. In addition, the Commission found some indications that PPDs could have been used as focal points for alignment of the majors. The Commission further found that the PPDs were rather transparent as they were available in the majors' catalogues. Monitoring of other majors' list pricing could therefore be possible. The Commission's analysis showed that transaction net prices were closely linked to gross prices (PPDs). However, the Commission found that the level of the different majors' discounts varied to some extent. Furthermore, it could not be established that invoice discounts were sufficiently aligned between the parties and although the Commission found that both Sony and BMG had set up a system of weekly reports by their salesforces, it could not be established that these reports ensured a sufficient degree of transparency of competitors' campaign discounts.

The Commission further analysed whether the markets for recorded music were characterized by features facilitating collective dominance. The heterogeneity in the content of recorded music, with its implications for pricing and reduced transparency in the market, rendered tacit collusion more difficult since it required some monitoring on the level of individual albums. Despite the fact that sales of albums take place in few price points, the variety of albums priced at different list prices could complicate the monitoring of a tacit agreement. In addition, the industry was characterized by long-term stable relationships between retailers and all majors. Moreover, a large part of the majors' sales of recorded music was channelled to a limited number of customers. This situation of a limited number of players in the market was conducive to the adoption of cooperative strategies on behalf of the majors and also facilitated the monitoring and information flow. The Commission could not prove, however, that by monitoring retail prices or by contacts with retailers, the majors had overcome in the past the deficits as regards the transparency of discounts.

As regards retaliation, the other majors could exclude the deviator from the conclusion of new joint ventures, they could refuse to license their songs for the deviator's compilations,[73] or they could even terminate some of the existing joint ventures. However, the Commission found no indications that, in response to a major's deviation from a common policy, other majors had been excluded from compilation joint ventures, that there had been a return to competitive behaviour as a retaliatory measure, or that retaliation had occurred in the online music market or music publishing markets. In addition, there was no evidence that threats of such retaliatory measures had been made, although the measures indicated earlier could represent credible retaliation mechanisms by recorded music market majors.

The Commission could not conclude from the observable degree of parallelism in average prices that there was an existing collective dominance of the majors in the markets for recorded music. The absence of fixed relationships between PPD and net price implied that coordination would be required at the level of invoice discounts. However, invoice discounts at album level exhibited significant variation and thus it would have been difficult to distinguish between deviation and adherence to the commonly adopted conduct.

The reduction of the majors from five to four, as a result of the merger, would lead to an increase in transparency as the number of bilateral competitive relations decreased from ten to six. However, as this analysis illustrates, the Commission did not find sufficient evidence that the five majors had held a collective dominant position in the past, in particular due to the deficits in actual transparency, the partly heterogeneous product characteristics and the lack of actual evidence as regards retaliatory action in the past. The Commission did not find sufficient evidence that a reduction from five to four majors would facilitate transparency and retaliation to such an extent that the creation of a collective dominant position of the remaining four majors would be anticipated as a likely outcome.

Third parties raised concerns that the joint venture would achieve a position of single dominance in the markets for recorded music due to the joint venture's vertical relationship to Bertelsmann's media interest in some member states.

Third parties raised further concerns that, as a result of the proposed transaction, Sony could obtain a position of single dominance in the national markets for distribution of online music via its Sony Connect music downloading service. The Commission did not allege any such anti-competitive effects as a result of the merger.

As regards the online music markets, the Commission concluded, given the emerging state of the market and the current structure of prices and usage conditions, that the reduction of the majors from five to four would increase neither transparency nor the possibility to retaliate to such an extent that these two factors would be likely to lead to the creation of a collective dominant position.

Thus, neither single firm nor collective dominance could be established as being the likely outcome of the merger. The Commission concluded that the concentration neither created nor strengthened a dominant position as a result of which effective competition would be significantly impeded in the common market or in a substantial part of it.[74]

Impala, the European association of independent music companies, in its appeal against the Commission's decision to approve the merger of Sony and BMG, alleged errors of law, as well as errors of assessment and reasoning, in relation to collective dominance in the recorded music market and the online wholesale licensing market. The General Court upheld Impala's appeal.

The Commission reassessed the merger based on the dominance test but taking into account the current market conditions, which are different (for example, online sales, the internet sales of music have gathered impetus) in comparison to the market conditions in 2004. The Commission was able to evaluate the actual impact of the merger on the market since 2004 and was not limited to an analysis of likely effects on the market in the future. It examined all national markets for recorded music in physical format and for the licensing of recorded music in digital format. The investigation focused in assessing the likelihood of the merger creating or reinforcing a collective dominant position of the major record producers. In its assessment of the merger, the Commission investigated all the various theories of price and non-price related coordination between major record companies.[75] It cleared the merger as it found no likely harm on competition.

It is the first time that the courts have upheld an appeal against a clearance decision of the Commission. The General Court argued that the Commission's decision was vitiated by a lack of reasoning and of supporting evidence. Thus, as is the case with prohibition decisions, the Commission must satisfy the high standard of proof in clearances.

The General Court decision arguably states that the *Airtours* criteria can also be established indirectly and seems to lower the threshold for a finding of collective dominance:

> [T]he three conditions defined by the Court of First Instance [General Court] in Airtours v Commission…may, however, in the appropriate circumstances, be established indirectly on the basis of what may be a very mixed series of indicia and items of evidence relating to the signs, manifestations and phenomena inherent in the presence of a collective dominant position.[76]

In particular, the General Court stated that:[77]

> [T]he alignment of prices, both gross and net, over the last six years, even though the products are not the same (each disc having a different content), and also the fact that they were maintained at such a stable level, and at a level seen as high in spite of a significant fall in demand, together with other factors (power of the undertakings in an oligopoly situation, stability of market shares, etc.), as established by the Commission in the Decision, might, in the absence of an alternative explanation, suggest, or constitute an indication, that the alignment of prices is not the result of the normal play of effective competition and that the market is sufficiently transparent in that it allowed tacit price coordination.

The General Court seems to say that presence of mere indicia of coordinated effects may be sufficient for the Commission to conclude that a dominant position already exists. It can be argued that the evidentiary burden could be shifted onto the parties faced with an issue of collective dominance to establish the type of alternative explanation referred to by the General Court in this paragraph.[78]

As regards transparency, the General Court argued that the argument that promotional discounts reduced transparency was not "supported by a statement of reasons of the requisite legal standard and [is] vitiated by a manifest error of assessment".

The General Court stated that:[79]

> [T]he findings made in the Decision concerning the transparency of the market are not supported by a statement of reasons of the

> requisite legal standard and are vitiated by a manifest error of assessment in that they do not rest on an examination of all the relevant data that must be taken into consideration and are not capable of supporting the conclusion that the market is not sufficiently transparent to permit a collective dominant position.

As regards retaliation, the General Court stated that:[80]

> [T]wo cumulative elements must be satisfied in order for the fact that no retaliatory measures have been employed to be taken to mean that the condition relating to retaliation is not satisfied, namely proof of deviation from the common course of conduct, without which there is no need to consider the use of retaliatory measures, and then actual proof of the absence of retaliatory measures.

The General Court argued that the Commission did not set out the necessary proof in the decision as regards these two cumulative elements. The Commission relied on the absence of evidence of retaliatory measures having been used in the past, whereas it is only sufficient that the deterrent mechanisms exist. The General Court stated that the decision and case file had revealed the existence of such mechanisms.

4.2.3.2 A gap case?

When investigating whether the merger would lead to non-coordinated effects in an oligopolistic market, it would be worth examining the degree of concentration in the recorded music market. The analysis will focus on the market shares of the parties as well as the concentration ratios and the HHIs.[81] The number of firms in the post-merger market would decrease from five to four players. The decision of the Commission refers to ranges of market shares of the merging parties as well as of their competitors. Thus, in this analysis the average of the range for each incumbent will be used in order to calculate the respective post-merger HHI, the change in the HHI, and concentration ratios.[82]

The post-merger HHI is equal to 2231.25, the change in the HHI is 312.5, the pre-merger CR3 is 60 per cent excluding Sony and BMG,[83] the pre-merger CR4 is 70 per cent, the post-merger CR3 is 65 per cent and the post-merger CR4 is 80 per cent. As is indicated by these figures, the market was concentrated. It should be noted at this point that, as already mentioned, the market shares as well as concentration ratios and HHIs can only provide an initial indication as to the effects of the merger and are not conclusive.

Non-coordinated effects might arise if the merger would remove any incentives among the members of the oligopoly to compete aggressively on price or in the A&R sector in the aftermath of the merger. Assuming a heterogeneous product, with limited supply and demand substitution, it is difficult for rivals to react to price changes. The market characteristics of the recorded music business and the heterogeneity of the product therefore might result in post-merger price increases since the incumbents might not be able to fully compensate for the decrease in the quantity by the other incumbents or benefit from the other incumbents' increase in price. In addition, the incumbents in the post-merger market would have more incentives to increase prices, since the loss in the demand of their product might not be substantial due to the heterogeneity of their product and thus due to the limited customer switching towards the other incumbents' products.

With product differentiation, firms are able to adjust prices without losing the entire market. In such cases, prices do not rapidly collapse to marginal cost (as would be the case under perfect competition) and hence mergers are profitable for all the firms in the market. Even if the differentiated products of the merging firms are not close substitutes, the adverse impact of the merger on competition in the market may in some circumstances be substantial. The bigger the number of firms in the market the less substantial, although it is likely to be as these firms account for small portion of the demand and thus may not find it profitable enough to increase prices, due to the risk of switching. On the contrary, if the market is oligopolistic and the merger increases concentration further, then the scope for the incumbents in the post-merger market to increase prices is greater, since even in the presence of some switching, the price increase will still be profitable as they account for a substantial portion of the demand.

When firms compete in prices, these prices are often complements, in the sense that an increase in the price of one good will typically lead competing firms to increase their own prices although probably to a lesser extent. An increase in the merging firms' prices triggers a positive response from the other firms, thereby further encouraging the merging firms to raise their own prices. Because of the complementarity of the prices, the direct impact of the merger on the behaviour of the new firm is exacerbated by the rival firms' adaptation to the new market structure.

Thus, there might be reduced incentives for the four remaining majors to compete aggressively on price or in the A&R sector, resulting in harm to consumers due to the likely higher prices for recorded music or likely restriction of the variety of output. The majors accounted for a large share of the market for recorded music, and especially for international acts.[84] There was some evidence that the influence of the independents[85] was lower. Particularly in the international segment, where, due to the necessity for a wide distribution network and significant marketing budget, barriers to entry might be higher, this merger was likely to lead to non-coordinated effects in such an oligopolistic market.[86]

In addition, the independents were not close competitors of the majors and could not impose effective competitive constraints. They were characterized by a much smaller organization, a focus on A&R and recording, more than on the rest of the value chain, by operations taking place mainly on a national scale, although a limited number of successful independents also had international operations that covered only a limited number of member states. For international representation of their artists, they needed to conclude licensing agreements with majors or other independents. In addition, they did not generally have their own manufacture and distribution facilities and for (international) distribution the independents often depended on the majors' distribution networks. Independents, furthermore, had a much more limited budget for promotional and marketing expenditure, which made them less attractive for international artists, had a frequent focus on a particular repertoire (classical, dance, etc.), and limited access to mass media, in particular radio and television.[87]

Thus, the dependence of independents on majors for distribution, manufacture, and international representation as well as the limited scope of the activities and of the product of independents (mainly national market and national artists) rendered them an ineffective competitor and imposed a weak competitive constraint.

In addition, neither countervailing buyer power nor *de novo* entry was likely to pose credible constraints on the likely harmful conduct of the incumbents in the post-merger market. As far as countervailing buyer power is concerned, in certain member states a large part of the majors' sales of recorded music was channelled to a limited number of customers and there was certain stability in the customer base of the majors.[88] The customer base might be relatively concentrated in some member states (for example the United Kingdom, France) with large customers such as supermarkets, and chains such as Virgin, FNAC, and HMV. However, this might not have been the case for other member states, where the customer base was significantly fragmented and smaller and thus specialized music retailers might not possess the same amount of buyer power that the larger retailers may hold. Finally, due to the complicated structure of the market, including licences, IP rights, etc., network effects, and the presence of four majors in the post-merger market, entry by a new firm might not have been likely in the event of an increase in prices.

The General Court criticized the Commission for the change in its position between the Statement of Objections and the decision. After five months of investigation, the Commission had concluded in the Statement of Objections that the concentration would lead to the creation or strengthening of collective dominance. After the oral hearing on 14 and 15 June 2004, the Commission altered its assessment and, two weeks later, circulated a draft decision approving the concentration. The input of the chief economist's team as well as of the devil's advocate panel seem to have played an essential role in proving that a collective dominance argument could not be sustained.[89] Their input did not prove the lack of any anticompetitive effects, but was focused on the sustainability of the theory of harm the Commission had used (that is to say, collective dominance). The General Court stated that the Commission could not fully explain this sudden change in the outcome of its assessment. The General Court concluded that the Commission had carried out a superficial analysis which was vitiated by an error of law, or at the very least by a manifest error of assessment.

The General Court's decision did not prove the sustainability of collective dominance. Rather it proved the inadequacy of the Commission's reasoning regarding the lack of the factors contributing to sustainable collective dominance. In addition, the market was not one that an allegation of single dominance could be sustained. However, this analysis illustrates that the merger may have led to anticompetitive effects in the post-merger market. The market characteristics of the recorded music business and the heterogeneity of the product therefore might result in post-merger price increases since the incumbents might not be able to fully compensate for the decrease in the quantity by the other incumbents or benefit from the other incumbents' increase in price. Furthermore, as already mentioned, the incumbents in the post-merger market would have more incentives to increase prices, since the loss in the demand of their product might not be substantial due to the heterogeneity of their product and thus due to the limited customer switching towards the other incumbents' products.

In my opinion, the inability of the Commission to block the merger under the dominance test led it to clear it rather than take the risk of prohibiting it, as was the case in the *Airtours/First Choice* merger, which was annulled by the General Court.[90] The Commission, as the General Court also noted, had identified harm to competition arising from that merger in the course of the investigation, culminating in the Statement of Objections. The inadequacy of explanation of the reasons for clearance, as also indicated by the sudden change in the Commission's approach which was criticized by the General Court, led the General Court to, correctly, annul the decision. Had the Commission been able to assess that merger under the SIEC test, it would have been able to block it (or request remedies)[91] without bearing the same risk of successful appeal by the parties.

As our analysis indicates, although the merger was not likely to lead either to single firm dominance or to collective dominance, it might have led to non-coordinated effects in the post-merger oligopolistic market. Post-merger the majors were likely to have less incentive to compete since they could benefit from price increases due to, inter alia, the heterogeneity of the product, the ineffective competitive constraints imposed by the independents, and the likely significant barriers to entry. These factors could contribute to the *Sony/BMG* merger inducing non-coordinated effects in the oligopolistic market for recorded music.

The results arising from the event study[92] indicated that the Commission's decision contradicts the investors' perception on the day of the initial significant dissemination of information. The market expected *Sony/BMG* to induce an adverse impact on competition in the post-merger market.

The *Sony/BMG* merger was also investigated by the FTC, which took no enforcement action. Throughout the course of their respective investigations, the FTC and the Commission consulted and cooperated. Unfortunately the closing letters sent by the FTC to the parties and a statement by Commissioner Mozelle W. Thompson are the only publicly available documents regarding this action.

Commissioner Thompson argued that:[93]

> The history of facilitating practices in the music industry, coupled with the elimination of Sony and BMG as independent competitors, causes me concern. The music industry has been scrutinized closely in the past by the Commission in connection with proposed mergers and with practices ranging from alleged anticompetitive Minimum Advertised Price ("MAP") programs[3] to agreements to fix prices and limit advertising.[4] The industry is highly concentrated among record labels, and the proposed joint venture will only enhance this concentration. Additionally, the history of parallel MAP policies in particular indicates a propensity for interdependent behavior among the major labels.

Since we do not have the FTC's reasoning in clearing the merger, no critical analysis can be made on the FTC's decision. From the publicly available documents we have Commissioner Thompson who argued that:[94] "The evidence tends to show growing clout among retailers that may be enough to undermine a potential collective exercise of market power on the part of the major labels."

Commissioner Thompson's argument is that increasing buyer power can mitigate any anticompetitive effects. The situation is the EU is slightly different, however, as regards buyer power. As mentioned already, the customer base might be relatively concentrated in some member states (for example the United Kingdom, France) with large customers such as supermarkets, and chains such as Virgin, FNAC, and HMV. However, this might not have been the case for other member states, where the customer base was significantly fragmented and smaller and thus specialized music retailers might not possess the same amount of buyer power that the larger retailers may hold. Thus, the Commission could have addressed any anticompetitive effects that may arise in these member states had it assessed the merger under an SLC/SIEC test.

In addition, the market structure of the EU is different to the United States. In the EU, there are multiple national markets with artists that are "constrained" to these national boundaries.[95] Thus, the merger of Sony/BMG would bring together some of these artists in each national market (the merged entity could have the biggest artists in some countries) and thus the merger could impede effective competition in these member states.[96] In the United States, there are no national boundaries and, thus, the sale of the songs of various artists are not constrained by any national boundaries.

It is also worth noting the wider likely implications of the uncertainty that is created from such occurrences where the Commission might have cleared or blocked a merger based on the wrong criteria. EMI and Warner had been in discussions about a possible merger. However, after the General Court's annulment the two companies announced that they would abandon their merger plans at that stage since the General Court's judgment cast doubt on whether regulators would allow further consolidation in the music industry. "Nothing can happen here until this antitrust case is redetermined and reassessed. It's pretty hard to do anything with the Sony BMG situation going on," a person familiar with the decision said. "Quite frankly there is a timing issue."[97] If the Commission had initially assessed the Sony/BMG merger under the SIEC test, then it might have imposed remedies to the parties and thus enhance legal certainty to the industry about the future of consolidation. In such a case, the EMI/Warner merger might have gone ahead in the expectation of, inter alia, a clearance with undertakings.

4.2.4 *Syngenta CP/Advanta*[98]

4.2.4.1 Analysis of the case

Syngenta and its subsidiaries were a multinational group of companies whose focus was on crop protection and seeds. Syngenta CP was a 100 per cent subsidiary of Syngenta. Advanta and its subsidiaries were active in the breeding, production, processing, packaging, and sale of various kinds of seed worldwide. Advanta operated across North America, Europe and Australia, Asia, and Africa. The ultimate purpose of the whole transaction was for Syngenta CP to acquire and retain the North American maize, soybean, and cereals business units of Advanta.[99]

The transaction affected the seed markets, (sugar beet seeds, maize seeds, sunflower seeds, oilseed rape seeds, spring barley seeds, pea seeds, and onion seeds in the EU), as well as markets for seed treatment products in the EEA.[100]

The seed industry can in general be described as a two stage industry: breeding and commercial production of seeds. The first stage comprises the breeding and biotechnology programmes leading to the development of seed varieties that are produced as "parent seeds". Breeders attempt to develop new varieties with desirable characteristics such as low production cost, high yield, low impurities, and resistance to disease.[101] The second stage comprises production of commercial quantities of the seed, including cleaning and processing, chemical treatment and pelleting, marketing, and distribution. These activities were less specialized and could be successfully carried out on a smaller scale by producer firms under licence agreements or contracts with breeders.

As mentioned earlier, the transaction affected several markets, for sugar beet seeds, maize seeds, sunflower seeds, oilseed rape seeds, spring barley seeds, pea seeds, and onion seeds in the EU. The Commission left open further segmentation of the oilseed rape seeds into winter and spring oilseed rape seeds since the merger did not raise any doubts. As regards the market pea seeds, the Commission further focused on the market for vining peas. As regards onion seeds, the Commission left open whether the market should be further divided into spring onions and common or ordinary onions.

As regards the relevant geographic market for the seed markets, prices and supply conditions to final consumers differed in various member states, and commercial seed was, to a substantial degree, customized (for example, disease resistance, chemical treatments, size of seeds, etc.) to suit the conditions of each country or regional area. In addition, official trials were conducted in the respective member states to assure quality control.[102] Thus, the Commission concluded that the relevant geographic market should be national in scope.

As regards the market for seed treatment, the Commission's market investigation indicated that seed treatment constituted a separate market. Seed treatment entails the treatment ("dressing") of seeds with specific formulations in order to protect the seeds in the early stages of their development.[103] Seed treatment producers such as Syngenta sold their products either to seed companies such as Advanta, to wholesalers, to dealers/cooperatives or directly to large farmers.[104] The seed treatment market could be subdivided into insecticides and fungicides and might again be split by crop since crop protection and seed treatment products targeted different pests, registration regulations differed and the customers and distribution channels were not identical. The Commission's market investigation indicated that the geographic scope was national but the Commission left the geographic definition open since the merger would not lead to any competition concerns in these markets.

HORIZONTALLY AFFECTED MARKETS

Sugar beet seeds This chapter turns now to the competitive assessment of these markets. The merger in the market for sugar beet seeds would lead to high combined market shares in Belgium (50 to 60 per cent), in Finland (70 to 80 per cent), in France (40 to 50 per cent), in the Netherlands (60 to 70 per cent), in Portugal (60 to 70 per cent), and in Spain (50 to 60 per cent). The market share in the EU would be 30 to 40 per cent. In Austria, Greece, Ireland and a proportion of the market in Italy, the parties licensed their basic seeds to the local sugar industry instead of supplying commercial seeds. The sugar industry then produced the commercial seeds itself and sold them to the local farmers. Thus, there was a relatively large discrepancy between the market share in volume and the market share in value (which was limited to only 10 to 30 per cent of the market value corresponding to the reported volume).[105]

The Commission further stated that that increases and decreases in market shares in the seeds business followed rather slow cycles and did not occur abruptly, which was related to the necessary timeframe for the development, breeding, testing and commercialization of a new variety.[106]

The main competitor of the merged entity was KWS with 40 to 50 per cent in Belgium, 15 to 20 per cent in Finland, 30 to 40 per cent in France, 30 to 40 per cent in the Netherlands, 10 to 15 per cent in Portugal and 15 to 20 per cent in Spain. Thus, in Finland, the Netherlands, Portugal, and Spain, the new combined entity would be more than double or three times the size of its closest competitor. In Belgium and France the parties would be the market leader. The remaining market shares would almost entirely be held by KWS.[107] In Austria, Ireland, and Italy, Syngenta was already the market leader before the proposed acquisition (a position that would be further enhanced following the acquisition), with more than double the market share of its closest competitor.

As these market share figures indicate, the sugar beet market was already a highly concentrated one. The Commission's investigation indicated that reducing the number of competitors in such an already highly concentrated market would lessen the ability of other companies to compete and thus act as competitive constraints on the new entity.[108]

Moreover, the seeds industry was a research-based industry (R&D plays a crucial role in the seed industry) and competition could be described more as "competition for the market" than "competition in the market". Companies that were active in the seeds business competed to develop a variety that would be the sole choice of the farmers.[109] As regards countervailing buyer power, the Commission suggested that sugar companies exercised a relatively strong bargaining power vis-à-vis the sugar producers. However, the Commission pointed out that this bargaining power might not be sufficiently strong to offset the market power of the already highly concentrated sugar beet suppliers.

The Commission concluded that the parties' high combined market shares and significant overlaps, and the reduction in the number of major sugar beet producers creating a strong market leader in a R&D-based industry, might significantly impede effective competition by the creation of a dominant position of the merged entity in the market for sugar beet seeds in Finland, the Netherlands, Portugal, Spain, Austria, Ireland, and Italy, and by the creation of non-coordinated effects in an oligopolistic market for sugar beet seeds in Belgium and France.[110]

Maize seeds Turning to the market for maize seeds: the proposed transaction would reduce the number of suppliers to five and create the second biggest supplier of maize seeds in Europe with a market share of 15 to 20 per cent (in 2003 value). However, the most important player at the European level was Pioneer, with a market share of 30 to 40 per cent; other competitors were Limagrain (10 to 15 per cent), KWS (10 to 15 per cent) and RAGT (5 to 10 per cent). Based on the Commission's analysis,[111] the merger might significantly impede effective competition by the creation of a dominant position of the merged entity in the market for maize seeds in Denmark, the Netherlands, and the United Kingdom.

Sunflower seeds The parties' combined market share would be 30 to 40 per cent. The parties' main competitors in the market for sunflower seeds on a Europe-wide market were Monsanto (20 to 30 per cent), Pau Euralis (10 to 15 per cent), Pioneer (5 to 10 per cent) and KWS (2 to 5 per cent). The Commission concluded that the merger would significantly impede effective competition by the creation of a dominant position of the merged entity in the market for sunflower seeds in Hungary and Spain.

Spring barley seeds – pea seeds As far as the markets for spring barley seeds and pea seeds were concerned, the Commission concluded that the merger might significantly impede effective competition in France for spring barley seeds and in the market for vining pea seeds in the United Kingdom.

Oilseed rape seeds – onion seeds As regards the markets for oilseed rape seeds and onion seeds, the Commission concluded that the merger would not lead to an adverse impact on competition.

VERTICALLY AFFECTED MARKETS

Turning to the vertical impact of the transaction, the Commission stated that vertically affected markets existed where Syngenta was a supplier of seed treatment destined to treat a certain seed crop, and Advanta was a supplier of the seed crop concerned; it also stated that either Syngenta had a market share of 25 per cent or more in the seed treatment market and the geographic market concerned, or that Advanta had either alone or together with Syngenta a market share of 25 per cent or more in the seed market and the geographic market concerned.[112] The Commission concluded that there was no likelihood of any foreclosure effects. In addition, the existence of competitors with a significant market share gave customers adequate alternatives. Thus, no competition concerns were identified.

The parties offered commitments to alleviate the Commission's concerns that consisted of the divestment of Advanta's European business. The divested business consisted of all companies belonging to the Advanta group incorporated in Europe (including Russia and Turkey), with the exception of Advanta Technology Ltd UK, a company that owned or had the right to certain IP rights related primarily to Advanta's North American maize and soybean operations.[113]

4.2.4.2 A gap case?

As mentioned earlier, the Commission argued that the merger might lead to the creation of non-coordinated effects in an oligopolistic market for sugar beet seeds in Belgium and France.[114] The merger would lead to high combined market shares in Belgium (50 to 60 per cent), and France (40 to 50 per cent). The main competitor was KWS with 40 to 50 per cent in Belgium, and 30 to 40 per cent in France. In Belgium and France, the parties would have been the market leader but the remaining market shares would almost entirely have been held by KWS.

The merger might not have been blocked by the Commission had it been assessed under the dominance test. It should be noted at this point that although the merged entity would have been the market leader in Belgium and France, the remaining market shares were attributed only to one competitor (KWS). Thus, in the post-merger market there were two main firms with roughly equal market shares.[115]

As the Commission mentioned, the seeds industry was a research-based industry (R&D plays a crucial role in the seed industry) and competition could be described more as "competition for the market" than "competition in the market". The aim of companies in this market was to compete in order to develop a variety that would be the sole choice of the farmers.[116] Furthermore, the market shares showed relative stability over time, countervailing buyer power was deemed insufficient to pose a significant constraint to the merged entity, and entry barriers were high due to the costly and time-consuming process of entry in such an innovative market. These factors, which would contribute to a significant impediment to competition, would have influenced the Commission's assessment of the merger under the dominance test as well.

Although the factors that would lead to an allegation that the merger would lead to single dominance were prevalent, had the Commission assessed the merger under the dominance test, it would not, in my opinion, have been able to allege that the merger leads to adverse effects on competition in Belgium and France. With the largest competitor in both markets having approximately equal market shares, the Commission would not be able to allege single firm dominance, since the market share of KWS was too high for the merged entity to be regarded as having the ability to unilaterally adversely affect competition.

In previous merger cases involving similar products and similar market conditions, the Commission alleged that the merger would have led to single firm dominance with the largest competitor having a much wider difference in the market share compared to the merged entity. The two following mergers, involving similar products, assessed under the dominance test illustrate the relative market shares that the Commission considered as indicative of single firm dominance.

In *Astra Zeneca/Novartis*,[117] as regards the cereal fungicide markets, the Commission believed that the merger would lead to the creation of a dominant position on the Spanish sugar beet fungicide market. The merged entity would have 50 to 60 per cent of the market. Dupont had a market share of 10 to 20 per cent. No producer had been identified by the parties for the remaining 30 to 40 per cent of the market. The market investigation indicated that Bayer and Cyanamid had each around zero to 5 per cent market share.

As regards the market for maize herbicides:[118]

> On the basis of ... the high market shares that the new combination will have, the fact that the new entity will typically be at least [.]* times as large as its next competitor and the strong and ubiquitous presence of the parties' products in all four segments of the maize herbicide market (preemergence and post-emergence, grass weed control and broadleaf control), the Commission concludes that the notified operation will lead to the creation of a dominant position in the market for maize herbicides in at least France, Germany, the Netherlands and Belgium.

In addition, the Commission concluded that the merger would lead to the creation of a dominant position on the Belgian and French markets for potato herbicides. In Belgium and France, the merged entity had a market share of 50 to 60 per cent, while the largest competitor had 20 to 30 per cent.

Moreover, the Commission concluded that the merger would lead to the creation of a dominant position on the Austrian botrytis market. The merged entity would have 50 to 60 per cent. The next competitor was Bayer with 10 to 20 per cent, and Agrolinz, Aventis and Cyanamid each having less than 5 to 10 per cent.[119]

In *Bayer/Aventis Crop Science*,[120] the Commission reached the conclusion that the proposed transaction would create or strengthen a dominant position on the market for soil insecticides for bananas in Spain. The parties' combined market share according to their own estimation amounted to 40 to 50 per cent. The largest competitor according to the parties was FMC 20 to 30 per cent while DuPont accounted for zero to 10 per cent of the market. Generic companies together had 20 to 30 per cent market share.[121]

Furthermore, the Commission concluded that the proposed transaction would create or strengthen a dominant position on the market for foliar insecticides for beets in France. The parties' combined market share was, according to their own estimate, 40–50 per cent, and was relatively stable over time. BASF was the largest competitor with 20–30 per cent of the market, followed by Syngenta with 20–30 per cent.

The Commission also concluded that the proposed transaction would create or strengthen a dominant position on the market for soil insecticides for beets in Italy. The parties' combined market share amounted to 40 to 50 per cent while Syngenta had 10 to 20 per cent of the market.[122] Moreover, the Commission reached the conclusion that the merger would create or strengthen a dominant position on the market for foliar insecticides for citrus fruit in Portugal. The parties' combined market share was 40 to 50 per cent, while Syngenta had 20 to 30 per cent.[123]

The Commission further concluded that the merger would create or strengthen a dominant position on the market for foliar insecticides for cotton in Greece where the parties' combined market share amounted to 40 to 50 per cent, BASF was the largest competitor with 10 to 20 per cent market share, Syngenta, Dow and Du Pont each had zero to 10 per cent, and were local and generic competitors accounted for 20 to 30 per cent of the market.

Thus, in *Bayer/Aventis Crop Science*, the Commission alleged that the merger would lead to single dominance since the merged entity would be the largest firm in the post-merger market having a significant difference in the market share from the second largest competitor.

As this analysis of the *Astra Zeneca/Novartis* and *Bayer/Aventis Crop Science* cases indicates, the Commission, in assessing these two mergers under the dominance test, alleged that the mergers in these cases would lead to single dominance with the merged entity and the second biggest competitor having a significant difference in the market shares of at least 20 per cent on average.[124]

Specifically, in *Bayer/Aventis Crop Science*, the Commission considered:[125]

> [T]hat competition concerns are unlikely to arise on these markets for one or more of the following reasons: ... and there are strong competitors who are likely to be able to provide effective competition on the market.

Thus, the Commission assessing the merger under the dominance test did not allege any anticompetitive effects due to the presence of strong competitors.

On the contrary, in *Syngenta CP/Advanta*, the Commission, in assessing the merger under the significant impediment to competition test stated:[126]

> The parties' combined share would be 50–60 per cent in Belgium, 40–50 per cent in France, 60–70 per cent ... The main competitor is KWS with [40–50] per cent in Belgium, [30–40] per cent in France ... In Belgium and France the parties would be the market leader ... The remaining market shares would almost entirely be held by KWS.

Thus, contrary to the Commission's argument regarding the strong competitors of the merged entity in *Bayer/Aventis Crop Science*, the Commission in *Syngenta CP/Advanta* alleged that the merger would lead to adverse competition effects by the creation of non-coordinated effects in an oligopolistic market, even though the merged entity and its largest competitor had roughly equal market shares. The Commission, based on the same argument (that is to say strong competitors), reached a different conclusion as regards the effects of the merger under the dominance and the SIEC test.

Although, as already mentioned, market shares are only indications of the likely adverse impact of the merger on competition, and assuming that the remaining factors that could contribute to an adverse effect on competition are the same in the *Syngenta CP/Advanta* under both substantive tests (for example, barriers to entry, stable market shares, buyer power), the Commission would not, in my opinion be able to block the merger under the dominance test. Contrary to the Commission's approach in *Astra Zeneca/Novartis* and *Bayer/Aventis Crop Science*, the approximately equal levels of market shares of the merged entity and its closest competitor in *Syngenta CP/Advanta* would prevent the Commission from concluding that the merger would lead to a creation or strengthening of a dominant position.

As regards collective dominance, it should first be noted that the Commission did not allege that the merger would lead to coordinated effects in the markets for Belgium and France, but rather to non-coordinated effects.[127] In addition, the markets involved in *Syngenta CP/Advanta* were innovative markets with competition being "for the market" rather than "in the market".[128]

Furthermore, the existence of IP rights rendered any successful coordination of the post-merger conduct of the merged entity and KWS difficult, since the IP rights provide a clear competitive advantage to the IP rights owner and thus reduce the incentives to coordinate his/her conduct. As the Commission stated in the decision, the success of a newly launched variety can be foiled in its entirety by a slightly better variety of a competitor.[129] Thus, the two members of the duopoly had a great incentive to produce a slightly better variety and gain increased market share. Companies in the Belgian and French market strived to develop a variety of seeds that would be the sole choice of the farmers. Thus, the firm that would develop such a variety was unlikely to have an incentive to coordinate its behaviour with a competitor since it had the ability to unilaterally capture a big share of the market due to its technological innovations.

A rapidly innovative market makes tacit collusion less likely since it alters several essential structural features of the market such as product range and quality. As the *Guidelines* mention: "[I]n markets where innovation is important, coordination may be more difficult since innovations, particularly significant ones, may allow one firm to gain a major advantage over its rivals."[130]

In addition, in an industry characterized by R&D, the cost structure of firms is likely to be asymmetric due to the variation in the investment that has been devoted to the development of new products. Different innovation rates contribute to variations in the range of products available and engender agreement on a set of prices or quantities for these products difficult to achieve and sustain. Thus, the market position of the firms is influenced by the asymmetry in costs; this renders tacit collusion an unlikely outcome. The Commission in *Nestlé*[131] argued that asymmetries in cost structure would inhibit parallel behaviour. In *Enso/Stora*,[132] the similarities in the cost structures of the firms constituted a significant indication of an increased likelihood of achieving a sustainable tacitly collusive outcome. Thus, the likely asymmetry in the costs involved in the production of the sugar beet seeds was a countervailing factor to the sustainability of a collective dominant position by the merged entity and KWS.

In addition, the products of the merged entity and KWS were differentiated due to, inter alia, the innovative nature of the market. As is stated in the decision, recommendations were of key importance for the market performance of the sugar beet seed products, as sugar beet seeds that were not listed in recommendation lists would normally not be saleable at all. Therefore, the launch of new varieties, which were included in the recommendation lists issued each year, usually led to substantial increases in market share. By the same token, the varieties that were replaced on the recommendation list would exit the market. Thus, each new variety could constitute a slightly differentiated product. The recommendation list included all the varieties of sugar beet seeds; all of these were slightly differentiated products due to their different qualities and attributes.

Differentiated products contribute to asymmetries in the market and lead to the creation of a considerable imbalance between the members of the oligopoly. This imbalance reduces the incentives for collusion. Heterogeneous products make comparison of prices more difficult, leading consequently to inefficient detection of cheating, and thus mitigate the sustainability of collusive outcomes.[133]

The results arising from the event study[134] indicated that the Commission's decision coincides with the investors' perception on the day of the initial significant dissemination of information regarding the adverse effects of *Syngenta CP/Advanta* on competition.

Thus, as the preceding analysis indicates, if the merger between Syngenta CP and Advanta had been assessed under the dominance test, the Commission might not be able, in my opinion, to allege that the merger would lead to either single firm dominance or collective dominance. Although, the Commission argued that the merger would lead to non-coordinated effects in the markets for sugar beet seeds in Belgium and France, it could not have alleged, if the merger had been assessed under the dominance test, that the merger would lead to adverse competition effects in the Belgian and French markets.

4.2.5 Johnson & Johnson/Guidant[135]

4.2.5.1 Analysis of the case

The Commission received a notification of a proposed concentration by which the undertaking Johnson & Johnson ("J&J") would acquire control of the whole of the undertaking Guidant Corporation ("Guidant") by way of a purchase of shares.

The transaction involved four main areas within the cardiovascular medical products business:

- interventional cardiology devices
- endovascular devices
- cardiac surgery devices
- cardiac rhythm management devices.
  All markets were deemed to be national in scope.

Interventional cardiology is a field of heart medicine dedicated to research and technology for minimally invasive procedures to treat coronary artery diseases. These procedures include the dilatation of narrowed or blocked coronary blood vessels using a balloon catheter and often a stent,[136] which is inserted into the cardiovascular system via an artery most often using the groin as an entry point.[137]

As regards interventional cardiology devices, the Commission found that coronary bare metal stents ("BMSs") and drug eluting stents ("DESs") constituted separate markets. In addition, the Commission concluded that coronary guiding catheters, coronary steerable guidewires and coronary percutaneous transluminal coronary angioplasty ("PTCA") balloon catheters formed relevant product markets. A guiding catheter is a long, hollow tube manufactured from a polymer blend that is inserted into the radial or femoral artery and is advanced to the origin of the coronary arteries. A steerable guidewire ("SGW") is a very thin and flexible wire that is advanced though the guiding catheter beyond the narrowed area of the artery that requires dilatation. A PTCA balloon catheter is a long, flexible, hollow tube with a balloon at the end.

Endovascular devices are used for the minimally invasive treatment of peripheral vascular (or endovascular) diseases. The Commission identified markets for endovascular stents, which are small expandable tubes designed to treat a narrowing or blockage in a peripheral artery. The market inquiry confirmed separate markets for balloon expandable stents ("BX") and self-expandable stents ("SX") due to the different applications, price (SX stents are more expensive than BX) and limited supply side substitutability between SX and BX stents (due to different design, material, deployment techniques, and manufacturing processes). Furthermore, within the SX stents, a separate market for carotid stents was defined.[138] The Commission concluded that there were separate product markets for carotid stents, for non-carotid SX stents and for BX stents. The last market in particular included highly differentiated products, such as renal stents and iliac-femoral stents.[139]

Moreover, the Commission identified separate product markets for the endovascular products: (i) guiding catheters, (ii) SGWs, (iii) percutaneous transluminal angioplasty ("PTA") balloon catheters.[140] The Commission further concluded that embolic protection devices ("EPDs") formed a relevant product market. EPDs are small umbrella-type devices that are mounted on a catheter and placed beyond the lesion with the aim of trapping any material or debris dislodged during the angioplasty procedure.[141]

As far as cardiac surgery devices are concerned, the Commission defined a market for beating-heart stabilization systems.[142] It also defined a market for blowers/misters and endoscopic vessel harvesting systems. Blowers/misters are ancillary products that are used in conjunction with the stabilization systems. Endoscopic vessel harvesting ("EVH") systems enable the surgeon to harvest the vein necessary for coronary artery bypass graft ("CABG") surgery procedure via a keyhole-sized incision in the leg or in the arm.

Finally, the Commission left open the market for cardiac rhythm management devices due to the inexistence of a horizontal overlap. Cardiac rhythm management devices are used for the treatment of severe heart rhythm disorders as arrhythmia (irregular heart beat), bradycardia (abnormally slow heartbeat), and tachycardia (abnormally fast heartbeat).[143]

As far as steerable guidewires are concerned, the merger would result in a quasi-monopoly situation in some member states. Guidewires in general are only moderately differentiated products.

The merger was likely to result in a significant impediment to effective competition in the common market and the EEA for steerable guidewires as a result of the strengthening of Guidant's dominant position.[144]

As far as the market for endovascular devices is concerned, J&J supplied the following endovascular devices in Europe: stents, PTA balloon catheters, guiding catheters, diagnostic catheters, catheter sheath introducers, steerable guidewires, diagnostic guidewires, embolic protection devices, venous products, thrombectomy systems, AAA stent graft systems, and accessories.[145] Guidant produced and sold a more limited line of endovascular products including stents, PTA balloon catheters, guiding catheters, steerable guidewires, and embolic protection devices.[146]

As far as the balloon expandable stents of the endovascular stents were concerned, J&J and Guidant were two of the strongest players, and there were high barriers to entry and insufficient countervailing buyer power. The merger would combine the leader and the number two in the BX stent markets. The Commission concluded that in the markets for BX stents in Austria, Belgium, France, Germany, Italy, Luxembourg, Netherlands, Portugal, and Spain, the concentration would result in the removal of the closest and strongest competitor to the market leader, J&J. The merger would therefore significantly impede effective competition in the markets for BX stents in these countries, in particular as a result of the creation of a dominant position.[147]

As far as the carotid stents of the endovascular stents were concerned, the three main players were J&J, Guidant, and Boston Scientific, together accounting for between 83 and 96 per cent of the market. The concentration would either reinforce the leadership of J&J or Guidant (in Austria, Finland, Netherlands, Portugal, and Spain), or combine the second and third player to create a new market leader (in Belgium, Germany, and Italy).

The Commission concluded that given the characteristics of the markets of carotid SX stents in Austria, Belgium, France, Finland, Germany, Italy, Luxembourg, Netherlands, Portugal, and Spain in terms of concentration, barriers to entry, customer loyalty, closeness of substitution, and as a result of the elimination of a major competitive constraint, the concentration would give rise to non-coordinated adverse effects in those national markets and would therefore impede effective competition in the common market and the EEA as a result of the creation or strengthening of a dominant position.[148]

As far as the non-carotid stents of the endovascular stents were concerned, both J&J and Guidant market non-carotid SX stents in the EEA. The Commission's market investigation indicated that J&J and Guidant products were considered to be the closest substitutes by the majority of respondents who procured non-carotid SX products. J&J and Guidant non-carotid SX stents were high-quality products, and close substitutes due to their superior performance compared to competing stents. The Commission concluded that given the characteristics of the markets of non-carotid SX stents in Austria, Belgium, Germany, and Netherlands in terms of concentration, barriers to entry, customer loyalty, closeness of substitution, and, as a result of the elimination of a major competitive constraint, the concentration would give rise to non-coordinated adverse effects in those national markets and therefore impede effective competition in the common market and the EEA as a result of the creation or strengthening of a dominant position.

In conclusion, in the market for endovascular stents the concentration would either consolidate an existing leadership position of one of the merging parties or create a new market leader. The relevant product markets were characterized by differentiated products with J&J's products being closer substitutes to Guidant's products. The Commission further stated that there were considerable barriers to entry in the form of IP rights, know how, access to customers and reputation of the firms, as well as large sunk costs.

As far as the market for cardiac surgery devices was concerned, J&J was active through products such as: minimally invasive access devices for valve surgery, stabilization systems for beating-heart surgery, stabilization system accessories, endoscopic vessel harvesting devices, and devices for non-surgical ablation. Guidant was active through stabilization systems for beating-heart surgery, stabilization system accessories, anastomosis assistance devices, and devices for surgical ablation.

The parties offered commitments to alleviate the Commission's concerns.[149] The Commission considered that the commitments were suitable for remedying the significant impediment to effective competition caused by the merger in the markets just mentioned.

The Commission concluded, on the basis of these remedies, that the notified operation whereby Johnson & Johnson would have acquired sole control of Guidant should be declared compatible with the common market and with the functioning of the EEA Agreement.[150]

4.2.5.2 A gap case?

In some of the markets analysed earlier, the Commission argued that the merger would significantly impede effective competition, however, it might not have concluded that the merger would lead to a creation or strengthening of dominant position if the merger had been assessed under the dominance test.

STEERABLE GUIDEWIRES

In the market for steerable guidewires used in interventional cardiology, the Commission stated in paragraph 196 that:[151]

> The concentration enables the merging parties to strengthen Guidant's uncontested leadership, by removing one of the only two main competitors in this market. On the basis of the information at the Commission's disposal, it seems unlikely that remaining competitors and potential entrants can constitute a sufficient and timely competitive constraint such as to prevent a unilateral increase in prices by the merged entity. Further, it cannot be excluded that the remaining firms in the market may even be expected to benefit from the reduction in competition which will result from the merger; the increase in concentration may provide them the opportunity to attain higher prices than would otherwise have been the case. The merger is therefore likely to result in a significant impediment to effective competition in the common market and the EEA for steerable guidewires as a result of the strengthening of Guidant's dominant position.

The Commission reached this conclusion by analysing the competitive landscape of the post-merger market. It reviewed the market shares of the merging parties and concluded that the significant market shares reinforced Guidant's uncontested leadership in the steerable guidewire markets. It added that Guidant's steerable guidewire was perceived by customers as being of superior quality to other guidewires and was their guidewire of choice. Customers valued the Guidant steerable guidewire product because of its superior nature but were also loyal to the Guidant brand because of its perception as a mark of quality and reliability.

The Commission concluded that post-merger there would clearly be a reduction in customers' competitive alternatives. If the merged entity raised prices post merger although Boston Scientific would be the only credible competitor it would not be able to provide sufficient competitive constraint such as to mitigate the significant impediment to effective competition induced as a result of the merger.

As paragraph 196 of the Commission's decision indicates, the Commission did not clearly articulate within which specific member states it considered that the merger would lead to a significant impediment to effective competition. As this paragraph further indicates, the Commission expected the competitors of the merged entity to be able to raise prices induced by the reduction of competition resulting from the merger. Thus, it expected the merger to have non-coordinated effects in oligopolistic markets.

In most member states, the merger represented the addition of the number one player, Guidant, with the number three player, J&J, and would lead to the post-merger entity having a market share between 55 and 100 per cent in certain member states. However, in Hungary, the merged entity would have 35 to 45 per cent combined share, with number two player Boston Scientific having 15 to 25 per cent. In Sweden, the merged entity would have a combined market share of 35 to 45 per cent. The HHI in the post-merger market in these two countries would be 3558 with a dHHI equal to 576 in Hungary and 4696 with a dHHI of 490 in Sweden.

Using the assumption that paragraph 196 indicates that the Commission considered that the merger would lead to a significant impediment to effective competition, inter alia, in Hungary and Sweden, it is arguable whether the Commission would be able to show that the merger would lead to a strengthening or creation of a dominant position had the merger been assessed under the dominance test of the original ECMR.

The product was moderately differentiated, broadly interchangeable, with no significant technical differences. The Commission mentioned that in the post-merger market there was a reduction in the customers' competitive alternatives and in response to a price increase customers would switch to other competitors (Boston Scientific) in proportion to their market shares. As the Commission further stated, the closeness of substitution did not play a significant role and the market shares remained a good indicator of market power. These factors would be conducive to an argument that the merger would led to a strengthening or creation of a dominant position.

However, the low market shares in Hungary and Sweden paint a different picture. The absolute level of the HHI can give an initial indication of the competitive pressure in the market post-merger. As the Commission noted, for moderately differentiated products, market shares remain a good indicator of market power.[152] Notwithstanding the HHI ratios and the increments, the low market shares might have prevented the Commission from concluding that the merger would have led to a creation or strengthening of dominance.

In the context of Article 102 TFEU, the threshold of market share for an allegation of single dominance to be upheld can be at 50 per cent, as has been identified in case law: *AKZO*.[153] In Recital 32 of the preamble of the ECMR, a reverse indication or presumption can be made that dominance exists where the market share of the undertakings exceeds 25 per cent. In the *Carrefour/Promodes*[154] case, most of the Commission's concerns essentially related to the absolute size of the merged entity. Buyer power arguments were used to suggest that a post-merger market share of 30 per cent could still raise serious dominance concerns.[155]

In *Johnson & Johnson/Guidant*, market shares of 35 to 45 per cent in Hungary, with number two player Boston Scientific having 15 to 25 per cent and market share of 35 to 45 per cent in Sweden,[156] in combination with the remaining features of the post-merger market mentioned earlier (for example, countervailing buyer power, innovative market),[157] do not give, in my opinion, much credibility to an argument of single firm dominance.

As regards collective dominance, an argument can be made that the incumbents in the post-merger market would engage in tacit coordination of their conduct and thus enjoy a position of collective dominance. The Commission did not allege that the merger would lead to coordinated effects but rather to non-coordinated effects. This in itself provides support to the argument that the post-merger market would not exhibit the features of collective dominance.[158] The degree of differentiation of the products and the variation in the post-merger incumbents' market shares, as well as the existence of IP rights,[159] would not lend credibility to the argument that the merger might have led to a creation or strengthening of a collective dominant position.

The Commission stated that, in general, interventional cardiology accessories tended to be more and more "commodity" like items, to the extent they were relatively simple and homogeneous products. As a consequence, compared to the market for stents, there was less differentiation and stronger price competition between a large number of suppliers, including some local players.[160] However, the trend towards commoditization was perhaps less accentuated for some of these items, such as, in particular, guidewires, where quality remained one of the key criteria driving customers' choice and constituted a differentiation factor of these products. Thus, arguably, the steerable guidewires were moderately differentiated products.

In addition, interventional cardiology accessories were low margin products, and dependent to some extent on the primary markets for stents. The Commission further stated that parties and their competitors' market shares across various segments of the interventional cardiology, that is to say, accessories and stents, were pretty uneven. Furthermore, some market share fluctuations within each segment were also recorded over time. This was explained by the fact that sourcing through formal tendering and by single item was also common, thus creating room for contestability.[161]

Thus, the discrepancy in the market shares of the merged entity and Boston Scientific (at least in Hungary where information is available), the fact that the steerable guidewires were moderately differentiated products, as well as the fluctuation in the market shares and the tendering form of procurement by customers (hospitals that can multi-source), do not lend credibility to the argument that the two post-merger firms might be able to successfully tacitly coordinate their behaviour and thus enjoy a collective dominant position in the post-merger market.

Thus, the Commission might not have been able to successfully argue that the merger would lead to a creation or strengthening of dominance in these two countries if it assessed the merger under the dominance test. However, the Commission would most likely have prohibited the merger or accepted remedies under the dominance test as well, since the merger would lead to a creation or strengthening of dominant position in a substantial part of the common market.[162]

CAROTID STENTS

Turning to the market for carotid stents of endovascular stents, the Commission concluded that:[163]

> Given the characteristics of the markets of carotid SX stents in Austria, Belgium, France, Finland, Germany, Italy, Luxembourg, The Netherlands, Portugal and Spain in terms of concentration, barriers to entry, customer loyalty, closeness of substitution, and as a result of the elimination of a major competitive constraint, the concentration will give rise to non coordinated adverse effects in those national markets and therefore impede effective competition in the common market and the EEA as a result of the creation or strengthening of a dominant position.

The merger would reduce the number of competitors from three to two in the carotid stents market. The merged entity would have a market share of 45 to 55 per cent in the EEA, with an HHI of 3663 and increment of 1176.[164] There were three main players in the carotid stent market: J&J, Guidant and Boston Scientific. Together they accounted for between 83[165] and 96 per cent of the market. In Belgium, Germany, and Italy the merger combined the second and third largest players and would have led to the biggest firm in the post-merger market with market shares of 45 to 55 per cent, 45 to 55 per cent, and 40 to 50 per cent respectively. Furthermore, in France, the post-merger entity had a market share of 35 to 45 per cent; in Spain, it was 45 to 55 per cent.[166] The other large firm, Boston Scientific can be conservatively estimated to have had a market share of 35 to 45 per cent in Belgium, 25 to 35 per cent in Germany, 30 to 40 per cent in Italy, 45 to 55 per cent in France, and 25 to 35 per cent in Spain.[167]

As already mentioned, the Commission stated that neither fast market growth nor new entry weakened the strong market presence of J&J and Guidant in the carotid stent markets. In addition, J&J and Guidant's positions were reinforced by the considerable financial resources they were devoting to the teaching of carotid stenting techniques, thereby increasing their market recognition and brand reputation. The Commission emphasized the high degree of differentiation of these products[168] and that the market shares of endovascular devices had been fairly stable over the previous three years. It also noted the significant barriers to entry in the market[169] (due, inter alia, to the existence of IP rights) and the low degree of innovation due to the differentiation of the products which induced highly diversified demand and lower expected returns from innovation.[170]

The demand for these products was constituted by hospitals that had strong countervailing buying power; this was particularly due to the fact that they had several alternatives at their disposal and were arguably able to play suppliers off against each other.[171] The great majority of buyers practiced multiple sourcing. There were infrequent problems of interoperability between products sourced from alternative suppliers. Multiple sourcing allowed the hospitals to obtain the best device for each medical application; it also allowed them to avoid any disruption to their activities in case of a problem in the supply of a specific device. The Commission acknowledged the countervailing buyer power of hospitals, but opined nonetheless that the closeness of substitution between Guidant and J&J undermined vigorously the alleged lack of competition concerns resulting from multiple-sourcing.

Had the Commission assessed this merger under the dominance test, it would have proved difficult to allege that the merger would lead to single firm dominance in Belgium, Germany, Italy, France, and Spain since the merger would lead to a market share for the combined entity of between 35 to 55 per cent and for the second largest firm, Boston Scientific, of between 25 to 55 per cent. Although the remaining factors that could substantiate an allegation that a merger could lead to single firm dominance were present (barriers to entry, low innovation, relatively stable market shares), taking into account the significant countervailing buyer power and the low market shares of the merged entity as well as of Boston Scientific in the post-merger market, the Commission would have taken a substantial risk of a successful appeal by the parties by concluding that the merger should have been prohibited under the dominance test based on the argument that the merger would lead to the creation or strengthening of a dominant position.

As regards collective dominance between the merged entity and Boston Scientific, the features of the post-merger market cannot, in my opinion, support such an allegation. The Commission did not allege that the merger would lead to coordinated effects, which in itself provides support for the argument that the post-merger market would not exhibit the features of collective dominance.[172] The significant degree of differentiation of the products, the substantial countervailing buyer power, the likely asymmetric cost structures due to the fact that the industry was characterized by innovation and R&D investments, and the existence of IP rights,[173] ensured the attainment and viability of a collectively dominant position would be difficult and unlikely.

Thus, as this analysis indicates, if the Commission had assessed the merger under the dominance test, it would have proved quite difficult to argue that the merger would lead to an adverse impact on competition in Belgium, Germany, Italy, France, and Spain, either on the grounds of single firm dominance or collective dominance.[174] The conclusion of the Commission's assessment would have been different under the dominance test. It might have resulted in a different set of remedies proposed by the merging parties.

NON-CAROTID STENTS

Finally, turning to the market for non-carotid stents of endovascular stents, the Commission stated that:[175]

> In conclusion, given the characteristics of the markets of non-carotid SX stents in Austria, Belgium, Germany and The Netherlands in terms of concentration, barriers to entry, customer loyalty, closeness of substitution, and as a result of the elimination of a major competitive constraint, the concentration will give rise to non coordinated adverse effects in those national markets and therefore impede effective competition in the common market and the EEA as a result of the creation or strengthening of a dominant position.

The merger would reduce the number of competitors from four to three in the non-carotid stents market. At EEA level, the combined entity had a market share of 30 to 40 per cent (J&J: 20 to 30 per cent, Guidant: 10 to 20 per cent). J&J's market share had been relatively stable for the past three years. Conversely, Guidant entered the market in 2000 and since then its market position constantly grew to reach 10 to 20 per cent. After the transaction the HHI would be 2691, with an increment of 600. In Belgium and the Netherlands. the combined market share would be 45 to 55 per cent; in Germany, it would be 40 to 50 per cent. In these markets, J&J was market leader, while Guidant was the third player in Belgium (after Bard) and the fourth in Germany and the Netherlands (after Boston Scientific and Bard). Together, J&J, Guidant, Boston Scientific, and Bard accounted for 85 to 95 per cent in Belgium, 80 to 90 per cent in Germany and 80 to 90 per cent in the Netherlands,[176] while the concentration ratio of the three largest firms was 70 to 80 per cent in Belgium, Germany, and the Netherlands.

The features of this market were very similar to the one for carotid stents as regards the high degree of product differentiation, significant barriers to entry, substantial countervailing buyer power and low degree of innovation and the existence of IP rights.[177] It is unlikely that the Commission would have been able to argue adverse impact on competition on the basis of single firm dominance had it assessed this merger under the dominance test. With such low market shares as well as countervailing buyer power and the presence of at least one more significant competitor in the post-merger market, the Commission would not, in my opinion, be able to allege that the merger would lead to single firm dominance.

As regards collective dominance between the incumbents in the post-merger market, the features of the post-merger market could not, in my opinion, support such an allegation. Furthermore, the Commission did not allege that the merger would lead to coordinated effects but rather to non-coordinated effects, which provides support to the argument that the post-merger market would not exhibit the features of collective dominance.[178] Similar to the market for carotid stents, the significant degree of differentiation of the products, the substantial countervailing buyer power, the likely asymmetric cost structures due to the fact that the industry was characterized by innovation and R&D investments, as well as the existence of IP rights, render the sustainability of a collusive equilibrium unlikely.

As regards the market for endovascular stents in general (including balloon expandable stents,[179] carotid and non-carotid stents),[180] the Commission noted that:[181]

> The concentration will reduce the number of most important competitors from three (the third being Boston Scientific) to two in the BX stents and carotid stents markets and from four (the third and fourth being Boston Scientific and Bard) to three in the non-carotid SX stent market. These restricted number of players account for the lion's share of the market in all countries considered above. Further competitors, although numerous, have failed so far to grab significant market shares. The concentration will either consolidate an existing

> leadership position of one of the merging parties or create a new market leader.

And concluded that:[182]

> [T]here is sufficient evidence showing with the requisite degree of confidence that the operation will give rise to important non-coordinated effects and will substantially impede effective competition in the Common Market and the EEA for the endovascular stents.

The merger between Johnson & Johnson and Guidant would lead to a significant impediment to effective competition. The transaction was allowed to proceed after substantial remedies were proposed by the parties and accepted by the Commission. In the market both for steerable guidewires and endovascular devices, the parties committed to divest the whole of the Guidant's operations in the EEA, an indication of the significant adverse competitive effects of the merger and the need to be rectified by an equally substantial remedy.

The results arising from the event study[183] indicated that the Commission's decision coincided with the investors' perception on the day of the initial significant dissemination of information regarding the adverse effects of *Johnson & Johnson/Guidant* on competition.

As the earlier analysis indicated, if the Commission had assessed the merger under the dominance test, it might not have been able to convincingly argue that the merger would have induced an adverse impact on competition in the markets analysed previously, mainly due to the differentiation of the products, asymmetric cost structure, the countervailing buyer power, and the low market shares of the merged entity. In these markets, the merger would give rise to neither single firm dominance nor collective dominance. However, the incumbents in the post-merger market would be able to unilaterally increase their prices and thus the merger would have non-coordinated effects in these oligopolistic markets.

This likely outcome was also acknowledged by the Commission when, in referring to the steerable guidewires of the interventional cardiology devices, it stated that:[184]

> [I]t cannot be excluded that the remaining firms in the market may even be expected to benefit from the reduction in competition which will result from the merger; the increase in concentration may provide them the opportunity to attain higher prices than would otherwise have been the case.

In addition, in referring to the endovascular devices, the Commission stated that:[185] "[T]here is sufficient evidence showing with the requisite degree of confidence that the operation will give rise to important non-coordinated effects."

This merger would likely have led to non-coordinated effects in oligopolistic markets, as suggested by the Commission. These adverse effects on competition might not have been able to be fully captured if the merger had been assessed under the dominance test as the above analysis illustrated.

4.2.6 T-Mobile/Tele.ring[186]

4.2.6.1 Analysis of the case

T-Mobile was a provider of mobile and fixed telephony services in Austria. Its parent company, Deutsche Telekom, was a world player in the telecommunications industry. Tele.ring was a provider of mobile and fixed telephony services in Austria.

The proposed transaction involved T-Mobile acquiring all the shares in EHG Einkaufs- und Handels GmbH, the sole owner of the Tele.ring group, which comprised Tele.ringTelekom Service GmbH, TRA 3G Mobilfunk GmbH and EKOM 3G Mobilfunk GmbH.

T-Mobile and Tele.ring operate mobile networks in Austria and were also active on related end customer and wholesale markets. They also both provided fixed network services; but the Commission argued that the merger had no effect on these markets.

As regards the provision of mobile telecommunications services to end customers, the Commission assessed previous cases on the basis of a single market for the provision of mobile telecommunications services to end customers.[187] It concluded that a single market existed for the provision of mobile telephony services to end customers, in so far as they could be provided on both a 2G and a 3G basis. The issue whether there was a separate market for specific applications available only on the basis of 3G technology was left open since, inter alia, multimedia services had recently become available on the market. The geographic scope of the market was defined as national.

As regards the wholesale market for call termination,[188] as established in previous Commission decisions,[189] there was no substitute for call termination on each individual network since the operator transmitting the outgoing call can reach the intended recipient only through the operator of the network to which the recipient is connected. The Commission thus argued that each individual network constituted a separate market for termination. According to the Commission, the geographic markets for call termination in mobile and fixed networks were national.[190]

Finally, concerning the wholesale market for international roaming,[191] demand for wholesale international roaming services came from foreign mobile operators who wished to provide their own customers with mobile services outside their own network and, downstream, from subscribers wishing to use their mobile telephones outside their own countries.

The Commission in earlier decisions reached the provisional conclusion that each network constituted a separate market for the provision of wholesale international roaming services.[192] However, network operators could to a great extent choose the network in which their customers can make calls abroad. Any foreign network operator may be selected.

As regards the geographic market, the Commission has previously[193] concluded that the market was national in scope. This analysis was based on the fact that wholesale international roaming agreements could be concluded only with companies that had an operating licence in the relevant country, and that licences to provide mobile services were restricted to national territory.

Turning to the competitive assessment, there were four main companies on the Austrian market operating mobile telephone networks based on GSM technology. They were Mobilkom (a subsidiary of Telekom Austria), T-Mobile, ONE and Tele.ring.

The market share of the merged entity was 30 to 40 per cent, while Mobilkom had 35 to 45 per cent, ONE had 15 to 25 per cent and H3G had under 5 per cent.[194] These market shares were calculated on the basis of turnover, but did not change if the market shares were calculated according to the number of customers.[195]

The Commission concluded that the elimination of Tele.ring as an independent network operator, the emergence of a market structure with two large network operators of similar size (Mobilkom and T-Mobile), a far smaller operator (ONE), and a very small operator (H3G)[196] would give rise to non-coordinated effects, even though T-Mobile would not have the largest market share after the merger.

The Commission analysed nine factors in order to assess the adverse impact of the merger on competition. It analysed the market shares, the HHI, customer switching, price development, incentive structures, importance of national network, network capacity, the role of other competitors, as well as the future development of Tele.ring.[197]

MARKET SHARES

In recent years, Tele.ring has more than doubled its market share, from 5 to 10 per cent in terms of turnover, or even almost tripled it, from 5 to15 per cent in terms of customers. By contrast, of the three established network operators Mobilkom, and T-Mobile in particular, had lost significant market shares in the same period. The proposed merger would lead to close symmetry between the two largest suppliers, Mobilkom and T-Mobile. The analysis of market shares alone showed not only that Tele.ring had played an active role on the market in the previous three years but also that it had been the only company to play such an active role, in terms of increased market share. Tele.ring, as a maverick, had a much greater influence on the competitive process in this market than its market share would suggest.[198]

HHI

The HHI and delta values were well above those defined as not giving rise to concern in the Commission's *Guidelines*.[199] The Commission argued that they showed that this was a highly concentrated market and that the proposed merger, in view of the high delta value, would bring about a significant change in market structures.

CUSTOMER SWITCHING

The market-share data in itself suggested that a large proportion of customers who had left T-Mobile and Mobilkom had become customers of Tele.ring. The data collected by the Austrian regulator on the basis of number portability further supported this interpretation. In 2005 more than half of all customers who switched provider and made use of number portability went to Tele.ring, and between 57 per cent and 61 per cent of those who left T-Mobile and Mobilkom with their telephone numbers switched to Tele.ring. In second place behind Tele.ring in 2005 was H3G, which picked up around some 20 per cent of all customers switching provider and using number portability.[200]

PRICE DEVELOPMENT

The Commission's analysis illustrated that, overall, prices constantly fell in the reference period and that Tele.ring offered its services since the third quarter of 2002 at significantly lower prices per minute than the other three network operators and that since the first quarter of 2002 at lower prices per minute than the market average. Tele.ring's prices were well below the per-minute prices charged by the three leading operators.

The Commission concluded that during the period under investigation (from 2002 to 2005) Tele.ring was the most active player in the market, and that it exerted considerable competitive pressure on T-Mobile and Mobilkom, in particular, and played a crucial role in restricting their freedom on pricing. The price analysis therefore suggested that Tele.ring's role in the market was that of a maverick.

INCENTIVE STRUCTURE

The incentives for an operator to attract new customers to an existing network by offering aggressive prices were determined by the size of the customer base. The mobile telephone industry was characterized by high investment costs in building up a network to cover 98 per cent of the population (a regulatory requirement for 2G services), network operating costs that were largely independent of the actual amount of airtime used, and relatively low variable costs. The initial incentive for network operators was therefore to exploit their capacity to the full by having as large a customer base as possible. This was particularly true of network operators that first have to build up their customer base in order to be able to recoup the network investment costs and cover the network operating costs.

It was therefore important for such network operators to attract new customers by adopting an aggressive pricing policy, as they did not have a secure and adequate customer base. In time, however, lower tariffs for new customers always had medium-term implications for the customer base, as existing customers would not tolerate discrimination over a longer period and might therefore go elsewhere. So, the bigger the customer base, the less likelihood of low price offers aimed at attracting new customers, as the threat of lost income from existing customers would no longer be offset by the additional income to be expected from new customers.

The Commission concluded that Tele.ring's incentive to charge very competitive prices was a consequence of the number of its existing customers. T-Mobile had not pursued such a strategy and the combination of T-Mobile and Tele.ring would have even less incentive to do so in future. Tele.ring's was regarded by customers as particularly inexpensive, but was not highly rated on other factors such as quality, innovation or service.

NATIONAL NETWORK

The importance of a national network with maximum possible network coverage stemmed in the first instance from customer demands. Investments and network operating costs did not constitute variable costs for a network operator and therefore had no direct bearing on the price of airtime sold to customers. With regard to these costs, the network operator had in particular an incentive to achieve economies of scale. There appeared to be no major differences in the incentives of Mobilkom, T-Mobile, ONE and Tele.ring as all these network operators had GSM networks with nationwide coverage of at least 98 per cent (a regulatory requirement).[201]

NETWORK CAPACITY

Sufficient network capacity[202] was a *sine qua non* for supplying services to existing customers and, in theory, an incentive to attract new customers. By the same token, if a mobile operator seeking to maximize profits had sufficient network capacity, this did not necessarily mean that when it had spare capacity it would lower its prices to attract new customers and use that capacity to the full, since this might reduce the profitability of its existing customer base.

Mobilkom's network was suitable as a reference here as it had the highest use of airtime. In comparison with Mobilkom's network, the current volume of traffic on Tele.ring's network was such that it could still absorb a limited amount of additional traffic, while T-Mobile's network was used to a much lesser extent and could still absorb significantly more traffic. ONE had spare network capacity somewhere between that of Tele.ring and T-Mobile and could therefore take up more new users than Mobilkom. From a structural point of view, Tele.ring's network was also suited to absorbing extra customers over and above its current capacity.

After completion of the proposed merger, not only would the Tele.ring network be eliminated, but, presumably, the T-Mobile network would be used to full capacity to a far greater extent than was then the case. The proposed merger would therefore lead to a situation where instead of there being three operators the considerable reduction in spare capacity would also reduce the incentives for network operators to attract new customers by offering low prices in order to use up significant spare capacity. Thus, the merger would lead to a significant overall reduction in capacity in the market. According to the Commission, this reduction in available capacity would suggest that the merger would have a considerable impact on competition.[203]

ROLE OF OTHER COMPETITORS

The Commission found no signs that a new network operator might be intending to enter the Austrian market. It concluded that it was unlikely that H3G or ONE/YESSS! would occupy a place in the market comparable with Tele.ring once the transaction was completed or that they would have been able to discipline the competitive behaviour of T-Mobile and Mobilkom in particular. Similarly, service providers would also not be able to assume such a role.

FUTURE DEVELOPMENT OF TELE.RING

The Commission concluded that Tele.ring would continue to operate in future as a price-aggressive service provider on the Austrian mobile telephone market.

CONCLUSION ON UNILATERAL EFFECTS ARISING FROM THE MERGER

As the preceding analysis indicates, as far as non-coordinated effects are concerned, the Commission concluded that, with the elimination of the maverick in the market and the simultaneous creation of a market structure with two leading, symmetrical network operators, it was likely that the merger would produce non-coordinated effects and significantly impede effective competition in a substantial part of the common market.

The Commission added that:[204]

> It is therefore probable that the proposed merger will have a tangible effect on prices in the Austrian end-customer market for mobile telephony services. Even if prices do not rise in the short term, the weakening of competitive pressure as a result of Tele.ring's elimination from the market makes it unlikely that prices will continue to fall significantly as in the past.

Turning to coordinated effects, the Commission argued that such effects may be induced as a result of the merger; but it did not offer definitive conclusions on this issue as the commitments proposed by the notifying party ruled out the possibility that the transaction would lead to coordinated effects.

After commitments submitted by the parties, the merger was declared compatible with the common market and with the EEA Agreement.

4.2.6.2 A gap case?

This is a case that clearly indicates the existence of gap cases. The Commission seems to analyse most of the factors that are essential in order for a merger to lead to non-coordinated effects in oligopolistic markets. The merged entity would have the second place in the post-merger market with 30 to 40 per cent, while Mobilkom would have 35 to 45 per cent. In addition, HHIs indicated a significant degree of concentration in the post-merger market. In the post-merger market, there would be limited customer switching between the merged entity and Mobilkom, since once Tele.ring disappeared from the market, H3G would be the major destination of customers who would like to switch as is indicated by eliciting the 20 per cent of all customers switching provider and using number portability.

Limited switching between the merged entity and Mobilkom, the two largest firms in the post-merger market, indicated that both firms were likely to increase prices without having any significant risk of customers switching to the other. Although customers of both firms could have switched to the other competitors, as the Commission argued, it was unlikely that H3G or ONE/YESSS! would occupy a place in the market comparable with that of Tele.ring once the transaction was completed, or that they would be able to discipline the competitive behaviour of the merged entity and Mobilkom. Thus, both these firms could unilaterally increase prices in the post-merger market.

This case shows that the finding of non-coordinated effects is not limited to a situation in which the merging parties are the closest competitors to each other. In addition, the merged entity had the second largest market share in the market, with Mobilkom being the largest firm. It is inconceivable that the Commission could allege that the merger would lead to the creation or strengthening of a dominant position, had the merger been assessed under the dominance test.

The Commission did not rule out the possibility that the proposed merger, besides producing the non-coordinated effects as described earlier, may also lead to a weakening of competitive pressure as a result of coordinated effects. These coordinated effects would result in prices on the market rising higher than if they were dictated only by the individual, non-coordinated, profit-maximizing behaviour of each individual competitor. The merger would lead to two network operators of roughly equal size, Mobilkom and T-Mobile, which together would account for a market share of 60 to 80 per cent on the Austrian mobile communications market. In addition, the merger would remove the price-aggressive maverick, leaving no other service provider that would be able to take over its role in the short to medium term. As mentioned already, the remaining competitors in the post-merger market were unlikely to pose significant constraints on the merged entity and Mobilkom.

Although the Commission alleged that coordinated effects could arise, it excluded their analysis from the decision.[205]

Although the Commission might not have been able to block the merger under the dominance test based on the allegation that the merger would lead to the creation or strengthening of a dominant position, the Commission might have been able to allege that the merger would lead to the creation or strengthening of a collective dominant position. Thus, it could have achieved the same outcome (that is to say, clearance with remedies) under the dominance test that it achieved under the SIEC test.

4.3 The United Kingdom

The UK cases[206] that will be analysed are *Littlewoods Organization Plc/Freemans Plc*[207] and *Lloyds TSB/Abbey National*.[208]

4.3.1 Littlewoods Organization Plc/Freemans Plc[209]

4.3.1.1 Analysis of the case

Littlewoods was first established as a football pools company in Liverpool in 1923. It moved into agency mail order a decade later and the first Littlewoods retail store was opened in 1937; it soon expanded into a chain selling food, clothing, and household goods. TLO, the holding company, had three main businesses: LHSG, which was a catalogue mail order operation; the chain of Littlewoods high street stores; and Littlewoods Leisure, which was the United Kingdom's leading football pools company.

Index, a chain of catalogue shops established in 1985, was transferred from the stores operation to LHSG early in 1997. The total turnover of TLO, which claimed to be the largest privately owned company in the United Kingdom, was £2.3 billion in 1996.[210] LHSG, the business with which the merger concerned, comprised the agency mail order, the direct mail order, and the Index catalogue operations of the group. It was the second largest home shopping business in the United Kingdom. The largest and most profitable part of LHSG's business was agency mail order.

Sears entered the mail order sector when in 1988 it acquired Freemans for £477 million. Formed in 1905, Freemans' business had been the sale of clothes and household goods by mail order catalogue. It was the third largest UK home shopping business. Freemans operated a single "big book" agency mail order catalogue under the Freemans name. Agency sales in the year to January 1997 amounted to £426 million, representing 86 per cent of all Freemans' sales. Freemans also ran a direct mail catalogue, "One to One". Freemans had an operating profit of £21 million in the year to January 1997. The balance of Freemans' turnover of £494 million during this period came from its export mail order business (Freemans International) and a business supplying goods for corporate awards schemes (Freemans Awards). All these businesses were included in the merger.[211]

Agency mail order was a traditional form of home shopping and had a number of distinguishing characteristics. These included the offer of a wide range of clothing; household and electrical goods through a free biannual colour catalogue (1000 page "big book"); the use of agents to place orders for themselves and their customers in return for a 10 per cent commission on all goods sold;[212] "bundled" prices, covering credit, delivery and the return of unwanted items; as well as the goods themselves, and a facility to pay the catalogue price either in a single payment or by instalments, described in the catalogue as "interest free". Catalogue prices were on average 15 to 20 per cent above those in the high street.

There were five firms operating in the agency mail order sector in the United Kingdom: the UK home shopping business of the Great Universal Stores PLC ("GUS"), the largest, with a share of agency mail order of 40.6 per cent in 1996; Littlewoods, with an agency mail order share of 27.9 per cent; Freemans, with 13.1 per cent; Grattan Plc ("Grattan") with 10.4 per cent; and Empire Stores Group ("Empire"), with 8.1 per cent. Total agency mail order sales amounted to £3.3 billion in 1996.[213]

For the purposes of determining the market, the UK Competition Commission examined, first, the extent to which other forms of home shopping, particularly direct mail order, and the high street, could be regarded as adequate substitutes for agency mail order; and second, whether alternative forms of credit were adequate substitutes for the agency mail order offer.

The UK Competition Commission concluded that agency and direct mail order differed markedly from each other; in particular, it concluded that direct mail order did not use agents to sell goods, prices were not bundled and were broadly comparable with high street prices, interest-free credit was not normally included as part of the catalogue price, the range of goods in many catalogues was far narrower, and many direct mail catalogues were more up market than those of agency mail order.

Agency mail order users in the lower income socioeconomic groups, who were the predominant users of this form of home shopping, were not very likely to have access to alternative sources of credit, especially credit and store cards. A lack of transparency in the agency mail order credit offer was eminent, as was a generally poor understanding on the part of agency mail order users of the nature of the credit terms offered.

As regards the role of the high street, agency mail order users were prepared to pay a significant premium above high street prices for the credit offered and the convenience of being able to choose items in their own home. The UK Competition Commission argued that high street prices exercised merely a broad upper constraint on the charges of agency mail order companies. As mentioned earlier, catalogue prices were on average 15 to 20 per cent above those in the high street.

After an extensive analysis of the relevant market,[214] the UK Competition Commission concluded that agency mail order was a distinct market. It based its conclusions on the following factors:[215]

(a) that agency mail order has distinctive features which distinguish it from other forms of home shopping, including direct mail order;
(b) that on the credit issue, on balance the agency mail order credit offer is sufficiently distinct as to be a factor in identifying the market, without being definitive on the matter; and
(c) that the high street represents some general constraint on the pricing of the agency mail order companies but is not a tight constraint on them.

The UK Competition Commission argued that the agency mail order market was broadly static and already highly concentrated. The proposed merger would raise concentration further, resulting in the merged company and the current market leader, GUS, having 82 per cent of agency sales between them. The UK Competition Commission expected this increase in concentration to reduce the level of existing competition significantly, thereby leading to a detrimental effect on choice, prices or efficiency in the agency mail order market. The two smallest companies, Grattan and Empire, with only 18 per cent of the agency mail order market, were unlikely to provide sufficient competitive constraint to the two largest players.

Furthermore, barriers to entry into agency mail order were still substantial, arising from the large economies of scale associated with this market. Benefits arising from the size of the large firms (in business areas such as purchasing power, warehousing, call centre and delivery systems) in this market rendered new entry unlikely. The substantial investment required to set up an agency mail order company was an additional factor that rendered new entry into the agency mail order market highly unlikely. It is worth noting that there had been no entry or exit for the last 30 years in that particular market.[216]

Although the UK Competition Commission acknowledged that there might have been some benefits, including cost savings to be derived from the merger, these were not likely to be passed on to consumers in such a concentrated market. Even if they were to be fully passed on, they would be insufficient to offset the detriment to competition.[217]

The UK Competition Commission concluded that the merger may be expected to operate against the public interest and thus it recommended that the merger should be prohibited.

4.3.1.2 A gap case?

The effect of the merger would be to add 13.1 per cent to Littlewoods' market share in the agency mail order market, generating a 41 per cent share for the merged company, while reducing the number of agency mail order companies from five to four. The second largest player, GUS, would have a market share of 40.6 per cent. Thus, not only was the increase in the market share of the second largest firm (pre-merger) substantial (13.1 per cent) but the already highly concentrated market would become even more concentrated.

GUS argued that the merger would create a stronger player within a highly competitive home shopping market that should now be considered as part of the wider European market. It argued that the merger reflected trends in the industry towards consolidation and the development of fewer but stronger players in an increasingly international market. According to GUS, although the merged entity would be able to achieve further economies of scale, it would not be able to exert undue pressure on its agency mail order competitors. Furthermore, the owners of Grattan and Empire gave these companies greater buying power than the merged company could exert.

On the contrary, Grattan and Empire viewed the merger with concern. Empire thought the resulting concentration would make it possible for the larger players to squeeze out the smaller companies with aggressive marketing and then to operate against customers' interests by cutting back on the service element of the agency mail order offer and the available credit options, or by setting higher prices than would otherwise be the case.[218]

It is worth noting that the major competitor of the merged entity (GUS) was, surprisingly, positive about the effects of the merger on competition. It can be argued that if GUS expected the merger to lead to increased competitive constraints, it might have raised some arguments in favour of the prohibition of the merger. One can infer from the main competitor's (with equal market shares to the merged entity) positive reaction to the merger that it might have expected the merger to lead to an enhancement of its ability to increase prices and/or reduce innovation and quality. Rather than creating a strong competitive constraint, GUS might have expected the merger to lead to a market where the incumbents would have reduced incentives to compete. Thus, GUS might have expected that the merger would lead to non-coordinated effects in the duopolistic post-merger market which would allow it to adopt practices having an adverse impact on competition.[219]

The UK Competition Commission in its analysis identified the possibility of the merger leading to non-coordinated effects in oligopolistic markets. As it stated:[220]

> In a concentrated market, we expect companies to assess not only the immediate costs and benefits of any competitive strategy but also the reactions of competitors. With two companies responsible for over 80 per cent of sales, the latter is likely to be an important factor. We have no reason to assume or predict that any form of collusion would occur between the two leading companies which would exist in this market after the merger, and we have discounted this possibility in our reasoning. But the existence of two companies each with over 40 per cent of the market would in our view be likely to create some reticence on their part about adopting vigorous competitive strategies against each other which, if successful, would be very likely to invoke an equally strong competitive response.

The UK Competition Commission in the above paragraph dismissed any collective dominance concerns.[221] Professor Davies argues that the market was static, and likely to become a declining one, especially as other forms of credit were becoming more readily available, even for lower income groups.[222] He further argues that the UK Competition Commission ruled out the possibility of explicit collusion, but then set out a scenario that can be identified as tacit collusion in paragraphs 2.112–2.120.

I respectfully disagree with Professor Davies' argument that the UK Competition Commission implicitly identified tacit collusion as the likely impact of the merger. In paragraph 2.116, the Competition Commission argued that the possibility of *any* form of collusion was discounted; thus both tacit and explicit collusion were not regarded as likely outcomes of the merger. The UK Competition Commission did not distinguish between tacit and explicit collusion. In addition, the UK Competition Commission did not analyse factors that would lead to the sustainability of tacit collusion such as transparency, retaliation, price symmetry etc.[223]

Professor Davies further argues: "[T[he market leader was in favour of the merger, but the two smaller firms were against – if tacit collusion were more likely, all should be in favour, if more intensive competition was likely, all should be against!"[224] Thus, the fact that only the two largest firms were positive about the impact of this merger on competition may indicate that the merger might have led to non-coordinated effects in the post-merger market, by reducing the competitive constraints in the post-merger market and thus allowing these two competitors to increase prices as well as reduce quantities and/or innovation.

The two smaller incumbents, Empire and Grattan might have chosen to take advantage of any tendency towards higher prices in order to gain market share, thereby offsetting any potential detriment to consumers. However, Empire and Grattan themselves argued that such a response was unlikely.[225] GUS and Littlewoods/Freemans would be four to five times larger than either of the smaller companies, which might inhibit the latter from counteracting the detriment to consumers by keeping prices steady or even lowering them, in the event that the two largest firms increase theirs. In addition, the advantages of the scale economies, which the larger companies would be likely to have achieved would add to the reluctance of the smaller players to adopt such an approach. Both the two largest firms and the smaller players would be likely, post-merger, to increase their prices. Thus, the merger would lead to non-coordinated effects in the oligopolistic market for agency mail order.

The UK Competition Commission argued:[226]

> Overall, we do not believe that less competition between the leading players is inevitable, particularly in the period immediately following such a merger. We do think, however, that a tendency towards less effective competition may be expected as a result of the increase in concentration.

Thus, the merger would reduce competition by inducing non-coordinated effects that might lead to a reduction in consumer choice over time, less incentive to generate further efficiency improvements or innovative activity, and a tendency over time for prices to be higher than they would otherwise have been. The UK Competition Commission did not regard behavioural remedies as adequate to remedy the adverse effects and thus recommended the prohibition of the merger. The Secretary of State for Trade and Industry adopted the UK Competition Commission's recommendation.

If the European Commission had assessed this merger under the dominance test, it is unlikely that it would have prohibited the merger. An allegation of single firm dominance would not be sustainable since in the post-merger market, GUS would have a market share of 40.6 per cent and Littlewoods/Freemans 41 per cent.[227] In addition, the post-merger market was not found to be prone to collective dominance. The UK Competition Commission clearly discounted the possibility of the duopolists engaging in collective dominance.[228]

Thus, the European Commission could have been faced with a merger, inducing an adverse impact on competition that would not be capable of being caught under the dominance test. As the preceding analysis indicated, and the UK Competition Commission emphasized, the *Littlewoods/Freemans* merger would have led to harm on competition in the oligopolistic market for agency mail order. However, this merger was not likely to be prohibited if it had been assessed by the European Commission under the dominance test.

4.3.2 Lloyds TSB/Abbey National

4.3.2.1 Analysis of the case

Lloyds TSB, and its predecessor Lloyds Bank Plc, had for many years been one of the four leading clearing banks in the United Kingdom (Barclays Plc, HSBC Holdings Plc, Lloyds TSB and Royal Bank of Scotland Plc (RBS)/National Westminster Bank Plc, referred to herein as the "big four"). In 2000 Lloyds TSB made a pre-tax profit of £3.9 billion. In 1989 Abbey National was the first building society to convert from mutual to public limited company (plc) status. In subsequent years it developed from being primarily a mortgage and savings account provider into a full-service retail and wholesale bank. In 2000 it made a pre-tax profit of £2.0 billion.

The operations of Lloyds TSB and Abbey National overlapped in the following categories of product market:

- markets for financial products sold to personal customers, notably personal current accounts ("PCAs"), mortgages and savings accounts
- markets for financial products sold to small and medium sized enterprises ("SMEs"), defined for this purpose as enterprises with annual turnover up to £25 million
- markets for financial products sold to larger firms
- wholesale banking.

Great Britain and Northern Ireland constituted two separate geographic markets.

The markets for financial products sold to larger firms and for wholesale banking were characterized by the presence of global competitors and strong buyers. The UK Competition Commission had no reason to believe that the merger might create competition problems in these areas.

As regards the PCA market, where the UK Competition Commission identified competition concerns, PCAs are the core product in personal banking and provide customers with money transmission and deposit-holding services and, through overdrafts, may act as a source of credit. Over 85 per cent of UK households were believed to have at least one current account. PCA services are delivered through a variety of means:

branches, automated teller machines ("ATMs"), telephone, internet, digital television, wireless application protocol ("WAP") phone and the Post Office.

They also served as a "gateway" through which suppliers could sell other financial products, such as credit cards and personal loans, as a result of the relationship established through the PCA. The constraints on the development of competition were considerable since the merger would increase the PCA share of Lloyds TSB, already the market leader, from 22 per cent to 27 per cent, and would raise the combined share of the big four banks from 72 per cent to 77 per cent.

There were several features of the PCA market such as homogeneity of products, small customers lacking buyer power and being unwilling to switch between banks, transparent prices, stable demand, similarity of size and cost structure among the main suppliers, limited new entry as well as suppliers' past behaviour, which made the market vulnerable to tacit collusion in pricing. These features would tend to exacerbate any adverse effects on competition arising from the loss of a significant player such as Abbey National. In this concentrated market structure well-established rivals to the traditional banks were important for competition.

Abbey National, along with Halifax, was one of the two most successful branch-based suppliers that had shown the capability to win a significant share of the PCA market. It offered a distinct alternative to the big four banks, had been reasonably innovative, and had to compete actively to maintain its position. Thus, it constituted an important force for competition in the PCA market.

The UK Competition Commission argued that the removal of Abbey National as a competitor, with the consequent dismantling of its branch network, would reduce incentives to compete:

- In respect of Lloyds TSB individually, by increasing its customer base and thereby encouraging it to attach more weight to the enhancement of margins than to the growth of market share.
- In respect of the big four banks collectively, by removing one of the two main sources of actual and potential competition.

This reduction in competition would lead to higher prices (that is, higher fees and overdraft rates, and lower interest on credit balances) and a loss of innovation in the PCA market, compared with the situation that could be expected in the absence of the merger.

Turning to the savings and mortgages markets: savings accounts are deposit-holding accounts, which, unlike PCAs, do not offer money transmission facilities; they are operated through branches, ATMs, post, telephone and internet.[229] Although the merger would significantly increase concentration on the supply side, the evidence indicated that these markets were competitive with low barriers to entry, an abundance of choices for customers and willingness to switch. While back-book pricing[230] was still an issue, customers were becoming increasingly ready to switch provider in order to obtain better terms.

The market for the supply of banking services to SMEs was highly concentrated and was dominated by the traditional banks, especially the big four, which together had about 85 per cent of the total market (Lloyds TSB had around 16 per cent). There were high barriers to entry, high barriers to switching, and there had been little change in suppliers' market shares. The structure and levels of prices charged by the traditional banks were similar. Some of the banking products supplied to SMEs were similar to those supplied to individuals, for example, current accounts (including overdrafts), deposit accounts. and secured and unsecured lending. However, SME current account customers usually had access to a relationship manager to advise them on their banking business.

Abbey National offered a restricted range of products and had less than 1 per cent of total supply. It was able to provide competition to the incumbents (an established brand name, a national network of branches and a presence in personal and some business banking markets) and it had publicly stated its ambitions to increase its market share. Among the other smaller players and possible entrants, only Halifax had comparable potential.

The acquisition of Abbey National by Lloyds TSB would reduce competition in the supply of banking services to SMEs, where there was a particular need for increased competition, because it would eliminate one of the very few players outside the big four which were able to contest this market. The merger would cause prices for SME banking services to be higher, and innovation lower, than would be expected in the absence of the merger.

The merger would lead to efficiency gains but the UK Competition Commission believed that these would not be passed on to consumers in the form of reduced prices. The UK Competition Commission further considered several remedies and rejected them. It concluded that the possible remedies short of prohibiting the merger would not adequately address the adverse effects in the PCA and SME markets.

The merger would reduce by one the number of separate providers of banking services available to consumers. In the PCA market it would remove one of only three competitors to the big four – the others being Halifax and Nationwide – which offered a broad range of personal banking services through a national branch network. It would also remove one of the two alternative suppliers in the SME market with a national branch network.[231]

The UK Competition Commission concluded that the merger would operate against the public interest with the specific adverse effects, in respect of both the PCA and SME markets, of higher prices, and of a reduction in customer choice and innovation, compared with the situation that could be expected to arise in the absence of the merger.[232]

4.3.2.2 A gap case?

As the UK Competition Commission stated regarding the PCA market, this merger would reduce incentives to compete both in respect of Lloyds TSB individually but also in respect of the big four banks collectively by removing one of the two main sources of actual and potential competition.[233] It also stated that the proposed merger between Abbey National and Lloyds TSB could be expected materially to reduce competitive pressure on the big four.[234]

Thus, according to the UK Competition Commission, this merger involved unilateral and coordinated effects at levels of market share well below normal dominance thresholds with the post-merger firm's share being around 27 per cent.[235] A further 50 per cent of the personal current accounts market was supplied by the other three principal rivals. The combined share of the big four would increase from 72 to 77 per cent. However, the UK Competition Commission alleged that the merger led to coordinated effects and analysed the factors contributing to the sustainability of a tacitly collusive equilibrium (homogeneity, stability, transparency). In its report the UK Competition Commission framed its conclusions within a structure that explicitly focused on the "market's vulnerability to tacit collusion". It concluded that:

> There are several features of the PCA market-homogeneity of products, many small customers lacking buyer power, trans-parent prices, stable demand, similarity of size and cost structure among the main suppliers, and suppliers' past behaviour-which make the market vulnerable to tacit collusion in pricing, that is, parallel pricing by rival firms, without any overt agreement between them, in ways which serve their common commercial interest.[236]

The factors for coordinated effects existed in the pre-merger market as well. The merger merely increased the market share of the leading bank in the post-merger market. Thus, the merger itself is likely to have induced the strengthening rather than the creation of coordinated effects, provided that the coordinated effects existed in the pre-merger market.

The merger may also have led to adverse non-coordinated effects by inducing the incumbents in the post-merger market to increase prices without necessarily reaching a tacitly collusive outcome.[237] The differentiation of the products (the UK Competition Commission acknowledges that strong branding can differentiate these products but argues that this fact does not alter the homogeneity of the products in question)[238] and the innovative nature of the market (where Abbey National was deemed as one of the most innovative incumbents) may indicate that the existence of non-coordinated effects resulting from this merger is more likely than coordinated effects, since for coordinated effects, features of the post-merger market such as homogeneity and maturity are essential. Furthermore, Fingleton (2002) argues that in *Lloyds TCB/Abbey National* tacit collusion could not have been alleged, since there was consumer inertia as well as switching costs, inducing no reaction of consumers to price cuts. Thus, no price coordination was necessary by the banks.[239] For example as regards the market for the supply of banking services to SMEs, the UK Competition Commission's report on the supply of banking services by clearing banks to small and medium-sized enterprises within the United Kingdom,[240] as we will see later, indicates the existence of limited switching.

In addition, Abbey National was held to have the features of a maverick firm; this argument was contested by Lloyds TSB.[241] The elimination of a maverick is likely to induce both non-coordinated[242] and coordinated effects. Maverick firms might be identified if they have won a higher proportion of their sales from new customers, might bid for more customers than other firms (depressing prices even if they do not win business), or win a higher share than rivals of the aggregate volume of business "lost" by suppliers over a period of time. Market shares may understate the competition issues if one of the parties to the merger is a "maverick" competitor.[243] Competition from the maverick does not necessarily affect one firm (for example, a close competitor) but may have a broader impact on many competitors in the market, causing them to compete more actively, thereby enhancing overall market competitiveness. Thus, the removal of the maverick was likely to have led to an enhancement of the motives and capability of the incumbents to adopt conduct having an adverse impact on competition, without tacitly colluding; consequently, the merger was likely to induce non-coordinated effects in such oligopolistic markets. Bishop and Ridyard (2003) argue that the *Lloyds TSB/Abbey National* merger was one that involved unilateral effects in low market shares.[244] In addition, Vickers (2002) seems to imply that this merger was a "gap" case,[245] although the UK Competition Commission chose to look at it under the coordinated effects theory.

The UK Competition Commission alleged that the merger would lead to coordinated effects. Had the case fallen under the original ECMR, the European Commission could have pursued the coordinated effects theory, although the merger would lead, inter alia, to non-coordinated effects in oligopolistic markets, and it could have blocked the merger as creating or strengthening a collectively dominant position.[246]

As regards, in particular, the market for the supply of banking services to SMEs: according to the UK Competition Commission, the merger would eliminate one of the very few players outside the big four that were able to contest this market leading to higher prices for SME banking services and lower innovation. Lloyds TSB was the third largest player with 19 per cent behind RBS/Natwest (29 per cent) and Barclays (21 per cent). The merged entity would still be the third largest player with 20 per cent market share.

As Abbey National suggested, its current account product was distinct from the equivalent products of other traditional banks. Thus, a certain degree of differentiation existed among the equivalent products of banks. This degree of differentiation was enhanced by the strong branding that was prevalent in these products since the possession of a known and trusted brand contributed to the success of these products (as was also the case for the PCA market).

The UK Competition Commission's report on the supply of banking services by clearing banks to small and medium-sized enterprises within the United Kingdom[247] indicated that the markets were characterized by a reluctance on the part of SMEs to switch banks, the reasons for which included the perceived complexity of switching for little financial benefit; the perceived significance of maintaining relationships with a particular bank or particular relationship manager; and the ability of the existing bank to negotiate lower charges or otherwise respond if there is a threat of switching. In addition, it concluded that the barriers to entry and expansion in the markets for liquidity management services and general purpose business loans were significant. Finally, it identified a number of practices, each carried out by some or all of the clearing banks, which constituted a monopoly situation in that they restricted and/or distorted price competition in the supply of the reference services. These included confining the provision of free banking services to start-ups and switching customers; not paying interest on current accounts; giving discriminatory discounts through negotiations; and refraining from price competition in setting prices such that they more than adequately financed an efficient SME banking business.[248]

The UK Competition Commission concluded that Abbey National was only a recent entrant to this market, but held that its brand name, national network of branches and presence in personal and some business markets made it one of the very few players outside the big four able to compete in the SME market. Thus, the merger would lead to adverse effects on competition by removing this significant source of competition. The UK Competition Commission recommended the prohibition of the merger; the Secretary of State for Trade and Industry adopted the UK Competition Commission's recommendation.

The RBS/Natwest merger had been approved creating the fourth player in the big four oligopoly. As the acquisition of Bank of Scotland by Halifax (occurring in the same period as the *Lloyds TSB/Abbey National* transaction)[249] was regarded as likely to be approved by the authorities, thus creating a strong fifth player, the acquisition of Abbey National should not have been blocked, regardless of its immediate implications.[250]

In addition, the suggestion that the authorities perceived Abbey National's market share of 1 per cent in the small business area as monopoly potential is, in my opinion, somewhat surprising taking into account the fact that the bank had been unable to increase market share significantly.

It is doubtful whether the European Commission could have argued that the market for the supply of banking services to SMEs was prone to either single firm or collective dominance: the market shares of the incumbents (apart from RBS/Natwest) was below the 25 per cent threshold identified in Recital 15 of the preamble of the original ECMR;[251] the market exhibited a certain degree of innovation in the products offered (with Abbey National being one of the major forces of innovation); the products were somewhat differentiated with a strong branding effect; and customers were not of an insignificant size.

Thus, the European Commission would not, in my opinion, be able to argue that the merger would lead to adverse effects on competition in the market for the supply of banking services to SMEs. Although the merger might lead to non-coordinated effects in the market for the supply of banking services to SMEs, the European Commission would not have been in a position to block the merger based on these adverse effects. However, the European Commission might have been able to block the merger or accept remedies based on the coordinated effects that would arise post-merger in the PCA market.

4.4 The United States

The US case that will be analysed is the baby foods merger. In this case, the second and third largest firm merged, with the resulting merged entity being the second biggest player in the post-merger market for prepared baby food.

4.4.1 Heinz/Beech-Nut[252]

4.4.1.1 Analysis of the case

Heinz was a worldwide producer and distributor of a wide variety of food products. Worldwide, Heinz was the largest seller of prepared baby foods, with over $1 billion in sales. Beech-Nut was a subsidiary of Milnot, a food product company. Beech-Nut had over $100 million in sales in prepared baby food sales.

The prepared baby food market had existed since the early 1930s when Beech-Nut created the first packaged baby food. For decades the market had consisted of only three firms: Gerber, Beech-Nut, and Heinz. Most prepared baby food sales were made through supermarkets, nearly all of which carried two main brands, Gerber and either Beech-Nut or Heinz. The direct competition between Heinz and Beech-Nut, at the wholesale level, for shelf space was intense, forcing these companies to compete aggressively, leading to better prices for consumers as well as to innovation, and forcing Gerber too to compete on price and innovation. There was extensive record evidence of this head-to-head competition as the merging firms sought to displace each other from existing accounts and be the second brand carried on retailers' shelves.

Heinz and Beech-Nut also competed at the retail level through advertising, couponing, loyalty card discounts, product quality, innovations, shelf positioning, and product variety.[253] The head-to-head competition for supermarket accounts resulted in very substantial price concessions to retailers and promotional programmes directed to consumers ("slotting fees" and "pay-to-stay arrangements").

The merger, between the second and third largest companies in the market, would eliminate the competition both at wholesale and retail level. This merger to duopoly raised very serious concerns that consumers would be harmed from higher prices, less innovation, and less consumer choice. Thus, Heinz's acquisition of Beech-Nut would eliminate the increasingly fierce competition between two of only three companies, and would thus lead to a substantial increase in market concentration. The result of the merger would be a duopoly, between Gerber and Heinz, representing 98 per cent of the market. The FTC challenged Heinz's proposed acquisition of Beech-Nut.

The FTC defined the market as the one for prepared baby food, or smaller segments thereof, consisting primarily of glass jars of food.[254] The relevant geographic framework was defined as the United States as well as smaller geographical markets within the United States. Heinz's share of the US jarred baby food market was approximately 17.4 per cent, while Beech-Nut's market share was approximately 15.4 per cent.[255] Heinz marketed itself as a "value brand" with a shelf price several cents below Gerber's. Beech-Nut maintained price parity with Gerber, selling at about one penny less and marketed its product as a premium brand.[256]

The FTC assembled evidence that the proposed merger would, in fact, substantially reduce competition in the prepared baby food market in two ways. First, the proposed merger would eliminate substantial head-to-head competition between Beech-Nut and Heinz, thus enabling the merged firm to increase its prices unilaterally. Second, by reducing the number of competitors in the prepared baby food market from three to two, the proposed merger would significantly increase the likelihood that the merged firm and Gerber would engage in coordinated behaviour.[257]

As we have just seen, Beech-Nut and Heinz were each other's most direct competitors. All retailers that sold baby food had Gerber and either Beech-Nut or Heinz. Thus, Beech-Nut and Heinz competed directly against one another to be the second baby food offered by retailers. This intense competition led to price reductions and offers for retailers and consumers. In the post-merger market, Heinz would have been in a position to exercise market power unilaterally, by increasing its prices, through its control of the combined Heinz and Beech-Nut baby food brands.

In addition, where both Heinz and Beech-Nut were present in the same areas, except from depressing each other's prices they also put downward pressure on the prices of Gerber, even though the three companies were very unlikely to be found in the same store. Moreover, Gerber's market share was lower in markets where both Heinz and Beech-Nut are significant players than when it faced significant competition from only Heinz or Beech-Nut. In the post-merger market, with the elimination of the Beech-Nut brand (since the products would be sold under the Heinz brand, which was considered lower quality by consumers than the brand of Gerber), Gerber would have the incentive to increase prices. Thus, the elimination of competitive constraints that both merging parties, and in particular Beech-Nut, imposed on Gerber, might have led the latter to unilaterally adopt conduct having an adverse impact on competition in the post-merger market.

The FTC further identified the likelihood of tacit collusion being induced by the merger. First, barriers to entry into the prepared baby food market were extremely high. For 60 years, no significant entry had occurred and the market had been stable or declining. In addition, the existence of a brand to ensure consumer acceptance and convey a reputation for quality was essential. Moreover, the proposed merger would reduce the number of effective competitors from three to two, and would increase the HHI by almost 400 points to over 5300.

In addition, demand for prepared baby food was relatively inelastic, and transactions were relatively frequent and pricing information was visible and collected regularly by the incumbents. There were a large number of smaller customers, and transactions were generally numerous and small both at wholesale and retail level, minimizing the incentive to cheat, as the gains from cheating would be small. The two remaining firms would be well positioned to detect any cheating by the other company. Furthermore, almost all retailers that carried baby food carried two brands of baby food – Gerber and either Beech-Nut or Heinz. Nearly all retailers were reluctant to carry only a single brand of baby food, for fear of not providing their customers a choice.

Thus, there would be significantly less incentive for the merged entity and Gerber to engage in head-to-head competition to displace each other, since there would be space on the shelves for both firms' products. As the above analysis indicates, there would be a significantly reduced incentive for the two remaining firms to either cheat on any tacit understanding they might reach, or to compete aggressively against one another.[258]

The defendants argued before the FTC that the proposed acquisitions would result in significant efficiencies. The defendants claim that this merger would result in substantial cost savings that ultimately would lead to lower prices for consumers.

The FTC sought a preliminary injunction to block Heinz's proposed acquisition of Beech-Nut, citing concerns that the transaction would inhibit competition both at wholesale and retail level, by reducing the number of competitors in the baby food market from three to two, creating a duopoly, and inducing either non-coordinated or coordinated effects.

The District Court denied a preliminary injunction.[259] The FTC appealed and sought a stay pending appeal. In its memorandum opinion granting the stay, the DC. Circuit stated that the FTC demonstrated a substantial probability of success on the merits. The Court of Appeals ("Court") noted that the pre-merger HHI of 4,775 and increase of 510 points would create by a wide margin a presumption that the merger will lessen competition at the retail level. The Court also noted that:

> [I]it is indisputable that the merger will eliminate competition between the two merging parties at the wholesale level, where they are currently the only competitors for what the district court described as the "second position on the supermarket shelves".[260]

As to the parties' efficiencies defence, the acting director of the FTC mentioned that in this case, the court concluded that, while:

> [A]ppellees' efficiencies defense may yet carry the day, ... only the grant of interim relief would both afford this court an opportunity to determine whether that should be the case and protect the public interest in the event that it is not.[261]

If the merger was allowed to proceed and the merger was ultimately found to violate the Clayton Act, it would be impossible to recreate pre-merger competition and the pre-merger market conditions.

The Court concluded that the FTC's showing on the merits was sufficient to establish that the public interest would be furthered by an injunction pending appeal. The parties abandoned the merger plans after the Court of Appeals decision.

4.4.1.2 A gap case?

As the FTC noted, the proposed merger would eliminate substantial head-to-head competition between Beech-Nut and Heinz, thus enabling the merged firm to increase its prices unilaterally. In addition, Gerber would increase prices unilaterally since the competitive constraints that were eminent prior to the merger would be decreased or eliminated by the acquisition of Beech-Nut by Heinz. Post-acquisition, both remaining incumbents would have the incentive to unilaterally increase prices as a result of the reduction in the competitive constraints posed on them. The merger would thus lead to non-coordinated effects in the oligopolistic market for prepared baby food.

This merger case has been identified in the academic literature as a likely gap case had it been assessed under the ECMR. Fingleton (2002) argued that the Court of Appeals mixed tacit collusion and unilateral effects in its decision.[262] As the preceding analysis indicated, in the post-merger market, both remaining incumbents would have the incentive to unilaterally increase prices as a result of the reduction in the competitive constraints posed upon them.

Certain scenarios have also been put forward on how the non-coordinated effects that arose from this case could have been dealt with under the dominance test. The dominance test could have been applied under the allegation that the merger would have led to collective dominance, as the Court also alleged. There are academic voices that support the argument that this case was not a gap case and that had it been assessed under the dominance test it would have resulted in the same outcome, that is, the prohibition of the merger. Boge and Muller (2002)[263] argue that the *Heinz* case proves that there is no gap in the application of the dominance test compared to the SLC test. The US competition authorities and courts assessed this merger in different ways although a uniform criterion, SLC, was applied. Thus, a merger may be evaluated differently by various institutions even if a uniform test is applied as the substantive prohibition criterion. As they argue, if the merger had been examined under the dominance test, it could have been prohibited based on the creation or strengthening of collective dominance.

However, in markets that do not exhibit a sufficient level of concentration and also lack market characteristics that contribute to the sustainability of collective dominance (highly differentiated products, innovative markets, lack of transparency, lack of retaliation, and lack of consumer and competitor constraints, etc.) an allegation of collective dominance is not credible and thus the adverse effects of the merger on competition will not be prevented. If the European Commission attempts to allege coordinated effects in such cases, it risks having its decision annulled by the courts (as happened in *Airtours*).[264]

An alternative scenario relates to a narrow definition of the relevant market; such a definition may ensure that the resulting market shares will be high enough to lead to a credible allegation of single dominance. In *Heinz*, the Commission could try to define a separate market for "second-in-shelf baby foods" in which the merged entity may have held a significant market share to be presumed dominant.[265] However, such narrow market definition may not always be accurate and may lead to complications as regards the creation of precedent for future merger cases. The market definition in a merger case should be done objectively, without being influenced by the impact of the merger on competition. Only after the market has been defined can there be an accurate assessment of the impact of the merger on competition.

A third scenario[266] would be to argue that the merger of the number two and three players decreases the competitive constraint that the market leader faces and, thus, strengthens its dominant position. This argument resembles the effect that the merger would have if it led to non-coordinated effects in the post-merger market. The Commission would have to show that the market leader already holds a position of single dominance, which will be difficult if the distance between the market shares of the market leader and merging entities is small. Moreover, it would also need to show that the removal of some residual pricing pressure from the market leader would be sufficient to reach the materiality threshold for finding a strengthening of a dominant position.[267]

None of these scenarios is, in my opinion, a solution to the inapplicability of the dominance test to mergers leading to non-coordinated effects in oligopolistic markets. Attempting to extend the application of the dominance test can only enhance the risks of successful appeals by the merging parties and can only lead to inefficiency in the Commission's assessment of mergers as well as to legal uncertainty.

Although the *Heinz* merger might have been caught under the dominance test as leading to the creation of a collectively dominant position, this case can provide the general market structure in which one would expect non-coordinated effects to arise as a result of a merger.[268] *Heinz* involved the merger of the number two and three competitors whose products were differentiated and which had a substantial combined market share but still were behind the market leader. If the market was not conducive to collective dominance,[269] then the Commission would not be able to address the non-coordinated effects of such mergers under the dominance test.

4.5 New Zealand

The case that will be analysed is *Progressive Enterprises/Woolworths*. This case was initially considered under the dominance test and was cleared. After a Court of Appeal decision the case was reconsidered under the SLC test and was prohibited. Thus, this case provides a useful example of the case being assessed the same case under the two substantive tests and reach different outcomes.

4.5.1 Progressive Enterprises/Woolworths

4.5.1.1 Analysis of the case

The proposed transaction concerned the acquisition of Woolworths (New Zealand) Limited ("Woolworths") by Progressive Enterprises Limited ("Progressive"), the country's third and second largest supermarket chains respectively. New Zealand's competition regulator, the Commerce Commission, was asked to assess the same business acquisition under the dominance test and again under the SLC test.

Progressive applied for clearance of the acquisition of Woolworths (New Zealand) with the Commerce Commission in May 2001, prior to the enactment of the Commerce Amendment Act 2001, which changed the substantive test for the assessment of mergers from the dominance test[270] to the SLC test. The Commerce Commission initially considered this transaction under the dominance test and, subject to divestments, cleared it. Foodstuffs, the remaining competitor in this market, then won a Court of Appeal decision to have the application considered under the SLC test. Subsequently, when considering the application under the SLC test, the Commerce Commission determined that the transaction could not proceed.

According to the annual report of major developments in competition law in New Zealand submitted to the OECD,[271] the key reason for the change in the decision was that under the SLC test the Commerce Commission was able to pay greater attention to the whole structure of a relevant market (rather than focusing on the resulting market share of the merged entity), and could take into account the effect the acquisition would have on coordinated market conduct.

Progressive enterprises was owned by Foodland Associated Limited ("FAL"), a public company incorporated in Western Australia. FAL conducted wholesale and retail supermarket operations in Western Australia and New Zealand.

Woolworths (New Zealand) and Denstree were ultimately owned by Dairy Farm International Holdings Limited ("Dairy Farm"). Dairy Farm operated supermarkets, hypermarkets, convenience stores, and drugstores throughout the Asia-Pacific region.

In the supermarket industry, there were three major competitors, Foodstuffs, Progressive and Woolworths. Foodstuffs comprised three independent cooperatives, Foodstuffs Auckland, Foodstuffs Wellington and Foodstuffs South Island. Foodstuffs held a market share in supermarket sales of approximately 58 per cent (163 stores) nationally. Progressive (inclusive of two small independent supermarket chains with wholesale/distribution links to Progressive) held around 24 per cent of sales (105 stores) nationally. Woolworths held 18 per cent of sales (81 stores) nationally.[272]

The Commerce Commission in the later decision ("448")[273] argued that although separate Foodstuffs stores may have competed to some extent in some areas, it was not to such a degree that they should be considered separate entities for the purposes of a competition analysis.[274] In the initial decision ("438"), the Commerce Commission considered the three Foodstuffs companies to be separate from each other; in doing so, it adopted the most conservative scenario in its assessment of the merger.[275]

In the initial decision, Progressive submitted with the application undertakings for certain divestitures in the geographic areas where high concentration was identified. The Commerce Commission in this decision defined the market as that for supermarkets. It further stated that convenience stores and specialist stores did not provide strong competition constraints to supermarkets and that "discount" supermarkets as well as full-service supermarkets constituted different market segments rather than different markets. As far as the geographic scope of the market was concerned, the Commerce Commission concluded that there was not a one sized market that applied to all areas. Stores within five kilometres of each other were generally substitutable for each other. Where there were competing stores within consecutive five-kilometre distances, by the chain of substitution those stores would fall within the one market and the market would, therefore be greater than five kilometres in dimension.

In addition, the Commerce Commission assessed the impact of the merger on the national market for the wholesale supply of groceries. It was concerned with the strong buying power of each supermarket due to the fact that supermarkets were a very important distribution outlet for "fast moving consumer goods".

In the market for supermarkets, the merged entity would have 42 per cent of supermarket shopping whereas the three Foodstuffs collectively would have 58 per cent. The Commerce Commission concluded that where Foodstuffs had a significant presence in a geographic market, it would provide an effective constraint on the merged entity. Foodstuffs would have the ability to expand that presence, inter alia, by increasing the size of its store in some instances. However, the Commerce Commission recognized that the construction of a new store could sometimes face a major barrier in obtaining the necessary consents. In addition, it mentioned that there was no *de novo* entry for at least the preceding 10 years. Furthermore, the Commerce Commission was not satisfied that *de novo* entry by a new chain was sufficiently likely to act as an effective competitive constraint. Neither could specialist and convenience stores as well as suppliers provide an effective constraint on supermarkets.[276]

The Commerce Commission analysed the impact of the merger in the markets with the highest post-merger concentration. It concluded that, as a result of either the divestments or the competitive constraints imposed from Foodstuffs, the merger would not lead to a creation or strengthening of a dominant position.[277]

As far as the national market for the wholesale supply of groceries is concerned, the Commerce Commission concluded as follows: that market shares were not indicative of dominance; that there were other distribution outlets; that Foodstuffs provided a strong competitive constraint; and that some large manufacturers might have had an influence on supermarkets and could thus countervail their market power.

In the later decision, the Commerce Commission, when defining the market, stressed the differentiated nature of the product; this was not done in the earlier decision. The Commerce Commission argued that the ability of supermarkets to vary the dimensions of service (location, variety, range of products, staff service, etc.) allowed them to compete on more grounds than just price.[278] According to the Commerce Commission, the service was likely to be somewhat differentiated. Thus, the market was spatially differentiated as well as in terms of price/service.[279]

In order to assess the likely unilateral effects arising from the merger, the Commerce Commission used a model of non-cooperative pricing behaviour in differentiated product markets. The results of the model were that price increases in the post-merger market would not be substantial, although as the Commerce Commission itself recognized, the assumptions that were considered in the construction of the model made any certain post-merger outcome unlikely. In addition, there would be several markets in which the merged entity would have market share outside the Commerce Commission's safe harbours.[280]

As regards the likely coordinated effects of the merger, the Commerce Commission concluded that the factors that facilitate tacit coordination (transparency, retaliation, high barriers to entry, cost symmetry, homogeneity of products, high concentration, mature markets, lack of countervailing buyer, and competitor power) were present. The reduction of three to two players was considered likely to materially increase the potential for coordinated market power, and to substantially lessen competition. The divestment undertaking would not alleviate these concerns.

As regards the national market for the wholesale supply of groceries, the Commerce Commission was satisfied that the merger would not lead to either unilateral effects (the 45 per cent market share was below the Commerce Commission's safe harbours) or to coordinated effects (no transparency, different sized firms, vertical integration as well as small and frequent sales).

The Commerce Commission blocked the merger based on the coordinated effects that would arise in the market for supermarkets. Progressive appealed to the Privy Council and the appeal was upheld. The Privy Council ruled that the old dominance test should have been applied. The merger was consummated as a result.[281]

4.5.1.2 A gap case?

The Commerce Commission in the decision analysed the change in the merger test that had been recently implemented. It argued that there was a level of market power that had been acceptable in the past but which was no longer so.[282] One can argue that this gap in the level of market power represents, inter alia, the creation of non-coordinated effects in oligopolistic markets as a result of the merger. The Commerce Commission continued by saying that it must take account the oligopolistic market structures and outcomes, which can imply competition concerns with a lower market share than under dominance.[283] Thus, it must take into account effects arising from mergers that do not satisfy the higher threshold of market power inherent in the dominance test.

As a numerical guide, the Commerce Commission mentioned that an increase in market power which would be likely to lead to a 4 to 5 per cent price increase (or reduction in conditions that was the equivalent of 4 to 5 per cent price increase) would suggest a substantial lessening of competition.[284] Prior to the change in the Act, the Commerce Commission had considered that a firm in a dominant position in a market was one which was in a position to increase prices above competitive levels by 5 to 10 per cent. The supermarket sector was one in which the Commerce Commission considered that it might be appropriate to apply a lower threshold. Thus, the inability of the Commerce Commission to apply the lower thresholds in the earlier decision does not stem from the inexistence of such market power, since the market conditions were arguably the same in both decisions, but rather from the inability of the Commerce Commission to apply the lower thresholds in assessing the merger under the dominance test.[285]

The reasoning of the Commerce Commission in the first decision was based on the fact that in the local markets where competition concerns were identified due to increased concentration, the competitive constraints were posed by each of the Foodstuffs individually in each locally defined geographic market rather than by the three Foodstuffs companies collectively.[286] Thus, the argument that a large and effective competitor was posing a significant competitive constraint, although accurate for the later decision (where the Commerce Commission considered Foodstuffs companies as a single entity), is not accurate according to the Commerce Commission's analysis about the first decision.

It is interesting that the Commerce Commission mentioned the differentiated nature of the products in the later decision only. In addition, it treated the Foodstuffs companies as separate entities in the earlier decision and as one entity in the later decision. However, this fact is not likely to have influenced the outcome of the assessment of the effects of the merger. The Commerce Commission in the earlier decision analysed local geographic markets where the existence of individual Foodstuffs companies posed significant competitive constraints. In the later decision, it focused on a national market, since, as it mentioned, if coordinated market power were to occur, it would most likely be facilitated at head office level. Thus, it argued, it would not be necessary to assess each geographic market separately, since one would expect many to be affected.[287] In both cases, the existence of individual Foodstuffs companies (at local level) or the Foodstuffs companies collectively (at national level) posed significant competitive constraints in the market. Under the same market conditions, the merger was cleared under the dominance test, and blocked under the SLC test.

Furthermore, as a result of the market definition in the earlier decision,[288] the Commerce Commission would not have adequate grounds to allege coordinated effects since in the post-merger market, Progressive/

Enterprises would have 42 per cent and the remaining 58 per cent would be attributed to the three Foodstuffs supermarkets separately.[289] Thus, the respective market shares of these entities are unlikely to be dispersed equivalently,[290] since judging from the number of stores that each of them has, Foodstuffs New World has 123 out of a total of 163 stores, Pak'N Save has 32 and Write Price has eight stores. The importance of the market share as an indication of collective dominance depends on the level relative to that of the nearest competitor, as well as on factors tending to entrench the leading position of the firm.[291] Thus, due to the discrepancy between the market shares of the incumbents in the post-merger market, the Commerce Commission, in my opinion, could not allege that the merger would lead to coordinated effects in the market for supermarkets.[292]

As the preceding analysis illustrates, in the earlier decision the Commerce Commission cleared the merger accepting undertakings. However, the Commerce Committee, in its report to the New Zealand Parliament on the Commerce Act Amendment Bill, recognized the limitations of the dominance test in assessing the effects of a merger.[293] Thus, the Commerce Commission would not be able to block a merger on the basis either of collective dominance or of non-coordinated effects in oligopolistic markets, since neither of these market situations entails a single firm being dominant.

The *Progressive Enterprises/Woolworths* merger may have involved, according to the Commerce Commission, coordinated effects, but it is clear that the adoption of the SLC test amended the capability of the Commerce Commission to block mergers with market shares lower than the ones relevant for the dominance test, especially in markets involving differentiated products (that is to say non-collusive oligopolies).

Had the Commerce Commission not been able to prove the sustainability of coordinated effects, it would still be able to block it under the SLC as the merger might have led to non-coordinated effects in the oligopolistic market for supermarkets. The Commerce Commission would not be able to block the merger under the dominance test.[294]

The argument of the Commerce Commission that under the SLC a lower threshold of market power applies,[295] indicates the newly acquired ability of the Commerce Commission not only to block merger inducing coordinated effects but also mergers leading to non-coordinated effects in oligopolistic markets. Thus, by amending the legal test, the Commerce Commission closed the "double" gap in the application of the dominance test of the New Zealand competition legislation.

4.6 Other jurisdictions

Australia is a very interesting example of a jurisdiction that changed from the SLC to the dominance test (in 1976), in an attempt by the government to encourage mergers leading to economies of scale and to enhanced international competitiveness. It amended again the test to the SLC in 1991.[296] The dominance test was deemed unable to capture certain types of merger having an adverse impact on competition.

Section 50 of the Trade Practices Act 1974 prohibits mergers or acquisitions that "substantially lessen competition in a substantial market for goods or services in Australia, or that are likely to do so".

During the period of the dominance test, a number of mergers had not been opposed and many argued that they had caused significant competitive harm. Those would have been likely to have been scrutinized and probably opposed under an SLC test. These likely gap cases included[297] *Coles-Myer, News Ltd and Herald & Weekly Times, Ansett Airlines/East West Airlines.*

In addition, mergers that were examined under the SLC test would not have been under the previous dominance test include *Retail Banking, Caltex/Ampol, Rank/Foodland Associated Ltd, Wattyl/Taubmans, Optus/AAPT, British American Tobacco Pty Ltd (W.D. & H.O. Wills)/Rothmans.*

A number of other mergers that did not infringe the dominance standard, but would have required examination under an SLC test, and many of which might have been opposed, were identified by the ACCC to the Cooney Committee.[298] They were *Allied Mills/Fielders Gillespie, Power Brewing, ICI (Dulux)*'s acquisition of *Berger* and *British Paints, BHP's* acquisition by *Tubemakers* of *McPherson, Mobil/Esso* and *Ampol/Solo.*

Unfortunately, the actual decisions for these gap cases have not been obtained.[299] However, the former Chairman of the ACCC, Alan Fells, indicates that the cases would have merited a different assessment under the dominance and SLC tests. This varied assessment has led to cases not being assessed or not being found to harm competition under the dominance test, whereas they would have been assessed or prohibited had they been assessed under the SLC test.

In Finland, the *SOK Corporation, Spar Finland Plc*[300] was cleared by the competition authority:

> The result might have been different depending on the test used by the competition authority. It is worth noting, that the FCA found that the legal requirement for intervention in merger control was exceeded in roughly 30 Finnish localities. Thus, the FCA imposed a condition that roughly 30 Spar outlets are divested from the S Group and sold to actual or potential competitors in the daily consumer goods trade. The FCA considered that this measure would relieve the competition concerns resulting from the planned deal to the retail trade market of daily goods. In a case where the FCA would have used the SIEC it is likely that the legal requirement for intervention may have had occurred in many other municipalities too.[301]

4.7 Conclusion

This chapter has addressed the issue of whether there is case law involving mergers which raised competition concerns due to the non-coordinated effects they would induce in post-merger oligopolistic markets. It has included a comparative approach of examining mergers that were prohibited as well as mergers that were allowed to proceed after the submission of undertakings by the parties,[302] under various legal systems. Several cases that were likely to be "gap" cases were identified. The chapter focused on the EU, by examining *Airtours/First Choice*, *Oracle/PeopleSoft*, *Sony/BMG*, *Johnson & Johnson/Guidant*, and *Syngenta CP/Advanta*; on the United Kingdom, by looking at *Lloyds TSB/Abbey National*, and *Littlewoods Organization Plc/Freemans Plc*; on Finland, by reviewing the *SOK Corporation*, *Spar Finland Plc*; on New Zealand, by reviewing the *Progressive Enterprises/Woolworths*, which was assessed under both substantive tests; and finally on the United States, by looking at the *Heinz/Beech-Nut* merger. In addition, the chapter briefly referred to likely gap cases in Australia, although without elaborating on the specifics of each case due to the lack of access to the actual decisions.

It can be argued that the Commission tried – in the cases mentioned that were dealt under the original ECMR – either at the stage of the Statement of Objections or at the decision, to stretch the concept and applicability of the dominance test to non-coordinated effects in oligopolistic markets, and aimed at having the courts confirm this expansion. However, the General Court appeal in *Airtours*, the criticisms during the *Oracle/PeopleSoft*, and the sudden change in the Commission's assessment in the *Sony/BMG* indicate that the aim of the Commission to expand the applicability of the dominance test was unlikely to be successful.

The aim of this chapter was to show that a different outcome of the assessment of these mergers could have been reached had the substantive test been different from the one that the relevant competition authority applied. This aim was achieved. This chapter has illustrated the inadequacy of the dominance test in dealing with mergers leading to non-coordinated effects in oligopolistic markets. Thus, the reform of the ECMR was justified and much needed.

As mentioned earlier, the number of cases analysed herein does not purport to be exhaustive. It clearly indicates, however, the existence of a gap in the application of the dominance test. The number of cases not only of the European Commission but also of the national competition authorities that apply the dominance test is likely to be significant.

Several member states still adhere to the traditional dominance test,[303] and thus are still likely to experience cases where they will be facing a merger that will have the features of a non-collusive oligopoly but the competition authorities will be unable to apply the dominance test, and will thus resort to other methods of trying to deal with the adverse effects on competition of a merger; this will lead to legal errors, uncertainty and likely (successful) appeals against the authorities' decisions. The evidence of cases in the case law that illustrate the existence of a gap in the application of the dominance test is a fact that needs to be taken into consideration by these member states in order to enable them to efficiently and accurately assess the adverse impact on competition.

In addition, complications may arise from the application of Articles 4(4) and 9 of the ECMR. According to Article 4(4):

> Prior to the notification of a concentration within the meaning of paragraph 1, the persons or undertakings referred to in paragraph 2 may inform the Commission, by means of a reasoned submission, that the concentration may significantly affect competition in a market within a Member State which presents all the characteristics of a distinct market and should therefore be examined, in whole or in part, by that Member State.

According to Article 9:

> The Commission may, by means of a decision notified without delay to the undertakings concerned and the competent authorities of the other Member States, refer a notified concentration to the competent authorities of the Member State concerned.

Under both these Articles a concentration may be referred to a member state for assessment. In case the merger is likely to lead to non-coordinated effects in oligopolistic markets, it will not be blocked in a member state that applies the dominance test, whereas it would have been blocked under the SIEC test of the Recast ECMR. Thus, a tendency may be observed of parties, where appropriate, requesting referrals to member states that apply the dominance test in the assessment of mergers, since mergers inducing non-coordinated effects in oligopolistic markets are unlikely to be blocked in these member states. The latter fact may create distortions in the merger referral and assessment process.

The next chapter will present the event study analysis that was conducted as a means to provide further evidence of the existence of gap cases. Through this analysis, the Commission's decisions were compared with the perception of the market as regards the impact of these mergers on competition.

Notes

1 A limitation in this chapter concerns the lack of information. The analysis of these cases was done based on publicly available material. The extent to which the authorities' decisions as well as other published material reflect accurately and fully the market conditions may vary on a case-by-case basis. Thus, in analysing these cases, certain assumptions as regards the market structure and

market features had to be made. Unfortunately, access to the authorities' file was not possible. Had such access been possible, the results of this chapter may have been further enhanced.

2 The main focus of this book is non-coordinated in oligopolistic markets, rather than non-coordinated effects in general. As the following analysis will illustrate, the gap in the application of the dominance test relates to oligopolistic markets characterized inter alia by differentiated products as compared to oligopolistic structures with homogeneous products which give rise to collective dominance concerns. Unless the market is oligopolistic, then the multitude of firms in the post-merger market, even with differentiated products, will imply that the demand is thinly spread to each of these firms and thus no unilateral conduct by any of these firms will amount to a significant impediment to effective competition.

3 Any inability of the dominance test to capture the mergers analysed herein, will be due to the gap in its application rather than due to any discrepancy in the quantitative methods used in the assessment of the market definition or of the merger's effects.

4 As the *Financial Times* mentioned in an article, "the Commission may be constrained by current rules, which do not explicitly permit it to ban mergers that could give rise to 'non-collusive oligopolies', such as the one Brussels suspects may arise between Oracle and SAP". See www.ft.com, article of 28 March 2004.

5 The SLC was adopted with the Enterprise Act 2002. See further: www.oft.gov.uk.

6 The SLC is applied according to Commerce Act 1986.

7 See further: Clayton Antitrust Act 1914, 15 USC §12–27, 29 USC §52–53.

8 The SLC was adopted with the Trade Practices Act 1974.

9 An additional gap case is Case C5422B, *Sai–Società Assicuratrice Industriale/La Fondiaria Assicurazioni*, 17 December 2002, Bull. No. 51–52/2002. This merger, which was assessed by the Italian Competition Authority, will not be analysed in this book any further, but is mentioned here for completeness. See further: Siragusa, M. et. al, in Kokkoris, I. (2007a), *Competition Cases from the European Union. The Ultimate Guide to Leading Cases of the EU and all 27 Member States*, Sweet & Maxwell, London.

10 Case M1524 *Airtours/First Choice* [2000] OJ L93/1 ("*Airtours/First Choice*").

11 Case M3216 *Oracle/PeopleSoft* [2005] OJ L218/6.

12 Case M3333 *Sony/BMG* [2005] OJ L62/30.

13 Case M3465 *Syngenta CP/Advanta* [2004] OJ C263/7 ("*Syngenta CP/Advanta*").

14 Case M3687 *Johnson & Johnson/Guidant* [2006] OJ L173/16 ("*Johnson & Johnson/Guidant*").

15 Case M3916 *T-Mobile/Tele.ring*, 26 April 2006 ("*T-Mobile/Tele.ring*").

16 These market shares are according to the shares provided by the research firm AC Nielsen, reproduced in Table 1 of the Commission's decision. According to the Commission's market shares the combined merger entity would have a market share of 32 per cent, with Airtours having 21 per cent and First Choice 11 per cent. Thomson had 27 per cent and Thomas Cook 20 per cent. There is insignificant divergence between the Commission's data and the data provided by AC Nielsen. This book employs the market shares provided by AC Nielsen.

17 See further: para. 54 of *Airtours/First Choice*.

18 Case T-342/99 *Airtours v Commission* [2002] ECR II-2585.

19 Case 62/86 *AKZO Chemie BV v Commission* [1991] ECR I-3359.

20 However, in Recital 32 of the preamble of the ECMR a reverse indication or presumption can be made that where the market share of the undertakings exceeds 25 per cent, then dominance will be assumed to exist.

21 Kolasky, W. (2002), "Co-ordinated Effects in Merger Review: From Dead Frenchmen to Beautiful Minds and Mavericks", http://www.usdoj.gov/atr/public/speeches/11050.htm, 28. A firm is defined as maverick when it declines to follow the industry consensus and thereby undermines effective coordination.
22 Case T-342/99 *Airtours v Commission* [2002] ECR II-2585, at §294.
23 Case T-342/99 *Airtours v Commission* [2002] ECR II-2585.
24 Paragraph 133, Case T-342/99 *Airtours v Commission* [2002] ECR II-2585.
25 Paragraph 147, Case T-342/99 *Airtours v Commission* [2002] ECR II-2585.
26 Whish, R. (2002), "Analytical Framework of Merger Review, Substantial Lessening of Competition/Creation or Strengthening of Sominance", International Competition Network, First Annual Conference, 28 September, Naples, www.internationalcompetitionnetwork.org/whish_icn_naples_full_version.pdf.
27 Paragraph 14, "*Guidelines on the Assessment of Horizontal Mergers under the Council Regulation on the Control of Concentrations between Undertakings*" ("*Guidelines*"), OJ C31, 05.02.2004, 5–18.
28 A more concrete analysis would need the calculation of diversion ratios. Market shares must be used with caution in drawing conclusions. In markets with homogeneous products, market shares can be used as proxies for diversion ratios.
29 Hildebrand, D. (2001), "EC&MC Comments on the Draft Guidelines on Market Analysis and the Calculation of Significant Market Power", www.ee-mc.com/files/Comment%20%20SMP%20Draft%20guidelines.pdf.
30 The concentration of the incumbents with the three highest market shares.
31 US Department of Justice and Federal Trade Commission Horizontal Merger Guidelines 1992, www.usdoj.gov/atr/public/guidelines/horiz_book/5.html, §1.5.
32 See further: "Merger Challenges Data, Fiscal Years 1999–2003", www.usdoj.gov/atr/public/201898.htm.
33 Paragraph 20, "*Guidelines on the Assessment of Horizontal Mergers under the Council Regulation on the Control of Concentrations between Undertakings*" ("*Guidelines*"), OJ C31, 05.02.2004, 5–18.
34 Cosmos/Avro (2.9 per cent), Manos (1.7 per cent), Kosmar (1.7 per cent) and others (8.2 per cent) have been grouped together.
35 It should be noted that the General Court found no likelihood of creation of collective dominance.
36 UK Competition Commission, Cm 3813, "Foreign Package Holidays: A Report on the Supply in the UK of Tour Operators' Services and Travel Agents' Services in Relation to Foreign Package Holidays", 19.12.97, www.competition-commission.org.uk.
37 Motta, M. (1999), "Economic Analysis and EC Merger Policy", European University Institute, www.iue.it/Personal/Motta?ECMergR.pdf, 27.
38 Nicholson, M. and Cardell, S. (2002), "Airtours v. Commission: Collective Dominance Contained", IBA EC Merger Control Conference, www.ibanet.org.
39 OXERA (2002), "Collective Dominance from an Economic Perspective", *Competing Ideas*, June.
40 Ehlermann, C-D., Völcker, S. and Gutermuth, A. (2005), "Unilateral Effects: The Enforcement Gap under the Old EC Merger Regulation", *World Competition*, 28(2), 193–203.
41 As mentioned, mergers inducing multilateral effects are equivalent to non-collusive oligopolies. Fingleton, J. (2002), "Does Collective Dominance Provide Suitable Housing for All Anti-competitive Oligopolistic Mergers", in

Hawk, B., *International Antitrust Law and Policy*, Fordham University Law School, Corporate Law Institute, 190.

42 Paragraph 54 of *Airtours/First Choice.*

43 Chapter 4 involves the implementation of an event study. In order to evaluate investors' perceptions and expectations, the abnormal increase/decrease of the share prices of the merging firms and their competitors on the official announcement day will be calculated by comparing the share price of both merging firms and their main competitors with an index of all market shares on the event day of the announcement of the merger in the news. Conducting an event study analysis for the merging parties as well as for rival firms, by comparing their actual stock price returns around the announcement date with a counterfactual measure of what the return would have been had the merger not taken place, would provide useful insights of the likely expectation of the market of the profitability of the firms resulting from a merger.

44 The author of this book has written extensively about merger assessment and this part of the chapter incorporates and some of his earlier work, including the following: Kokkoris, I. (2009), "Was There a Gap in the ECMR", in *Concurrences*, 1.

45 Case M3216 *Oracle/PeopleSoft* [2005] OJ L218/6.

46 The Commission used proxies to describe those customers and the transactions for such software applications. As a first suitable proxy for the "complexity" of the requirements of such large organizations, the Commission considered a net licence value of €1 million to be appropriate. The Commission further complemented this threshold by a delineation of large and complex enterprises as customers. The market investigation showed that thresholds of 10,000 employees or of revenues exceeding €1 billion might be an appropriate proxy for a rough qualification of large and complex undertakings.

47 Judge Walker found that the US government failed to prove the unilateral effects case, since they failed to show an area of localized competition between Oracle and PeopleSoft. He argued that the relevant markets were not limited to high function HRM and FMS software as the DOJ had suggested. He further suggested that the market included, inter alia, outsourcing, mid-market vendors and that the competitors in the relevant market were not limited to Oracle, PeopleSoft and SAP, although the DOJ had relied heavily on the testimony of customer witnesses to formulate its market definition. The DOJ had contended that only three vendors competed in the market, Oracle, PeopleSoft, and SAP and that Oracle and PeopleSoft were the two strongest players and closest substitutes, with SAP lagging considerably behind. Judge Walker found the DOJ's evidence on the market as unconvincing and rejected the DOJ's product and geographic markets, and thus argued that no likely harm on competition would occur. The flaws of the Judge's view are, in my opinion, the same as the flaws of the Commission's analysis on the market. Had the judge accepted the DOJ's market definition, he would probably have prohibited the merger under the SLC test. The Commission on the other hand could not have prohibited the merger under the dominance test, a fact that would illustrate the gap in the application of the dominance test.

48 See paragraph 184 of *Oracle/PeopleSoft.*

49 Paragraph 186 of *Oracle/PeopleSoft.*

50 Paragraph 201 of *Oracle/PeopleSoft.*

51 Paragraph 203 of *Oracle/PeopleSoft.*

52 Paragraph 205 of *Oracle/PeopleSoft.*

53 The products are very heterogeneous to the extent that they differ between products sold between the same vendor to different customers.
54 Baxter, S. and Dethmers, F. (2005) "Unilateral Effects Under the European Merger Regulation: How Big is the Gap?", *ECLR*, 26(7), 380–89.
55 Ehlermann, C-D., Völcker, S. and Gutermuth, A. (2005), "Unilateral Effects: The Enforcement Gap under the Old EC Merger Regulation", *World Competition*, 28(2), 193–203.
56 Paragraph 81 of *Oracle/PeopleSoft*.
57 Paragraph 26 of *Oracle/PeopleSoft*.
58 Paragraph 37 of *Oracle/PeopleSoft*.
59 In such a context, the incumbent supplier (for example the one who supplied and maintains the existing EAS system) can be expected to have an informational advantage: the less "informed" the contenders are relative to the incumbent supplier, the more leeway the incumbent has in terms of pricing for the new bid.
60 Oracle's software only runs on Oracle's database, while PeopleSoft and SAP's software also run on other databases.
61 Paragraph 189 of *Oracle/PeopleSoft*.
62 Paragraph 135 of *Oracle/PeopleSoft*.
63 In addition, as the event study analysis of Chapter 4 will illustrate, both Lawson and QAD had much lower positive abnormal returns compared to SAP, an indication that the positive impact of the merger, according to the investors, would be greater on SAP than on the smaller competitors QAD and Lawson. Thus, It can be argued, that the latter fact indicates that Oracle and PeopleSoft were constrained by SAP more than they were constrained by the two smaller players.
64 "*Microsoft-Revolutionizing Enterprise Application Software*", 2003, www.cw360ms.com/research/Ovum/Microsoft_business_apps.pdf.
65 IP/04/1312, 26 October 2004.
66 Paragraph 1 of the DOJ decision.
67 Paragraph 30 of the DOJ decision.
68 Werden, G. (2005) "Unilateral Effects from Mergers: the Oracle Case", British Institute of International and Comparative Law, 5th Annual Transatlantic Antitrust Dialogue, 10 May, London.
69 Chapter 4 involves the implementation of an event study. In order to evaluate investors' perceptions and expectations, the abnormal increase/decrease of the share prices of the merging firms and their competitors on the official announcement day will be calculated by comparing the share price of both merging firms and their main competitors with an index of all market shares on the event day of the announcement of the merger in the news. Conducting an event study analysis for the merging parties as well as for rival firms, by comparing their actual stock price returns around the announcement date with a counterfactual measure of what the return would have been had the merger not taken place, would provide useful insights of the likely expectation of the market of the profitability of the firms resulting from a merger.
70 Case M3333 *Sony/BMG* [2005] OJ L62/30.
71 The worldwide active record companies that is to say BMG, Sony, Universal Music Group, EMI, and Warner Music Group.
72 The Commission analysed the development of average net prices on a quarterly basis for the top 100 single albums of each major in the five largest member states.
73 Multi-artist compilations such as "Hits 2003" and "Bravo Hits" required the approval of the record labels of all artists involved. It appeared from the market investigation that the combination of artists from different labels

made it possible to cover a broader range of the charts, or of the genre to which the compilation refers. Therefore, the appearance of artists from more than one record company appeared to be a key factor for the success of a compilation. See further: para. 115 of *Sony/BMG*.

74 Case T-464/04 *IMPALA v Commission*, 13 July 2006 ("*IMPALA*"). The parties appealed to the Court of Justice. C-413/06 P *BMG&Sony v Commission* [2006] OJ C326/25 (pending).

75 These theories included alleged coordination on budgets, on the pricing of each title, on pricing policy, on chart album prices, on access to retailers, on access to airplay, on chart rules, on release date, on coordination at the level of publishing activities and alleged negative impact on cultural diversity. http://europa.eu/rapid/pressReleasesAction.do?reference=IP/07/1437&format=HTML&aged=0&language=EN&guiLanguage=en.

76 *IMPALA*, para. 251.

77 *IMPALA*, para. 253.

78 SJ Berwin, *Community Week*, issue 286, 28 July 2006, www.sjberwin.com.

79 Paragraph 459, *IMPALA*.

80 Paragraph 469, *IMPALA*.

81 Shares for the majors refer to "owned content" sales. "Owned Content" refers to trade sales of finished music product by the Member Company (that is to say the record company) to retailers or to intermediate wholesalers, net of returns and discounts and excluding exports (in accordance with IFPI Market Data Reporting Definitions). The following do not qualify as "Owned Content" sales: (i) sales by minority owned labels; (ii) sales of finished product from distribution deals; (iii) sales of finished music product by Member Company's licensees; (iv) all other forms of revenue that are not wholesale sales or finished music product, for example licence income fees or royalty based income, etc.

82 This analysis uses Table 2 of the Commission's decision. The market shares of the Others (including the independents) have been grouped together. Using the lowest or highest market shares of the range leads to higher margin of error. Based on the publicly available documents an analysis of market shares and concentration ratios is a tractable method of evaluating the anticompetitive effects of a merger. Had there been access to the sources of data the Commission had at its disposal, more elaborate quantitative techniques could be used, such as critical loss analysis and merger simulation that were analysed above.

83 UMG had 25 to 30 per cent, EMI had 15 to 20 per cent, WMG had 10 to 15 per cent, Others (including the independents) had 20 to 25 per cent, SMEI had 10 to 15 per cent and BMG had 10 to 15 per cent.

84 See further: para. 53 of *Sony/BMG*.

85 Independents are smaller record companies which often specialize in certain specific genres.

86 See further: paras 53–54 of *Sony/BMG*.

87 See further: para. 54 of *Sony/BMG*.

88 See further: para. 112 of *Sony/BMG*.

89 See further: http://howrey.com/docs/EC_Merger_Developments.pdf, http://lathamandwatkins.com/upload/pubContent/_pdf/pub1063_1.pdf.

90 It is interesting to note that in *Tetra Laval* (Case 12/03 *Commission v Tetra Laval* [2005] ECR I-987), Advocate General Tizzano had suggested that in "grey" zone cases, that is to say in situations of uncertainty as to whether or not the transaction is compatible with the common market, the Commission ought to lean towards authorising the merger. Herbert Smith, "*Court of First Instance annuls Sony/BMG Decision (Case T-464/04 Impala v Commission)*",

www.herbertsmith.com/NR/rdonlyres/D488A886–7214–4EC4-AE25–8C0E9B115B67/2329/euc_140 706_updated_250706.html.

91 A possible remedy might have been the divestiture of some of the artists who account for a large share of the market.

92 Chapter 4 involves the implementation of an event study. In order to evaluate investors' perceptions and expectations, the abnormal increase/decrease of the share prices of the merging firms and their competitors on the official announcement day will be calculated by comparing the share price of both merging firms and their main competitors with an index of all market shares on the event day of the announcement of the merger in the news. Conducting an event study analysis for the merging parties as well as for rival firms, by comparing their actual stock price returns around the announcement date with a counterfactual measure of what the return would have been had the merger not taken place, would provide useful insights of the likely expectation of the market of the profitability of the firms resulting from a merger.

93 www.ftc.gov/os/caselist/0410054/040728mwtstmnt0410054.pdf.

94 www.ftc.gov/os/caselist/0410054/040728mwtstmnt0410054.pdf.

95 Due to, inter alia, factors such as language, culture, etc.

96 Table 1 of the Commission's decision depicts the market shares in the national markets.

97 *Financial Times*, 27 July 2006, www.ft.com/cms/s/1bde5a0a-1ce4–11db-9780–0000779e2340.html.

98 Case M3465 *Syngenta CP/Advanta* [2004] OJ C263/7.

99 This included a company incorporated in Europe which held a number of IP rights (maize germplasm, a molecular marker database, know-how and probes, specific maize transformation technology and IT systems) primarily used for the North American business. Paragraph 5 of *Syngenta CP/Advanta*.

100 The concentration did not meet the thresholds set out in Articles 1(2) and 1(3) of the ECMR. The case had been referred to the Commission upon Syngenta's request under Article 4(5) of the ECMR.

101 Paragraph 10 of *Syngenta CP/Advanta*.

102 Before seeds can be sold, they must pass two series of tests: (i) DUS: distinctness, uniformity and stability; and (ii) VCU: value for cultivation and use. Paragraph 24 of *Syngenta CP/Advanta*.

103 Seed treatment therefore targets seed or soil born diseases or soil dwelling or early season insects.

104 Paragraph 27 of *Syngenta CP/Advanta*.

105 The parties receive royalties for each unit sold by the sugar industry. Such royalties are in the range of 10 to 30 per cent of the selling price. See further: para. 35 of *Syngenta CP/Advanta*.

106 The breeding and testing phase for new hybrids, such as sugar beet seeds, was 7 to 10 years, the commercial preparation phase 1 to 2 years, and the commercial phase around 7 years (with peak sales for 3 to 4 years, followed by a declining period until phase out). Thus, the argument that the shares were too volatile for contributing to a significant impediment of competition was not accepted by the Commission.

107 Paragraph 42 of *Syngenta CP/Advanta*.

108 Paragraph 45 of *Syngenta CP/Advanta*.

109 Paragraph 46 of *Syngenta CP/Advanta*.

110 Paragraph 52 of *Syngenta CP/Advanta*.

111 In addition, the Commission concluded that barriers to entry in these markets were high. The market for seed development and production is a research-based industry, and there was a long and costly process before a variety of a product line is put on the market. Furthermore, no new entry had taken place

in the past number of years. Finally, market shares tended to remain stable, demand side was fragmented and no new varieties from competitors were in the pipeline.

112 Paragraph 86 of *Syngenta CP/Advanta.*
113 Paragraph 105 of *Syngenta CP/Advanta.*
114 See para. 52 of *Syngenta CP/Advanta.*
115 This is the case predominantly for France according to the information available. According to the Commission in *Sony/BMG*, "on the basis of these market shares the proposed joint venture does not reach the threshold of single dominance, in particular given that Universal is, by and large, an equally strong competitor in the markets for recorded music in Germany, the Netherlands, Belgium, Luxembourg and France".
116 Paragraph 46 of *Syngenta CP/Advanta.*
117 Case M1806 *Astra Zeneca/Novartis* [2004] OJ L110/1 (*Astra Zeneca/Novartis*).
118 Paragraph 367 of *Astra Zeneca/Novartis.*
119 Paragraph 287 of *Astra Zeneca/Novartis.*
120 Case M2547 *Bayer/Aventis Crop Science* [2004] L107/1 (*Bayer/Aventis Crop Science*).
121 Paragraph 214 of *Bayer/Aventis Crop Science.*
122 Paragraph 267 of *Bayer/Aventis Crop Science.*
123 Paragraph 304 of *Bayer/Aventis Crop Science.*
124 Unfortunately, more accurate data were not available in the published decisions.
125 Paragraph 212 of *Bayer/Aventis Crop Science.*
126 Paragraph 42 of *Syngenta CP/Advanta.*
127 The Commission had access to all the information provided by the parties and based on this information concluded that the merger would not lead to coordinated effects, but to non-coordinated effects. The decision is not, in my opinion, fully explanatory of why the Commission did not choose the route of coordinated effects.
128 Paragraph 46 of *Syngenta CP/Advanta.*
129 Paragraph 39 of *Syngenta CP/Advanta.*
130 "*Guidelines on the Assessment of Horizontal Mergers under the Council Regulation on the Control of Concentrations between Undertakings*" ("*Guidelines*"), OJ C31, 05.02.2004, 5–18, para. 45.
131 M190 *Nestlé/Perrier* [1992] OJ L356/1.
132 Case M1225 *Enso/Stora* [1999] OJ L254/9.
133 Other features of products that competition can be based on include quality and service. If the products are heterogeneous in such aspects, competition may rely on these aspects rather than on prices, thus making tacit collusion difficult to sustain.
134 Chapter 4 involves the implementation of an event study. In order to evaluate investors' perceptions and expectations, the abnormal increase/decrease of the share prices of the merging firms and their competitors on the official announcement day will be calculated by comparing the share price of both merging firms and their main competitors with an index of all market shares on the event day of the announcement of the merger in the news. Conducting an event study analysis for the merging parties as well as for rival firms, by comparing their actual stock price returns around the announcement date with a counterfactual measure of what the return would have been had the merger not taken place, would provide useful insights of the likely expectation of the market of the profitability of the firms resulting from a merger.
135 Case M3687 *Johnson & Johnson/Guidant* [2006] OJ L173/16.

136 A stent is a small expandable wire tube that is used to support the walls of the coronary artery.
137 See para. 9 of *Johnson & Johnson/Guidant.*
138 As the Commission noted, no other stent can be marketed as a carotid stent, and stents designed for carotid applications are usually not used for any other procedure. Thus, there was neither demand-side nor supply-side substitutability between carotid and other endovascular stents.
139 See para. 47 of *Johnson & Johnson/Guidant.*
140 Endovascular guiding catheters, SGWs, and PTA balloon catheters performed a similar function to the corresponding products in interventional cardiology. Each of these endovascular accessories was sold in different sizes and dimensions, there was no supply side substitutability across accessories, and they were in distinct markets from the coronary corresponding products (guiding catheters, SGWs, and PTCA balloon catheters). In addition, prices between the two lines of products tended to differ significantly and, from the supply side point of view, there was not a high degree of substitution between endovascular and cardiology devices.
141 Paragraph 53 of *Johnson & Johnson/Guidant.*
142 Beating-heart CABG stabilization systems enable the surgeon to perform coronary artery bypass graft ("CABG") surgery on the heart while beating.
143 The Commission did not analyse the competitive effects in this market since there were no horizontal overlaps.
144 Paragraph 198 of *Johnson & Johnson/Guidant.*
145 Paragraph 197 of *Johnson & Johnson/Guidant.*
146 Paragraph 199 of *Johnson & Johnson/Guidant.*
147 Paragraph 287 of *Johnson & Johnson/Guidant.*
148 Paragraph 301 of *Johnson & Johnson/Guidant.*
149 The parties' commitments in the steerable guidewires business consisted of the parties' proposal to divest the assets associated predominantly with the supply, marketing and sale of J&J's steerable guidewires business in the EEA. In the Endovascular area, the parties proposed to divest the entire operations (products, logistics, inventory, customer list, sales force, brand names, and IP divest any of the following: (i) J&J's endoscopic vessel harvesting products and endoscopic radial artery harvesting; (ii) Guidant worldwide assets and personnel of cardiac surgery business division; or (iii) Guidant's endoscopic vessel harvesting products, namely procedural kits for EVH.
150 On 5 December 2005, Boston Scientific preliminary offered $25 billion to buy Guidant. J&J raised its offer to $24.2 billion. Subsequently, Boston Scientific raised its offer to $27 billion, which was accepted by Guidant. Thus, Guidant paid J&J a termination fee of $705 million to withdraw from that deal.
151 Paragraph 196 of *Johnson & Johnson/Guidant.*
152 Paragraph 192 of *Johnson & Johnson/Guidant.*
153 Case 62/86 *AKZO Chemie BV v Commission* [1991] ECR I-3359.
154 Case M1684 *Carrefour/Promodés* [2000] OJ C164/5.
155 Although the merger did not raise issues of single firm dominance. Collective dominance was also ruled out. Lexecon (2001), "Buyer Power", www.lexecon.co.uk/assets/buyer_power.pdf, 2.
156 There is no evidence available of the second largest firm in the post-merger market in Sweden.
157 Albeit a low degree of innovation.
158 The Commission might have evidence of transparency, monitoring possibilities as well as of the countervailing impact of buyers and competitors and based on this evidence it decided not to pursue a possible allegation of collective dominance.

159 IP rights can provide asymmetric market power to the firms engaging in collective dominance and thus, undermine the sustainability of the collective dominant equilibrium.
160 Paragraph 171 of *Johnson & Johnson/Guidant.*
161 Paragraph 173 of *Johnson & Johnson/Guidant.*
162 Excluding Hungary and Sweden.
163 Paragraph 301 of *Johnson & Johnson/Guidant.*
164 J&J would have 15–25 per cent and Guidant 20–30 per cent.
165 70–80 per cent in the tiny Luxembourg market.
166 The merger reinforces the leadership of J&J or Guidant.
167 Based on tables J and P of the Commission's decision *Johnson & Johnson/Guidant.*
168 Paragraph 265 of *Johnson & Johnson/Guidant.*
169 Paragraph 232 of *Johnson & Johnson/Guidant.*
170 Paragraph 205 of *Johnson & Johnson/Guidant.*
171 Paragraph 237 of *Johnson & Johnson/Guidant.*
172 The Commission might have evidence of transparency, monitoring possibilities as well as of the countervailing impact of buyers and competitors and based on this evidence it decided not to pursue a possible allegation of collective dominance.
173 IP rights can provide asymmetric market power to the firms engaging in collective dominance and thus undermine the sustainability of the collective dominant equilibrium.
174 The extent to which these countries may have constituted a substantial part of the common market in which the merger would lead to a creation or strengthening of dominant position is unclear.
175 Paragraph 311 of *Johnson & Johnson/Guidant.*
176 Paragraph 306 of *Johnson & Johnson/Guidant.*
177 IP rights can provide asymmetric market power to the firms engaging in collective dominance and thus undermine the sustainability of the collective dominant equilibrium.
178 The Commission might have had evidence of transparency, monitoring possibilities as well as of the countervailing impact of buyers and competitors and based on this evidence it decided not to pursue a possible allegation of collective dominance.
179 The merger will therefore significantly impede effective competition in the markets for BX stents, in particular as a result of the creation of a dominant position (see para. 287 of the Commission's decision). The merger would lead to a firm with market shares ranging between 35 to 45 per cent and 90 to 100 per cent in the member states.
180 The Commission looks at the subsegments of the stents (carotid, non-carotid and balloon expandable stents). It analyses the impact of the merger in each of this segments and in paras 312–323 concludes on the whole market after conducting a per-segment assessment.
181 Paragraph 312 of *Johnson & Johnson/Guidant.*
182 Paragraph 323 of *Johnson & Johnson/Guidant.*
183 Chapter 4 involves the implementation of an event study. In order to evaluate investors' perceptions and expectations, the abnormal increase/decrease of the share prices of the merging firms and their competitors on the official announcement day will be calculated by comparing the share price of both merging firms and their main competitors with an index of all market shares on the event day of the announcement of the merger in the news. Conducting an event study analysis for the merging parties as well as for rival firms, by comparing their actual stock price returns around the announcement date

with a counterfactual measure of what the return would have been had the merger not taken place, would provide useful insights of the likely expectation of the market of the profitability of the firms resulting from a merger.

184 Paragraph 196 of *Johnson & Johnson/Guidant.*

185 Paragraph 323 of *Johnson & Johnson/Guidant.*

186 Case M3916 *T-Mobile/Tele.ring,* 26 April 2006.

187 Case M3530 *TeliaSonera/Orange* [2004] OJ C263/7 and Case M3776 *Vodafone/Oskar Mobile,* 25 May 2005.

188 Call termination is the service provided by network operator B to network operator A whereby a call originating in operator A's network is delivered to the user in operator B's network.

189 Case M1493 *Telia/Telenor* [2001] OJ L40/1, Case M2803 *Telia/Sonera* [2002] OJ C201/19, and Case M3806 *Telefónica/Cesky Telecom,* 10 June 2005.

190 This is essentially owing to regulatory barriers as the geographical scope of licences is in principle limited to areas which do not extend beyond the borders of a member state.

191 International roaming is a service which allows mobile subscribers to use their mobile handsets and SIM cards to make and receive calls/texts/data services even when abroad. In order to be able to offer this service to their customers, mobile network operators conclude wholesale agreements with one another providing access and capacity on mobile networks in the foreign country.

192 See IP/05/161 "Commission Challenges International Roaming Rates for Mobile Phones in Germany" and IP/04/994 "Commission Challenges UK International Roaming Rates".

193 Case M2726 *KPN/E-PLUS* [2002] OJ C79/12, Case M2469 *Vodafone/Airtel* [2001] OJ C207/1, Case M1863 *Vodafone/BT/Airtel* [2001] OJ C42/11, Case M2803 *Telia/Sonera* [2002] OJ C201/19, and Case M3806 *Telefónica/Cesky Telecom,* 10/6/2005.

194 H3G (a subsidiary of Hutchison) entered the market in May 2003 and provides mobile telephony services purely on the basis of a UMTS network. H3G buys airtime access to Mobilkom's GSM network on the basis of a national roaming agreement. In the areas not covered by H3G's own network, H3G's customers therefore make their calls using Mobilkom's GSM network.

195 The market shares expressed in terms of turnover relate to all revenue from mobile telephony and therefore include turnover from international roaming and call termination. With respect to the end-customer market, the parties could only provide the Commission with data based on market research. The end-customer market shares established during the market investigation essentially correspond to the market shares by turnover given above. The same problem does not arise with respect to the market shares by customer number, as this is the figure that relates to the end-customer market.

196 Another service provider was YESSS!, which, after entering the market in April 2005, by December 2005 had a market share of around 5 per cent (in customer terms). However, it should be noted that YESSS! was not an independent service provider, but a subsidiary of the network operator ONE and also offered its services over ONE's network. YESSS! offered only pre-paid packages and only through a discount food store and the internet.

197 This case presents a structure for the analysis of unilateral anticompetitive effects especially in network industries.

198 The use of the term "maverick" has been criticized as misleading. This term is unconventional as it is usually used in the context of coordinated effects. www.crai.com/ecp/assets/Tele.ring_Mobile.pdf. However, the Horizontal Merger Guidelines in the analysis of unilateral effects refer to mergers eliminating an important competitive force (that is to say maverick) and state that: "Some

firms have more of an influence on the competitive process than their market shares or similar measures would suggest" (paragraphs 37–38).

199 Post-merger HHI was 3000–3500 with a Delta of 500–600 both by turnover and by customers.

200 The Commission assumed that the data collected by the Austrian regulator on switching behaviour based on number portability related to a representative section of the market as a whole and constituted a more reliable sample than customer surveys by commercial market research institutes, which necessarily included a smaller number of customers.

201 H3G, whose network covers around 50 per cent of the Austrian population purchases airtime under a national roaming agreement with Mobilkom in order to cover the rest of the population. As a result, H3G has variable costs for each minute used by its customers outside its own network, and this has implications for its pricing. H3G's incentives are also fundamentally different here as it cannot achieve economies of scale for that airtime comparable with those of a network operator.

202 Network capacity is determined on the basis both of the frequency spectrum available and of the number of carriers within a cell that transmit the radio signal between the mobile terminal equipment and the antenna.

203 The setting of prices and acquisition of new customers did not necessarily depend on the (spare) capacity available but were determined primarily by the incentives in the light of the existing customer base. So the existence of spare capacity among competitors amounting to 10 per cent of T-Mobile and Tele.ring customers did not point to the conclusion that the competitors would inevitably plan to attract those customers at the expense of the profitability of their own customer base.

204 Paragraph 125 of the Commission's decision.

205 www.internationallawoffice.com. As mentioned in the Introduction, although non-coordinated and coordinated effects are unlikely to occur simultaneously, it is possible that the merger may lead to non-coordinated and coordinated effects occurring sequentially.

206 The paragraph numbers in this part of the chapter refer to the respective UK Competition Commission report. In addition, to the cases below, in the *Stonegate Farmers Ltd/Deans Food Group Ltd*, the UK Competition Commission, in addition to the unilateral effects of the merger – any increased prices by the merged company alone – they considered whether the merger could result in a multilateral increase in prices to retailers – that is to say increased prices not only by the merged company but also by other suppliers. Several factors suggested multilateral effects are likely to arise. Although prices were not transparent, but negotiated with both suppliers and customers, it was nonetheless easy for suppliers to identify the effects of each other's actions when an order is lost, if not necessarily during the process of negotiation. It would be likely to be in the interests of other suppliers of shell, of free range and of organic eggs to retailers, particularly given their difficulty in acquiring eggs in the short term, at least in part to follow a price increase by the merged company rather than maintain, or reduce, their prices to increase market share. In their view, therefore, the merger would be expected to have the effect of enabling other suppliers of shell, of free range and of organic eggs to retailers to attain higher prices than would otherwise be the case. The above outcome did not require any form of coordinated behaviour, but could emerge purely from the actions of the suppliers in the market responding to one another's prices. The market shares and features of the market were likely though to lead to the submission of undertakings/prohibition of the merger under the dominance test as well.

207 Cm 3761, *Littlewoods Organization Plc and Freemans Plc (a subsidiary of Sears Plc): A Report on the Proposed Merger*, 1997.

208 Cm 5208 *Lloyds TSB Group Plc and Abbey National Plc: A Report on the Proposed Merger*, 2001. The summary of this case in this chapter draws from the summary of the report cited above.

209 The summary of the *Littlewoods/Freemans* merger in this chapter draws from the summary of the UK Competition Commission's report. The paragraphs in this part of the chapter refer to this report.

210 At para. 2.6.

211 At para. 2.5.

212 According to the UK Competition Commission, there were around 2.5 million traditional agents in 1996, that is to say agents having customers outside their own household, and around 6 million agents' customers. They accounted for about 70 per cent of all sales or around £2.3 billion. Such agents represented one-third of all agents, the remaining two-thirds being "personal shoppers", that is to say agents who buy only for themselves and their own household. These lower income groups accounted for around 70 per cent of all agency mail order sales.

213 Table 4.10 of the CC report.

214 As a means of illustration, in Chapter 2 of the report, which incorporates the conclusions of the UK Competition Commission, the analysis of the market and the definition of the relevant market occupied 73 per cent of the chapter, whereas the analysis of the merger on public interest occupied a mere 15 per cent.

215 Paragraph 2.109.

216 Paragraph 4.166.

217 Paragraph 2.126.

218 Paragraphs 2.114 and 2.115.

219 As it will be illustrated in the following paragraphs of this chapter the UK Competition Commission discarded any concerns about coordinated effects.

220 Paragraph 2.116.

221 The UK Competition Commission did not substantiate this argument. The merger was from five firms to four firms. Regarding the impact of the number of firms on the attainment and sustainability of collective dominance see Europe Economics (2002), "One's a Monopoly, Two's Collectively Dominant, Three's Alright?", www.europe-economics.com. In addition, the agency prices are fixed six months in advance and are somewhat inflexible (see para. 4.120). Thus, retaliation through lower prices is not a viable option for one of the firms that engage in collective dominance to punish the other. These are only some of the factors that do not contribute to the sustainability of collective dominance.

222 "Report by Professor Davies" in "Comments by Academic Economists: Covering Note", www.competition-commission.org.uk/rep_pub/pdf/reports.pdf, 9.

223 There is an obvious difference between the analysis of the UK Competition Commission in the assessment of the *Lloyds TSB/Abbey* merger, analysed earlier and the analysis in the *Littlewoods/Freemans* merger. In the *Lloyds TSB/Abbey*, the Commission alleged that the merger would lead to coordinated effects and analysed the factors that would contribute to such adverse effects on competition in the post-merger market (transparency, retaliation, price symmetry, stability in demand, cost symmetry, etc.). In the *Littlewoods/Freemans*, there is no such analysis of the UK Competition Commission.

224 "Report by Professor Davies" in "Comments by Academic Economists: Covering Note", www.competition-commission.org.uk/rep_pub/pdf/reports.pdf, 13.

225 Paragraph 2.117.

226 Paragraph 2.118.

227 The market shares showed stability over time and the products did not exhibit any substantial differentiation.
228 At para. 2.116.
229 The savings and mortgage markets had historically been closely linked since the building society movement developed in order to hold members' savings and use them to provide mortgages.
230 Customers are said to be on the back book if they receive terms and conditions different from (in many cases, worse than) those that are offered to new customers. See further: www.competition-commission.org.uk/rep_pub/reports/2001/fulltext/458glossary.pdf.
231 At para. 2.222.
232 At para. 2.241.
233 At para. 2.161.
234 At para. 2.160.
235 It should be noted that the UK Competition Commission assessed the merger using the "public interest test", which was the predecessor of the SLC test.
236 At the summary.
237 The UK Enterprise Act uses the SLC test, which resembles the SIEC test and does not have any gap in its applicability as the dominance test did. Prices could rise as a result of coordination. In addition, non-merging firms in the same market (with differentiated products) can also increase their prices since they benefit from the reduction of the competitive pressure resulting from the merger, since the merging firms' price increase may switch some demand to the rival firms, which, in turn, may find it profitable to increase their prices (non-collusive oligopoly scenario). Thus, even if rival firms pursue the same competitive strategies as they did prior to the merger, this can result in them increasing prices in the post-merger market. In such cases, the firms in the marketplace are not coordinating their competitive behaviour, but merely reacting to changes in each other's behaviour.
238 Paragraph 2.55.
239 Fingleton, J. et al (2002), "Substantive Standards for Mergers and the Role of Efficiencies", in Hawk B., *International Antitrust Law and Policy*, Fordham University Law School, Corporate Law Institute.
240 www.competition-commission.org.uk/reports/462banks.htm.
241 Paragraph 2.133.
242 For example see paras 37–38 of the *Guidelines*. If we see the maverick as a potential competitor, then the elimination of a potential competitor may still induce anticompetitive effects. See further: M1630 *AIR LIQUIDE/BOC*, M3440 *ENI/EDP/GDP* (4064). Other cases in which the harm on potential competition has been assessed includes: *Anticipated Acquisition by the Nasdaq Stock Market, Inc. of London Stock Exchange Group Plc*, 24 January 2007, *Deutsche Börse AG, Euronext NV and London Stock Exchange Plc*, November 2005 ("LSE bids"), *SvitzerWijsmuller A/S/Adsteam Marine Ltd*, February 2007, in the United Kingdom as well as, CCD/368/06 *Maltacom Plc/Multiplus Limited*, 26.01.07, in Malta and Ccent 16/2005 – *Enernova/Ortiga*Safra*, 11 November 2005, in Portugal.
243 www.iclg.co.uk/index.php?area=4&show_chapter=582&ifocus=1&kh_publications_ id=27.
244 Bishop, S. and Ridyard, D. (2003), "Prometheus Unbound: Increasing the Scope for Intervention in EC Merger Control", *ECLR*, 25(7), 395–409, 359.
245 Vickers, J. (2002), "How to Reform the EC Merger Test?", speech at the EC/IBA merger control conference, 8 November, Brussels, www.oft.gov.uk/NR/rdonlyres/80E5D0FE-7CF0–4606-A502-DD42FDD06AAF/ 0/spe0802.pdf, 2.

246 As analysed some of the factors conducive to coordinated effects are ambiguous.

247 www.competition-commission.org.uk/reports/462banks.htm.

248 Summary of the report: UK Competition Commission, Cm 5319, "The Supply of Banking Services by Clearing Banks to small and medium-sized Enterprises within the UK", 2002, www.competition-commission.org.uk/reports/462banks.htm.

249 On 4 May 2001 Halifax Group plc and Bank of Scotland announced terms for a recommended nil premium merger. The transaction received regulatory approval on 19 July 2001 and completed successfully on 10 September 2001.

250 The UK Competition Commission argued that that there were major uncertainties surrounding the HBOS merger. Moreover the dominance of the big four banks in the SME market was such that, even if that merger proceeded and HBOS became a strong competitor in the SME market in England and Wales, the competition from Abbey National would still be important (para. 2.199). If the authorities had approved the acquisition of NatWest – considered a much more portentous decision since in effect it created the fourth player in the Big Four oligopoly – and if the acquisition of Bank of Scotland could be expected to create a strong fifth player then there was no reason to block the acquisition of Abbey National, regardless of its immediate implications. See further: www.m-a-monitor.co.uk/xam-bin/m?mah03164.

251 According to Recital 15: "Whereas concentrations which, by reason of the limited market share of the undertakings concerned, are not liable to impede effective competition may be presumed to be compatible with the common market; whereas, without prejudice to Articles 85 and 86 of the Treaty, an indication to this effect exists, in particular, where the market share of the undertakings concerned does not exceed 25 per cent either in the common market or in a substantial part of it." Thus, a merger leading to a post-merger entity with a market share less than 25 per cent was unlikely to be considered incompatible with the Common Market under the dominance test of the original ECMR.

252 *FTC v H.J. Heinz Co.,* 116 F.Supp. 2d 190 (DDC 2000), appeal pending, No. 00–5362 (DC Cir.).

253 *FTC v H.J. Heinz Company, et al.*, Brief for Plaintiff-Appellant Federal Trade Commission, No. 00–5362, 8.

254 *FTC v H.J. Heinz Company, et al.*, Civ. No. 1:00CV01688 JR, Memorandum in Support of Plaintiff's Motion for Preliminary Injunction, www.ftc.gov/os/2000/07/heinzmemo.htm.

255 *FTC v H.J. Heinz Company, et al.*, Brief for Plaintiff-Appellant Federal Trade Commission, No. 00–5362, 6.

256 *FTC v H.J. Heinz Co. and Milnot Holding Corporation,* No. 00–5362, Appeal from the United States District Court for the District of Columbia No. 00cv01688.

257 *FTC v H.J. Heinz Company, et al.*, Civ. No. 1:00CV01688 JR, Memorandum in Support of Plaintiff's Motion for Preliminary Injunction, www.ftc.gov/os/2000/07/heinzmemo.htm.

258 *FTC v H.J. Heinz Company, et al.*, Civ. No. 1:00CV01688 JR, Memorandum in Support of Plaintiff's Motion for Preliminary Injunction, www.ftc.gov/os/2000/07/heinzmemo.htm.

259 *FTC v H.J. Heinz Co.,* 116 F.Supp. 2d 190 (DDC 2000), appeal pending, No. 00–5362 (DC Cir.). www.ftc.gov/speeches/other/boastmollys.htm_N_15_.

260 No. 00–5362, *FTC v H.J. Heinz Co., et al.*

261 Prepared Remarks of Molly S. Boast before the American Bar Association Antitrust Section Spring Meeting 2001 Washington, DC, 29 March 29, www.ftc.gov/speeches/other/boastmollys.htm.

262 Fingleton, J. et al. (2002), "Substantive Standards for Mergers and the Role of Efficiencies", in Hawk, B., *International Antitrust Law and Policy*, Fordham University Law School, Corporate Law Institute.
263 Boge, U. and Muller, E. (2002), "From the Market Dominance Test to the SLC Test: Are There Any Reasons for a Change?", *ECLR*, 23(10), 495–8.
264 Case T-342/99 *Airtours v Commission* [2002] ECR II-2585.
265 US District Court, Columbia, *FTC v HF Heinz Company, et al.*, 00–5362a, 2000.
266 Levy, N. (2003), "European Merger Control Law: A Guide to the Merger Regulation", LexisNexis, para. 10.04[6][c].
267 Boge, U. and Muller, E. (2002), "From the Market Dominance test to the SLC Test: Are There Any Reasons for a Change?", *ECLR*, 23(10), 495–8.
268 An analysis of a market structure conducive to non-coordinated effects is presented in the concluding chapter.
269 The features that make a market conducive to collective dominance have been analysed in earlier parts of this book.
270 Commerce Act 1986 (NZ).
271 www.oecd.org/dataoecd/56/32/28324700.pdf.
272 Table 1, Commerce Commission, *Progressive Enterprises Limited and Woolworths (New Zealand) Limited, Decision No. 438* (13 July 2001) ("438").
273 Commerce Commission, *Progressive Enterprises Limited and Woolworths (New Zealand) Limited, Decision No. 448* (14 December 2001) ("448").
274 Paragraph 107 of 448.
275 Paragraph 18 of 438.
276 Paragraphs 112–115 of 438.
277 Section 47(1) of the Commerce Act prohibits certain business acquisitions: "No person shall acquire assets of a business or shares if, as a result of the acquisition, –

(a) That person or another person would be, or would be likely to be, in a dominant position in a market; or
(b) That person's or another person's dominant position in a market would be, or would be likely to be, strengthened."

278 Paragraph 35 of 448.
279 Paragraph 118 of 448.
280 Paragraph 275 of 448.
According to the new test, under the safe harbours, a business acquisition is considered unlikely to substantially lessen competition in a market where, after the proposed acquisition, either of the following situations exist:

- where the three-firm concentration ratio (with individual firms' market shares including any interconnected or associated persons) in the relevant market is below 70 per cent, the combined entity (including any interconnected or associated persons) has less than in the order of a 40 per cent share; or
- where the three-firm concentration ratio (with individual firms' market shares including any interconnected or associated persons) in the relevant market is above 70 per cent, the market share of the combined entity is less than in the order of 20 per cent.

See further: para. 109 of the 448.
According to the old test, The *Business Acquisitions Guidelines* specify certain "safe harbours" which can be used to assess the likely impact of a merger in terms of s 47 of the Act: "In the Commission's view, a dominant position in a market is generally unlikely to be created or strengthened where, after the proposed acquisition, either of the following situations exist:

- the merged entity (including any interconnected or associated persons) has less than in the order of a 40 per cent share of the relevant market;
- the merged entity (including any interconnected or associated persons) has less than in the order of a 60 per cent share of the relevant market and faces competition from at least one other market participant having no less than in the order of a 15 per cent market share." See further: para. 82 of the 438.

281 Following the Court of Appeal decision a technical amendment was made to the Commerce Act. The Commerce (Clearance Validation) Amendment Act 2001 clarified the law with respect to applications for clearance of business acquisitions that spanned the date of the changes in legislation.
282 Paragraph 84 of 448.
283 Paragraph 99 of 448.
284 Paragraph 87 of 448.
285 Goddard and Curry (2003) mention that under the former New Zealand dominance test the proposed merger between the second and third largest supermarket chains was cleared predominantly on the basis of the competitive constraints of a large and effective remaining competitor. They further mention that the concept of joint dominance was adopted in Europe to try and overcome this deficiency, but that it was never a feature of the former New Zealand dominance test for mergers. Goddard, G. and Curry, E. (2003), "New Zealand's New Mergers Test: A Comparison of Dominance and Substantial Lessening of Competition in the Supermarket Industry", *ECLR*, 24(7), 300–11.
286 The Commerce Commission considered the three Foodstuffs companies to be separate entities. See further: para. 18 of 438.
287 Paragraph 100 of 448.
288 In the initial decision ("438"), the Commerce Commission considered the three Foodstuffs companies to be separate from each other; in doing so it adopted the most conservative scenario in its assessment of the merger.
289 Since the Commerce Commission alleged that the Foodstuffs supermarkets should be assumed to constitute three separate entities.
290 The 438 decision does not contain information relating to the market shares of each of the Foodstuffs companies.
291 Hildebrand, D. (2001), "EC&MC Comments on the Draft Guidelines on Market Analysis and the Calculation of Significant Market Power", www.ee-mc.com/files/Comment%20%20SMP%20Draft%20guidelines.pdf.
292 As Chapter 4 illustrates, a firm's incentive to cheat is significantly influenced by the contribution margin and thus the level of its individual critical loss. The extent of this incentive is measured by the level of sales an individual firm can afford to lose or expect to win before the price increase becomes unprofitable or profitable respectively. Irrespective of whether the actual loss will be low or high, its importance for the firms will depend on the market share of the firms. If a firm expects that cheating will increase sales by more than its critical loss, it will cheat on the price agreement. The incentive of the firm with the smaller market share to cheat makes the tacitly collusive equilibrium unlikely to sustain and thus the merger is unlikely to lead to collective dominance.
293 "[T]he definition of dominance … does not allow coordinated anticompetitive effects to be considered. Only one firm can be dominant in the market." Commerce Committee, Report to Parliament on the Commerce Amendment Bill (October 2001), 16. See further: Goddard, G. and Curry, E. (2003), "New Zealand's New Mergers Test: A Comparison of Dominance and Substantial Lessening of Competition in the Supermarket Industry", *ECLR*, 24(7), 300–11.

294 Under the same market definition, especially as regards whether Foodstuffs companies are considered to be three separate entities (438 decision) or a single entity (448 decision).

295 Paragraph 84 of 448.

296 This part of the chapter draws from Fels, A. et al. (2002), "The Change from a Dominance to a Substantial Lessening of Competition Test in Australia's Merger Law", in Hawk, B., *International Antitrust Law and Policy*, Fordham University Law School, Corporate Law Institute, as well as from Fels, A. (2002), "Merger Law in Australia", ICN Merger Review Working Group, www.internationalcompetitionnetwork.org/afsgaustralia.pdf. Unfortunately, although several attempts have been made, it has not been possible to obtain copies of the decisions of the cases mentioned in this part of the chapter. Thus, this chapter will refer to these cases as likely gap cases, without providing any further analysis as has been done for the other jurisdictions analysed herein. Had the decisions of these cases been publicly available, further research would be conducted on them, and more concrete conclusions could have been derived.

297 Fels, A. et al. (2002), "The Change from a Dominance to a Substantial Lessening of Competition Test in Australia's Merger Law", in Hawk, B., *International Antitrust Law and Policy*, Fordham University Law School, Corporate Law Institute.

298 Fels, A. (2002), "Merger Law in Australia", ICN Merger Review Working Group, www.internationalcompetitionnetwork.org/afsgaustralia.pdf.

299 Several attempts (written and by phone) were made to source the original decisions from the ACCC. The ACCC confirmed that they do not have the actual decisions.

300 *SOK Corporation, Spar Finland Plc*, the FCA Decision (case number 657/81/2005), 4 January 2006.

301 *SOK Corporation, Spar Finland Plc*, the FCA Decision (case number 657/81/2005), 4 January 2006. This case is taken from Marjo Ojala, in Kokkoris, I. (2007a), *Competition Cases from the European Union. The Ultimate Guide to Leading Cases of the EU and all 27 Member States*, Sweet and Maxwell, London.

302 The request for submission of undertakings implies that the merger was found to be incompatible with the common market and was allowed after the proposed remedies would rectify the adverse impact on competition.

303 See further: Appendix.

5 Event studies in assessing the gap

> [I]t boils down to whether you trust the agencies or the stock market. I'll take the stock market any day.[1]

5.1 Introduction

As mentioned in the Introduction, one particular method that could be used to assess whether the Commission was correct in its assessment of the non-collusive oligopolies identified in Chapter 4, is the evaluation of the market perception of the competitive effects of such mergers.[2]

Event study methodology provides an ex-ante evidentiary tool of merger assessment. Although it cannot solely determine the outcome of the merger, event studies can provide useful insights in the likely impact of the merger on competition.

The aim of this chapter[3] is twofold:[4] first, evaluating mergers that would lead to non-coordinated effects in oligopolistic markets and were not prohibited. The movement of the share prices of the merged firms and their competitors on the announcement day indicates whether customers expected these mergers to be profitable for the firms. An assumption is made that firms increase profitability mainly by increasing prices (reducing output) in the market, thus adopting conduct having an adverse impact on competition.

Second, this chapter will examine cases that would lead to non-collusive oligopolies and which were prohibited in order to evaluate whether prohibiting the merger was correct according to investors' perceptions. Similarly, the movement of the share prices of the merged firms and their competitors on the announcement day indicates whether customers expected these mergers to be profitable for the firms.

This analysis will involve the implementation of an event study. In order to evaluate investors' perceptions and expectations, the abnormal increase/decrease[5] of the share prices of the merging firms and their competitors on the official announcement day will be calculated by comparing the share price of both merging firms and their main competitors with an index of all market shares, on the event day of the announcement of the merger in the news.[6] An assumption is made that the market is informationally efficient. Thus, share prices have absorbed all the information up to the announcement date and thus have not increased (at least not significantly),[7] due to any information that has been disseminated before the official announcement of the merger.

In an agreed merger the share price of the target will be expected to indicate positive abnormal returns[8] because firms' investors should not oppose the merger, expecting the merger to be profitable and increase their returns. The impact of the merger announcement on the acquirer is ambiguous. The acquirer's share price may indicate positive abnormal returns, but it is more likely that the share price of the acquirer will indicate negative abnormal returns since a substantial investment is needed for the acquisition.

An important assumption is that the likely increase in the share prices of the firms to be merged is not due to prospective efficiencies that will be passed on to consumers and result from the merger. Such likely efficiencies are not likely to be significant except in industries with high innovation and research such as pharmaceuticals. Efficiencies arising from a merger are not always passed on to consumers, thus even if share prices increase due to efficiencies, these efficiencies may be internalized by the merged entity rather than passed on in the form, of lower prices, higher quality, etc.

In addition, an assumption is made that the market is informationally efficient. Thus, the share prices of the merging firms have absorbed all the information up to the announcement date and thus have not increased (at least not significantly)[9] due to any information that has been spread before the official announcement of the merger.

The analysis in this chapter will attempt to assess the stock market's perception of the non-collusive oligopolies identified in Chapter 4[10] and examine whether the Commission's decisions to prohibit or allow these mergers are reflected in the stock market's expectations. As mentioned earlier, since investors' perception is an indication of whether the merger is expected to have adverse effects on competition, it will illustrate whether the Commission's assessment was correct. Thus, it will provide a technical method of proof of the existence of gap cases, in addition to the theoretical support provided in Chapter 4.

The chapter will initially provide a review of the academic literature related to the application of event studies in merger assessment and after presenting the rationale of event study analysis for the purposes of this book, it turns to the implementation of event study analysis in the gap cases identified in Chapter 4. Finally, the limitations of event studies are presented.

5.2 Efficient market hypothesis and event study analysis

One of the important underlying assumptions of event studies will be the existence of informationally efficient markets. The Efficient Market Hypothesis ("EMH") addresses the issues raised, relevant to the degree that share prices reflect all known information. The EMH has been the core proposition of finance. The concept of market efficiency has been and is likely to continue to be a dominant theme in academic literature and an issue of intense debate in the investment community.

The concept of market efficiency has several distinct varieties.[11] As Sharpe, Alexander and Bailey (1998) state, "a market is efficient with respect to a particular set of information if it is impossible to make abnormal profits (other by chance) by using this set of information to formulate buying and selling decisions".[12] Thus, in an efficient market no abnormal returns can be earned. Information is of utmost importance to the determination of the prices of securities. Hence, markets are efficient if the prices of securities on average quickly and with accuracy fully reflect all known information. All investors operating in an efficient market should expect to obtain an equilibrium rate of return. The aforementioned notion depicts the EMH.

Market efficiency is an essential issue for investment professionals and analysts of the market. Market efficiency depends on the types of information that are reflected in the securities' prices. According to these types, the EMH has three versions that depend on the extent and type of the information that share prices reflect: the weak, the semi-strong and the strong forms.

Depending on what is regarded as information, Fama (1970)[13] defines the weak form tests of the EMH that stress that securities' prices fully reflect the information included in the past returns. Hence, information cannot be exploited to achieve abnormal returns. Under the weak form of the efficient market hypothesis "securities (stocks) prices already reflect all information that can be derived by examining market trading data such as history of past prices, trading volume or short interest".[14] According to the semi-strong version of the EMH stock (securities') prices already reflect all publicly available information relevant to the prospects of the firm including past data, earning forecasts, reports related to the state of the economy, accounting reports, and balance sheet reports. The strong form version of the efficient market hypothesis states that "prices reflect all information public and private".[15] Arguably, the latter form of market efficiency is the most difficult to sustain. Fama (1991)[16] refers to the weak form tests as tests for return predictability, to the semi-strong as event studies, and to the strong ones as tests for private information.

There are a number of features that characterize an efficient market: investors are price takers with no individual influence on the security's price, they behave in a rational, profit maximizing way, and they are capable analysts. In addition to that, access to currently available information about the future is costless and investors monitor market prices and react quickly and fully to new information by adjusting their holdings appropriately and causing similar adjustments to securities' (stock) prices. In addition, expected security returns cannot be predicted by past deviations from the equilibrium rates of return.

There are multitudes of methodologies for conducting tests which determine the degree of efficiency in a market. Semi-strong form tests deal with the speed of adjustments of stock prices to new information. One method of examining this adjustment and assessing the importance of an event for the security (stock) price is an event study. An event study is a research methodology designed to measure the impact of an event of interest on stock returns.[17]

Event studies can have many applications in accounting and finance research. "Event studies are now an important part of finance, especially corporate finance. The results stand up to replication and the empirical regularities, some rather surprising, are the impetus for theoretical work to explain them".[18] They can be used to evaluate the impact of several economic events on stock prices by examining the firms' stock returns. Such events are stock splits, a debt-for-equity swap executed by a company, earnings announcements, mergers and acquisitions and announcements of macroeconomic variables important to the firm.

5.3 Literature review of event studies in mergers

The notion that mergers that are harmful for competitors will tend to be pro-competitive has long been recognized and has been first exploited by Eckbo (1983)[19] and Stillman (1983).[20] They propose to use an "event study" to assess the stock market reaction to the announcement of a merger as a means to evaluate the impact of the merger on competitors' profits. A positive reaction will normally indicate that the merger is expected to enhance competitors' profits and hence that it will have an adverse impact on competition (and vice versa).[21]

Eckbo and Wier (1985)[22] argue that abnormal returns to the merging firms and their rivals are associated with events that either increase or decrease the probability that a merger will be full consummated. Probability increasing events are merger proposal announcements and announcements of decisions of the competition authorities that support the merger. Events that decrease the probability of consummation of the merger are announcements of merger complaints against mergers and decisions of the competition authority adverse to the merger.

The authors assess, inter alia, the validity of the "market power" hypothesis. According to the "market power" hypothesis, a horizontal merger will encourage industry-wide collusion or dominant firm pricing, which causes an increase in (quality–adjusted) product price and/or a reduction in factor prices. The resulting price change benefits all firms in the industry. Thus, the stock prices of the merging firms and their rivals' rise. The two studies by Eckbo (1983) and Stillman (1983) reject the market power hypothesis because rival firms do not show the predicted sequence of abnormal performance. Eckbo (1983) finds that rival firms, in mergers challenged by the FTC, show statistically significant gains in response to the complaint announcement that is inconsistent with the collusion argument. However, Duso, Neven and Röller (2003) find evidence in support of the market power hypothesis.[23]

In a later paper, Eckbo and Wier (1985) argued that rivals firms in challenged mergers earn significantly positive abnormal returns around merger proposal announcements, while the typical antitrust complaint and pro-government final outcome announcement fails to significantly reduce the equity value of rival firms.

Cox and Portes (1998)[24] described both flawed and correctly implemented event studies submitted in the merger application of SBC Communications and Pacific Telesis. On 1 April 1996 SBC Communications, Inc. (SBC) and Pacific Telesis Group (PacTel) announced their intention to merge. PacTel's stock price closed at more than 20 per cent higher than its previous close. SBC stock, by way of contrast, declined in value on the day of the announcement. In the cases they analysed, the relevant event is the announcement of a merger and the relevant variable is usually the combined market value of the merging companies. They considered a one-day and five-day event window. Their results indicated that the estimated one-day excess return of the combined entity varied between 1.1 per cent and −1.25 per cent. In four of the six models they used, estimated one-day excess returns were negative. Statistically significant negative excess returns would indicate that the market's evaluation of the merger was negative.

They also considered the merger between BT and MCI. On 4 November 1996 British Telecom (BT), the largest British telecommunications operator, and MCI Communications (MCI), the second largest US long-distance company, announced their intention to conclude a full merger. Although MCI and BT had already undertaken joint ventures, the market did not learn of their merger discussions until the afternoon of 1 November 1996. At MCI's request, NASDAQ halted trading of MCI stock at approximately 13:35 EST, by which time the London market had already closed.[25] The formal announcement of merger discussions did not occur until 4 November 1996. On 31 October 1996, the approximate market capitalization of MCI was \$17.2 billion and the approximate market capitalization of BT was \$36.3 billion. At the close of trading on 4 November 1996, the market capitalizations of MCI and BT were \$21.1 billion and \$38.8 billion, respectively.

The increase in the capitalization, which indicates an increase in the stock price of the companies, implies that markets concluded that the shareholders of this new merged entity would be substantially benefited. This positive market movement encompassed the probability of the merger's success, the prospects for its competitors, and the expected future of the global telecommunications industry.

To assess the competitive impact of the merger the authors looked at the stock prices of competitors. If these companies exhibited statistically significant negative price reactions, one might view this as evidence that a BT-MCI merged entity would have increased efficiency and competitiveness, hence reducing competitors' profits. The results indicated that for both one-day and five-day valuations, three of the four companies had negative price reactions; however, none of these reactions was significant. The authors concluded that the price reactions of the BT-MCI competitors could not be used to distinguish between competitive efficiencies or collusive profits as the explanation for BT-MCI's substantial positive stock price reaction.

Panayides and Gong (2002) used event study methodology to empirically investigate the reaction of the stock market to the announcement by listed liner shipping companies of a planned merger or acquisition. The results obtained from a number of analytical tests provided support for the hypothesis that the announcement of a merger or acquisition had significant impact on the stock price behaviour of the liner companies involved. They concluded that the behaviour exhibited by the share price of the two companies after the event (announcement of merger) was quite similar, in that almost synchronic movements in the share prices could be observed. It must be noted that such behaviour could be observed immediately after the announcement of the merger (which was quite some time away from the actual implementation of the merger). The authors concluded that events affecting one company also affect the other even though the merger has not actually taken place.[26]

The economic consultancy OXERA undertook a study of the market reaction to a referral by the UK OFT to the UK Competition Commission of a merger for second-phase investigation.[27] They concluded that the market's reaction to a second-phase referral is highly negative for merger targets and mixed for bidders. The reaction to an OFT merger clearance is muted, indicating that the market expects most mergers to be cleared at the first stage. The small reaction to merger clearance decisions relative to the reaction to referrals indicated that there could be a general market perception that mergers will be cleared. OXERA mentions that one reason for the expectation of clearance is that around 84 per cent of mergers have been cleared in the past. A number of clearance decisions led to negative share price reactions, suggesting that the risk of UK Competition Commission referral was not fully priced into the target's stock.

Duso, Gugler and Yurtoglu (2006)[28] analyse the economic effects of ECMR decisions and distinguish between prohibitions, clearances with commitments (either behavioural or structural) and outright clearances.

They implement an event study on merging and rival firms' stocks to quantify the profitability effects of mergers and merger control decisions.

The authors argue that after the merger, insider firms' profitability should rise due to higher market power and efficiency. Hence, their cumulative average abnormal returns around the announcement of the merger should be positive. Rival firms' profitability – hence their cumulative average abnormal returns around the merger announcement – should rise only if the merger increases product market prices (that is to say, the market power effect is larger than the efficiency effect), and should diminish if the reverse is true.

Their results suggest that outright blockings solve the competitive problems generated by the merger. By the same token, remedies, on average, are not always effective in solving the market power concerns. However, both structural (for example divestitures) and behavioural remedies help restore effective competition when correctly applied to mergers having an adverse impact on competition during the first phase investigation. In contrast, when applied after the second phase investigation, they seem to be ineffective. Finally, remedies, especially behavioural ones, seem to constitute a rent transfer from merging firms to rivals when mistakenly applied to pro-competitive mergers.[29]

Duso, Neven and Röller (2003)[30] evaluated the adverse consequences of mergers on competition from the reaction of the stock market price of competitors and of the merging firms. They identified instances where the Commission has prohibited mergers that the stock market regarded as pro-competitive (type I errors) as well as instances where the EU has failed to prevent mergers that were regarded as having an adverse impact on competition (type II errors).

Their data suggest that the Commission made a type I error in four of the 14 prohibitions (28 per cent). They identified as type I errors two cases that have later been overturned on appeal (*Airtours/First Choice* and *Tetra Laval/Sidel*)[31,32] and one case (*General Electric/Honeywell*)[33] that has been highly controversial and was successfully appealed by the merging parties, as regards the non-horizontal competitive harm that, allegedly, induced.[34] Regarding type II errors, the authors suggest that the Commission made an error in about 23 per cent of the cases that it has allowed without conditions.[35]

In addition, their results suggest that the Commission's decisions cannot be explained solely in terms of a motivation to protect consumer surplus and are not sensitive to firms' interests while the institutional and political environment plays an influencing role. Factors such as country and industry effects, as well as market definition and procedural aspects also play significant roles.

5.4 Rationale of event study in this book

In the event study that will be carried out in this chapter, an attempt will be made to assess whether the Commission's decision in allowing or blocking the mergers that would or could have led to non-coordinated effects in oligopolistic markets, identified in Chapter 4, was perceived as accurate according to the stock market reaction on the announcement of the merger.[36]

Röller and Neven (2002)[37] conducted an event study analysis and identified three reasons for the type II discrepancies: the concept of dominance; the lack of an explicit efficiency defence in the original ECMR; and the influence that third parties can bring to bear on the Commission.[38] As regards the concept of dominance, the authors argue that mergers could lead to a price increase even if they do not create or strengthen dominance. Thus, the authors identified the existence of a gap in the application of the dominance test, as one of the likely reasons for instances where the Commission allowed mergers having an adverse impact on competition. As for the lack of the efficiency defence, the authors argue that if the benchmark level of efficiency that is assumed by the Commission exceeds average efficiency gains, then mergers inducing adverse effects on competition are likely to be cleared. Finally, as regards the influence that third parties can bring to bear on the Commission, the authors argue that under such influence the Commission may not always follow the objective of protecting consumer welfare.

Stock markets' reactions to news can be a particularly valuable source of information for inferences about the nature of a merger or a takeover.[39] The idea underlying these studies is that the reaction of share prices – which reflect expectations about a firm's stream of future profits – will allow the testing of the alternative hypotheses as to the consequences of a merger. By examining who gains and loses when mergers or merger challenges are announced, different hypotheses can be tested regarding expectations about market power or efficiency.

A merger between two companies may induce two possible outcomes in the product market. First, if market power increases substantially after a merger, the product price will increase and so will profits for both the merger partners and the other firms operating in the market, at least in the short run (that is, prior to entry by new players). Thus, provided that the stock market is efficient, the share prices of the merging firms and horizontal rival firms in the industry should earn positive abnormal returns when a merger having an adverse impact on competition is announced.[40]

Second, if the merger generates cost efficiencies, then the merged firm is likely to be more profitable than the sum of the pre-merger entities. Such higher profitability, however, will not extend to other firms in the industry. Merging partners should gain positive abnormal returns around the date of the merger announcement. Generally, such an increase in cost efficiencies will induce the merging firms to reduce their prices in an attempt to increase sales and market share.

The situation for rival firms is, however, more complex. An increase in efficiency of the merging parties will result in downward pressure on competitors' prices and competing firms would expect to see margins and profits reduced and, therefore, negative abnormal returns.[41] However, if the market expects the cost efficiencies to be easily passed along to other players in the industry, then rival firms should also earn positive abnormal returns when news about the merger is disseminated.

Thus, positive abnormal returns[42] for the merging partners at the time of the merger announcement do not distinguish between a merger that is expected to raise prices and one that is expected to lower costs. Similarly, positive abnormal returns for the horizontal rivals do not distinguish between the two hypotheses of a price-increasing versus cost-reducing merger. However, in the analysis herein, an assumption is made that these cost reductions are not passed on to consumers in the form of lower prices or higher quality. In concentrated markets, where incumbents have sufficient market power, and produce differentiated products, passing on of such cost synergies to the final consumers is unlikely. It should also be noted that competition authorities have very rarely accepted such efficiency defences.[43]

Insignificant or negative abnormal returns for the rivals around the announcement date are a sufficient condition to conclude that the market expects the merger to be cost reducing, not price increasing.[44]

An increase in the market value of all firms may mean that concentration in the relevant antitrust market has increased. Such an increase in stock prices[45] of all firms may be due to an increase in the ability of firms in the relevant market to coordinate production and pricing decisions or adopt other conducts having an adverse impact on competition. Thus, the merger is likely to increase prices and competing firms will experience a windfall increase in profits, either because they will leave their prices unchanged, and experience an increase in the demand for their products, or because they will also raise prices. In other words, an increase in the market value of all firms indicates that the merger may lead to adverse effects on competition.

Conducting an event study analysis for the merging parties as well as for rival firms, by comparing their actual stock price returns around the announcement date with a counterfactual measure of the market return would provide useful insights of the likely expectation of the market of the profitability of the merging parties and competitors in the post-merger market.

Event studies can assist in assessing the change in the market's valuation of the company. The change in the stock price and thus in the market value of the company that occurs as a result of the announcement of an "event" is the *single best estimate*, based on publicly available information, of the impact of the occurrence of the event on the future profits of the company.[46] This estimate incorporates all the information relevant to this event, such as the impact of this event in the profitability of the company, the likelihood that the event will occur etc. In principle, abnormal movements in share prices signals a change in long-term earnings expectations. Such a change reflects the impact of the merger on competition in the post-merger market.

Thus, the analysis of price changes of the stocks of the merged company does not indicate whether two firms, merged, are more efficient or whether the merger will result in the new firm being able to profitably raise prices. These two effects will have very different impacts on competition and consumer welfare and, hence, have different regulatory and antitrust implications. However, stock price movements of firms that compete with the merging companies in the relevant markets or are likely potential competitors, can be used, as will be illustrated, in order to indicate which of the two effects mentioned earlier is more likely.

In addition, it should be noted that the market takes into account the antitrust procedure at the time of announcement.[47] Hence, the change in the value of the stock at the time of the announcement is equal to the probability that the deal will be cleared times the value that will accrue if the merger is realized. Following Duso, Neven and Röller (2003),[48] in order to identify whether deals are perceived as having an adverse impact on competition, the event study in this chapter employs only the sign of the abnormal return of the stock price on the day of the event. Hence, the fact that the market may anticipate the outcome of the antitrust procedure does not introduce a bias in this analysis.[49]

Table 5.1 provides a summary of how event studies can be used to indicate the effects of mergers.[50]

The abnormal return for an asset can be calculated based on the capital asset pricing model ("CAPM") or the market index model. Following Röller and Neven (2002)[51] a simple approach will be followed, in this analysis, where the abnormal return is computed as the difference between the return on the stock and the return on an appropriate index on the day of announcement. In addition, following OXERA,[52] this analysis uses the relevant stock market index as the counterfactual and assumes that all stocks in the sample have the same sensitivity to the market[53] with respect to the relevant stock market index.

The event in the analysis herein is the announcement of the merger.[54] The date that will be taken into account in determining the stock price reaction to the announcement of the merger, the event date, will be the first date that news about the merger circulated in the financial press. The "announcement date" or "event date" was identified using Factiva,[55] customizable business news and research product that integrates content from newspapers, newswires, journals, research reports, and websites. This

Table 5.1 Use of event studies

*Value of merging companies**	*Value of competing companies*	*Possible economic interpretations of market's valuation*
Increase	Increase	Reduced competition, higher prices, lower consumer welfare or no change in competitive conditions but reevaluation by market
Increase	Decrease	Increased efficiency of merged firm, lower prices, higher consumer welfare
Decrease	Increase	Decreased efficiency in merged firm, higher prices, reduced competition, lower consumer welfare
Decrease	Decrease	Increased competition, lower prices, higher consumer welfare or no change in competitive conditions but reevaluation by market

Note
* Changes in the value of merging companies and of competing companies are net of market effects.

approach has the advantage of reducing the uncertainty in identifying the correct event, but the measure of abnormal returns may be downward biased since there is still uncertainty whether the merger will take place.[56] In addition, the main competitors of the merging parties in the affected markets of interest[57] will be identified from the Commission's decision in each merger case.[58]

The event study in this chapter will, in most cases, include an event window of at least three days prior to announcement to three days after the announcement.[59] Cox and Portes (1998) argue that there is a trade-off between using longer and shorter time horizons. The argument in favour of a large event window is that investors may need some time to react to the news, even in the most efficient markets. However, a larger event window implies a likely larger number of events affecting the stock price and thus the valuation of the company. They add that one-day reaction is frequently used, but there does not appear to be any sound empirical basis for choosing one day as the time that minimizes such pitfalls.[60]

5.5 Event study implementation

This part of the chapter will present the empirical results of the event study for each of the gap cases that were assessed by the European Commission, and identified in Chapter 4.[61] Thus, the following cases will be analysed: *Airtours/First Choice*, *Oracle/PeopleSoft*, *Sony/BMG*, *Syngenta CP/Advanta*, *Johnson & Johnson/Guidant*, and *T-Mobile Austria/Tele.ring*.

It would be useful to present the steps of conducting an event study.

The initial task is to define the particular event (merger announcement, decision of the authority) and collect a sample of firms that experience this event (merging parties and the competitors) and thus are included in the study. Second, the date of the announcement of the event (date of initial dissemination of the news) is indicated as "date zero" and the period over which the stock prices of the firms in the sample are examined is called the "event window". This period can be from a date before the actual date of the event up to a certain date after the event takes place. The use of very small period intervals such as daily or intraday data, increases the accuracy of the measure of market efficiency and is frequently used in event studies (five days prior and after the event is generally a widely used event window). Finally, the calculation of the abnormal return consists of the difference of the return of the share price of each firm in the sample for each time interval (for example, one day) from the return of the index (for example, stock market index).

5.5.1 Airtours/First Choice[62]

On 29 April 1999 Airtours Plc, a UK company whose main activity was as a tour operator and supplier of package holidays, announced its intention to acquire all the shares in the UK tour operator, First Choice Plc, one of its competitors. The major tour operators were Thomson (30.7 per cent of the market), Airtours (19.4 per cent of the market), Thomas Cook (20.4 per cent of the market), and First Choice (15 per cent of the market).[63] The Commission concluded that the proposed operation would create a dominant position in the market for short-haul foreign package holidays in the United Kingdom, as a result of which competition would be significantly impeded.

Airtours presented an empirical analysis to the Commission evaluating the reaction of share prices to the announcement of the merger. If the merger were viewed by the stock market as mainly increasing the efficiency of the merging companies, then it would be expected that the share prices of competitors would fall in reaction to the announcement of the merger, because the merger would create a more efficient competitor. If, by way of contrast, the merger would lead to collective dominance, then it would be expected that the share prices of all companies would increase in reaction to the merger.

Thomas Cook will not be included in the analysis in this chapter, since it was controlled by Preussag. Since Thomas Cook was not a separate entity, it did not have a separate share price distinct from Pressuag's share price. The share price of Pressuag may have been influenced by various factors, which may be related to the other business activities or subsidiaries that it may had at the time. Thus, any change in the share price of Pressuag would not be exclusively due to the rumours of an Airtours bid for First Choice.

The analysis in this chapter follows the same principle for all companies that may be controlled by another company and thus those not having their own individual listing. Unless a merging party or a competitor has its own listing, then the share price of the parent or controlling company is not taken into account, as it would introduce significant "noise" in the estimation. Share price data are often full of extraneous "noise" due to many other events affecting the parent or controlling entity, which may be completely unrelated to the market, the subsidiary or the event in question.

Initial widespread rumours of an Airtours bid arose on 23 February 1999. Newspapers reported ongoing rumours of consolidation among tour operators. Shares in Airtours, First Choice and Eurocamp all rose strongly on 23 February 1999. Further news in the leisure sector involved the announcement, on 23 February 1999, of merger plans between European Leisure and Allied Leisure. On 17 March the *Daily Mail* newspaper's market column mentioned that rumours persisted of a counter-bid following Kuoni Reisen's agreed merger offer for First Choice. The newspaper said Airtours might still lodge a bid.[64] First Choice stock price rose from 161 pence (17 March) to 178.5 pence (18 March) to 182.5 pence on 19 March.

The first significant rumours about the likely bid of Airtours for First Choice were evident on 18 March 1999. Shares in UK travel company First Choice Holidays were up 12 per cent on that day on speculation that package tour operator Airtours would make a bid for the company. At 15:45 GMT,[65] shares in Airtours were lower by 5.5 pence, or 1.1 per cent, to 490.5 pence. Shares in Kuoni were down CHF60, or 1.1 per cent, to CHF5500. On 18 March 1999, the First Choice stock price was almost 11 per cent higher to close at 178.5 pence, close to its five-year peak. Airtours decreased 6 pence to 490 pence as investors were concerned with the costs of the bid.[66] Thomson's share price decreased 8 pence to 179 pence.

On 19 April 1999 shares in tour operator First Choice increased amid speculation that Airtours would launch a hostile £750 million bid. Thomson, the market leader in the supply of package holidays announced that it would not stand by and see its position usurped. First Choice's share price increased, whereas both Airtours' and Thomson's share prices decreased.

On 20 April Thomson announced that if Airtours made a hostile counter-bid for First Choice, it would fight to defend its market share, which was the highest in the UK's tour business. Thomson's stock dropped over 9 per cent following the announcement, due to fear that the company would start a price war to maintain its market share. Airtours' share price dropped just over 7 per cent the same day, while First Choice remained steady at 192 pence. Airtours and Thomson share prices increased mildly later in that week, but some analysts feared that if Thomson held true to its claims, the entire industry could suffer.

Airtours announced its bid on 29 April 1999. At 08:30 GMT, First Choice was up 18 pence, or 9.3 per cent, at 211 pence, making it the best performer in the FTSE 250 index. Airtours shares were down 1.5 pence at 456.5 pence. At 13:17 GMT, First Choice was the best performing stock in the FTSE 250 index, gaining 15.5 pence, or 8.0 per cent, to 208.5 pence. It was also the most actively traded stock in the index, with about 25 million shares changing hands. Airtours shares had tumbled 15 pence to 443 pence, and Thomson was down 15 pence at 139.5 pence. In Zurich, Kuoni shares were up CHF85 at CHF5490. Thomson immediately pledged to start selling summer 2000 holidays with "substantially increased capacity and very attractive prices". Its shares ended 24 pence lower at 130.5 pence. Thomson was regarded as more vulnerable to a price war than Airtours because 90 per cent of its profits came from the UK, compared with 65 per cent for Airtours. Shares in First Choice closed 7 1/2 pence higher at 200 1/2 pence, while those of Airtours fell 27 pence to 431 pence.

The economic consultant of Airtours, Lexecon, conducted an analysis using the developments in the share price of Thomson, which was presented to the Commission. In particular the study found that the share price of Thomson fell significantly when the Airtours' bid for First Choice was announced. The study concluded that this is evidence that the stock market viewed the Airtours bid as pro-competitive. Otherwise, if the merger had been seen as leading to less competition, the announcement of the bid would have led to an increase in the share price of Thomson.

The Commission concluded that the fact that Thomson immediately announced plans of aggressive capacity additions at the same time as Airtours launched its bid was seen as having a tremendous negative effect on the share price of Thomson (as well as Airtours) because capacity utilization was the crucial driver of profitability in the foreign package holiday sector. It further argued that this was the key event influencing the share price of Thomson and constituted an alternative explanation of the share price movement of Thomson to the pro-competitive impact of the merger.

However, the Commission failed to note that the aggressive response of Thomson was a reaction of the company to the news of the merger and to the possibility that the merger would lead to Thomson having the second place in the market. This reaction would lead to lower prices for consumers. In addition, a decrease in Thomson's share price was also experienced as early as 19 March 1999 when news of a likely Airtours' bid surfaced, more than one month before Thomson announced its price reducing plans for the summer of 2000. Thus, the merger would induce the main competitor of the merging parties to lower its prices, a beneficial outcome for consumers.

As the preceding analysis indicated, there were a number of events influencing the stock prices of the main players. Since the rumours of a bid of Airtours for First Choice were announced, the stock prices reacted favourably for First Choice and, as expected, negatively for Airtours, being the bidder in a hostile bid, and having to make substantial investment to acquire First Choice. The rumours of the hostile bid lasted for over two months (24 February to 29 April), with a wide impact on share prices.

The general trend of the movement of share prices was increasing for First Choice, and decreasing for Kuoni, Airtours, and Thomson. First Choice's share price increase was due to the fact that there was another bidder for the company. A higher bid from Airtours might have led to increased value for the shareholders of First Choice. When First Choice dampened hopes of a counter-bid on 15 March 1999, its shares fell almost 8 per cent to 173 pence.

Kuoni's share price decrease can be explained due to the fact that Kuoni was the initial bidder for First Choice and the merger plans were likely to fail after Airtours' intervention. Kuoni's share price had also fallen on announcement of its merger with First Choice, as Kuoni was the acquirer and made a significant investment. Airtours' share price decrease was expected as the investment that Airtours would make for its hostile bid for First Choice would be substantial. Such a share price reaction is normally expected for bidders/acquirers, especially in hostile bids. Thomson's share price followed a decreasing pattern.

As a report prepared for the UK OFT claimed, negative returns for the rivals around the announcement date are a sufficient condition to conclude that the market expects the merger to be cost reducing, not price increasing.[67] According to our earlier analysis of the share price movements of the companies involved in the *Airtours/First Choice* merger, the market did not expect the merger to lead to adverse competitive effects in the post-merger market.

Duso, Neven and Röller (2003)[68] evaluated the adverse consequences of these mergers on competition from the reaction of the stock market price of competitors to the merging firms. They identified *Airtours/First Choice* as one case where the Commission has prohibited mergers that the stock market regarded as pro-competitive.

If the merger had been likely to lead to an adverse impact on competition, the share prices of Thomson should have increased. The decrease of Thomson's share price, emanating, inter alia, from the announced price reduction for summer 2000 holiday packages, was an indication of the likely enhanced competition in the post-merger market. Thus, the results of the event study confirm the theoretical conclusions drawn in Chapter 4, as regards the lack of adverse effects on competition arising from the *Airtours/First Choice* merger.

5.5.2 Oracle/PeopleSoft

Oracle was a publicly listed company that was active in the design, development, manufacture, and distribution of enterprise application software, database and application server software and related services. PeopleSoft was a publicly listed company active in the design, development, manufacture, and distribution of enterprise application software and related services. The Commission received a notification of a proposed concentration by which the undertaking Oracle Corporation would acquire sole control of the undertaking PeopleSoft Inc. by way of a public bid.

The Commission's initial concerns about this merger were based on a definition of the market which, post-merger, would consist of only Oracle/PeopleSoft and SAP. The Commission did not uphold its preliminary conclusion that customers would be confronted with a de facto absence of choice after the merger, since vendors such as Microsoft, Lawson, and QAD would also constitute, according to the Commission, alternative options. The Commission initially based its concerns on the finding of non-coordinated effects in the post-merger oligopolistic market.[69] However, the Commission, consequently, in clearing the merger, focused and justified the lack of adverse impact on competition on the existence of smaller players in the markets for high-function FMS and HR for large enterprises.

Oracle's hostile takeover bid[70] for PeopleSoft induced a sharp increase in the stock price of PeopleSoft on 6 June 2003. PeopleSoft shares increased $3.24, or nearly 22 per cent, to $18.35 after Oracle CEO Larry Ellison made an offer of $16 a share for PeopleSoft.[71] Oracle shares increased 23 cents, or 1.6 per cent, to $13.56 after the bid was announced. SAP's, one of Oracle's biggest rivals, shares increased $2.15, or more than 7 per cent, to $31.55 amid speculation that the German company might consider a rival bid rather than face the prospect of competing against an Oracle-PeopleSoft combination.[72]

Oracle's buyout offer came less than a week after PeopleSoft announced its intention to acquire rival JD Edwards for $1.7 billion in stock. The deal between PeopleSoft and JD Edwards, announced Monday 2 June 2003, would have created the world's second largest seller of applications software to businesses.

The dynamics and reaction of the stock market to the news of the merger is noteworthy. The news of the deal boosted shares in SAP and other software stocks across Europe. At 16:55 GMT on 6 June 2003, SAP's share price increased 8.7 per cent at €107 and Software AG's was up 6.2 per cent at €13.28. In London, Sage Group, a competitor of the merging parties, saw its share price increase 5.8 per cent at 177.25 pence. NASDAQ added 12.16 to 1658.17, boosted by news of Oracle's bid for software peer PeopleSoft (and an upbeat US labour market report). In trading on 9 June 2003 on the NASDAQ stock market, PeopleSoft shares rose 8 cents to close at $17.90 US. Oracle shares fell 23 cents to $12.86 and JD Edwards shares decreased by 13 cents to $13.07.

On 12 June 2003 PeopleSoft board formally rejected Oracle's hostile $5.1 billion bid. PeopleSoft shares closed down 25 cents, or 1.4 per cent, to $17.37. The rejection was widely expected because Oracle's initial offer was less than PeopleSoft's stock price at the time. Antitrust experts suggested that an Oracle-PeopleSoft combination would likely face a lengthy review, but was unclear then whether regulators would block such a takeover.[73]

The initial announcement date of the merger was 6 June 2003. Table 5.2 illustrates the abnormal returns of the stock prices of the merging parties and their competitors around that event date. The abnormal returns of the stock prices are calculated taking either the NYSE composite or the NASDAQ composite as the benchmark.[74]

Table 5.3 provides the abnormal returns of the four stocks traded on NASDAQ, taking as benchmark the NASDAQ composite index.

The results that can be drawn from these two tables, as regards the abnormal returns of the stock prices of the merging parties and their competitors, are similar. Oracle experienced negative abnormal returns, as did Microsoft, while PeopleSoft, QAD, and Lawson indicated positive abnormal returns.

Arguably, the NASDAQ composite index provides a more accurate benchmark of the return of the market index, since it incorporates all the stocks traded on NASDAQ and thus, on average, any particular trend identified in any particular industry sector is countervailed by the return on the remaining industry sectors, providing thus an overall accurate representation of the expected return of the market as the benchmark in this analysis.[75]

As Table 5.2 illustrates, on 6 June Oracle stock price indicated a significant negative abnormal return of around 5 per cent. This is an expected response of the stock market to the share price of the acquirer in a hostile acquisition. The share price of PeopleSoft strongly increased as is shown by the 14.9 per cent positive abnormal return. SAP, the main competitor

Table 5.2 Abnormal returns in *Oracle/Peoplesoft* event study

Date	*Oracle*	*Peoplesoft*	*SAP*	*Microsoft*	*Lawson*	*QAD*
3 June 2003	3.107001	1.85585322	−0.11338	2.362277	7.626783	5.670019
4 June 2003	3.349964	0.1127189	2.116306	−0.9913	2.330409	−0.95111
5 June 2003	−2.6139	−1.585973811	−1.57119	−4.13018	−1.66276	0.463085
6 June 2003	**−5.05898**	**14.89711762**	**4.002607**	**−4.78149**	**1.84413**	**1.400618**
9 June 2003	1.059051	3.265050858	3.038118	3.154098	7.149985	5.941117
10 June 2003	1.973065	0.728897104	4.573416	4.644687	−0.80956	2.668291

Table 5.3 Other abnormal returns in *Oracle/Peoplesoft* event study

Date	*Oracle*	*Peoplesoft*	*Microsoft*	*Lawson*	*QAD*
3 June 2003	0.413901	0.551004	1.057428	4.933683	4.36517
4 June 2003	2.360209	−1.82815	−2.93217	1.340653	−2.89198
5 June 2003	−1.42206	−1.38801	−3.93221	−0.47093	0.66105
6 June 2003	**−1.33802**	**15.58005**	**−4.09855**	**5.56509**	**2.083552**
9 June 2003	−0.69854	4.323573	4.21262	5.392391	6.999639
10 June 2003	−0.858	−1.37327	2.542519	−3.64063	0.566124

of the merging parties, experienced a 4 per cent positive abnormal return on its share price, similar to the 1.8 per cent positive abnormal return for Lawson and 1.4 per cent positive abnormal return for QAD.

Only Microsoft had a negative abnormal return of 4.8 per cent, while on 5 June it had a negative abnormal return of 4.13 per cent. Microsoft had a negative abnormal return prior to the announcement of Oracle's bid. Although its negative trend might have been influenced by Oracle's bid, the bid was not be the sole and major factor inducing the negative abnormal returns for Microsoft's share price.

In addition, on 5 June Microsoft CEO Steve Ballmer used his annual memo to Microsoft's employees to bring up the challenge from open-source software in general, and the Linux operating system in particular. Investor reaction was swift. Microsoft shares decreased 78 cents, or 3 per cent, to close at $24.09 on 5 June, and were the second most active issues on the NASDAQ composite index with 112 million shares trading hands.[76] In addition, on 5 June 2003, research firm Gartner Dataquest released server revenue figures showing that worldwide sales of Linux-based servers hit $609 million in the first quarter of 2003, a 51 per cent increase over the previous year. Victor Raisys, a software analyst with SoundView Technology estimated that 23 per cent of Microsoft's revenue comes from server software sales.[77] Thus, the negative abnormal returns of Microsoft on 6 June 2003 might have been significantly influenced by its CEO announcement, as well as by the announcement of increased sales of Linux-based servers.

The fact that both Lawson and QAD had much lower positive abnormal returns compared to SAP, indicates that the positive impact of the merger on SAP, according to the investors, would be greater than the impact on the smaller competitors QAD and Lawson. It can be argued that the latter fact indicates that Oracle and PeopleSoft were constrained by SAP more than they were constrained by the two smaller players. This conclusion casts doubt on the Commission's argument that the two smaller firms were effective competitors of Oracle and PeopleSoft. That factor was one of the Commission's factors for the clearance of the merger, since it argued that the smaller competitors would provide adequate competitive constraints on the merger entity. The same argument applies for Microsoft as well, whose share price due to a series of events around the announcement date, indicated a negative abnormal return.

As this analysis indicates, the fact that, in general, competitors' share price illustrated positive abnormal returns indicates that investors expected the merger to be profitable for competitors and thus, based on the theoretical underpinnings of the event study undertaken in this article, the merger would likely induce adverse effects on competition in the post-merger oligopolistic market. Such effects were eloquently expressed by a Goldman Sachs analyst who said, referring to the next 12 to 18 months that SAP might be able to win customers away from Oracle/

PeopleSoft and added that "it takes away a competitor and anytime you do that, it helps the pricing environment".[78]

The Commission failed to block a merger that the market perceived as having an adverse impact on competition. The clearance of the merger was due to the inability of the Commission to block it under the dominance test, as it was illustrated in Chapter 4. As we also saw in that chapter, had the Commission been able to use the SLC/SIEC test, it would have been able to block the merger and thus conform with the perception of the market as regards the adverse effects of the *Oracle/PeopleSoft* merger on competition in the post-merger market.

5.5.3 Sony/BMG

The Commission received notification of a proposed concentration by which the undertakings Bertelsmann AG and Sony Corporation of America ("parties") belonging to the Sony group would merge their global recorded music businesses. The joint venture companies, which would be operated under the name SonyBMG, would be active in the discovery and the development of artists ("A&R") and the subsequent marketing and sale of recorded music. SonyBMG would not engage in related activities such as music publishing, manufacturing, and distribution.

The world-wide active record companies were Bertelsmann ("BMG"), Sony, Universal Music Group ("UMG"), EMI and Warner Music Group ("WMG"). UMG had 25 to 30 per cent, EMI had 15 to 20 per cent, WMG had 10 to 15 per cent, "Others" (including the independents) had 20 to 25 per cent, Sony had 10 to 15 per cent and BMG had 10 to 15 per cent.[79] The Commission concluded that the concentration did not create or strengthen a dominant position as a result of which effective competition would be significantly impeded in the common market or in a substantial part of it.

Rumours about a possible merger between Sony and BMG started as early as 12 March 2003. The *New York Post* wrote that BMG was considering Sony Music as a possible backup merger partner in case BMG's move to acquire EMI failed. BMG was concerned about being left out of the merger game, so the company would seek a deal with Sony Music – either a merger or a joint venture – should Warner and EMI merge. A deal between BMG and Sony was considered a long shot at the time, and BMG would prefer to agree a deal with the smaller EMI, which would raise fewer regulatory issues.[80]

On 23 September 2003 the *New York Post* wrote that, unable to reach deals with either Warner Music or EMI, BMG had begun exploring a merger with Sony Music.[81] Meanwhile, London-based EMI issued a statement confirming that it was in talks with Warner. EMI had bid about $1 billion in cash, plus a reported $600 million in stock, for 75 per cent of Warner Music. As a result, ratings agency Standard & Poor's mentioned on 22 September that it was putting EMI on notice for a possible debt downgrade to "junk" status. Its shares fell more than 4 per cent in trading in London on that day.

On 24 September 2003 Reuters News announced that BMG had approached Sony Music executives to explore a possible merger after failing to conclude a deal with rival music company Warner Music. BMG, the smallest of the top five music companies aimed at holding talks with Sony Music as Warner turned its attention to a possible deal with EMI Group Plc.[82]

On 1 November 2003 news were spread that Bertelsmann AG and Sony, respectively the fifth and second largest music companies in the world, signed in early November a non-binding letter of intent to form a jointly owned company to be called Sony BMG.[83] Finally, on 6 November, news agencies reported that BMG and Sony signed a preliminary deal to form a 50:50 joint venture company to be called SonyBMG. EMI shares fell on 6 November on word of the Sony/BMG deal, closing at 177 pence, decreased by 3 pence. A key issue was whether the prospect of two mergers occurring between four of the five music majors heightened the regulatory risk.[84]

The date that best indicates the initial dissemination of significant information about the merger is 24 September 2003. Universal was part of the conglomerate entity Vivendi and thus, as was mentioned earlier, is not taken into account in the assessment of the abnormal returns emanating from this merger.[85] In addition, Bertelsmann was privately held. WMG initiated a listing on 11 March 2005. Table 5.4 illustrates the abnormal return for the stocks of Sony and EMI.

As Table 5.4 demonstrates, the stock price of Sony indicated a positive abnormal return on 24 September, whether the benchmark is the composite NYSE index or the NYSE international subindex.[86] EMI experienced a positive abnormal return.

As regards EMI's negative abnormal returns prior to the announcement date, EMI had refreshed a bid it made for Warner Music earlier that year, which included $1 billion of cash and would give AOL Time Warner a 25 per cent stake in a combination. On 19 September 2003 EMI interrupted merger talks between BMG, the music group of Bertelsmann, and Time Warner's Warner Music with a new proposal to merge. EMI shares increased 4 per cent, or 6 pence, to 158 pence on expectations that the

Table 5.4 Abnormal returns in *Sony/BMG* event study

Date	*EMI–FTSE250*	*Sony–NYSE*	*Sony–NYSE Intl*
19 September 2003	3.957713022	−2.1743609	−1.82704
22 September 2003	−3.171832214	−2.2204004	−2.50281
23 September 2003	−2.039820114	−0.2217042	0.955051

British group would drive a wedge between Warner Music and BMG, which have failed to strike a deal despite months of dogged negotiations. On 22 September, London-based EMI's shares ended 4.1 per cent lower at 152 pence, adding to an initial decline amid uncertainty over the outcome of the Warner talks, after Standard & Poor's placed the company's ratings on CreditWatch with negative implications.

Thus, the negative abnormal return of EMI prior to 24 September, can be explained due to the events surrounding the dissemination of information regarding the Sony/BMG merger.

The positive reaction of EMI constitutes an indication that investors expected the merger to be profitable for the company, as was the expectation for Sony, whose stock price indicated positive abnormal returns. Thus, according to the market perception, the Sony/BMG merger would be profitable and lead to adverse effects on competition.

The Commission, contrary to the market perception, allowed the merger, a decision which was quashed by the CFI in the IMPALA[87] appeal. Had the Commission been able to employ the SLC/SIEC test, it would have been able, as illustrated in Chapter 4, to block the merger as it was likely to lead to non-coordinated effects in the oligopolistic post-merger market.

The parties after IMPALA's successful appeal renotified to the Commission. The Commission initiated a Phase II investigation, an indication that competition concerns, if proved through the Phase II investigation, remain. Thus, the outcome of the event study would be an accurate prediction for the impact of the initial Sony/BMG merger on competition.

5.5.4 Syngenta CP/Advanta

The Commission argued that the merger might lead to the creation of non-coordinated effects in an oligopolistic market for sugar beet seeds in Belgium and France. The merger would lead to high combined market shares in Belgium (50 to 60 per cent) and France (40 to 50 per cent). The main competitor was KWS with 40 to 50 per cent in Belgium, and 30 to 40 per cent in France. In Belgium and France, the parties would have been the market leader but the remaining market shares would almost entirely have been held by KWS. The Commission cleared the merger after the submission of satisfactory remedies.

On 12 May 2004 Syngenta AG announced that it has entered an agreement with Fox Paine & Co. LLC to buy Advanta BV, a Dutch seed company, for a total of €400 million. Syngenta also announced on the same day the purchase of glyphosate tolerance technology for corn, called GA21, from Bayer CropScience. This purchase, together with the acquisition of Advanta's North American corn and soybean business, would enable Syngenta to market a complete range of biotech input traits in both corn and soybean from 2005.

Table 5.5 illustrates the abnormal return of the acquirer and the main competitors on the event date of 12 May 2004.

Syngenta's share price had a positive reaction to the announcement of the merger. The two announcements on 12 May, of the merger as well as of the acquisition of the tolerance technology for corn, explain the positive abnormal return of the stock price of Syngenta. Investors expected Syngenta to benefit from these two acquisitions. Advanta was a private company and, as such, it was not listed on any stock exchange. Danisco, a competitor of the merging parties, had a share price that showed a positive abnormal return on the announcement of the news of the merger. Finally, KWS' stock price, a significant competitor of the two merging parties, experienced a negative abnormal return.

Certain explanations can be put forward for the negative abnormal return of KWS's stock price. If the merger is expected by the market to lead to adverse effects on competition in the market, the stock prices of the competitors should, in theory, as analysed previously, indicate positive abnormal returns. KWS had a significantly low volume of trading during these days. As Table 5.6 illustrates, the volume of KWS stocks that were traded during this period was significantly lower compared to the volume of stocks that were traded of the other companies. On some days, KWS's stock did not trade at all.

This low level of trading cannot provide an accurate response of KWS's share price to the news of the merger. The inaccuracy of the abnormal

Table 5.5 Abnormal returns in *Syngenta/Advanta* event study

Date	*Syngenta–Virt–X*	*Syngenta–NYSE*	*Danisco*	*KWS*
17 May 2004	0.306200528	0.922616855	0.78781186	2.046412
14 May 2004	−0.226445362	0.084676745	1.18411372	0.469566
13 May 2004	−1.234742865	−1.146959814	−1.2344896	−1.94726
12 May 2004	**1.36639234**	**0.874036023**	**1.63310972**	**−3.37597**
11 May 2004	−0.691029459	0.525464296	−1.9915474	3.195368
10 May 2004	1.470035991	0.024117659	0.78722101	−0.35411

Table 5.6 Other abnormal returns in *Syngenta/Adventa* event study

Date	*Syngenta–Virt–X*	*Syngenta–NYSE*	*Danisco*	*KWS*
17 May 2004	386946	156200	77586	50
14 May 2004	612681	66300	243582	0
13 May 2004	633172	177600	190623	50
12 May 2004	**573891**	**231100**	**215356**	**50**
11 May 2004	532726	214700	162973	0
10 May 2004	1050247	294500	287026	100
7 May 2004	616397	99400	0	0

Table 5.7 Closing prices of KWS stock used in *Syngenta/Adventa* event study

Date	*Close price*	*Volume*
14 May 2004	61.9	50
13 May 2004	61.9	0
12 May 2004	61.9	50
11 May 2004	62.5	50
10 May 2004	65	0

returns of KWS's stock price is also indicated by the movement in the close price of the stock. As Table 5.7 illustrates, the stock of KWS closed at the same price on three consecutive days from the announcement of the Syngenta's acquisition of Advanta.

The analysis of KWS's stock price indicates that the abnormal returns of the stock around the announcement of the acquisition cannot be safely taken into account, as the conclusions drawn from these abnormal returns may not be accurate and representative of the market perception of the adverse effects of the merger on competition.

As mentioned earlier, both Syngenta's and Danisco's stock price experienced positive abnormal returns. This result indicates that investors expected the merger to be beneficial for the acquirer as well as the competitor. Based on the theory analysed in this chapter, positive abnormal returns for competitors would indicate that, according to the market's perception, the merger would be profitable for competitors and thus would likely lead to adverse effects on competition in the post-merger market. This perception coincided with the Commission's assessment of the merger, which was cleared subject to remedies.

Positive abnormal returns may indicate enhanced efficiencies as a result of the merger that would be beneficial for the competitors as well. If the market expects efficiencies to be easily passed along to other players in the industry, then rival firms should also earn positive abnormal returns when the merger is announced. In this particular case, no efficiency arguments were suggested to the Commission by the merging parties to indicate that any efficiencies arising from the merger would benefit the consumers.

5.5.5 Johnson & Johnson/Guidant

Chapter 4 argued that non-coordinated effects were likely to have been created in the oligopolistic markets for steerable guidewires in Hungary and Sweden as well as in the markets for carotid and non-carotid stents. As regards the market for steerable guidewires used in interventional cardiology, in Hungary the merged entity would have a 35 to 45 per cent combined share, with number two player Boston Scientific having 15 to 25 per cent. In Sweden, the merged entity would have a combined market share of 35 to 45 per cent.

The Commission concluded that the merger was likely to result in a significant impediment to effective competition in the Common Market and the EEA for steerable guidewires as a result of the strengthening of Guidant's dominant position. It was argued in Chapter 4 of this book that the Commission might not have been able to successfully argue that the merger would lead to a creation or strengthening of dominance in these two countries if it assessed the merger under the dominance test.

In addition, the merger would reduce the number of most important competitors from three (the third being Boston Scientific) to two in the carotid stents markets and from four (the third and fourth being Boston Scientific and Bard) to three in the non-carotid SX stent market. This restricted number of players accounted for the lion's share of the market in all countries considered earlier.

The Commission concluded that:[88]

> [T]here is sufficient evidence showing with the requisite degree of confidence that the operation will give rise to important non-coordinated effects and will substantially impede effective competition in the Common Market and the EEA for the endovascular stents.

The Commission, after submission of satisfactory remedies, cleared the merger. The following analysis will illustrate the perception of the market about the adverse effects of the merger on competition.

It would be interested to present a series of events affecting the share price of the merging parties and their competitors. On 1 December 2004, in its mid-quarter financial update, Guidant failed to reveal a replacement for its chief executive, Ron Dollens, who was set to retire at the end of the month.[89] That sparked speculation among analysts that Dollens might stay longer or that the company might be considering a merger. Investors pushed up Guidant's share price as the delay in a succession announcement fuelled rumours that Guidant might be acquired, perhaps by Johnson & Johnson, which lacked a cardiac rhythm management franchise of its own. Guidant was the second largest maker of implantable cardioverter defibrillators.

On 7 December the *New York Times* reported that Johnson & Johnson was in advanced talks to buy cardiovascular device maker Guidant Corp. for more than $24 billion. It was reported that a final deal could be reached in the following week. Guidant shares rose more than 5 per cent by midday. In midday trading on the New York Stock Exchange, Guidant shares increased $3.66 to $72.41, while Johnson & Johnson fell 72 cents to $61.11. Guidant shares closed at $3.66, or 5.3 per cent, higher at $72.41 on 7 December. On that day Guidant shares rose to near 52-week highs. Johnson & Johnson decreased by $1.42, or 2.3 per cent, to $60.41.

The details of the deal were announced late on 15 December. According to the deal, each Guidant share would be exchanged for $30.40 in cash and $45.60 in Johnson & Johnson stock. The $76 price was a 5.5 per cent premium over Guidant's closing price of $72.05 on 15 December. Shares of Johnson & Johnson increased $1.03 to $61.93 on 16 December morning trading on the New York Stock Exchange, where Guidant shares fell 3 cents to $72.02. In the afternoon Guidant decreased by 8 cents to $71.97. Shares of Johnson & Johnson reached a 52-week high on 16 December, rising $3.01, or 5 per cent, during afternoon trading, to $63.91. Boston Scientific shares fell 94 cents to $35.55 in afternoon trading on that day. This movement of the stock prices can be attributed to the reaction of investors to the particular details (price, cost) of the deal.

Thus, the initial day that news about the merger was made public was 7 December 2004.[90] Table 5.8 illustrates the abnormal returns of the two merging parties as well as of Boston Scientific and Bard, two main competitors.

As the table shows, J&J, being the acquirer, had its share price decrease on the announcement of the merger; J&J's share also indicated a negative abnormal return. Guidant's shares indicated a 6.19 per cent positive abnormal return which can be attributed to the news of the merger. In addition, Bard's share prices increased significantly, while, Boston Scientific's share price indicated a negative abnormal return.

Boston Scientific recalled approximately 100,000 coronary stents in summer 2004 and lowered its fourth quarter profit forecast. Analysts cut estimates, inducing a decrease in the share price from $46 in May to $33.36 in late November. Furthermore, it was announced on 6 December 2004, that Medinol and Boston Scientific Corp. both responded positively over the weekend of 4 and 5 December 2004 to a US court decision that the two former partners should go to trial to solve a case that could involve as much as $1.5 billion in payments for damages.[91] A US District Court judge in Manhattan ruled that Medinol was entitled to try its claims that Boston Scientific's sale of express and taxus stents was in breach of the firms' contract, and that Medinol was entitled to royalties on those sales. Shares of Boston

Table 5.8 Abnormal returns in *Johnson & Johnson/Guidant* event study

Date	*J&J*	*Guidant*	*Boston Scientific*	*Bard*
2 December 2004	0.915182	3.380674	0.429634	1.347949
3 December 2004	0.007513	−0.46805	−3.11999	−2.32533
6 December 2004	0.012336	−0.4369	0.025748	−1.2534
7 December 2004	**−1.33849**	**6.194489**	**−0.05637**	**1.946706**
8 December 2004	1.007563	1.717638	0.514664	0.440828
9 December 2004	0.003756	−0.2579	−0.75208	0.5637
10 December 2004	−1.45097	−2.7051	0.36559	1.042956

Table 5.9 Other abnormal returns in *Johnson & Johnson/Guidant* event study

Date	*J&J*	*Guidant*	*Boston Scientific*	*Bard*
10 December 2004	–0.79851	–2.05264	1.018053	1.69542
9 December 2004	–0.54927	–0.81092	–1.3051	0.010678
8 December 2004	0.031734	0.741809	–0.46116	–0.535
7 December 2004	**–0.75927**	**6.773717**	**0.52286**	**2.525933**
6 December 2004	0.42578	–0.02345	0.439193	–0.83996
3 December 2004	0.040045	–0.43551	–3.08746	–2.2928

Scientific Corp. fell 2.9 per cent to $34.54 on Friday 3 December 2004 following the announcement. Thus, the negative abnormal return of Boston Scientific's share price on the announcement of the merger might have been, inter alia, due to this generally negative trend in the stock price over the recent months arising from the events mentioned earlier.

Furthermore, if the abnormal return of the stock prices of J&J, Guidant, Bard and Boston Scientific is calculated with respect to the NYSE healthcare index, the adverse effects of the merger are more obvious. As Table 5.9 illustrates, J&J showed a negative abnormal return, being the acquirer, while the target as well as the main competitors indicated a positive abnormal return.[92]

Compared to the composite NYSE index, the abnormal returns of the stock prices in relation to the NYSE healthcare index are higher. The analysis of stock price returns, based on both indices, indicates that the merger was perceived by the market as inducing an adverse impact on competition in the post-merger market.

Table 5.8 may lead to somewhat ambiguous conclusions as regards the overall adverse impact of the merger on competition in the post-merger market, since compared to the NYSE composite index, the stock price of Boston Scientific illustrated a negative abnormal return. However, a number of possible explanations and illustrations have been provided indicating that, based on the investors' perception, as indicated by the stock price movements, the merger would likely lead to adverse effects on competition in the post-merger market.

5.5.6 T-Mobile Austria/Tele.ring

In this case, the Commission concluded that, with the elimination of the maverick in the market and the simultaneous creation of a market structure with two leading, symmetrical network operators, it is likely that the merger would produce non-coordinated effects and significantly impede effective competition in a substantial part of the common market.

The Commission argued that it was unlikely that either H3G or ONE/YESSS! would occupy a place in the market comparable with Tele.ring once the transaction is completed. It added that neither H3G nor ONE/YESSS! would be able to discipline the competitive behaviour of the merged entity and Mobilkom. Thus, both these firms could unilaterally increase prices in the post-merger market.

As was argued in Chapter 4, the post-merger entity had the second highest market share in the post-merger market. Had the Commission assessed this merger under the dominance test, it would have been unable to allege any competition concerns arising from unilateral conduct.

Information regarding the sale of Tele.ring was public on 11 May 2005.[93] Reports mentioned that parties, including Swisscom AG, Belgacom SA, Denmark's TDC, and Tele2 AB, have shown an interest in the sale. None of the main competitors of Tele.ring in the Austrian market was identified as a possible buyer. News about T-Mobile's being a potential buyer of Tele.ring arose on 30 May 2005. Since no competitor of Tele.ring was identified as a potential buyer of Tele.ring on the first announcement of the event of the sale (11 May 2005), the reaction of the share prices of Tele.ring's competitors is unlikely to provide the most accurate representation of future profitability (and thus of likely competition concerns). On 30 May 2005, however, a competitor in the Austrian market was identified as a potential buyer of Tele.ring. Thus, the reaction of the market may be more representative of future profitability (and thus of likely competition concerns) arising from the merger.

The event date used for the event study in this case will be 30 May 2005. Table 5.10 indicates the abnormal return of Deutsche Telekom (owner of T-Mobile), Hutchison (owner of H3G) and Telekom Austria (owner of Mobilkom).[94]

The share price of Deutsche Telekom, owner of T-Mobile, indicated a negative abnormal return, which as illustrated earlier, is expected, as Deutsche Telekom was the acquirer of Tele.ring. Hutchison's share price had a positive abnormal return, whereas Telekom Austria's share price indicated a negative abnormal return.

The negative return of Telekom Austria's share price may be attributed to the fact that on 27 May 2005 Telekom Austria (TA) and its subsidiary

Table 5.10 Abnormal returns in *T-Mobile Austria/Tele.ring* event study

Date	*Deutsche Telekom/ XETRA*	*Hutchison/ XETRA*	*Telekom Austria/ ATX*
3 June 2005	0.15	0.48	0.34
2 June 2005	–0.37	1.22	0.02
1 June 2005	–0.96	–1.49	1.23
31 May 2005	–0.22	–0.87	–0.23
30 May 2005	**–0.27**	**0.53**	**–1.74**
27 May 2005	–0.64	1.17	–2.67
26 May 2005	–0.81	–1.07	N/A
25 May 2005	–0.04	0.16	–0.60

Mobilkom Austria announced that they had finalized the takeover of Bulgarian mobile operator MobilTel earlier than expected. This was the largest acquisition by an Austrian company at the time. This significant acquisition is likely to have exerted significant downward pressure on the share price of Telekom Austria.

The Commission alleged that the T-Mobile/Tele.ring merger would induce non-coordinated effects in the post-merger market. Thus, the incumbents could unilaterally increase prices in the post-merger market. As this analysis illustrates, the share prices of Hutchison (parent company of H3G) illustrated a positive abnormal return, whereas the share price of Telekom Austria (parent company of Mobilkom) indicated negative abnormal returns which may be explained due to the acquisition of MobiTel, occurring at the same time as the announcement of the merger between Deutsche Telekom's T-Mobile and Western Wireless' Tele.ring.

These movements of the share prices illustrate that such non-coordinated effects alleged by the Commission were, based on the reaction of the market to the merger, likely.

It should be noted that all the share prices used in the analysis of this case are share prices of the parent companies, rather than of the competitors of Tele.ring. Thus, as already explained in this chapter, the returns identified for these share prices may not constitute an accurate representation of the competition impact of the merger, since they are likely to incorporate the reaction to events that may not have affected the competitors directly, but that affected their parent companies. Thus, as far as the *T-Mobile/Tele.ring* merger is concerned, the conclusion as regards the impact of the merger on competition may not be an accurate representation of the market's expectation.

Although event studies can provide very useful results in the assessment of a merger, such studies entail limitations that need to be taken into account in conducting such an analysis.

5.6 Limitations of event study analysis

There are several advantages in using stock market data. The stock market's reaction is an independent assessment of the effects of a merger. Second, stock market reactions are available whether the merger is cleared or not. Stock market data thus avoid a potential censoring problem (that is to say the impact of a merger is only observed if the merger is cleared). Another advantage of stock market data is that they are relatively easy to obtain and relative to accounting data, stock market data are inherently prospective and hence better suited to capture dynamic effects of mergers on firm performance. In addition, the collection process is rapid so analysis using stock market evidence can be implemented quickly and separately from the rest of the merger investigation.

Although event studies can provide a useful insight in the adverse effects of the merger on competition, they also entail certain drawbacks. The assumption of capital market efficiency is not always accurate. Thus, stock market data may not fully capture the truth about market power or cost reduction possibilities.

In addition, there may be abnormal return prior and after the event date, attributable to the event in question. Provided that insider trading rules were obeyed and suitably enforced, there should be no abnormal return around the event date. However, there are instances where information is revealed to a small number of individuals before the actual announcement date and thus the stock price changes before the event date. The individuals with access to important information may reveal it and thus cause significant movement of securities' prices. The abnormal return after the event date can occur because the event was announced after the markets close on the event day – and thus the impact of the event on prices and trades can be reflected on the day after the event day. Moreover the abnormal return after the date of event is due to the time it takes for the released information to have an impact on prices.

It can be argued that the initial reaction of the stock market to the announcement of the merger may be biased due to the stock market's expectation of the competition authority's decision. The market takes into account the antitrust procedure at the time of announcement.[95] Hence, the change in the value of the stock at the time of the announcement is equal to the probability that the deal will be cleared times the value that will accrue if the merger is realized.

However, even if that were the case, the results of the event study employed in this chapter do not change. If the market expects the merger to be cleared, the share price of the target firm is likely to illustrate a higher positive abnormal return. If the market expects the merger to be prohibited, then the reaction of the market is likely to be neutral (in the unlikely event that the market is certain about the competition authority's prohibition decision),[96] or positive (if the market is not certain about the result of the competition assessment). In the latter case, the stock price of the target firm will not exhibit as strong a positive abnormal return as it would indicate if the market expects the merger to be cleared.[97] The methodology employed in this article has focused on the sign of the return of stock prices rather than the magnitude. Thus, the bias incurred by the expectation of the competition assessment does not alter the results of the analysis herein.

Additional concerns have been raised as regards the delegation of antitrust enforcement decisions to the stock market. Stock market analysts often do not take a fully sophisticated approach to competition analysis, and do not have access to the information that antitrust authorities have. Furthermore, if inferences about the competitive effects of particular mergers are drawn from the stock market response to the mergers' announcement, once stock markets become aware of that they may choose their reaction in a way that will not indicate that they expect the merger to harm competition.

Moreover, shareholders may react differently to a merger between competitors operating in a similar geographical market than between those operating in different geographical markets.[98] Hence, there are strategic factors that may be used to explain the variation in wealth gains and stock prices that may be observed depending on particular characteristics of the firms involved. We should note that the announcement of the merger may have a small impact on stock prices of competitors if the merger affects only a small part of the business of the firms being considered.

The EMH suggests that the market's estimate is not systematically biased, that is to say, today's market estimate incorporates all publicly available information, until today. The EMH does not imply that the market is always right, rather that the market is not *systematically* wrong. Event studies do not convey any information about the rationality of the residual divergence generated by deviations from the average settlement of securities' prices. Although there are a large number of event studies verifying the efficiency in the markets, efficiency issues are never completely resolved.[99]

Academic research has also identified a number of drawbacks in the implementation of event studies. Event studies may experience the joint hypothesis problem. Event studies involve market efficiency tests and validity tests of asset pricing models. Thus, there is a joint hypothesis problem in the sense that a particular result of an event study may be attributed to the existence of inefficiency in the market or to the use of an unsuitable asset pricing model. However, the use of daily or intraday data in the procedure of an event study in order to measure precisely the speed of the stock prices adjustment can enfeeble the joint hypothesis problem.

In addition, post-announcement drift constitutes evidence of market inefficiency and is common in event studies examining mainly the impact of earnings announcement and merger announcements on securities' prices. Post-announcement drift can be attributed to the bias in measured abnormal returns, the drift may be sample specific and there may be problems measuring abnormal returns. Thus, in designing an event study the precise definition of the event date as well as whether the event date is partially predicted or not is of crucial importance.

A further indication of market inefficiency is the identification of certain pattern that stock prices follow. Such patterns are classified as empirical regularities or market anomalies. Famous market anomalies are the "calendar effect"[100] (such as the January Effect, the September Effect, the Week of the Month Effect, the Monday Blues, the Hour of the Day Effect), the small firm or size effect, the high earnings/price ratio effect, the closed-end mutual fund paradox, the seasonal equity offerings. The existence and significance of these anomalies are controversial and subject to much debate. Most importantly, the research that identifies such anomalies is likely to contribute to their destruction, since it suggests the existence of profitable trading strategies not yet exploited. Market participants are likely to attempt to implement such strategies, and, by so doing, arbitrage them away.[101]

An event study very similar to the one analysed herein was used in *Airtours/First Choice.* The Commission in *Airtours/First Choice* was presented with the Eckbo-Stillman test. The basic principle of the test resembles an event study. The aim was to analyse the reaction of share prices to major new developments. If, for example, a merger were viewed by the stock market as mainly increasing the efficiency of the merging companies, then it would be expected that the share prices of competitors would fall in reaction to the announcement of the merger, because the merger would create a more efficient competitor. If, by way of contrast, the merger would lead to collective dominance, then it would be expected that the share prices of all companies would increase in reaction to the merger. The study indicated that the share price of Thomson fell significantly, when the Airtours' bid for First Choice was announced and that this is evidence that the stock market viewed the Airtours bid as pro-competitive.

The Commission argued that:

> Analysis of share prices can in some circumstances provide valuable information about the competitive impact of mergers. However, share price developments are in any case only indirect evidence, since the data do not relate directly to the market concerned. Furthermore, it is also clear that share price data are often full of extraneous "noise" due to many other events, which may or may not be completely unrelated to the market in questions. The presence of "noise" can be expected to be higher than normal during a period when numerous rumours about possible mergers are circulating.

Taking into account this study, the Commission concluded that apart from methodological problems, the study failed to explain all of the main movements in the share prices of Airtours, First Choice, and Thomson.

Fridolfsson and Stennek (2000) take a more radical stance and argue that event studies cannot detect mergers having an adverse impact on competition. They argue that while an increase in the competitors' share prices indicate that a merger has an adverse impact on competition, a decrease in their share prices does not indicate that a merger is procompetitive.[102] When participants in the stock market contemplate several possible mergers, the announcement of a particular merger will change the likelihood of many alternative configurations. Thus, a fall in the stock price of a competitor may reflect that the market anticipated an increase in the value of the competitor in merger configurations that become irrelevant when the merger is announced.

Moreover, the announcement of a merger may increase the likelihood that competitors will themselves be involved in subsequent mergers. Thus, a change in the value of stock price of competitors may not always be reliable indicator that the merger has an adverse impact on competition. Duso, Neven and Röller (2003) argue, however, that it is not clear whether the latter effect is important empirically.[103] Salinger and Shumann (1988)[104] argue that although such contradictory effects on the share prices of competitors may matter in some cases, on average across a sample of cases, such effects are not important.

A number of studies have tried to compare *ex ante* predictions through event studies with *ex post* realizations. Using different samples of mergers, Ravenscraft and Scherer (1989),[105] Healy, Papepu and Ruback (1992),[106] as well as Kaplan and Weisbach (1992)[107] found that the *ex ante* stock market returns are positively and significantly correlated with *ex post* performance. Existing studies typically report that the announcement of mergers triggers relative large changes in stock market prices.[108] A change in stock prices is likely to provide an unbiased estimate of the change in profitability.

Event study analysis is an *ex ante* method assessing the anticipation by stock market of the adverse consequences of particular mergers on competition and the impact of this anticipation on share prices. The reliability of this method should though not be overemphasized since potential pitfalls of this method have also been identified.

5.7 Conclusion

Event study analysis aims at assessing the stock market's perception of mergers and examines whether the Commission's decisions to prohibit or allow such mergers are reflected in the expectation of the stock market.

The reliability of this method should not be overemphasized, however, since potential pitfalls of this method have also been identified. The limitations that event studies involve notwithstanding, the event study employed in this chapter provides an interesting and useful insight on the accuracy of the Commission's decisions as they are assessed based on the perception of the market of these mergers. As regards *Syngenta CP/Advanta*, *Johnson & Johnson/Guidant*, and *T-Mobile/Tele.ring* the Commission's decisions coincide with the investors' perception of the effects of these mergers on the day of the initial significant dissemination of information related to them. Investors expected these mergers to lead to adverse effects on competition, and the mergers were allowed by the Commission after the submission of satisfactory undertakings.

However, as regards the merger cases *Airtours/First Choice*, *Oracle/PeopleSoft*, and *Sony/BMG* which were assessed by the Commission under the original ECMR, the market perception contradicts the Commission's decisions. As was analysed in Chapter 4, had the Commission applied the

SIEC substantive test to the last two mergers, it would have prohibited the merger or cleared it with commitments, a decision which would coincide with the perception of the market.

Specifically, the merger of *Airtours/First Choice* was not expected to lead to adverse effects on competition based on the market perception, although the merger was blocked by the Commission, whose decision was overturned on appeal by the CFI. *Oracle/PeopleSoft* would have an adverse impact on the post-merger market, but the Commission failed to block it, or request undertakings. Finally, *Sony/BMG* was expected to lead to adverse effects on competition in the post-merger market, but was cleared by the Commission without any undertakings.

In all these three merger decisions, assessed under the dominance test, the Commission's decisions contradicted the market perception of the effects of the mergers. The market perception, as illustrated by the results of the event study analysis, constitutes a further indication that two of these mergers might have had an adverse impact on competition (*Oracle/PeopleSoft* and *Sony/BMG*), and that one merger (*Airtours/First Choice*) might have been pro-competitive, as the theoretical analysis in Chapter 4 indicated. The inability of the Commission to block the *Oracle/PeopleSoft*, and *Sony/BMG* mergers was due to the inadequacy of the dominance test to block mergers leading to non-coordinated effects in oligopolistic markets. Thus, as both the qualitative analysis in Chapter 4 and the quantitative one in Chapters 3 and 5 indicate, had the Commission applied the SIEC test, these mergers would have been either blocked, or allowed after the submission of satisfactory undertakings.

Notes

1 Bruce Kobayashi, former economist at the US Federal Trade Commission (FTC) and DOJ (Antitrust Division) quoted in *Fortune Magazine*, 14 April 1997. In Duso, T., Röller, L-H. and Neven, D. (2003), "The Political Economy of European Merger Control: Evidence using Stock Market Data", http://skylla.wz-berlin.de/pdf/2002/iv02–34.pdf. Some parts of this chapter have been published in: Kokkoris, I. (2007c), "Event Studies in Merger Assessment. Successes and Failures", *European Competition Journal*, July.

2 The UK Competition Commission has commissioned a research report on the use of event studies in merger assessment, illustrating thus the possible importance and use of event studies in merger analysis. The author of this book has written extensively about merger assessment and this part of the chapter incorporates some of his earlier work, including the following: Kokkoris, I. (2007c), "Event Studies in Merger Assessment. Successes and Failures", *European Competition Journal*, July.

3 I would like to thank David Stalibrass and Mario Marinelli, economists at the UK OFT, Kyriakos Papadakis, analyst at JP Morgan, as well as Claudio Calgano, economist at CRA International. The data have been obtained from Bloomberg, as well as Yahoo Finance. The information about the announcement of the mergers in the press has been obtained from Factiva (www.factiva.com).

4 The event study herein does not purport to identify unilateral from coordinated effects. It is used as a method of predicting the anticompetitive effects of a merger. Since Chapter 4 identified likely non-coordinated effects in oligopolistic markets being induced by some mergers, this event study aims at confirming whether the market expected the merger to have this anticompetitive impact.

5 The abnormal return is computed as the difference between the return on the stock and the return on an appropriate index on the day of announcement. A normal rate of return for the stock would be the same return as the one for the index.

6 Data on share prices will be taken from databases such as Datastream, Bloomberg, Factset as well as from public information data sources such as the *Financial Times.*

7 This argument refers to the semi-strong efficiency of markets. According to the semi-strong version of the efficient market hypothesis, stock (securities') prices already reflect all publicly available information relevant to the prospects of the firm including past data, earning forecasts, reports related to the state of the economy, accounting reports, balance sheet reports. Fama, E. F., Fischer, L., Jensen, M. and Roll R. (1969) "The Adjustment of Stock Prices to new Information", *International Economic Review,* 10, 1–21.

8 The abnormal return is computed at the difference between the return on the stock and the return on an appropriate index on the day of announcement.

9 This argument refers to the semi-strong efficiency of markets. According to the semi-strong version of the efficient market hypothesis, stock prices already reflect all publicly available information relevant to the prospects of the firm including past data, earning forecasts, reports related to the state of the economy, accounting reports, balance sheet reports. Fama, E. F., Fischer, L., Jensen, M. and Roll, R. (1969), "The Adjustment of Stock Prices to new Information", *International Economic Review,* 10, 1–21.

10 The event study analysis herein will focus only on the cases decided under the ECMR.

11 In an allocationally efficient (Pareto efficient) market any re-allocation that makes one or more individuals better off would result in at least one individual being made worse off. Operational efficiency in a market deals with the determination of commission fees, the degree of competition between financial market centres and among financial service providers. According to informational efficiency 'a market is said to be efficient if it fully and correctly reflects all relevant information in determining security prices'. Newman, P., Milgate, M. and Eatwell, J. (1992), *The New Palgrave Dictionary of Money and Finance,* vol. 1, Macmillan, London, 739.

12 Sharpe, W., Alexander, G. and Bailey, J. V. (1998), *Investments,* 6th edn, Prentice Hall, Upper Saddle River, NJ, 93.

13 Fama, E. F. (1970), "Efficient Capital Markets: A Review of Theory and Empirical Work", *Journal of Finance,* 25(2), 383–417.

14 Bodie, Z., Kane, A. and Marcus, A. (1999), *Investments,* 4th edn, Irwin McGraw-Hill, Singapore, 331.

15 Jones, C. (1994), *Investments,* 4th edn, John Wiley & Sons, Hoboken, NJ, 628.

16 Fama, E. F. (1991), "Efficient Capital Markets II", *Journal of Finance,* 46, 1575–617.

17 Bodie, Z., Kane, A. and Marcus, A. (1999), *Investments,* 4th edn, Irwin McGraw-Hill, Singapore, 933.

18 Fama, E. F. (1991), "Efficient Capital Markets II", *Journal of Finance,* 46, 1575–617.

19 Eckbo, B. E. (1983), "Horizontal Mergers, Collusion, and Stockholder Wealth", *Journal of Financial Economics*, 11, 241–73.
20 Stillman, R. (1983), "Examining Antitrust Policy Towards Horizontal Mergers", *Journal of Financial Economics*, 11, 225–40.
21 Duso, T., Röller, L-H. and Neven, D. (2003), "The Political Economy of European Merger Control: Evidence using Stock Market Data", http://skylla.wz-berlin.de/pdf/2002/iv02–34.pdf, 6.
22 Eckbo, B. E. and Wier, P. (1985), "Antimerger Policy under the Hart-Scott-Rodino Act: A Reexamination of the Market Power Hypothesis", *Journal of Law and Economics*, 28, 119–49.
23 See further: Duso, T., Röller, L-H. and Neven, D. (2003), "The Political Economy of European Merger Control: Evidence using Stock Market Data", http://skylla.wz-berlin.de/pdf/2002/iv02–34.pdf, 7.
24 Cox, A. and Portes, J. (1998), "Mergers in Regulated Industries: The Uses and Abuses of Event Studies", *Journal of Regulatory Economics*, 14, 281–304.
25 This request is an indication of the possible impact of the merger news on stock prices.
26 Panayides, P. and Gong, X. (2002), "The Stock Market Reaction to Merger and Acquisition Announcements in Liner Shipping", *International Journal of Maritime Economics*, 4, 55–80.
27 OXERA (2006), "Blocking the Deal. How Do Merger Decisions Affect Share Prices", March 2006, www.oxera.co.uk.
28 Duso, T., Gugler, K. and Yurtoglu, B. (2006), "How Effective is European Merger Control?", http://homepage.univie.ac.at/klaus.gugler/public/dgy.pdf.
29 Duso, T., Gugler, K. and Yurtoglu, B. (2006), "How Effective is European Merger Control?", http://homepage.univie.ac.at/klaus.gugler/public/dgy.pdf, 1.
30 In Duso, T., Röller, L-H. and Neven, D. (2003), "The Political Economy of European Merger Control: Evidence using Stock Market Data", http://skylla.wz-berlin.de/pdf/2002/iv02–34.pdf.
31 Case M1524 *Airtours/First Choice* [2000] OJ L93/1 ("*Airtours/First Choice*").
32 T-5/02, T-80/02, *Tetra Laval BV/Sidel v Commission*, judgment of 22 October 2002.
33 T-210/01 *General Electric v Commission*, judgment of 14 December 2005.
34 The CFI upheld the Commission's analysis as far as the horizontal issues were concerned.
35 In Duso, T., Röller, L-H. and Neven, D. (2003), "The Political Economy of European Merger Control: Evidence using Stock Market Data", http://skylla.wz-berlin.de/pdf/2002/iv02–34.pdf, 25.
36 The event study in this chapter focuses on the non-coordinated effects arising from horizontal mergers, rather than their coordinated effects.
37 Röller, L-H. and Neven, D. (2002), "Discrepancies Between Markets and Regulators: an Analysis of the First Ten Years of EU Merger Control", http://hei.unige.ch/sections/ec/pdfs/Working_papers/HEIWP10–2002.pdf. For a full literature review behind event studies, see: Kokkoris, I. (2007c), "Event Studies in Merger Assessment. Successes and Failures", *European Competition Journal*. Duso, Neven and Röller (2003) evaluated the adverse consequences of mergers on competition from the reaction of the stock market price of competitors and of the merging firms. They identified instances where the Commission has prohibited mergers that the stock market regarded as pro-competitive (type I errors) as well as instances where the EU has failed to prevent mergers that were regarded as having an adverse impact on competition (type II errors). Their data suggest that the Commission made a type I

error in four of the 14 prohibitions (28 per cent). They identified as type I errors two cases that have later been overturned on appeal (*Airtours/First Choice* and *Tetra Laval/Sidel*) and one case (*General Electric/Honeywell*) that has been highly controversial and was successfully appealed by the merging parties, as regards the non-horizontal competitive harm that, allegedly, induced. Regarding type II errors, the authors suggest, that the Commission made an error in about 23 per cent of the cases that it has allowed without conditions.

38 Ibid., p. 27. The two last factors can also lead to type I errors.

39 OFT (1999), "Quantitative Techniques in Competition Analysis", Research Paper 17, October 1999, www.oft.gov.uk, 107. It can be argued that the initial reaction of the stock market to the announcement of the merger may be biased due to the stock market's expectation of the competition authority's decision. The market takes into account the antitrust procedure at the time of announcement. Hence, the change in the value of the stock at the time of the announcement is equal to the probability that the deal will be cleared times the value that will accrue if the merger is realized. However, even if that is the case, the results of the event study employed in this chapter do not change. The stock market is more likely to base its reaction on factors that it is more certain of their occurrence. Due to the complexity and unpredictability of the merger assessment process as well as due to the ignorance of competition law, investors are more likely to base their reaction on their expectation of the merged entity's profitability arising from the merger, rather than on the uncertain outcome of the merger assessment. If the market expects the merger to be cleared, the share price of the target firm is likely to illustrate a higher positive abnormal return. If the market expects the merger to be prohibited, then the reaction of the market is likely to be neutral (in the unlikely event that the market is certain about the competition authority's prohibition decision), or positive (if the market is not certain about the result of the competition assessment). In the latter case, the stock price of the target firm will not exhibit as strong positive abnormal return as it would indicate if the market expects the merger to be cleared. (Similarly, as regards the stock price of the acquirer, it is likely to show negative abnormal returns, which will not be materially influenced by the expectation of the competition authority's assessment.) The methodology employed in this article has focused on the sign of the return of stock prices rather than the magnitude. Thus, the bias incurred by the expectation of the competition assessment does not alter the results of the analysis herein.

40 As mentioned earlier, the share price of the acquirer may illustrate negative abnormal returns.

41 An assumption is made that competitors will not be weakened to the point that they would prefer to leave the industry. If such an event occurs, then both consumers and competitors could be harmed as a result of the merger. In the mergers assessed in this analysis, there is little likelihood that one of the competitors would exit the market as the result of the merger.

42 The abnormal return is computed as the difference between the return on the stock and the return on an appropriate index on the day of announcement.

43 In Case M4000 *Inco/Falconbridge*, 20 January 2006, the Commission addressed the efficiency arguments raised by the parties.

44 OFT (1999), "Quantitative Techniques in Competition Analysis", Research Paper 17, October 1999, www.oft.gov.uk, 108. Judge Posner (Posner, R. (2001), *Antitrust Law*, 2nd edn, University of Chicago Press, Chicago) also claims that lower rivals' stock prices on the merger announcement day indi-

cate that the merger is likely to be pro-competitive. However, Baker (2002) (Baker, J. (2002), "Horizontal Merger Analysis Grows Up: A Review of Article 5 of Richard Posner's Antitrust Law (2nd edn 2001)", *The Antitrust Source*, January, 1–5) argues that interpreting lower stock market prices for rival shares as suggesting that the merger creates efficiencies rather than an adverse impact on competition is correct only if the theory of harm involves collusive rather than exclusionary effects. A merger that harms competition by excluding rivals would also lower the price of rival shares.

45 The term "stock price" and "share price" are used interchangeable herein.

46 Cox, A. and Portes, J. (1998), "Mergers in Regulated Industries: The Uses and Abuses of Event Studies", *Journal of Regulatory Economics*, 14, 281–304.

47 Aktas, N., de Bodt, E. and Roll, R. (2003), "Market Response to European Regulation of Business Combinations", in Duso, T., Röller, L-H. and Neven, D., "The Political Economy of European Merger Control: Evidence using Stock Market Data", http://skylla.wz-berlin.de/pdf/2002/iv02–34.pdf.

48 Duso, T., Röller, L-H. and Neven, D. (2003), "The Political Economy of European Merger Control: Evidence using Stock Market Data", http://skylla.wz-berlin.de/pdf/2002/iv02–34.pdf.

49 The expected change is of the same sign as the conditional change given that the merger takes place.

50 Adapted from Duso, T., Röller, L-H. and Neven, D. (2003) "The Political Economy of European Merger Control: Evidence using Stock Market Data", http://skylla.wz-berlin.de/pdf/2002/iv02–34.pdf, 290.

51 Röller, L-H. and Neven, D. (2002), "Discrepancies Between Markets and Regulators: an Analysis of the First Ten Years of EU Merger Control", http://hei.unige.ch/sections/ec/pdfs/Working_papers/HEIWP10–2002.pdf. The CAPM equation can be written as $Rs = Rf + b(Rm-Rf) + \varepsilon$. Rf is the risk-free rate of return, Rs is the return of the stock and Rm is the return of the market index. b represents the sensitivity of the stock price to the market index. An assumption is made that $b = 1$, that is to say stocks in the sample have the same sensitivity to the market with respect to the relevant stock market index. Thus, this equation turns to $Rs = Rm + \varepsilon$. Any discrepancy indicated by ε indicates the abnormal return of the stock price in the event of a merger announcement.

52 OXERA (2006), "Blocking the Deal. How Do Merger Decisions Affect Share Prices", March 2006, www.oxera.co.uk.

53 This implies that beta ('b") is equal to 1. This assumption will bias the magnitude of the negative or positive reaction that will be identified. For the purposes of this analysis, importance is given to whether the market anticipated the merger to be beneficial or harmful for competition. This will be indicated by whether the reaction was positive or negative respectively, rather than by the magnitude of the coefficient itself.

54 In addition, rather than taking as event date the date of the merger announcement, event study methodology can employ the date of the announcement of the decision of the competition authority as regards the clearance or prohibition of the merger. If the latter approach is followed then, the event study will assess the impact of the competition authority's decision on the likelihood of completing the merger, rather than the impact of the merger on the profitability of the incumbents, and thus the impact on competition in the post-merger market.

55 www.factiva.com.

56 Duso, T., Gugler, K. and Yurtoglu, B. (2006), "How Effective is European Merger Control?", http://homepage.univie.ac.at/klaus.gugler/public/dgy.pdf, 17.

57 The affected markets of interest will include the markets where non-coordinated effects in oligopolistic market were identified.

58 In cases where a particular company is listed on more than one exchanges, the stock price taken into consideration for the analysis in this chapter, is the stock price at the exchange where the stock exhibited the highest trading volume.

59 OXERA used –1 to day 0, –3 to day 0 and –1 to day +3, where 0 is the announcement day. Capkun and Semenova (2004) (Capkun, V. and Semenova, M. (2004), "Market Reaction to Merger Approval process of the European Commission", http://papers.ssrn.com/sol3/papers.cfm?abstract_id=634583) used –5 to +1 working days. Panayides and Gong (2002) used –5 to +5 event window. Duso, Gugler and Yurtoglu (2006) used –50 to +5 as event window.

60 Cox, A. and Portes, J. (1998), "Mergers in Regulated Industries: The Uses and Abuses of Event Studies", *Journal of Regulatory Economics*, 14, 281–304.

61 The aim of this part of the chapter is to use event study methodology to assess the expectation of the stock market as regards the impact of merger on the profitability of the firms in the post-merger market. Thus, the movement of stock prices around the event date will be illustrated.

62 For all the cases, except *Airtours/First Choice*, the analysis will include an assessment of the abnormal returns of the stock prices of the merging parties and the competitors. For the *Airtours/First Choice*, the analysis focused on the actual movements of share prices. The reason for following this approach is that the share prices of the companies as well as the stock index were subject to several events. There were many dates (from 23 February until 29 April) that could be identified as the event dates and thus as the benchmarks for the relevant event windows. In addition, the sector was prone to several events occurring in the same period (for example Kuoni bid for First Choice, merger plans between European Leisure and Allied Leisure) influencing the level of the stock index. Thus, the noise in the market during this period was significant. Rather than following an inaccurate approach of conducting an event study on these event dates, and assessing the abnormal returns emanating from these share price movements as compared to the stock index movements, a more accurate approach would be to follow the actual share price movements.

63 These market shares are, according to the shares provided by the research firm AC Nielsen, reproduced in Table 1 of the Commission's decision. According to the Commission's market shares the combined merger entity would have a market share of 32 per cent, with Airtours having 21 per cent and First Choice 11 per cent. Thomson had 27 per cent; Thomas Cook 20 per cent. There is insignificant divergence between the Commission's data and the data provided by AC Nielsen. This book employs the market shares provided by AC Nielsen.

64 Reuters news, "UK stocks – Factors to watch on March 17", www.factiva.com.

65 Greenwich Mean Time.

66 *The Independent* on 19 March 1999 wrote that "The smart money was on a 220p-a-share hostile bid for First Choice, owner of Unijet and Hays & Jarvis. The offer would value the UK travel group at a sunny #742m, leaving Kuoni, the posh holiday specialist, out in the cold", www.factiva.com.

67 OFT (1999), "Quantitative Techniques in Competition Analysis", Research Paper 17, October 1999, www.oft.gov.uk, 108. Judge Posner (Posner, R. (2001), *Antitrust Law*, 2nd edn, University of Chicago Press, Chicago) also claims that lower rivals' stock prices on the merger announcement day indicate that the merger is likely to be pro-competitive. However, Baker (2002) (Baker, J. (2002), "Horizontal Merger Analysis Grows Up: A Review of Chapter 5 of Richard Posner's Antitrust Law (2nd edn 2001)", *The Antitrust Source*, January, 1–5) argues that interpreting lower stock market prices for rival

shares as suggesting that the merger creates efficiencies rather than an adverse impact on competition is correct only if the theory of harm involves collusive rather than exclusionary effects. A merger that harms competition by excluding rivals would also lower the price of rival shares. An assumption is made that competitors will not be weakened to the point that they would prefer to leave the industry. If such an event occurs, then both consumers and competitors could be harmed as a result of the merger.

68 In Duso, T., Röller, L-H. and Neven, D. (2003), "The Political Economy of European Merger Control: Evidence using Stock Market Data", http://skylla.wz-berlin.de/pdf/2002/iv02–34.pdf.

69 See further: paragraph 187, *Oracle/PeopleSoft*.

70 Oracle's offer represented a 5.9 per cent premium to PeopleSoft's closing price on 5 June 2003.

71 PeopleSoft stock, which had started in 2003 at $18.30, was trading at $15.11 before Oracle announced its offer. However, part of the surge in PeopleSoft shares was the result of arbitrageurs unwinding positions they had set up on the PeopleSoft-JD Edwards deal. "Oracle Makes $5.1B Bid For Rival PeopleSoft", 6 June 2003, 17:53, Dow Jones News Service. www.factiva.com.

72 Oracle also disclosed that it expects to report fiscal fourth-quarter earnings of 14 to 15 cents a share.

73 "Update(3): PeopleSoft Board Rejects Oracle Hostile Offer", 12 June 2003, 22:26 Dow Jones News Service. www.factiva.com.

74 Some stocks are listed on NYSE and some on NASDAQ.

75 In case there is a general trend (positive or negative) in the stocks in a particular industry, it may be worth using the industry as benchmark, in order to address this trend.

76 "Microsoft's Ballmer reiterates Linux threat – Update 3", 5 June 2003, AFX International Focus.

77 "Microsoft slips on Ballmer's Linux comments – Update 4", 5 June 2003, AFX UK Focus. www.factiva.com.

78 Stockwatch "SAP breaches 107 eur, seen benefiting from Oracle's PeopleSoft bid", 6 June 2003, AFX Asia. www.factiva.com.

79 The "Others" have not been included in this analysis, as they would not influence the outcome of the analysis.

80 "Plan B for BMG BMG Booby Prize: Label Eyes Sony Play Lest Warner Snare EMI", by Tim Arango, 12 March 2003, *New York Post*, www.factiva.com.

81 "BMG Eyes Sony Deal – New Talks Start as Race to Music Merger Begins", Tim Arango, 23 September 2003, *New York Post*, www.factiva.com.

82 At a board meeting that week, BMG's German parent Bertelsmann AG approved an approach of Sony Music. "BMG looks to Court Sony in Merger Musical Chairs", by Merissa Marr, 24 September 2003, 09:47, Reuters News. www.factiva.com.

83 "Bertelsmann, Sony to Form Joint Music Group", 1 November 2003, Medialine, www.factiva.com.

84 Sony shares decreased 78 cents to $35.99 in early afternoon trading on 6 November.

85 Share price data are often full of extraneous "noise" due to many other events affecting the parent or controlling entity, which may be completely unrelated to the market, the subsidiary or the event in question.

86 Sony is listed in the NYSE international as well as the NYSE composite. The return of any particular industry sector is countervailed by the return on the remaining industry sectors, providing thus overall an accurate representation of the expected return of the market as the benchmark in this analysis. Thus, in case there is a general trend (positive or negative) in the stocks in a par-

ticular industry, it may be worth using the industry as benchmark, in order to address this trend.

87 Case T-464/04 *IMPALA v Commission*, 13 July 2006. The parties appealed to the ECJ. C-413/06 P *BMG&Sony v Commission* [2006] OJ C326/25 (pending).

88 Paragraph 323 of *Johnson & Johnson/Guidant*.

89 It also announced that it expects to report fourth quarter earnings of 63 cents to 68 cents a share on sales of $925 million to $965 million.

90 Reuters News, "J&J in talks to buy Guidant for $24 bln – NY Times", 7 December 2004, 06:15, www.factiva.com.

91 Jerusalem-based stent maker Medinol claimed that Boston Scientific Corp., the world's largest stent maker, had secretly set up a factory in Ireland to manufacture Medinol stents without Medinol's permission.

92 The return of any particular industry sector is countervailed by the return on the remaining industry sectors, providing thus overall an accurate representation of the expected return of the market as the benchmark in this analysis. Thus, in case there is a general trend (positive or negative) in the stocks in a particular industry, it may be worth using the industry as benchmark, in order to address this trend.

93 The date were identified through www.factiva.com.

94 Tele.ring was owned by Western Wireless, which in August 2005 was acquired by Alltel. Thus, no share price information for Western Wireless could be acquired. This does not affect the analysis herein, since the share price of the target, as the analysis in this chapter has illustrated, is expected to show positive abnormal return. In addition, what is essential in using stock price date in order to assess the competition concerns of a merger is the reaction of the competitors' share prices. ONE is owned by the German EON (50.10 per cent), the Norwegian Telenor (17.45 per cent), the French Orange (17.45 per cent) and the Danish TDC (15 per cent). Due to the multiplicity of shareholders, the abnormal return of the stock prices has been excluded from this analysis, as it would not provide an accurate and meaningful outcome as regards the impact of the merger on profitability (and thus on competition) in the Austrian market. All the three share prices used are share prices of the parent companies. Although, in the previous cases analysed herein only share prices of the subsidiaries are used, in this case the use of the parent companies was for two reasons. The first is that the share prices of the parent companies have been used for all the three subsidiaries, and second, the parent companies are involved strictly in the telecommunication sectors.

95 Aktas, N., de Bodt, E. and Roll, R. (2003), "Market Response to European Regulation of Business Combinations", in Duso, T., Röller, L-H. and Neven, D. (2003), "The Political Economy of European Merger Control: Evidence using Stock Market Data", http://skylla.wz-berlin.de/pdf/2002/iv02–34.pdf.

96 The stock market is more likely to base its reaction on factors that it is more certain of their occurrence. Due to the complexity and unpredictability of the merger assessment process as well as due to the ignorance of competition law, investors are more likely to base their reaction on their expectation of the merged entity's profitability arising from the merger, rather than on the uncertain outcome of the merger assessment.

97 Similarly, as regards the stock price of the acquirer, it is likely to show negative abnormal returns, which will not be materially influenced by the expectation of the competition authority's assessment.

98 Panayides, P. and Gong, X. (2002), "The Stock Market Reaction to Merger and Acquisition Announcements in Liner Shipping", *International Journal of Maritime Economics*, 4, 55–80.

99 Schwert (1996) confirmed that there is a lot of evidence in support of the semi-strong hypothesis of market efficiency with respect to mergers. Schwert, W. (1996), "Markup Pricing in Mergers and Acquisitions", *Journal of Financial Economics*, 41, 153–192. (Also in Duso T., Röller L-H., Neven D., (2003), "The Political Economy of European Merger Control: Evidence using Stock Market Data", http://skylla.wz-berlin.de/pdf/2002/iv02–34.pdf.)

100 Kokkoris, I. (2005e), "Weak-Form Tests of Market Efficiency in Corporate Debt Restructuring", *International Corporate Rescue*, 2(6), 337–43.

101 Cox, A. and Portes, J. (1998) "Mergers in Regulated Industries: The Uses and Abuses of Event Studies", *Journal of Regulatory Economics*, 14, 281–304.

102 Fridolfsson, S-O. and Stennek, J. (2000), "Why Event Studies Do Not Detect Anticompetitive Mergers", WP, Research Institute of Industrial Economics, Stockholm, http://swopec.hhs.se/iuiwop/papers/iuiwop0542.pdf, 6.

103 In Duso, T., Röller, L-H. and Neven, D. (2003), "The Political Economy of European Merger Control: Evidence using Stock Market Data", http://skylla.wz-berlin.de/pdf/2002/iv02–34.pdf, 9.

104 Salinger, M. and Schumann, L. (1988), "Horizontal Mergers and the Market Value of Rivals: The 'In Play' Effect", Columbia First Boston Series in Money, Economics and Finance Working Paper: FB-88–03. (Also in Duso, T., Röller, L-H. and Neven, D. (2003), "The Political Economy of European Merger Control: Evidence using Stock Market Data", http://skylla.wz-berlin.de/pdf/2002/iv02–34.pdf.)

105 Ravenscraft, D. and Scherer, F. M, (1987), "Life after Takeovers", *Journal of Industrial Economics*, 36, 147–156. In Duso, T., Röller, L-H. and Neven, D. (2003), "The Political Economy of European Merger Control: Evidence using Stock Market Data", http://skylla.wz-berlin.de/pdf/2002/iv02–34.pdf.

106 Healy, P., Palepu, K. and Ruback, R. (1992), "Does Corporate Performance Improve After Mergers?", *Journal of Financial Economics*, 31, 135–75. In Duso, T., Röller, L-H. and Neven, D. (2003), "The Political Economy of European Merger Control: Evidence using Stock Market Data", http://skylla.wz-berlin.de/pdf/2002/iv02–34.pdf.

107 Kaplan, S. and Weisbach, M. (1992), "The Success of Acquisitions: Evidence from Divestitures", *Journal of Finance*, March 1992, 47(1), 107–38. In Duso, T., Röller, L-H. and Neven, D. (2003), "The Political Economy of European Merger Control: Evidence using Stock Market Data", http://skylla.wz-berlin.de/pdf/2002/iv02–34.pdf.

108 Aktas, N., de Bodt, E. and Roll, R. (2003), "Market Response to European Regulation of Business Combinations", in Duso, T., Röller, L-H. and Neven, D. (2003) "The Political Economy of European Merger Control: Evidence using Stock Market Data", http://skylla.wz-berlin.de/pdf/2002/iv02–34.pdf.

6 Market structure – assessment criteria of gap cases

The most robust argument against the dominance test was that it may fail to forbid mergers between non-dominant firms having an adverse impact on competition.[1] The "gap" corresponds to the situation where the post-merger entity's market share falls below the level required for dominance but the merger may however lead to non-coordinated effects.

The European Commission faced intense criticism after the *Airtours/First Choice*[2] case, a case which appears to illustrate the existence of the so-called "gap" in the application of the original ECMR. The "gap" was a result of the application of the dominance test as the legal substantive test in the assessment of mergers.[3] It corresponds to the situation where the post-merger entity's market power would not amount to single firm or collective dominance but where the merger may nonetheless lead to non-coordinated effects in the post-merger oligopolistic market. This chapter presents the market structure as well as a non-exhaustive list of assessment criteria that the Commission may employ in examining whether a merger is likely to lead to non-coordinated effects in oligopolistic markets.

Mergers that are deemed "gap" mergers lead to non-coordinated effects in oligopolistic markets if they result in the elimination of important competitive constraints on one or more firms apart from the merging parties. As a report prepared for the Commission by Ivaldi, Jullien, Rey, Seabright and Tirole (2003)[4] ("Report") emphasizes, unilateral effects include not only the impact of the merger on the merging firms but also the equilibrium effect resulting from the adjustment of the decisions of the incumbents to the decisions of the merged entity. The post-merger market structure will be oligopolistic and comprise of a small number of firms, whose products are not close substitutes.[5] In addition, the competitors of the merged entity are not likely to be in a position to expand their capacity or switch their production and new firms have no incentives to enter the market in the presence of an increase in the price or a reduction in the quantity produced by the merged entity.

The two terms "mergers leading to non-coordinated effects in oligopolistic markets" and "non-collusive oligopolies" refer to situations in which the remaining firms in the post-merger market have the incentive and ability to adopt conduct inducing an adverse impact on competition, and thus profit from exerting their market power in the post-merger market, without being dependent on a coordinated response on the part of the other members of the oligopolistic market structure.[6]

An increase in price by the post-merger firm will enhance demand for competing firms' products as consumers switch their demand towards these alternatives, and will, therefore, encourage rival firms to raise prices too. This turns the "unilateral" effect into what can be called a "non-coordinated" effect or a "multilateral" effect of price increases. The evaluation of the latter type of effect is essential in the assessment of mergers leading to non-coordinated effects in oligopolistic markets. The post-merger equilibrium is reached when no firm in the market has an incentive to unilaterally change its prices.

Nicholson and Cardell (2002)[7] argue that the CFI in *Airtours* ruled out the assessment of multilateral effects under the original ECMR. As Ehlermann, Völcker and Gutermuth (2005)[8] mention that, in this case, the Commission appears to have viewed non-coordinated effects as a category of collective dominance. Fingleton (2002)[9] argues that the *Airtours/First Choice* was incorrectly characterized as a tacit collusion case instead of a multilateral effects case. It is clear, that unilateral effects should be distinguished from non-coordinated effects.

In *Oracle/Peoplesoft*, the Commission clearly stated in paragraph 187 that the initial concerns it had concerned the likely non-coordinated effects arising from the merger:

> In the Statement of Objections the Commission based its concerns in part on the finding that significant non-coordinated effects would arise from the transaction. In the reply to the statement of objections, Oracle contested the Commission's competence to assess such effects under the dominance test incorporated in Regulation (EEC) No. 4064/89. It is not necessary to address Oracle's submission on the lack of competence as, on the basis of the new evidence obtained after the Oral Hearing, it has been concluded that no such anticompetitive effects are likely to result from the merger.

In *J&J/Guidant*, the market for carotid stents of endovascular stents, the Commission concluded that:[10]

> Given the characteristics of the markets of carotid SX stents in Austria, Belgium, France, Finland, Germany, Italy, Luxembourg, The Netherlands, Portugal and Spain in terms of concentration, barriers to entry, customer loyalty, closeness of substitution, and as a result of the elimination of a major competitive constraint, the concentration will give rise to non coordinated adverse effects in those national markets and therefore impede effective competition in the common market and

> the EEA as a result of the creation or strengthening of a dominant position.

In the market for non-carotid stents of endovascular stents, the Commission stated that:[11]

> In conclusion, given the characteristics of the markets of non-carotid SX stents in Austria, Belgium, Germany and The Netherlands in terms of concentration, barriers to entry, customer loyalty, closeness of substitution, and as a result of the elimination of a major competitive constraint, the concentration will give rise to non coordinated adverse effects in those national markets and therefore impede effective competition in the common market and the EEA as a result of the creation or strengthening of a dominant position.

The Commission in this case refers to unilateral effects in some markets and to non-coordinated effects in some others (e.g. noncarotid stents). Thus, the Commission identified two different types of anticompetitive harm arising from this merger. Other gap cases have also used this distinction between the two types of effect.

The most direct impact of a merger on competition will be the elimination of the competitive constraints that the merging firms exerted on each other prior to the merger. In addition, non-merging firms can also benefit from the reduction of competitive pressure that results from the merger since the merging firms' price increase or output reduction may induce the switching of some demand to the rival firms, which, in turn, may find it optimal to increase prices. This might happen in particular in differentiated product markets[12] where a merger can lead to incentives for conduct having an adverse impact on competition, without creating a single leading player, and without significantly increasing the feasibility of tacit collusion.

The elimination of competitive constraints enables merging parties, inter alia, to profitably raise prices as well as reduce output. Other firms may then find it profitable to raise prices because of some switching of demand towards their products/services. The extent of this switching depends on the closeness of competition between the merging parties and between them and other firms. This tendency in turn will depend on the degree of heterogeneity between the parties' products and those of their competitors. The more heterogeneous they are the fewer consumers will tend to switch between them and thus the more profitable the post-merger price increase by the incumbents will be. Thus, the incumbents in the post-merger market are prone to increase prices unilaterally, in the post-merger market, without tacitly coordinating.[13]

Non-coordinated effects in oligopolistic markets may arise in a concentrated market with differentiated products where, because of the small number of firms, the incumbents are able to adopt conduct having an adverse impact on competition, without the need to coordinate their behaviour and thus without adopting collectively dominant conduct. Attempting to capture non-collusive oligopolies by applying the single firm dominance concept is inadequate since it omits the incumbents' responses to the actions of the merged entity. In addition, collective dominance may not be applicable due to the fact that in the post-merger market the incumbents do not act in a collusive manner, but individually adopt conduct having an adverse impact on competition.

In markets characterized by homogeneous products and capacity constraints faced by the incumbents mergers may lead to a similar adverse impact on competition as non-collusive oligopolies. When the merger takes place in such a market it is possible that the merged entity as well as its rivals may raise prices and that no firm will be able to increase capacity in order to absorb the switching of demand attributed to that price increase. In the post-merger market all firms may increase prices due to the capacity constraints. However, the merger induces neither such constraints nor the price increase, and thus, such price increase is likely to happen in the absence of the merger as well. In addition, as Willig (2002) argues, this post-merger effect is unilateral, in the sense that the action that creates harm for consumers in the post-merger market, and is induced by the merger, is the likely price increase by the merged entity, rather than the likely responses of the incumbents.[14]

Thus, gap cases are cases that strictly satisfy neither the criteria for single firm dominance nor for collective dominance.[15] Such mergers will lead to a significant impediment to effective competition by reducing the competitive constraints not only between the merging parties but also the competitive constraints exerted on the rival firms in the market. In the case of such a merger, in the post-merger market the oligopolistic interdependence is altered and thus the incumbents may adopt a pricing or production structure that may have an adverse impact on competition. The incumbents will find it individually profitable to increase prices taking into account the higher prices charged by the merged entity.

The gap in the application of the dominance test could, in theory, be rectified if the threshold of dominance was lowered or if the authorities weakened the link between dominance and market power in their assessment of mergers.[16] In such case, mergers leading to non-dominant firms in the post-merger market engaging in unilateral conducts having an adverse impact on competition may be prohibited. In addition, in a market with differentiated products a narrow market definition may rectify the gap of the dominance test. However, these approaches are undesirable since they are an inaccurate assessment of the true competition conditions in the market and lead to legal uncertainty.

The possible existence of cases which can be alleged as leading neither to single firm nor collective dominance is emphasized in Recital 25 of the

Recast ECMR. In addition, Recital 25 emphasizes that the original ECMR was not interpreted in a way that would render mergers to lead to non-coordinated effects in oligopolistic markets incompatible with the common market.

At this point it would be worth presenting the text of Recital 25:

> In view of the consequences that concentrations in oligopolistic market structures may have, it is all the more necessary to maintain effective competition in such markets. Many oligopolistic markets exhibit a healthy degree of competition. However, under certain circumstances, concentrations involving the elimination of important competitive constraints that the merging parties had exerted upon each other, as well as a reduction of competitive pressure on the remaining competitors, may, even in the absence of a likelihood of coordination between the members of the oligopoly, result in a significant impediment to effective competition.
>
> The Community courts have, however, not to date expressly interpreted Regulation (EEC) No. 4064/89 as requiring concentrations giving rise to such non-coordinated effects to be declared incompatible with the common market. Therefore, in the interests of legal certainty, it should be made clear that this Regulation permits effective control of all such concentrations by providing that any concentration which would significantly impede effective competition, in the common market or in a substantial part of it, should be declared incompatible with the common market. The notion of 'significant impediment to effective competition' in Article 2(2) and (3) should be interpreted as extending, beyond the concept of dominance, only to the anticompetitive effects of a concentration resulting from the non-coordinated behaviour of undertakings which would not have a dominant position on the market concerned.

There are several scenarios and examples regarding the features of market structures voiced in the academic literature where, in the post-merger market, a merger may lead to non-coordinated effects without the post-merger firm enjoying a situation either of single dominance or collective dominance.

Sir Derek Morris[17] suggested that where a new entrant appears with advanced technology and innovative ideas and one of the non-dominant companies buys this new entrant, the acquisition may not lead to the creation or strengthening of dominance. However, the merger may not only have a significant adverse impact on potential competition but may lead to a significant impediment to competition by creating the firm with the second highest market share. Morris' argument is very similar to the "maverick" argument that has been incorporated in the *Guidelines.*[18]

Whish (2002)[19] refers to a market structure where a three to two merger in a market with a small number of players may not lead to single firm dominance, and the post-merger market structure does not seem to be prone to collective dominance. However, there is a possibility that the remaining firms in the market may be able unilaterally to increase prices or decrease the quantity of their products; thus, their conduct may have an adverse impact on competition. Such mergers can produce non-coordinated effects in oligopolistic markets if non-merging firms in the same market can also benefit from the reduction of the competitive pressure resulting from the merger, since the merging firms' price increase may switch some demand to the rival firms, which, in turn, may find it profitable to increase their prices. This can result in them increasing prices in the post-merger market. In such cases, the firms in the marketplace are not coordinating their competitive behaviour, but merely reacting to changes in each other's behaviour. Although the dominance test will not prove useful in blocking this type of merger, the SIEC test will.

Additional examples of non-collusive mergers include a merger between two small players in which a third firm is dominant,[20] a merger in a stable oligopoly where one firm buys a smaller rival or entrant,[21] as well as a merger between small players that make the market more symmetric and in which the merged firm does not join the "big" players.[22]

A report[23] prepared for DG Competition provides an example of an oligopolistic market structure in which a merger may induce non-coordinated effects. The authors mention the negative effect of a merger between two firms having a market share of 20 per cent with the dominant firm having a market share of 60 per cent. In the post-merger market the authors predict that all prices increase, with the merged firm having less than 40 per cent market share.[24] Such a merger would not be blocked under the dominance test but could be blocked under the SIEC test.

As was mentioned earlier in this book, mergers between competitors can produce non-coordinated effects if the elimination of the competitive constraints that the merging firms exercised on each other increases the combined firm's market power. Thus, the merged group is able to profitably reduce choice or innovation through its own acts, without the need for a cooperative response from competitors. Furthermore, non-merging firms in the same market can also benefit from the reduction of the competitive pressure resulting from the merger, since the merging firms' price increase may switch some demand to the rival firms, which, in turn, may find it profitable to increase their prices (non-collusive oligopolies). Thus, even if rival firms pursue the same competitive strategies as they did prior to the merger, this can result in them increasing prices in the post-merger market. In such cases, the firms in the marketplace are not coordinating their competitive behaviour, but merely reacting to changes in each other's behaviour. The reduction in these competitive constrains could lead to significant competitive harm in the relevant post-merger market.

Turning to the features that one expects to find in a market in which gap cases may arise, as regards market shares, what one would expect to find is market shares in the post-merger market similar to those in a market that is prone to collective dominance. Thus, the post-merger firm may not be the one with the highest market share. In addition, the post-merger firm may have the highest market share but that market share may not be adequate for single firm dominance to be established.[25] Features that would render a post-merger market prone to anticompetitive conduct need to be present in order to allege that the merger case is a gap case. Such features include barriers to entry and exit, a small number of firms. In addition, consumers and competitors must be unable to counterbalance the anticompetitive behaviour by switching demand or by increasing their capacity respectively in response to a reduction in supply by the post-merger dominant firm. These criteria depend on features such as product homogeneity, low demand growth, low price sensitivity of demand, symmetric cost structures and multi-market contacts.[26] If these features are present, then the merger is more likely to lead to collective dominance rather than to non-coordinated effects in oligopolistic markets to the extent that the products are homogeneous.

Specifically, the market structure in which mergers are likely to lead to non-coordinated effects in oligopolistic markets resembles the market structure in which mergers could lead to unilateral effects.[27] The factors that need to be present for unilateral effects to be likely in the post-merger market include:[28]

- Merging firms have large market shares.
- Merging firms are close competitors.
- Customers have limited possibilities of switching supplier.
- Competitors are unlikely to increase supply if prices increase.
- Merged entity is able to hinder expansion by competitors.
- Merger eliminates an important competitive force.

Similarly, several conditions typically reduce the likelihood that a merger will result in significant unilateral effects:

- Merging parties are not close/closest substitutes.
- Differentiation between products is limited.
- Repositioning of market players is likely and/or entry is easy.
- Post-merger synergies (efficiencies).

Unilateral effects potentially arise whenever the merging parties' products are substitutes. The stronger the substitutability between the merging products, the greater the diversion between them, and the stronger/more likely unilateral effects become. In this case pre-merger market shares may not be a good indicator of levels of rivalry between the merging parties, (for example their products may be differentiated such that they are not close competitors but they still form part of the same relevant market).

The magnitude of any unilateral effects from a merger depends in part on the extent to which the merger allows the parties to recapture customers that would otherwise have been lost. In general, this recapture rate will be measured by the *diversion ratio* between the two firms. This diversion ratio is calculated by looking at customers' choices if they switch away from a firm that increases its price. If the products are differentiated, so that products sold by different participants in the market are not perfect substitutes for one another, a merger between firms in a market for differentiated products may diminish competition by enabling the merged firm to profit by unilaterally raising the price of one or both products above the pre-merger level, without at the same time incurring substantial switching of customers from its products to rivals' products.

Entry by new competitors or expansion by existing competitors must be sufficient in time, scope and likelihood to deter or defeat any attempt by the merging parties to exploit the reduction in rivalry following the merger. Even firms with very high market shares may not be in a position, post-merger, to exercise market power if customers possess countervailing buyer power. The factors to consider in making an assessment of buyer power would be (i) whether or not the customer can credibly threaten to resort, within a reasonable timeframe, to alternative sources of supply; and (ii) whether or not the buyer is able to refuse to buy products produced by the supplier or (in the case of durable goods) delay purchases.[29] Sometimes buyers choose their suppliers through a bidding or auction process (for example, through procurement auctions or tenders). A merger would not produce significant unilateral effects even if the merged entity had a high market share, where tenders are large and infrequent, where suppliers are not subject to capacity constraints, and are not significantly differentiated.

If there are a number of alternative suppliers to whom a significant number of customers are willing to turn, the threat of losing these customers may be adequate to place a constraint on the merging parties. However, product differentiation as well as the inability of competitors to react by either increasing output (if spare capacity is limited), or repositioning in order to place a constraint on the parties post-merger, is conducive to the creation of unilateral effects in the post-merger market.

Furthermore, the acquisition or merger with a maverick firm not only leads to the creation of a larger combined entity in the longer term but may also have additional adverse effects on competition by reducing the competitive dynamics. As regards efficiencies, the greater the likely unilateral effects from a merger, the greater the efficiencies necessary to offset those effects.

These factors are all relevant for the analysis of mergers leading to non-coordinated effects in oligopolistic markets as well. Particular market features make the creation of non-coordinated effects in oligopolistic markets more likely.

Non-coordinated effects can arise in concentrated markets in which firms compete with differentiated products and the products of the merging firms are particularly close substitutes. Similarly, they may arise if competitors are close competitors because of their close geographic location. In the case where products are differentiated based on brand image, technical specifications, quality, or level of service, customers often prefer different suppliers. If firms producing close substitutes merge, the combined entity is more likely to increase price post-merger than if competitors that do not produce close substitutes merge. If the incumbents can alter their product line and become close substitutes to the merged entity, the induced non-coordinated effects will be mitigated. Furthermore, in case competitors are located within close proximity, even if a relevant geographic market is relatively large, competition can be localized and the geographic location of suppliers will play a significant competitive factor.

Finally, concerns of non-coordinated effects in oligopolistic markets can also arise if the suppliers' capacities are the main driver of competition, rather than product differentiation, and competitors would be unlikely to increase output in response to a price increase (and output reduction) of the combined entity due to capacity constraints they may be facing.[30]

As far as the relevant importance and weight of the assessment criteria are concerned, Lindsay, Lecchi and Williams (2003)[31] examined the factors which the Commission took into consideration under the original ECMR in assessing whether a merger would lead to the creation or strengthening of dominance. The decisions they used in their sample were adopted between 1 January 2000 and 30 June 2002. The authors concluded that market shares are highly significant in determining whether a merger will be cleared by the Commission, although the Commission has argued that the market shares are only initial indicators of the likely adverse effects on competition of a merger. Low barriers to entry contribute to the clearance of concentrations with high market share, while buyer power does not seem to be too significant. The geographic coverage influences the assessment if the Commission. Finally, the HHI was not significant but the authors argued that this might be attributed to inaccuracies in the data.

Bergman, Jakobsson and Razo (2003),[32] using a sample of 96 mergers notified to the Commission, analysed the Commission's decision process. They found that the probability of a Phase 2 investigation and of a prohibition of the merger increases with the parties' market shares. The probability also increases when the Commission finds either high entry barriers or that post-merger collusion is easy. The nationality of the merging firms or the identity of the commissioner did not seem to affect the Commission's decisions.

After a brief analysis of the assessment criteria for mergers leading to non-coordinated effects in oligopolistic markets, some concluding remarks should be presented. The purpose of this book was to address the issue of mergers leading to non-coordinated effects in oligopolistic markets. The two terms "mergers leading to non-coordinated effects in oligopolistic markets" and "non-collusive oligopolies" referred to situations in which the remaining firms in the post-merger market have the incentive and ability to adopt a conduct which will have an adverse impact on competition. The incumbents profit from exerting their market power, without being dependent on a coordinated response on the part of the other members of the oligopolistic market structure. This conduct of the post-merger firms is a result of the removal of competitive constraints placed on them prior to the merger.

Notes

1 EEA Standing Committee of the EFTA States (2002), "EEA EFTA Comments on the Commission's Green Paper on the review of Council Regulation (EEC) No 4064/89 (COM(2001) 745/6 Final)", http://secretariat.efta.int/Web?EuropeanEconomicArea/OngoingWork/100w149.doc, 7.

2 The Commission faced criticism because it did not make an efficient use of evidence, for example, by not taking into consideration the conclusions of the UK Competition Commission in 1997 according to which the market was competitive with no significant barriers to entry. In addition, the Commission attempted to extend the law by applying the collective dominance concept in a merger between the second and third largest firms, in a market which did not exhibit the features that render it likely to be conducive to collective dominance. Furthermore, the merger would not lead to a situation of single firm dominance. See: UK Competition Commission, Cm 3813, "Foreign Package Holidays: A Report on the Supply in the UK of Tour Operators' Services and Travel Agents' Services in Relation to Foreign Package Holidays", 19.12.97, www.competition-commission.org.uk.

3 It can also be argued that the *Airtours* decision (Case T-342/99 *Airtours v Commission* [2002] ECR II-2585) came at the right moment for the European Commission. The limitations of the dominance test and the benefits of adopting an SLC-type test were identified from the application of the SLC test in other jurisdictions, such as the United States. It can arguably be said that *Airtours* provided an "opportunity" to reform the substantive test.

4 Ivaldi, M., Jullien, B., Rey, P., Seabright, P. and Tirole, J. (2003), "The Economics of Unilateral Effects", IDEI, Toulouse, Interim Report for DG Competition, European Commission, http://europa.eu.int/comm/competition/mergers/review/the_economics_of_unilateral_effects_en.pdf#search="Economics%20of%20Unilateral%20Effects", 7.

5 Non-collusive oligopolies have some typical features including a small and stable number of firms, each firm is profit maximizing taking into account the other firms' reactions and the market reaches a static equilibrium from which no firm has any incentive to deviate. Fingleton, J. (2002), "Does Collective Dominance Provide Suitable Housing for All Anti-competitive Oligopolistic Mergers", in Hawk, B., *International Antitrust Law and Policy*, Fordham University Law School, Corporate Law Institute.

6 See further: para. 25, ECMR.

7 Nicholson, M. and Cardell, S. (2002), "Airtours v. Commission: Collective Dominance Contained", IBA EC Merger Control Conference, www.ibanet.org.
8 Ehlermann, C-D., Völcker, S. and Gutermuth, A. (2005), "Unilateral Effects: The Enforcement Gap under the Old EC Merger Regulation", *World Competition*, 28(2), 193–203.
9 Mergers inducing multilateral effects are equivalent to non-collusive oligopolies. Fingleton, J. (2002), "Does Collective Dominance Provide Suitable Housing for All Anti-competitive Oligopolistic Mergers", in Hawk, B., *International Antitrust Law and Policy*, Fordham University Law School, Corporate Law Institute, 190.
10 Paragraph 301 of *Johnson & Johnson/Guidant*.
11 Paragraph 311 of *Johnson & Johnson/Guidant*.
12 The significance of product differentiation may be diminished if it is possible for competitors to reposition their products to compete directly with the merging parties' products (e.g. by engaging in brand repositioning or introducing new brands).
13 The main feature of an oligopolistic market is the existence of a possibly sustainable mechanism of coordination of behaviour that may lead to parallelism of prices and capacity. In an oligopolistic market, there are a small number of operators who are able to behave in a parallel manner and derive benefits from their collective market power, without necessarily entering into an agreement or concerted practice. This phenomenon is called *tacit collusion*. The CFI in *Gencor* implicitly equated the notion of collective dominance with the notion of tacit collusion, broadening thus the reach of the ECMR.
14 Willig, R. et al. (2002), "Substantive Standards for Mergers and the Role of Efficiencies", in Hawk, B., *International Antitrust Law and Policy*, Fordham University Law School, Corporate Law Institute.
15 A more detailed analysis of the criteria will be presented in the concluding chapter of this book.
16 OECD (2003), "Substantive Criteria Used for the Assessment of Mergers", www.oecd.org, 31.
17 House of Lords Select Committee on the European Union, "The Review of EC Merger Regulation", Thirty-Second Report, Pt 4: Substantive Issues. www.parliament.the-stationery-office.co.uk/pa/ld/ldeucom.htm, paragraph 148.
18 See for example: *T-Mobile/Tele.ring* (analysed later in this chapter) for a merger case involving a maverick player.
19 Whish, R. (2002), "Analytical Framework of Merger Review, Substantial Lessening of Competition/Creation or Strengthening of Dominance", International Competition Network, First Annual Conference, 28 September, Naples, www.internationalcompetitionnetwork.org/whish_icn_naples_ full_version.pdf.
20 See the *Heinz* case analysed in Chapter 4.
21 See the *Lloyds TSB/Abbey* analysed in Chapter 4.
22 See the *Airtours/First Choice* analysed in Chapter 4. If the merged entity joined the big players, then the post-merger market may be prone to collective dominance.
23 Ivaldi, M., Jullien, B., Rey, P., Seabright, P. and Tirole, J. (2003), "The Economics of Unilateral Effects", IDEI, Toulouse, Interim Report for DG Competition, European Commission, http://europa.eu.int/comm/competition/mergers/review/the_economics_of_unilateral_effects_en.pdf#search="Economics&20of%20Unilateral%20Effects".
24 The requirements (for example, absence of efficiency gains) for the model may be too strict for the model to have wide practical application by the authorities in the assessment of mergers.

25 As an indicators, in Case 62/86 *AKZO Chemie BV v Commission* [1991] ECR I-3359, dominance was alleged with a market share of 50 per cent.

26 Kokkoris, I. (2005d), "The Reform of the European Community Merger Regulation in the Aftermath of the Airtours Case. The Eagerly Expected Debate: SLC v Dominance Test", *ECLR*, 26(1), 37–47.

27 In this context, unilateral effects refer to mergers that induce unilateral actions of the merged entity which are harmful for competition. Non-coordinated effects refer to mergers that induce not only the merged entity but also the other incumbents in the post-merger market to increase their prices and/or adopt other conducts which are harmful to competition.

28 See further: "*Guidelines on the Assessment of Horizontal Mergers under the Council Regulation on the Control of Concentrations between Undertakings*" ("*Guidelines*"), OJ C31, 05.02.2004, 5–18.

29 ICN (2006), "ICN Merger Working Group: Investigation and Analysis Subgroup ICN Merger Guidelines Workbook", prepared for the Fifth Annual ICN Conference, April 2006, Cape Town, www.internationalcompetitionnetwork.org, 42.

30 WilmerHale, *Guide To EC Merger Regulation*, 4th edn, www.wilmehale.com, 51.

31 Lindsay, A., Lecchi, E. and Williams, G. (2003), "Econometrics Study into European Commission Merger Decisions Since 2000", *ECLR*, 24(12), 673–82.

32 Bergman, M, Jakobsson, M. and Razo, C. (2003), "An Econometric Analysis of the European Commission's Merger Decisions", 3 February, www.ne.su.se/research/seminars/pdf/041104_1.pdf#search='n%20Econometric%20Analysis%20of%20the%20European%20Commission%E2%80%99s%20Merger%20Decisions'.

7 Conclusion

This book has embarked on an analysis of mergers inducing non-coordinated effects in oligopolistic markets. The book commenced with an illustration of the emergence of the gap in the application of the dominance test. Then, this book assessed the amendments in the ECMR aimed at rectifying this gap. Subsequently, essential steps and methods in the assessment of non-collusive oligopolies under the two substantive tests (dominance and SLC tests) were addressed. Evidence of gap cases was then presented focusing on jurisdictions that employ either the dominance test or the SLC test in assessing mergers. Finally, the market perception of the market about these non-collusive oligopolies was illustrated, as further proof of the inability of the European Commission to block non-collusive oligopolies under the dominance test, and then the market structure in which gap mergers are likely to occur was presented.

This book is structured so that each chapter would answer certain questions relevant to non-collusive oligopolies. The first chapter addressed the question of whether there is a "gap" in the application of the dominance test. The *Airtours/First Choice* case provided an example of where the Commission, under the impression that the merger would lead, inter alia, to non-coordinated effects in oligopolistic markets,[1] blocked the merger based on the allegation of creation or strengthening of collective dominance. This decision was appealed to the CFI, which annulled the decision and set out criteria that need to be satisfied before an allegation of collective dominance can be made by the Commission.

The second chapter addressed the issue of whether there is EU legislation that deals with "gap" cases. It analysed the Recast ECMR and illustrated how the Commission, after intense debate, changed the substantive test for assessing mergers, in an attempt to address and rectify the "gap". The Commission adopted the SIEC test as the substantive test for the assessment of mergers. According to this test, a concentration which would "significantly impede effective competition, in the common market or in a substantial part of it, in particular as a result of the creation or strengthening of a dominant position, shall be declared incompatible with the common market".[2] This test allows the Commission to block mergers that lead to non-coordinated effects in oligopolistic markets; it was not able to prohibit such mergers under the dominance test of the original ECMR.

The third chapter addressed some necessary steps in the assessment of mergers leading to non-coordinated effects in oligopolistic markets. The chapter addressed quantitative methods for the assessment of such mergers. The analysis of the merger simulation and critical loss analysis focused on the way that these methods have been applied in mergers being assessed under the SLC and dominance tests in the EU, the United States and the United Kingdom. No differences were identified, not only in the application of these methods under the two substantive tests but also in their efficiency, accuracy and predictability for the assessment of non-collusive oligopolies. Any inability of the dominance test to capture mergers leading to non-coordinated effects in oligopolistic markets will be due to its limited scope of application, rather than due to the quantitative method that lawyers, economists and competition practitioners will employ to assess the effects of such mergers.

The fourth chapter sought to provide evidence of mergers leading to non-coordinated effects in oligopolistic markets. Several cases which were likely to be "gap" cases were identified: in the EU, *Airtours/First Choice, Oracle/PeopleSoft, Sony/BMG, Syngenta CP/Advanta, Johnson & Johnson/Guidant*, and *T-Mobile/Tele.ring*; in the United Kingdom, *Lloyds TSB/Abbey National* and *Littlewoods Organization Plc/Freemans Plc*; in Finland, *SOK Corporation, Spar Finland Plc*; in New Zealand, *Progressive Enterprises/Woolworths*, which was assessed under both the SLC and dominance tests; and finally, in the United States, the *Heinz/Beech-Nut* merger. Furthermore, in Australia, a significant number of cases were identified as likely gap cases, but due to lack of access to publicly available decisions, detailed analysis of these cases was not possible. If the mergers identified in the fourth chapter were assessed under a different substantive test (either the dominance test or the SLC/SIEC test) from the one that was actually applied, the assessment of these mergers would have resulted in different outcomes.

In most of these cases, the post-merger market structure, in some markets, consisted of a small number of incumbents, with similar market shares, producing differentiated products. In these markets, the criteria for collective dominance were not satisfied (for example transparency, retaliation, monitoring, countervailing buyer power). In addition, the post-merger market was not conducive to the creation of unilateral effects either. However, the reduction in the competitive constraints in the market might have led to an adverse impact on competition, since the incumbents in the post-merger market would have the incentive to unilaterally increase prices, reduce quality, and adopt conduct having an adverse impact on competition.

The fifth chapter dealt with the issue of whether the Commission's assessment of a gap merger is supported by the stock market reaction to the announcement of the merger. A positive abnormal return indicates that customers expected these mergers to be profitable for the firms.

Firms increase profitability mainly by increasing prices (reducing output) in the market, and thus adopting conducts harming competition. If investors believed that the merger would not be profitable for the merging firms (that is to say, firms are not likely to increase prices/reduce output, and thus are not likely to adopt a conduct having an adverse impact on competition), the merging firms' share prices are likely to have exhibited negative abnormal returns on the day of announcement. The event study used as a sample the cases decided by the Commission that have been identified as gap cases in Chapter 4.

The results indicated that the Commission's decision coincides with the investors' perception on the day of the initial significant dissemination of information regarding the adverse effects of three of these mergers on competition, *Syngenta CP/Advanta*, *Johnson & Johnson/Guidant*, and *T-Mobile/Tele.ring*. However, as regards the mergers *Airtours/First Choice*, *Oracle/PeopleSoft*, and *Sony/BMG*, which were assessed by the Commission under the dominance test of the original ECMR, the market perception contradicts the Commission's decision. The market did not expect the *Airtours/First Choice* to have an adverse impact on competition, while it regarded both *Oracle/PeopleSoft*, and *Sony/BMG* as leading to adverse effects on competition in the post-merger markets. Thus, the conclusions of the event study coincide with the conclusions of the theoretical case law analysis elaborated in Chapter 4. According to these conclusions, *Oracle/PeopleSoft* and *Sony/BMG* were gap cases.

As mentioned in Chapter 4, a limitation of this book concerns the lack of information. The analysis of some cases in this book was done based on publicly available material. The extent to which the authorities' decisions, as well as other published material accurately, fully reflect the market conditions may vary on a case-by-case basis. Thus, in analysing these cases, certain assumptions as regards the market structure and market features had to be made. Unfortunately, access to the competition authorities' file and documents was not possible. Had such access been possible, the accuracy of the results of this chapter might be further enhanced. Provided the authorities are able to provide access to certain information (market conditions, market structures, market shares, etc.) contained in the documents relevant for these mergers, a more accurate analysis can be carried out in the future.

In particular, future research can focus on EU member states and Australia. This book referred to likely non-collusive oligopolies identified in Finland and Australia, without providing any further analysis as has been done for the other jurisdictions analysed herein, due to the lack of publicly available decisions. Since Australia presents such an interesting example of a jurisdiction which initially employed the SLC test, then changed to the dominance test and then reverted to the SLC, it would be useful to conduct further research on these likely gap cases.

In addition, the event study methodology that was used in this book is generally subject to limitations arising from the assumptions of both the theoretical and technical model. Notwithstanding strong assumptions such as that all stocks in the sample have the same sensitivity to the market,[3] as well as issues such as the existence of "noise" in the data, event studies constitute a useful and tractable indication of the impact of a merger, but cannot solely constitute sufficient evidence of the effects of the merger in the post-merger market. Further analysis may be necessary in order to "insulate" the share price movements from events occurring around the event date, in order to enhance the accuracy and predictability of event study analysis.

The substantive test was amended as regards the ECMR. Thus, the gap in the dominance test was rectified as the European Commission is currently able to capture non-collusive oligopolies under the SIEC test. However, several member states still adhere to the traditional dominance test,[4] and thus are still likely to experience cases in which the competition authorities will be facing a merger that will have the features of a non-collusive oligopoly but they will be unable to apply the dominance test, and will thus resort to other methods of trying to deal with the adverse effects of such mergers on competition. Such an approach is likely to lead to legal errors, uncertainty and successful appeals against the authorities' decisions. Evidence of cases illustrating the existence of a gap in the application of the dominance test is a fact that needs to be taken into consideration by these member states in order to enable them to efficiently and accurately assess the adverse impact of mergers on competition.

Improved understanding of mergers leading to non-coordinated effects in oligopolistic markets as well as of the contributing factors, firmly rooted in economic theory, is essential in three respects: reducing the number of transactions having an adverse impact on competition that are cleared, reducing the number of beneficial transactions that might be prohibited, as well as reducing the uncertainty surrounding merger approval.

The amendment in the substantive test in particular and, in general, the amendments included in the Recast ECMR, is of paramount importance in the accurate assessment of mergers in the EU. Similar amendments need to be followed in the 11 member states and other jurisdictions that still adhere to the dominance test.

Notes

1 As illustrated in para. 54 of *Airtours/First Choice*.
2 Article 2(3), Council Regulation (EC) No. 139/2004 of 20 January 2004 on the Control of Concentrations between Undertakings (the EC Merger Regulation), ("Recast ECMR"), OJ L24, 29.01.2004, 1–22.
3 This implies that beta is equal to 1. This assumption will bias the magnitude of the negative or positive reaction that will be identified. For the purposes of this book, importance is given to whether the market anticipated the merger to be beneficial or harmful for competition. This will be indicated by whether the reaction was positive or negative respectively, rather than by the magnitude of the coefficient itself.
4 See Appendix.

Appendix: substantive tests for the assessment of mergers in EU member states

Table A.1

Dominance test	*SIEC*	*SLC/SRC/SDC*[1]
Austria	Belgium	Estonia
Bulgaria	Czech Republic	Hungary
Cyprus	Denmark	Ireland
Finland	France	Malta
Germany	Greece	Poland
Italy	Latvia	United Kingdom
Latvia	Netherlands	
Lithuania	Spain	
Portugal	Sweden	
Romania		
Slovak Republic		
Slovenia		

Austria

Federal Act of 19 October 1988 on Cartels and Other Restrictive Trade Practices
(1988 Cartel Act – KartG 1988)
Section 42b

(2) If the examination of the concentration pursuant to para 1 was applied for, the Cartel Court shall:

1. if there is no concentration pursuant to Section 41, make a statement to this effect;
2. prohibit the concentration, if it is to be expected that the concentration will cause or strengthen a market-dominating position (Section 34); or, if this is not the case,
3. declare that the concentration is not prohibited.

Belgium

Law of 10 June 2006 on the Protection of Economic Competition and Law of 10 June 2006 establishing a Competition Council consolidated by a Royal Decree of 15 September 2006 (the Belgian Competition Law)
Article 8

§1. A concentration which would not significantly impede effective competition in the Belgian market or in a substantial part of it, in particular by the creation or strengthening of a dominant position, shall be declared permissible.

§2. A concentration which would significantly impede effective competition in the Belgian market or in a substantial part of it, in particular by the creation or strengthening of a dominant position, shall be declared non-permissible.

Bulgaria

Law on Competition Protection
(Published in the SG No 52/1998, as amended, SG Nos. 112/1998, 81/1999, 28/2002, 9/2003 and 107/2003)
Article 28. (1) (Amended, SG No. 9/2003)

> The Commission shall authorise the concentration provided that the latter does not result in the creation or strengthening of a dominant position that would significantly impede effective competition on the market concerned.

Cyprus

Number 22(I) of 1999 a Law to provide for the Control of Concentrations between Enterprises for the Purposes of Protection of Effective Competition

> 10. A concentration which creates or strengthens a dominant position in the affected markets within the Republic shall be declared incompatible with the requirements of the competitive market.

Czech Republic

Consolidated Act on the Protection of Competition
ACT No. 143/2001 Coll. of 4 April 2001 on the Protection of Competition and on Amendment to Certain Acts (Act on the Protection of Competition) as amended by Act No. 340/2004 Coll. of 4 May 2004, Act No. 484/2004 Coll. of 5 August 2004, Act No. 127/2005 Coll. of 22 February, Act No. 361/2005 Coll. of 19 August 2005 and Act No. 71/2007 Coll. of 4 April 2007

Article 17 Assessment of concentrations

(3) The Office shall not approve a concentration provided it would result in a substantial distortion of competition in the relevant market particularly because it would result in or would strengthened a dominant position of the undertakings concerned or any of them.

Denmark

Consolidated Competition Act No. 539 of 28 June 2002
Part 4 Merger control

12c (2). A merger that will not significantly impede effective competition, in particular due to the creation or strengthening of a dominant position, shall be approved. A merger that will significantly impede effective competition, in particular due to the creation or strengthening of a dominant position, shall be prohibited.

Estonia

Competition Act passed 5 June 2001 (RT[1] I 2001, 56, 332), entered into force 1 October 2001

§ 22. Appraisal of concentrations
The Director General of the Estonian Competition Board (ECB) or his or her deputy shall prohibit a concentration if it is likely to significantly restrict competition in the goods market, above all, by creating or strengthening a dominant position.

Finland

Act on Competition Restrictions (480/1992), incl. Amendment (318/2004)
Article 11 d (1529/2001)

(1) The Market Court may, upon the proposal of the Finnish Competition Authority, prohibit or order a concentration to be dissolved or attach conditions to the implementation of a concentration, if, as a result of such a concentration, a dominant position shall arise or be strengthened which significantly impedes competition in the Finnish markets or a substantial part thereof.

France

Code of Commercial Law on the Freedom to set Prices and to Compete
Legislative Section Book IV
Art. L. 430–6

> If a merger operation has been subject, pursuant to III. of article L. 430–5, to a referral to the Competition Council (Conseil de la concurrence), the latter ascertains whether such an operation may undermine competition, especially through the creation or reinforcement of a dominant position or through the creation or reinforcement of purchasing power creating economic dependence at the supplier's expense.

Germany

Gesetz gegen Wettbewerbsbeschränkungen
Act against Restraints of Competition, ARC in the version of 15 July 2005 (Bundesgesetzblatt (Federal Law Gazette) I 2005), p. 2114 (in the following referred to as BGBl), last amended by Article 8 of the Act of 17 March 2009 (BGBl. I 251, p. 550)
Section 36

> Principles for the Appraisal of Concentrations
> A concentration which is expected to create or strengthen a dominant position shall be prohibited by the Federal Cartel Office unless the participating undertakings prove that the concentration will also lead to improvements of the conditions of competition, and that these improvements will outweigh the disadvantages of dominance.

Greece

Article 4c
Control of Concentration of Undertakings [Art.2 §. 4 *v.* 2296/95]

> With decision of the Competition Commission any concentration of undertakings which is subject to pre-notification and may significantly impede competition in the national market or, in relation to the products' or services' features, in a substantial part of it, in particular as a result of the creation or strengthening of a dominant position is prohibited.

Hungary

Act LVII of 1996 on the Prohibition of Unfair and Restrictive Market Practices
Article 30(2)

(2) The Hungarian Competition Authority may not refuse to grant authorization for a concentration where, with a view to the provisions of Section (1), the concentration would not significantly reduce competition on the relevant market (Article 14), in particular as a result of the creation or strengthening of a dominant position. To the extent that the creation of a joint venture pursuant to point c) of Article 23(1) has as its object or effect the coordination of the market conduct of the creating groups of undertakings, such coordination shall be assessed in accordance with the criteria of Article 17.

Ireland

Competition Act, 2002

22 (3) On completion of a full investigation in relation to the merger or acquisition concerned, the Authority shall make whichever of the following determinations it considers appropriate, namely that the merger or acquisition—
(*a*) may be put into effect,
(*b*) may not be put into effect, or
(*c*) may be put into effect subject to conditions specified by it being complied with, on the ground that the result of the merger or acquisition will or will not, as the case may be, be to substantially lessen competition in markets for goods or services in the State or, as appropriate, will not be to substantially lessen such competition if conditions so specified are complied with.

Italy

Law No. 287 of 10 October 1990 Competition and Fair Trading Act
Section 6
Prohibition on concentrations restricting free competition

1. The Authority shall appraise concentrations subject to notification under section 16, to ascertain whether they create or strengthen a dominant position on the domestic market with the effect of eliminating or restricting competition appreciably and on a lasting basis. This situation shall be appraised taking into account the possibilities of substitution available to suppliers and users, the market position of

the undertakings, the access conditions to supplies or markets, the structure of the relevant markets, the competitive position of the domestic industry, barriers to the entry of competing undertakings and the evolution of supply and demand for the relevant goods or services.

Latvia

Competition Law
Section 16. Procedure for Examination of Market Participants Merger notifications

(3) The Competition Council by its decision shall prohibit merger that creates or strengthens dominant position, which will significantly hinder, restrict, or distort competition in any relevant market. The Competition Council may permit such merger, at the same time determining provisions, which prevents negative consequences of the merger and which are binding upon the respective market participants.

Lithuania

Law on Competition 23 March 1999 No VIII-1099 Vilnius
Chapter One: General Provisions
Article 14. Resolutions of the Competition Council on Concentration

1. Upon completing the examination of notification, the Competition Council shall take one of the following decisions:
2. to permit the implementation of concentration attaching to its decision conditions and obligations for the participating undertakings or controlling persons in order to prevent creation or strengthening of a dominant position;

Malta

Subsidiary Legislation: 379.08
Control of Concentrations Regulations 1 January 2003
LEGAL NOTICE 294 of 2002, as amended by Legal Notice 299 of 2002

4. (1) Subject to subregulation (4), concentrations that might lead to a substantial lessening of competition in the Maltese market or a part thereof are prohibited.

The Netherlands

Act of 22 May 1997, providing New Rules for Economic Competition (Competition Act) [Version applicable as of 1 August 2004]

§ 4. Licences
Section 41
2. A licence shall be refused if, as a result of the proposed concentration, effective competition on the Dutch market or a part thereof would be appreciably impeded, specifically as a result of the creation or strengthening of a dominant economic position. Section 37(3) shall apply mutatis mutandis if the application for a licence concerns a concentration, as referred to in section 27(2), aimed at or resulting in coordination of the competitive behavior of the effecting undertakings.

Poland

Act of 16 February 2007 on Competition and Consumer Protection
Chapter II. Decisions in cases of concentration

Article 17. The President of the Office shall, by way of decision, issue a consent to perform a concentration, which shall not result in restrictions to competition in the market, in particular, by emergence or strengthening of dominant position in the market.

Portugal

Assembly of the Republic Law No. 18/2003 of 11 June Approving the Legal Framework for Competition
Article 12 Appraisal of concentrations

4 – A prohibition shall be imposed on concentrations that create or strengthen a dominant position that results in significant barriers to effective competition in the Portuguese market or in a substantial part of it.

Romania

Competition Law No. 21/1996
Article 13

Economic concentrations are illegal which, having the effect of creating or consolidating a dominant position, lead to or are likely to lead to a significant restriction, prevention or distortion of competition on the Romanian market or on a part of it.

Slovak Republic

136/2001 Coll. ACT of 27 February 2001 on Protection of Competition and on Amendments and Supplements to Act of the Slovak National Council No. 347/1990 Coll. on Organization of Ministries and Other Central Bodies of State Administration of the Slovak Republic as amended
Amendment: 465/2002 Coll.
Amendment: 204/2004 Coll.

> Article 12 (6) The Authority shall prohibit a concentration if it creates or strengthens a dominant position resulting in significant barriers to effective competition in the relevant market.

Slovenia

Prevention of the Restriction of Competition Act
Part IV – Concentration of Undertakings
Article 11
(Prohibited concentrations)

> (1) Concentrations which strengthen the power of one or more undertakings, individually or jointly, as a result of which effective competition on the relevant market would be significantly impeded or excluded, shall be prohibited.

Spain

Competition Act 15/2007 of 3 July
(Official State Gazette No. 159, of 4 July 2007)
Article 10

> 1. The National Competition Commission shall assess the economic concentrations in light of the possible impediment to the maintenance of effective competition in all or part of the national market.

Sweden

Swedish Competition Act
Prohibition against concentrations etc.
Article 34 a

> (2) A concentration shall be prohibited, if:
>
> 1. it creates or strengthens a dominant position which significantly impedes, or is liable to significantly impede the existence or development of effective competition in the country as a whole, or a substantial part thereof; and

2. a prohibition can be issued without significantly setting aside national security or essential supply interests. Act (2000: 88).

United Kingdom

Mergers – Substantive Assessment Guidance

3.2 The test for reference will be met if the OFT has a reasonable belief, objectively justified by relevant facts, that there is a realistic prospect that the merger will lessen competition substantially.

Note

1 SRC stands for significant restriction of competition and SDC stands for significant distortion of competition.

Bibliography

Akman, P. (2007), "To Abuse, or not to Abuse: Discrimination between Consumers", *European Law Review*, 32(4), 492–512.

Aktas, N., de Bodt, E. and Roll, R. (2003), "Market Response to European Regulation of Business Combinations", mimeo, University of Louvain, Belgium.

Alfter, M. (2003), "Tetra Laval/Sidel and the Future of EC Merger Control", *Lawyers' Europe*, Winter, 17–20.

Anderson, A. (2001), "Collective Dominance in E.C. Merger Control: An Analysis of Legal and Economic Arguments", Law Institute, Göteborg University, www.kkv.se/epdf/uppsats2002_ andersson.pdf.

Andrews, P. (1998), "Is Meeting Competition a Defence to Predatory Pricing? The Irish Sugar Decision Suggests a New Approach", *ECLR*, 49.

Armstrong, M. (2005), "Recent Developments in the Economics of Price Discrimination", October Working Paper, http://129.3.20.41/eps/io/papers/0511/0511004.pdf.

Armstrong, M. and Vickers, J. (1993), "Price Discrimination, Competition and Regulation", *Journal of Industrial Economics*, 41, 335.

Assonime, "Comments on the Draft EC Commission Notice on the Appraisal of Horizontal Mergers", http://europa.eu.int/comm/competition/mergers/review/contributions.html.

Azevedo, J. P. and Walker, M. (2001), "Dominance: Meaning and Measurement", CRA Competition Policy Discussion Papers, www.crai.co.uk, 1–8.

Azevedo, J. P. and Walker, M. (2002), "Dominance: Meaning and Measurement", *ECLR*, 23(7), 363–7.

Baker, J. (2002), "Horizontal Merger Analysis Grows Up: A Review of Chapter 5 of Richard Posner's Antitrust Law (2nd edn 2001)", *The Antitrust Source*, January, 1–5.

Baker, S. (2002), "Unilateral effects in retail chain mergers: an application to supermarkets", *ECLR*, 3(4), 180–92.

Baker, S. (2003), "The Treatment of Captive Sales in Market Definition: Rules or Reason?", *ECLR*, 24(4), 161–4.

Bannock, G., Baxter, R. E. and Rees, R. (1985), *The Penguin Dictionary of Economics*, 3rd edn, Penguin Books, Basingstoke.

Baxter, S. and Dethmers, F. (2005), "Unilateral Effects Under the European Merger Regulation: How Big is the Gap?", *ECLR*, 26(7), 380–89.

Baxter, S. and Dethmers, F. (2006), "Collective Dominance Under EC Merger Control – After Airtours and the Introduction of Unilateral Effects is There Still a Future for Collective Dominance", *ECLR*, 27(3), 148–60.

Begg, D., Fischer, S. and Dornbusch, R. (1997), *Economics*, 5th edn, McGraw-Hill, Maidenhead.

Bergman, M., Jakobsson, M. and Razo, C. (2003), "An Econometric Analysis of the European Commission's Merger Decisions", 3 February, www.ne.su.se/research/seminars/pdf/041104_1.pdf#search='An%20Econometric%20Analysis %20of%20the%20European%20Commission%E2%80%99s%20Merger%20Decisions'.

"Bertelsmann, Sony to Form Joint Music Group", 1 November 2003, Medialine, www.factiva.com.

Biggar, D. (2000), "Airline Mergers and Alliances", *OECD Journal of Competition Law and Policy*, 2(2), 122–220.

Bishop, S. and Ridyard, D. (2003), "Prometheus Unbound: Increasing the Scope for Intervention in EC Merger Control", *ECLR*, 25(7), 395–409.

Bishop, S. and Walker, M. (2002), *The Economics of EC Competition Law: Concepts, Application and Measurement*, Sweet & Maxwell, London.

Black, O. (2003), "Collusion and Co-ordination in EC Merger Control", *ECLR*, 24(8), 408–11.

Blumenthal, W. (2004), "Why Bother? On Market Definition under the Merger Guidelines", statement before FTC/DOJ Merger Enforcement Workshop, 17 February, Washington, DC,

"BMG Eyes Sony Deal – New Talks Start as Race to Music Merger Begins", 23 September 2003, *New York Post*, www.factiva.com.

"BMG looks to court Sony in merger musical chairs", 24 September 2003, 09:47, Reuters News, www.factiva.com.

Bodie, Z., Kane, A. and Marcus, A. (1999), *Investments*, 4th edn, Irwin McGraw-Hill, Singapore.

Boge, U. and Muller, E. (2002), "From the Market Dominance Test to the SLC Test: Are there any Reasons for a Change?", *ECLR*, 23(10), 495–8.

Briones, J. and Padilla, A. J. (2001), "The Complex Landscape of Oligopolies under EU Competition Policy. Is Collective Dominance Ripe for Guidelines?", *World Competition*, 24(3), 307–18.

Cabral, L. (2000), *Introduction to Industrial Organization*, MIT Press, Cambridge, MA.

Carlton, D. (2001), "A General Analysis of Exlusionary Conduct and Refusal to Deal – Why Aspen and Kodak Are Misguided", NBER Working Paper No. 8105, www.nber.org/papers/w8105.

Capkun, V. and Semenova. M. (2004), "Market reaction to merger approval process of the European Commission", http://papers.ssrn.com/sol3/papers.cfm?abstract_id=634583.

Chen, Z., Ross, T. and Stanbury, W. T. (1998), "Refusals to Deal and Aftermarkets", *Review of Industrial Organization*, 13, 131.

Church, J. and Ware, R. (2000), *Industrial Organization Strategic Approach*, McGraw-Hill, Singapore.

Clark, J. (1999), "Efficiency Claims in Horizontal Mergers", *OECD Journal of Competition Policy*, 1(3), 245–62.

Clifford Chance (2002), "Green Paper on the Merger Regulation. A Summary of the Main Issues", January 2002, www.cliffordchance.co.uk/uk/pdf/ECMR_Summary_of_Main_issues.pdf.

Coate, M. B. (1992), "Economics, the Guidelines and the Evaluation of Merger Policy", *Antitrust Bulletin*, 37(4), 997–1024.

Coleman, M. and Sheffman, D. (2004), "Quantitative Analysis of Potential Competitive Effects from a Merger", in Evans, D. and Padilla, J. (eds), *Global Competition Policy, Economic Issues and Impacts*, LECG, Emeryville, CA.

Competition Commission, Cm 3813, "Foreign Package Holidays: A Report on the Supply in the UK of Tour Operators' Services and Travel Agents' Services in Relation to Foreign Package Holidays", 19.12.97, www.competition-commission.org.uk.

Competition Commission, Cm 5319, "The Supply of Banking Services by Clearing Banks to Small and Medium-sized Enterprises within the UK", 2002, www.competition-commission.org.uk/reports/462banks.htm.

Cook, C. J. and Kerse, C. S. (2000), *E.C. Merger Control*, 3rd edn, Sweet & Maxwell, London.

Coscelli, A. and Van Reenen, J. (2004), "Empirical Analysis of Unilateral Effects in Merger Control", presentation to the IBC Conference on "The Use of Economics in Competition Law", 11 March.

Cox, A. and Portes, J. (1998), "Mergers in Regulated Industries: The Uses and Abuses of Event Studies" *Journal of Regulatory Economics*, 14, 281–304.

Crooke, P., Froeb, L., Tschantz, S. and Werden, G. (1997), "Draft: Comments Solicited, Properties of Computed Post-merger Equilibria", http://www2.owen.vanderbilt.edu/fmrc/pdf/wp9712.pdf.

Dethmers, F. and Dodoo, N. (2006), "The Abuse of Hoffmann-La Roche: The Meaning of Dominance under EC Competition Law", *ECLR*, 27(10), 537–49.

Dobbs, I. and Richards, P. (2005), "Output Restriction as a Measure of Market Power", *ECLR*, 26(10), 572–80.

Doherty, B. (2001) "Just What Are Essential Facilities?", *CMLR*, 38, 397.

Duso, T., Gugler, K. and Yurtoglu, B. (2006), "How Effective is European Merger Control?", http://homepage.univie.ac.at/klaus.gugler/public/dgy.pdf.

Duso, T., Röller, L-H. and Neven, D. (2003), "The Political Economy of European Merger Control: Evidence using Stock Market Data", http://skylla.wz-berlin.de/pdf/2002/iv02–34.pdf.

Eckbo, B. E. (1983), "Horizontal Mergers, Collusion, and Stockholder Wealth", *Journal of Financial Economics*, 11, 241–73.

Eckbo, B. E. and Wier, P. (1985), "Antimerger Policy under the Hart-Scott-Rodino Act: A Reexamination of the Market Power Hypothesis", *Journal of Law and Economics*, 28, 119–49.

EEA Standing Committee of the EFTA States (2002), "EEA EFTA Comments on the Commission's Green Paper on the review of Council Regulation (EEC) No. 4064/89 (COM(2001) 745/6 Final)", www.secretariat.efta.int/Web?EuropeanEconomicArea/OngoingWork/100w149.doc.

Ehlermann, C-D., Völcker, S. and Gutermuth, A. (2005), "Unilateral Effects: The Enforcement Gap under the Old EC Merger Regulation", *World Competition*, 28(2), 193–203.

Eilmansberger, T. (2005), "How to Distinguish Good From Bad Competition Under Article 82 EC: In Search of Clearer and More Coherent Standards for Anti-competitive Abuses", *CMLR* (PP), 129.

Elliott, D. (2007), "What is an Excessive Price?", *Competition Law International*, 6(8), 13–15.

Epstein, R. and Rubinfeld, D. (2004) "Technical Report Effects of Mergers Involving Differentiated Products", COMP/B1/2003/07, http://europa.eu.int/

comm/competition/mergers/others/effects_mergers_involving_differentiated_products.pdf.

Europe Economics (2001), "Study on Assessment Criteria for Distinguishing between Competitive and Dominant Oligopolies in Merger Control", http://europa.eu.int/comm/enterprise/library/lib-competition/libr-competition.html.

Europe Economics (2002), "One's a Monopoly, Two's Collectively Dominant, Three's Alright?", www.europe-economics.com.

Fama, E. F. (1970), "Efficient Capital Markets: A Review of Theory and Empirical Work", *Journal of Finance*, 25(2), 383–417.

Fama, E. F. (1991), "Efficient Capital Markets II", *Journal of Finance*, 46, 1575–617.

Fama, E. F., Fischer, L., Jensen, M. and Roll, R. (1969), "The Adjustment of Stock Prices to new Information", *International Economic Review*, 10, 1–21.

Farrell, L. (2002), "Airtours PLC v EC Commission", *Competition Law Journal*, 1(3), 207–15.

Faull, J. and Nikpay, A. (2007), *The EC Law of Competition*, Oxford University Press, Oxford.

Fels, A. (2002), "The Change from a Dominance to a Substantial Lessening of Competition Test in Australia's Merger Law", in Hawk, B., *International Antitrust Law and Policy*, Fordham University Law School, Corporate Law Institute.

Fels, A. (2002), "Merger Law in Australia", ICN Merger Review Working Group, www.internationalcompetitionnetwork.org/afsgaustralia.pdf.

Field Fisher Waterhouse (2002), "Collective Dominance: The Airtours Appeal", www.ffwlaw.com/download/Docs1944387_1.PDF.

"Financial Times", 28/1/2005, www.ft.com.

"Financial Times", 29–30/1/2005, www.ft.com.

Fingleton, J. (2002), "Does Collective Dominance Provide Suitable Housing for All Anti-competitive Oligopolistic Mergers", in Hawk, B., *International Antitrust Law and Policy*, Fordham University Law School, Corporate Law Institute.

Fingleton, J. et al. (2002), "Substantive Standards for Mergers and the Role of Efficiencies", in Hawk, B., *International Antitrust Law and Policy*, Fordham University Law School, Corporate Law Institute.

Fingleton, J. (2003), "Competition for the Merger Test Market", presentation to the CRA Conference on Economics and Merger Policy for the 21st Century, 4 June, www.crai.com/.%5CAgenda%5CFingletonpr.pdf.

Fountoukakos, K. and Ryan, S. (2005), "A New Substantive Test for EU Merger Control", *ECLR*, 5, 277–96.

Freshfields Bruckhaus Deringer (2001), "EC merger regulation Green Paper: The Best of all Possible Worlds?", www.freshfields.com/practice/corporate/publications/pdfs/2322.pdf.

Fridolfsson, S-O. and Stennek, J. (2000), "Why Event Studies do not Detect Anti-competitive Mergers", Research Institute of Industrial Economics, Stockholm, http://swopec.hhs.se/iuiwop/papers/iuiwop0542.pdf.

Froeb, L., Tenn S. and Tschantz, S. (2004), "Mergers When Firms Compete by Choosing both Price and Promotion", FTC working paper.

Furse, M. (2004), "Article 82, Microsoft and bundling, or 'The Half Monti'", *Competition Law Journal*, 3(3), 169–78.

Furse, M. (2004), *Competition Law of the UK & EC*, 4th edn, Oxford University Press, Oxford.

Gal, M. (2007), "Below-cost Price Alignment: Meeting or Beating Competition? The France Telecom Case", *ECLR*, 28(6), 382–91.

Gandhi, A., Froeb, L., Tschantz, S. and Werden, G. (2004), "Post-Merger Product Repositioning", University of Chicago working paper.

Geradin, D. and Rato, M. (2006), "Excessive Pricing: In Reply", *Competition Law International*, 5(10), 3–5.

Gerard, D. (2005), "Price Discrimination under Article 82(c) EC: Clearing up the Ambiguities", in Global Competition Law Centre Research Papers on Article 82 EC 133.

Glader, M. and Larsen, S. (2006), "Article 82: Excessive Pricing", *Competition Law International*, 5(7), 3–5.

Goddard, G. and Curry, E. (2003), "New Zealand's New Mergers Test: A Comparison of Dominance and Substantial Lessening of Competition in the Supermarket Industry", *ECLR*, 24(7), 300–311.

Gordon, C. and Richardson, R. (2001) "Collective Dominance: The Third Way?", *ECLR*, 22(10), 416–423.

Goyder, D. G. (1998), *EC Competition Law*, 3rd edn, Oxford University Press, Oxford.

Gravengaard, M. (2006), "The Meeting Competition Defence Principle – A Defence for Price Discrimination and Predatory Pricing?", *ECLR*, 27(12), 658–77.

Harkrider, J. (2004), "Operationalizing the Hypothetical Monopolist Test", www.avhlaw.com.

Harris, B. (2004), "Recent Observations about Critical Loss Analysis", www.ftc.gov/bc/mergerenforce/presentations/040217harris.pdf.

Harris, B. and Simons, J. (1989), "Focusing Market Definition: How Much Substitution is Necessary?", *Research in Law and Economics*, 12, 207–26.

Harris, B. and Veljanovski, C. (2003), "Critical Loss Analysis: Its Growing Use in Competition Law", *ECLR*, 24(5), 213–18.

Haupt, H. (2002), "Collective Dominance under Article 82 EC and EC Merger Control in the Light of the Airtours Judgment", *ECLR*, 23(9), 434–44.

Healy, P., Palepu, K. and Ruback, R. (1992), "Does Corporate Performance Improve After Mergers?", *Journal of Financial Economics*, 31, 135–75.

Herbert Smith, "Court of First Instance annuls Sony/BMG Decision (Case T-464/04 *Impala v Commission*)", www.herbertsmith.com/NR/rdonlyres/D488A886–7214–4EC4-AE25–8C0E9B115B67/2329/euc_140 706_updated_ 250706.html.

Hewitt, G. (1999), "The Failing Firm Defence", *OECD Journal of Competition Law and Policy*, 1(2), 113–33.

Hildebrand, D. (2001), "EC&MC Comments on the Draft Guidelines on Market Analysis and the Calculation of Significant Market Power", www.ee-mc.com/files/Comment%20%20SMP%20Draft%20guidelines.pdf.

House of Lords Select Committee on the European Union, "The Review of EC Merger Regulation", Thirty-Second Report, Pt 4: Substantive Issues, www.parliament.the-stationery-office.co.uk/pa/ld/ldeucom.htm.

Hungarian Office of Economic Competition (2002), "Comments of the Hungarian Office of Economic Competition to some issues by the Green Paper of the Commission on the Review of Council Regulation No 4064.89", http://europa.eu.int/comm/competition/mergers/review/comments/ref029hungarianoffice.pdf.

ICN (2004), "ICN Report on Merger Guidelines", April, www.internationalcompetitionnetwork. org.

ICN (2006), "ICN Merger Working Group: Investigation and Analysis Subgroup ICN Merger Guidelines Workbook", prepared for the Fifth Annual ICN Conference, April, Cape Town, www.internationalcompetitionnetwork.org.

International Chamber of Commerce (2002), "Comments on the EC Green paper on the Review of Merger Regulation 4064/89", www.iccwbo.org/home/statements_rules/statements/2002/ review_of_merger_regulation.asp.

Ivaldi, M. and Verboven, F. (2001), "Quantifying the Effects from Horizontal Mergers in European Competition Policy", www.cepr.org/pubs/dps/DP2697.asp.

Ivaldi, M. and Verboven, F. (2002), "Quantifying the Effects from Horizontal Mergers in European Competition Policy", September, www.idei.fr/doc/by/ivaldi/iv_merger_v04.pdf.

Ivaldi, M., Jullien, B., Rey, P., Seabright, P., Tirole, J., (2003), "*The Economics of Unilateral Effects*", IDEI, Toulouse, Interim Report for DG Competition, European Commission, http://europa.eu.int/comm/competition/mergers/review/the_economics_of_unilateral_effects_en.pdf#search="Economics%20of%20Unilateral%20Effects".

"J&J in talks to buy Guidant for $24 bln – NY Times", 7 December 2004, 06:15, www.factiva.com.

Jayaratne, J. and Shapiro, C. (2000), "Simulating Partial Asset Divestitures to Fix Mergers", *International Journal of the Economics of Business*, 7, 179–200.

Jephcott, M. and Withers, C. (2001), "Where to go now for EC Oligopoly Control?", *ECLR*, 22(8), 295–303.

Jones, A. (2006), "A Dominant Firm's Duty to Deal: EC and US Antitrust Law Compared", in Marsden, P. (ed.), *Handbook of Research in Transatlantic Antitrust*, Edward Elgar, Cheltenham.

Jones, A. and Sufrin, B. (2004), *EC Competition Law*, 2nd edn, Oxford University Press, Oxford.

Jones, C. (1994), *Investments*, 4th edn, John Wiley & Sons, Hoboken, NJ.

Kaplan, S. and Weisbach, M. (1992), "The Success of Acquisitions: Evidence from Divestitures", *Journal of Finance*, 47(1), 107–38.

Katz, M. and Shapiro, C. (2003), "Critical Loss: Let's Tell the Whole Story", *Antitrust*, Spring, 50.

Kloosterhuis, E. (2001), "Joint Dominance and the Interaction between Firms", *ECLR*, 22(3), 79–92.

Kokkoris, I. (2005a), "The Concept of Market Definition and the SSNIP test in the Merger Appraisal", *ECLR*, 26(4), 209–14.

Kokkoris, I. (2005b), "Critical Loss Analysis: Critically Ill?", *ECLR*, 26(9), 518–25.

Kokkoris, I. (2005c), "Merger Simulation: A Crystal Ball for Assessing Mergers", *World Competition*, 28(3), 327–48.

Kokkoris, I. (2005d), "The Reform of the European Community Merger Regulation in the Aftermath of the Airtours Case. The Eagerly Expected Debate: SLC v Dominance Test", *ECLR*, 26(1), 37–47.

Kokkoris, I. (2005e), "Weak-Form Tests of Market Efficiency in Corporate Debt Restructuring", *International Corporate Rescue*, 2(6), 337–43.

Kokkoris, I. (2006a), "Buyer Power Assessment in Competition Law", *World Competition*, 29(1), 139–64.

Kokkoris, I. (2006b), "Do Merger Simulation and Critical Loss Analysis Differ Under the SLC and Dominance Test?", *ECLR*, 27(5), 248–59.

Kokkoris, I. (2006c), "Failing Firm Defence in the European Union. A Panacea for Mergers?", *ECLR*, 27(9), 494–509.

Kokkoris, I. (2007a), *Competition Cases from the European Union. The Ultimate Guide to Leading Cases of the EU and all 27 Member States*, Sweet & Maxwell, London.

Kokkoris, I. (2007b), "The Development of the Concept of Collective Dominance in the ECMR. From its Inception to its Current Status", *World Competition*, 30(3), 419–48.

Kokkoris, I. (2007c), "Event Studies in Merger Assessment. Successes and Failures", *European Competition Journal*, 3(1), 65–100.

Kokkoris, I. (2009), "Was There a Gap in the ECMR?", *Concurrences*, 1, 23214.

Kolasky, W. (2002), "Coordinated Effects in Merger Review: From Dead Frenchmen to Beautiful Minds and Mavericks", www.usdoj.gov/atr/public/speeches/11050.htm.

Kon, S. and Turnbull, S. (2003), "Pricing and the Dominant Firm: Implications of the Competition Commission Appeal Tribunal's judgment in the Napp case", *ECLR*, 24(2), 70–86.

Korah, V. (1997), *An Introductory Guide to EC Competition Law and Practice*, Hart Publishing, Oxford.

Korah, V. (2001), *Cases and Materials on EC Competition Law*, 2nd edn, Hart Publishing, Oxford.

Kühn, K. U. (2002), "Closing Pandora's Box? Joint Dominance after the Airtours Judgment", in *The Pros and Cons of Merger Control*, Swedish Competition Authority, www.kkv.se/epdf/skrift_proscons.pdf.

Kühn, K. U., Stillman, R. and Caffarra, C. (2005), "Economic Theories of Bundling and their Policy Implications in Abuse Cases: An Assessment in Light of the Microsoft Case", *European Competition Journal*, 1(1), 85–121.

Lane, R. (2000), *EC Competition Law*, Pearson Education, Harlow.

Lang, J. T. (1994), "Defining Legitimate Competition: Companies' Duties to Supply Competitors and Access to Essential Facilities", *Fordham International Law Journal*, 18, 437.

Lang, J. T. (2002) "Defining Legitimate Competition: How to Clarify Pricing Abuses Under Article 82", *Fordham International Law Journal*, 83.

Lang, J. T. (2005) "Fundamental Issues Concerning Abuse Under Article 82 EC", Regulatory Policy Institute 19.

Lang, J. T. and O'Donoghue, R., (2002), "Defining Legitimate Competition: How to Clarify Pricing Abuses under Article 82EC", *Fordham International Law Journal*, 26, 83.

Langenfeld, J. and Li, W. (2004), "Critical Loss Analysis in Evaluating Mergers", in Evans D. and Padilla, J. (eds), *Global Competition Policy, Economic Issues and Impacts*, LECG, Emeryville, CA.

Lao, M. (2005) "Aspen Skiing and Trinko: Antitrust Intent and Sacrifice", *Antitrust Law Journal*, 73, 171.

Levy, N. (2003), *European Merger Control Law: A Guide to the Merger Regulation*, LexisNexis, London.

Levy, N. (2003), "EU Merger Control: From Birth to Adolescence", *World Competition*, 26(2), 195–218.

Lexecon (2001), "Buyer Power", www.lexecon.co.uk/assets/buyer_power.pdf.

Lexecon (2003), "*Quantitative Techniques in Competition Analysis*", www.lexecon.co.uk/assets/quantitative_techniques.pdf, 01/11/2003.

Lindsay, A. (2003), *The EC Merger Regulation: Substantive Issues*, Sweet & Maxwell, London.

Lindsay, A., Lecchi, E. and Williams, G. (2003), "Econometrics Study into European Commission Merger Decisions Since 2000", *ECLR*, 24(12), 673–82.

Livingston, D. and Scott, J. (1995), *Competition Law and Practice*, FT Law & Tax, London.

Lorenz, M., Lübbig, M. and Russel, A. (2005), "Price Discrimination: A Tender Story", *ECLR*, 355.

Lowe, P. (2002), "Competition Policy in the European Union", speech at the American Antitrust Institute, Washington, DC, 1 July, www.eurunion.org/news/speeches/2002/020701phillowe.htm.

Lowe, P. (2002), "Review of the EC Merger Regulation – Forging a Way ahead", European Merger Control Conference, Conrad Hotel, 8 November, Brussels, http://europa.eu.int/comm/competition/speeches/text/sp2002_035_en.pdf.

Lowe, P. et al. (2002), "Substantive Standards for Mergers and the Role of Efficiencies", in Hawk, B., *International Antitrust Law and Policy*, Fordham University Law School, Corporate Law Institute.

Mas-Colell, A., Whinston, M. and Green, J. (1995), *Microeconomic Theory*, Oxford University Press, New York.

McDavid, J. (2002), "Proposed Reform of the EU Merger Regulation: A US Perspective", *Antitrust*, 17, 52–5.

"Microsoft's Ballmer reiterates Linux threat – Update 3", 5 June 2003, AFX International Focus, www.factiva.com.

"Microsoft-Revolutionising Enterprise Application Software" (2003), www.cw360ms.com/reserach/Ovum/Microsoft_business_apps.pdf.

"Microsoft slips on Ballmer's Linux comments – Update 4", 5 June 2003, AFX UK Focus, www.factiva.com.

Ministry of Industry, Employment and Communications (2002), "Statement of opinion on Green Paper COM(2001) 745 Final on the Review of Council Regulation (EEC) No. 4064/89 (the so-called Merger Regulation)", Sweden, www.industry.ministry.se/pdf/eun2002_880_nl.pdf.

Monti, M. (2002), "Review of the EC Merger Regulation – Roadmap for the Reform Poject", Conference on Reform of European Merger Control, British Chamber of Commerce, 4 June, Brussels, http://europa.eu.int/rapid/start/cgi/guesten.ksh?paction.gettxt=gt&doc=SPEECH/02/252|0|RAPID&lg=EN&display=.

Monti, M. (2002), "Merger Control in the European Union: A Radical Reform", European Commission/IBA Conference on EU Merger Control, 7 November, Brussels, http://europa.eu.int/rapid/start/cgi/guesten.ksh?p_action.gettxt=gt&doc=SPEECH/02/545|0|RAPID&lg=EN&display=.

Motta, M. (1999), "Economic Analysis and EC Merger Policy", European University Institute, www.iue.it/Personal/Motta?ECMergR.pdf. 28 July 2003.

Motta, M. (2000), "EC Merger Policy and the Airtours Case", *ECLR*, 21(4), 206–207.

Motta, M. (2004), *Competition Policy – Theory and Practice*, Cambridge University Press, Cambridge.

Muysert, P. (2004) "Price Discrimination – An Unreliable Indicator of Market Power", *ECLR*, 6, 350.

Nagy, C. (2007), "Refusal to Deal and the Doctrine of Essential Facilities in US and EC Competition Law: A Comparative Perspective and a Proposal for a Workable Analytical Framework", *European Law Review*, 32(5), 664–85.

Nazerali, J. (2002), "A Merger of Minds or Split Opinion – Does the European Commission Address Current EU Merger Concerns?", *ICCLR*, 13(12), 480–84.

Newman, P., Milgate, M. and Eatwell, J. (1992), *The New Palgrave Dictionary of Money and Finance*, vol. 1, Macmillan, London.

Newmark, C. (2004), "Price-Concentration Studies: There You Go Again", prepared for the DOJ/FTC Merger Workshop, "Concentration and Market Shares" panel, www.ftc.gov/bc/mergerenforce/presentations/040217 newmark.pdf.

Nicholson, M. and Cardell, S. (2002), "Airtours v. Commission: Collective Dominance Contained", IBA EC Merger Control Conference, www.ibanet.org.

Niels, G. (2001), "Collective Dominance: More than just Oligopolistic Interdependence", *ECLR*, 22(5), 168–72.

Nikpay, A. and Houwen, F. (2003), "Tour de Force or a Little Local Turbulence? A Heretical View on the Airtours Judgment", *ECLR*, 24(5), 193–202.

Nourry, A. (2003), "EU Merger Control: Application and Recent Developments", in *PLC Global Competition Law Handbook*, 7th edn, www.practicallaw.com/comphandbook, 19–33.

Nucara, A (2003), "Schneider/Legrand and Tetra Laval/Sidel: Fast Track towards Merger Reform?", *EBL Review*, 14(2), 193–200.

O'Brien, D. and Wickelgren, A. (2003), "A Critical Analysis of Critical Loss Analysis", www.ftc.gov/be/workpapers/wp254.pdf.

OECD (2003), "Competition Policy Roundtable on Loyalty and Fidelity Discounts and Rebates", 4 March, 1–239.

OECD (2003), "Substantive Criteria Used for the Assessment of Mergers", www.oecd.org.

OECD (2005), "Competition Policy Roundtable on Predatory Foreclosure", 15 March, 1–279.

OECD, "The Essential Facilities Concept", Background Note, OCDE/GD (96)113.

OFT (1999), "Quantitative Techniques in Competition Analysis", Research Paper 17, October, www.oft.gov.uk.

Oliver, P. (2006) "The Concept of 'Abuse' of a Dominant Position under Article 82 EC: Recent Developments in Relation to Pricing", *European Competition Journal*, 1(2), 315–39.

"Oracle Makes $5.1B Bid For Rival PeopleSoft", 6 June 2003, 17:53, Dow Jones News Service, www.factiva.com.

Ottolenghi, I. and Rose, I. (2003), "Packaging: CFI annuls Commission Decision on Tetra Laval/Sidel Merger", *Lawyers' Europe*, Spring, 26–7.

OXERA (2002), "Collective Dominance from an Economic Perspective", *Competing Ideas*, June.

OXERA (2006), "Blocking the Deal. How Do Merger Decisions Affect Share Prices", March, www.oxera.co.uk.

Padilla, J. (2004), "The Economics of Merger Control. An Overview of Quantitative Methods for the Assessment of Competitive Effects", a presentation to the UK Competition Commission, www.lecg.com.

Panayides, P. and Gong, X. (2002), "The Stock Market Reaction to Merger and

Acquisition Announcements in Liner Shipping", *International Journal of Maritime Economics*, 4, 55–80.

Parker, D. (2006), "A Screening Device for Tacit Collusion Concerns", *ECLR*, 27(8), 424–33.

Perrot, A. (2005), "Towards an Effects-based Approach of Price Discrimination" in *The Pros and Cons of Price Discrimination*, Swedish Competition Authority.

Pindyck, R. and Rubinfeld, D. (1998), *Microeconomics*, 4th edn, Prentice Hall, Upper Saddle River, NJ.

"Plan B for BMG BMG Booby Prize: Label Eyes Sony Play Lest Warner Snare EMI", 12 March 2003, *New York Post*, www.factiva.com.

Posner, R. (2001), *Antitrust Law*, 2nd edn, University of Chicago Press, Chicago.

Prepared Remarks of Molly S. Boast before the American Bar Association Antitrust Section Spring Meeting 2001 Washington, DC, 29 March, www.ftc.gov/speeches/other/boastmollys.htm.

Prete, L. and Nucara, A. (2005), "Standard of Proof and Scope of Judicial Review in EC Merger Cases: Everything Clear after Tetra Laval?", *ECLR*, 26(12), 692–704.

Rabassa, V. and Christensen, P. (2001), "The Airtours Decision: Is there a new Commission Approach to Collective Dominance?", *ECLR*, 22(6), 227–37.

Ragolle, F. (2003), "Schneider Electric v Commission: The CFI's Response to the Green Paper on Merger Review", *ECLR*, 24(4), 176–81.

Ravenscraft, D. and Scherer, F.M. (1987), "Life After Takeovers", *Journal of Industrial Economics*, 36, 147–56.

RBB Economics (2004), "Assessing Unilateral Effects in Practice: Lessons from GE/Instrumentarium", RBB Brief 14, www.rbbeconomics.com/publications/downloads/rbb_brief14.pdf, May .

Regulatory Policy Institute (2001), "Developments in Competition Policy: Mergers and Oligopolies", International Competition Policy Conference, 26 June, http://216.239.37.104/search?q=cache:u8EUV_TO3TYJ:www.competition-commission.org.uk/inquiries/rpiconf.pdf+developments+in+ competition+polic y:+Mergers+and+Oligopolies&hl=el&ie=UTF-8.

Report by Professor Davies in "Comments by Academic Economists: Covering Note", www.competition-commission.org.uk/rep_pub/pdf/reports.pdf.

Reuters news, "UK stocks- Factors to watch on March 17", www.factiva.com.

Ridyard, D. (2002), "Exclusionary Pricing and Price Discrimination Abuses under Article 82 – An Economic Analysis", *ECLR*, 6, 286.

Ridyard, D. (2004), "The Commission's New Horizontal Merger Guidelines – An Economic Commentary", http://gclc.coleurop.be/documents/DR%20GCLC%20 paper%20March%2004.pdf.

Ridyard, D. (2005), "Tying and Bundling – Cause for Ccomplaint?", *ECLR*, 26(6), 316–19.

Robinson, C. K. (1996), "Quantifying Unilateral Effects in Investigations and Cases", US DOJ before the George Mason Law Review Symposium Antitrust in the Information Revolution: New Economic Approaches for Analyzing Antitrust Issues, George Mason University School of Law, 11 October, Arlington, Virginia.

Robinson, G. (2002), "On Refusing to Deal with Rivals", *Cornell Law Review*, 87, 1177.

Rodger, B. and MacCulloch, A. (2001), *Competition Law and Policy in the EC and UK*, 2nd edn, Cavendish Publishing, London.

Röller, L-H. and Neven, D. (2002), "Discrepancies Between Markets and Regulators: An Analysis of the First Ten Years of EU Merger Control", http://hei.unige.ch/sections/ec/pdfs/Working_papers/HEIWP10–2002.pdf.

Roth, P. (2001), *Bellamy and Child European Community Law of Competition*, 5th edn, Sweet & Maxwell, London.

Rubinfeld, D., Roy, J. and Epstein, R. (2001), "Merger Simulation: A Simplified Approach with New Applications", paper CPC01–026, Institute of Business and Economic Research, Competition Policy Center, University of California, Berkeley, http://repositories.cdlib.org/cgi/viewcontent.cgi? article=1000&context= iber/cpc.

Salinger, M. and Schumann, L. (1988), "Horizontal Mergers and the Market Value of Rivals: The 'In Play' Effect", Columbia First Boston Series in Money, Economics and Finance Working Paper: FB-88–03.

Schmalensee, R. (1981) "Output and Welfare Implications of Monopolistic Third-Degree Price Discrimination", *American Economic Review*, 71, 242.

Schwert, W. (1996), "Markup Pricing in Mergers and Acquisitions", *Journal of Financial Economics*, 41, 153–92.

Scott, A. (2002), "An Immovable Feast? Tacit Collusion and Collective Dominance in Merger Control after Airtours", www.ccr.uea.ac.uk/workingpapers/ccr02–6.pdf.

Shapiro, C. (1995), "Mergers with Differentiated Products", before the American Bar Association International Bar Association "The Merger Review Process in the US and Abroad", Willard Inter-Continental Hotel Washington, DC, 9 November, www.usdoj.gov/atr/public/speeches/shapiro.spc.

Sharpe, W., Alexander, G. and Bailey, J. V. (1998), *Investments*, 6th edn, Prentice Hall, Upper Saddle River, NJ.

Sheffman, D. and Simons, J. (2003), "The State of Critical Loss Analysis: Let's Make Sure We Understand the Whole Story", www.antitrustsource.com.

Siclen, S. V. (1999), "Abuse of Dominance and Monopolization", *OECD Journal of Competition Law and Policy*, 1(4), 160–204.

SJ Berwin Community Week, 286, 28 July 2006, www.sjberwin.com.

Snelders, R. and Dolmans, M. (2002), "Cross-Border Mergers in Company Law and Competition Law: Removing the Final Barriers", at the XX Congress of the Féderation Internationale pour le Droit Européen (FIDE), 30 October–2 November, London, www.fide2002.org/pdfs/cbmnetherlands.pdf.

Spector, D. (2006), "From Harm to Competitors to Harm to Competition: One More Effort, Please!", *European Competition Journal*, 2(1) Supp. (Special issue), 145–62.

Stigler, G. (1982), "The Economists and the Problem of Monopoly", *American Economic Review*, 72, May.

Stiglitz, J. E. and Driffill, J. (2000), *Economics*, W. W. Norton & Company Ltd, New York.

Stillman, R. (1983), "Examining Antitrust Policy towards Horizontal Mergers", *Journal of Financial Economics*, 11, 225–40.

Stockwatch (2003), "SAP breaches 107 eur, seen benefiting from Oracle's Peoplesoft bid", 6 June, AFX Asia, www.factiva.com.

Stratakis, A., (2006), "Comparative Analysis of the US and EU Approach and Enforecement of the Essential Facilities Doctrine", *ECLR*, 27, 434.

Stroux, S. (2002), "Collective Dominance under the Merger Regulation: A Serious Evidentiary Reprimand for the Commission", *European Law Review*, 27(6), 736–46.

Sweet & Maxwell (2003), "In Competition", February, www.smlawpub.co.uk/online/newslet/incm/.

Temple Lang, J. (2003), "Two Important Merger Regulation Judgments: The implications of Schneider-Legrand and Tetra Laval-Side", *European Law Review*, 28(2), 259–72.

The Independent, 19 March 1999, www.factiva.com.

Tom, W. (2004), "Market Definition under the Merger Guidelines: Some Modest Proposals", comments submitted to the FTC/DOJ Merger Enforcement Workshop, Washington, DC, 17 February.

"UK Response to the Commission Green Paper on the Review of Council Regulation (EEC) No. 4064/89", www.dti.gov.uk/ccp/topics2/pdf2/ukresponsetoecmegersgp.pdf.

"Update(3): PeopleSoft Board Rejects Oracle Hostile Offer", 12 June 2003, 22:26, Dow Jones News Service, www.factiva.com.

US DOJ, "Merger Challenges Data, Fiscal Years 1999–2003", www.usdoj.gov/atr/public/201898.htm.

Varian, H. R. (1985) "Price Discrimination and Social Welfare", *American Economic Review*, 75, 870.

Venit, J. (2005) "Article 82: The Last Frontier – Fighting Fire with Fire?", *Fordham International Law Journal*, 28, 1157.

Vickers, J. (2002), "How to Reform the EC Merger Test?", speech at the EC/IBA merger control conference, 8 November, Brussels, www.oft.gov.uk/NR/rdonlyres/80E5D0FE-7CF0-4606-A502-DD42FDD06AAF/0/spe0802.pdf.

Vickers, J. (2003) "Competition Economics and Policy", *ECLR*, 24(3), 95–102.

Voigt, S. and Schmidt, A. (2004), "Switching to Substantial Impediments to Competition (SIC) can have Substantial Costs", *ECLR*, 25(9), 584–90.

Volcker, S. (2004) "Mind the Gap: Unilateral Effects Analysis arrives at the Merger Control", *ECLR*, 25(7), 395–409.

Volcker, S. and O'Daly, C. (2006), "The Court of First Instance's Impala Judgement: A judicial Counter-Reformation in EU Merger Control", *ECLR*, 27(11), 589–96.

Walker, M., (2004), "The Use of Empirical Analysis in Antitrust: Lessons from Merger Simulation Models", Network of Industrial Economists Meeting, 14 December, Nottingham University Business School.

Werden, G. (2005),"Unilateral Effects from Mergers: The Oracle Case", British Institute of International and Comparative Law, 5th Annual Transatlantic Antitrust Dialogue, 10 May, London.

Werden, G. and Froeb, L. (2002), "Calibrated Economic Models Add Focus, Accuracy, and Persuasiveness to Merger Analysis", www2.owen.vanderbilt.edu/luke.froeb/papers/sca10.pdf.

Werden, G. and Froeb, L. (2006), "Unilateral Competitive Effects of Horizontal Mergers", in Buccirossi, P. (ed.), *Handbook of Antitrust Economics*, MIT Press, Cambridge, MA.

Werden, G., Froeb, L. and Sheffman, D. (2004) "A Daubert Discipline for Merger Simulation", www.ftc.gov/be/daubertdiscipline.pdf.

Whish, R. (2002), "Substantive Analysis under the EC Merger Regulation: Should the Dominance Test be replaced by Substantial Lessening of Competition"?, in "EU Competition Law and Policy, Developments and Priorities", Hellenic Competition Commission Conference, 19 April, Athens.

Whish, R. (2002), "Analytical Framework of Merger Review, Substantial lessening of competition/creation or strengthening of dominance", International Competition Network, First Annual Conference, 28 September, Naples, www.internationalcompetitionnetwork.org/whish_icn_ naples_full_version.pdf.

Whish, R. (2008), *Competition Law,* 6th edn, Butterworths, London.

William, Cutler and Pickering (2002), "The European Commission Adopts Merger Control Reform Package", www.wilmer.com/docs/frameset.cfm?SECTION=practice&P.=index.

Willig, R. et al. (2002), "Substantive Standards for Mergers and the Role of Efficiencies", in Hawk, B., *International Antitrust Law and Policy,* Fordham University Law School, Corporate Law Institute.

WilmerHale, *Guide To EC Merger Regulation,* 4th edn, www.wilmehale.com.

Wu, L., Williams, M. and Hofer, P. (2004) "The Increasing Use of Empirical Methods in European Merger Enforcement: Lessons from the Past and a Look Ahead", www.nera.com.

Websites

http://europa.eu.int/comm/competition/mergers/review/contributions.html

http://finance.yahoo.com/q/hp?s=WMG

http://howrey.com/docs/EC_Merger_Developments.pdf

http://lathamandwatkins.com/upload/pubContent/_pdf/pub1063_1.pdf

www.bundeskartellamt.de/wDeutsch/index.shtml?navid=27

www.factiva.com

www.ft.com, article of 28/03/2004 on Oracle/PeopleSoft

www.ft.com/cms/s/1bde5a0a-1ce4–11db-9780–0000779e2340.html

www.ftc.gov/be/hilites/ftcbeababrownbag.pdf

www.ftc.gov/os/caselist/0410054/040728mwtstmnt0410054.pdf

www.iclg.co.uk/index.php?area=4&show_chapter=582&ifocus=1&kh_publications_id=27

www.internationallawoffice.com/ld.cfm?Newsletters__Ref=7850#substantive

www.m-a-monitor.co.uk/xam-bin/m?mah03164

www.oecd.org/dataoecd/56/32/28324700.pdf

www.oft.gov.uk

Index